# Jewish Research Literature
## by
## Shimeon Brisman

Volume I:   A History and Guide to Judaic Bibliography
Volume II:  A History of Jewish Encyclopedias
Volume III: Jewish Dictionaries and Concordances

# BIBLIOGRAPHICA JUDAICA 7

*A bibliographic series of the Library of*
*Hebrew Union College-Jewish Institute of Religion*
*Edited by Herbert C. Zafren, Professor of Jewish Bibliography*

Bibliographica Judaica

# A HISTORY AND GUIDE TO

# JUDAIC

# BIBLIOGRAPHY

Shimeon Brisman

VOLUME ONE
of
JEWISH RESEARCH LITERATURE

Hebrew Union College Press · *Cincinnati*
Ktav Publishing House, Inc. · *New York*

1977

**Library of Congress Cataloging in Publication Data**

Brisman, Shimeon.
  A history and guide to Judaic bibliography.

  [His Jewish research literature ; v. 1]
[Bibliographica Judaica ; 7]
  Includes bibliographical references and index.
    1.  Bibliography—Bibliography—Jews—History.
2.  Jews—Bibliography—History.    3. Jews—Bibliography—
Periodicals—History.  4. Jews—Indexes—History.
I. Title.  II. Series: Bibliographica Judaica ; 7.
Z6366.B8  1977  vol. 1  (DS102.5)  016.909'04'924
ISBN 0-87820-900-X                    77-26149
ISSN 0067-6853

MANUFACTURED IN THE UNITED STATES OF AMERICA

*To Sara and
the children
with love*

# Contents

# Preface

Jewish literature began with one religious-historical book—The Bible; in about three millennia this literature has grown into hundreds of thousands of publications covering all conceivable topics of Jewish and universal interest. It is curious that while the ancient Jewish nation—whether concentrated in one or in two kingdoms—led a more or less independent life, its literature was slow in developing; but when that nation went into exile its literary activity accelerated. This literary activity continues unabated even in our own day; it encompasses almost the entire globe and uses almost every language of civilization.

Through the ages, many Jewish communities, in their places of dispersion, gradually relinquished their native Hebrew language and began to develop dialects based on the languages of their neighbors. Some of these dialects were developed into full-fledged languages, with their own literature written in Hebrew characters. The existence of Jewish communities in the midst of non-Jewish populations was also instrumental in the development of a literature on Jewish themes written by non-Jews. Thus the term "Jewish literature" includes books written in Hebrew characters, commonly referred to as "Hebraica," and books on Jewish themes written by Jews or non-Jews in non-Hebrew characters, commonly referred to as "Judaica."

About a decade ago, A. M. Habermann in his *Hasefer Ha'ivri Behitpatchuto,* estimated the number of Hebraica books (Hebrew, Yiddish, Ladino, Judeo-Arabic, and Judeo-Persian) printed since 1475 to be around 140,000, of which eighty thousand were printed since 1850. An equal number of Judaica may also have been produced during the same period. Since that estimate of printed Hebraica was made, Jewish literature has continued to grow with unprecedented speed, reaching an annual output of more than two thousand titles, excluding periodicals.

The existence of such a large literature necessitated the creation of a variety of bibliographic reference tools to guide and assist the potential users of these books. Indeed, during the last two and a half centuries numerous efforts have been made—with varying degrees of success—to bring the fast-growing Jewish literature under bibliographic control. During his years as a Jewish Studies librarian and lecturer in Hebrew bibliography, the author has noticed with disappointment that the average Jewish scholar, student, or even librarian is totally unaware of the existence of such tools; but he has been pleasantly surprised as a lecturer to notice students' fascination with Jewish bibliography, a subject usually considered "dry." It seems that Jewish bibliography, when presented in the realm of Jewish cultural and literary history, can become an exciting topic for scholars and students.

Some eighteen years ago the author began to collect material for a three-volume work to be entitled *Jewish Research Literature.* The purpose of the planned work was to acquaint the scholar and student of Jewish literature with the history and development of a branch of Jewish literature unfamiliar to most of them. Volume One was to be devoted to Jewish bibliography, Volume Two to Jewish encyclopedias, and Volume Three to Jewish language dictionaries and concordances. The accumulated material later became the basis for a three-part course in Hebrew bibliography and methods of research, given by the author for graduate students of the Department of Near Eastern Languages at the University of California at Los Angeles. A grant of sabbatical leave by the Regents of the University of California (made possible by the efforts of UCLA's former University Librarians, Robert Vosper and Page Ackerman), and a Sir Simon Marks Fellowship by the Los Angeles Jewish Community Foundation, enabled the author to prepare an "Experimental Edition" (limited to forty-five copies) of the first volume of his planned three-volume work. The volume was published in Jerusalem in 1973 and was received with enthusiasm by the author's colleagues in Israel and in the United States. The enthusiastic reception given the "Experimental Edition" encouraged the author to prepare this entirely revised and enlarged edition for the general public.

The present volume, the first in a series of three, is divided into eight chapters. Each of the first four chapters deals with a specific type of bibliography (general, catalogs, bio-bibliographies, subjects), chapter five discusses Judaica bibliographies, chapter six turns toward Jewish bibliographical periodicals, chapter seven relates the development of indexes to Jewish literature, and chapter eight is devoted to miscellaneous Jewish bibliographical works. Only those works devoted entirely to Jewish bibliography are discussed; general sources, which also include Jewish bibliography, are not dealt with in this volume. In each category, an effort was made to include works published up to the end of December, 1975. The romanization of Hebrew words, phrases, and titles is according to the General-Purpose romanization style prepared by the American National Standards Institute (ANSI Z39.25), published in New York in 1975, but all names of authors are given in the form established by the Library of Congress. Hebrew words, phrases, or titles beginning with the article *ha* were alphabetized in the lists and indexes in this volume under the letter following the article (e.g., *Hadoar* under D). Yiddish is romanized according to the YIVO/Library of Congress rules.

Since this work has no antecedent in Jewish literature, it may have certain defects. The author is aware of the inequality of treatment given to various works and personalities. Perhaps some discussions are too lengthy and others too brief; some statements might be overdocumented and others might be insufficiently documented. Since some sections in the book are based on work done in class and on materials collected over a long period of time, occasional errors may have been included. The author will be pleased to have these called to his attention in order to correct them in subsequent volumes.

———————————◆●◆————————————

I would like to acknowledge with thanks the assistance of the following individuals in preparing this volume. My wife, Sara, participated with suggestions and criticism at every stage of the writing of this book; without her encouragement and help this volume would never have been completed. Jonas C. Greenfield, Professor of Ancient Semitic Languages at the Hebrew University in Jerusalem, offered helpful suggestions on the first draft of the Experimental Edition. The Israeli scholars and bibliographers, Professor Meir Benayahu, Getzel Kressel, and Shlomo Shunami, suggested many sources. My colleagues at the Department of Near Eastern Languages at UCLA, Professors Herbert Davidson and Moshe Perlmann, offered sound stylistic suggestions; my colleague at the University of California (Berkeley) Library, Bibliographer Sheldon R. Brunswick, contributed linguistic suggestions; and my colleague at the University of California (Los Angeles) Research Library, Richard Zumwinkle, carefully read and corrected the entire final draft. Herbert C. Zafren edited the final version of the manuscript and supervised the entire production of this work; and Ruth Glushanok, Emilie Sulkes, and Elizabeth Levine prepared the manuscript for the printer.

עד־הנה עזרנו ה'.

Los Angeles, Iyar 5736-May 1976

# List of Abbreviations

For complete bibliographical details on the titles listed here, please consult the List of Sources below.

| | |
|---|---|
| *AJYB* | *American Jewish Yearbook* |
| *EE* | *Evreiskaia Entsiklopediia* |
| *EI* | *Ha'entsiklopedyah Ha'ivrit* |
| *EJ* | *Encyclopaedia Judaica* (German) |
| *EJ (1971)* | *Encyclopaedia Judaica* (English) |
| *HB* | *Hamazkir-Hebraeische Bibliographie* |
| *HJ* | *Historia Judaica* |
| *HUCA* | *Hebrew Union College Annual* |
| *JBA* | *Jewish Book Annual* |
| *JE* | *The Jewish Encyclopedia* |
| *JJGL* | *Jahrbücher für jüdische Geschichte und Litteratur* |
| *JJLG* | *Jahrbuch der Jüdisch-Literarischen Gesellschaft* |
| *JL* | *Jüdisches Lexikon* |
| *JQR* | *Jewish Quarterly Review* |
| *JQR* n. s. | *Jewish Quarterly Review*, new series |
| *JSS* | *Jewish Social Studies* |
| *KS* | *Kiryat Sefer* |
| *Leksikon* | *Leksikon fun der Nayer Yidisher Literatur* |
| *MGWJ* | *Monatsschrift für Geschichte und Wissenschaft des Judentums* |
| *OY* | *Otsar Yisrael* |
| *OYS* | *Otsar Yehude Sefarad* |
| *PAAJR* | *Proceedings of the American Academy for Jewish Research* |
| *PAJHS* | *Publications of the American Jewish Historical Society* |
| *REJ* | *Revue des Études Juives* |
| *SB* | *Soncino-Blätter* |
| *SBB* | *Studies in Bibliography and Booklore* |
| *UJE* | *The Universal Jewish Encyclopedia* |
| *YB* | *Yivo Bleter* |
| *YL* | *Yad Lakore* |
| *ZfGJ* | *Zeitschrift für die Geschichte der Juden* |
| *ZfHB* | *Zeitschrift für hebraeische Bibliographie* |
| *ZGJD* | *Zeitschrift für die Geschichte der Juden in Deutschland* |

# List of Sources

## (Selection)

*Ale Hadas,* edited by M. E. Belinson. Odessa: Belinson, 1865.

*Alexander Marx Jubilee Volume.* 2 vols. New York: Jewish Theological Seminary of America, 1950.

*American Jewish Yearbook.* New York: American Jewish Committee and Jewish Publication Society of America, 1899/1900-

*Areshet; Sefer Shanah Lecheker Hasefer Ha'ivri.* Jerusalem: Mosad Harav Kuk, 1958-

*Asupot.* Afikim: Archiyon Afikim, 1969-

Bader, Gershom, *Medinah Vechachameha.* New York: National Booksellers, 1934.

Baron, Salo Wittmayer, *History and Jewish Historians.* Philadelphia: Jewish Publication Society of America, 1964.

Benayahu, Meir, *Rabbi Chayim Yosef Azulai.* Jerusalem: Mosad Harav Kuk, 1959.

Bialik, Hayyim Nahman, *Igrot.* 5 vols. Tel-Aviv: Dvir, 1937-39.

*Bitsaron.* New York: 1939-

Brainin, Reuben, *Kol Kitve.* 3 vols. New York, Va'ad Hayovel, 1922-1940.

*Chochmat Yisrael Bema'arav Eropah,* edited by S. Federbusch. 3 vols. Jerusalem: M. Neuman, 1958-65.

*Hadarom.* New York: Rabbinical Council of America, 1957-

Deinard, Ephraim, *Zichronot Bat Ami.* 2 vols. Arlington-New Orleans: Printed by Moinester, 1920.

*Deot.* Jerusalem: Ha'akadema'im Hadatiyim, 1957-

*Devarim Atikim,* edited by Isaac Benjacob. 2 vols. Leipzig: Printed by Fr. Nies, 1844-46. [Reprinted, Jerusalmem: Tsiyon, 1969/70.]

*Hadoar.* New York: Histadruth Ivrith of America, 1921-

Dubnow, Semen Markovich, *Dos Bukh fun Mayn Lebn.* 3 vols. Buenos Aires-New York: Congress for Jewish Culture, 1962/63.

Eisenstadt, Benzion, *Dor Rabanav Vesofrav.* 4 vols. Warsaw-Vilna: Printed by Halter and Eisenstadt, 1895-1903.

*Eleh Ezkerah.* 7 vols. New York: Research Institute of Religious Jewry, 1956-1972.

*Encyclopaedia Judaica.* 10 vols. Berlin: Verlag Eschkol, 1928-1934.

*Encyclopaedia Judaica.* 16 vols. Jerusalem: Encyclopaedia Judaica, 1971-72.

*Ha'entsiklopedyah Ha'ivrit, Kelalit, Yehudit, Ve'artsiyisre'elit.* 27 vols. Jerusalem: Chevrah Lehotsa'at Entsiklopedyot, 1949-

Epstein, Baruch ha-Levi, *Mekor Baruch.* 3 vols. Vilna: Romm, 1928. [Reprinted, New York: L. Goldman, 1954.]

*Evreiskaia Entsikolopediia.* 16 vols. St. Petersburg: Brockhaus-Efron, 1906-1913.

Federbusch, Simon, *Chikre Yahadut.* Jerusalem: Mosad Harav Kuk, 1965.

*Forschungen zur Judenfrage.* 7 vols. Hamburg: Hanseatische Verlagsanstalt, 1937-1943.

Fünn, Samuel Joseph, *Kneset Yisrael.* Warsaw: Baumritter, 1886.

*Fun Noentn Ovar.* 2 vols. Warsaw: Literarishe Bleter, 1937-38.

*Hagat,* edited by L. Rabinovitch. St. Petersburg: Hamelits, 1897.

*Gedenkbuch zur Erinnerung an David Kaufmann,* edited by M. Brann and F. Rosenthal. Breslau: Schles. Verlags-Anstalt, 1900.

*Genazim.* Tel-Aviv: Agudat Hasofrim Haivrim Beyisrael, 1961-

*Gilyonot,* edited by I. Lamdan, 31 vols. Tel-Aviv: 1933-1954.

Gordon, Judah Loeb, *Igrot.* 2 vols. Warsaw: Schuldberg, 1894.

Habermann, Abraham Meir, *Anshe Sefer Ve'anshe Ma'aseh.* Jerusalem: Rubin Mass, 1974.

Harkavy, Abraham Elijah, *Chadashim Gam Yeshanim.* Jerusalem: Karmiel, 1970.

*Harry Austryn Wolfson Jubilee Volume.* 2 vols. Jerusalem: American Academy for Jewish Research, 1965.

*Hebrew Union College Annual.* Cincinnati: 1924-

Heiber, Helmut, *Walter Frank und sein Reichsinstitut für Geschichte des neuen Deutschlands.* Stuttgart: Deutsche Verlags-Anstalt, 1966.

Henish, Meir, *Mibayit Umichuts.* Tel-Aviv: 1961.

*Historia Judaica.* 23 vols. New York: 1938-1961.

*Ishim Udemuyot Bechochmat Yisrael Be'eropah Hamizrachit Lifne Sheki'atah,* edited by S. K. Mirsky. New York: Ogen, 1959.

*Jahrbuch der Jüdisch-Literarischen Gesellschaft.* 22 vols. Frankfort: Jüdisch-Literarische Gesellschaft, 1903-1931/32.

*Jahrbücher für jüdische Geschichte und Litteratur.* 10 vols. Frankfort: N. Brüll, 1874-1890.

*Jewish Book Annual.* New York: Jewish Book Council of Ameirica, 1942-

*The Jewish Encyclopedia.* 12 vols. New York and London: Funk and Wagnalls Company, 1901-1906 [etc.] [Reprinted, New York: Ktav Publishing House, 1964?]

*The Jewish Quarterly Review.* 20 vols. London and New York: D. Nutt and Macmillan, 1888-1908. [Reprinted, New York: Ktav Publishing House, 1966.]

*The Jewish Quarterly Review,* new series. Philadelphia: The Dropsie College, 1910-

*Jewish Social Studies.* New York: Conference on Jewish Relations, 1939-

*Jewish Studies in Memory of Gerorge A. Kohut,* edited by S. W. Baron and

A. Marx. New York: The Alexander Kohut Memorial Foundation, 1935.

*Jewish Studies in Memory of Israel Abrahams.* New York: Jewish Institute of Religion, 1927.

*The Joshua Bloch Memorial Volume,* edited by A. Berger, L. Marwick and I. S. Meyer. New York: The New York Public Library, 1960.

*Jüdisches Lexikon.* 5 vols. Berlin: Jüdischer Verlag, 1927-1930.

*Hakarmel.* 8 vols. Vilna: S. J. Fünn, 1860-71.

*Katif.* Petach-Tikva: Iriyah, Hamachlakah Letarbut, 1953/54-

*Hakerem.* Warsaw: E. Atlas, 1887.

*Hakinus Haolami Lemada'e Hayahadut.* Jerusalem: Magnes Press, 1952.

*Kiryat Sefer.* Jerusalem: Magnes Press, 1924-

Klausner, Joseph, *Historyah Shel Hasifrut Ha'ivrit Hachadashah.* 6 vols. Jerusalem: Magnes Press, 1930-1950.

Kressel, Getzel, *Leksikon Hasifrut Ha'ivrit Bedorot Ha'acharonim.* 2 vols. Merchavya: Sifriyat Poalim, 1965-67.

Lachover, Fischel, *Toldot Hasifrut Ha'ivrit Hachadashah.* 3 vols. Tel-Aviv: Dvir, 1936-1948 [etc.]

*Leksikon fun der Nayer Yidisher Literatur.* 7 vols. New York: Congress for Jewish Culture, 1956-

*Literarishe Bleter.* 16 vols. Warsaw: B. Kletzkin, 1924-1939.

*Hamagid.* 36 vols. Lyck: 1856-1892.

*Hamagid Leyisrael.* 12 vols. Cracow-London, 1892-1903.

*Magid Mishneh.* 3 vols. Lyck: 1879-81.

Mann, Jacob, *Texts and Studies in Jewish History and Literature.* 2 vols. Cincinnati: Hebrew Union College Press, 1931-35. [Reprinted, New York: Ktav Publishing House, 1972]

*Hamaor.* Brooklyn, N. Y.: 1950-

Marx, Alexander, *Essays in Jewish Biography.* Philadelphia: Jewish Publication Society of America, 1947.

Marx, Alexander, *Studies in Jewish History and Booklore.* New York: Jewish Theological Seminary of America, 1944.

*Hamazkir-Hebraeische Bibliographie,* edited by M. Steinschneider. 21 vols. Berlin: 1858-1882.

*Metsudah,* edited by S. Rawidowicz. 7 vols. London: 1943-1954.

*Mizrach Uma'arav,* edited by A. Elmaleh. 5 vols. Jerusalem: 1919-1932.

*Monatsschrift für Geschichte und Wissenschaft des Judentums.* 83 vols. Frankfort: J. Kauffmann et. al., 1851-1939.

*Moznayim.* 5 vols. Tel-Aviv: Agudat Hasofrim Ha'ivrim Beyisrael, 1929-1933.

*Moznayim.* Tel-Aviv: Agudat Hasofrim Beyisrael, 1933-
*The Occident and American Jewish Advocate.* 26 vols. Philadelphia: 1843-1869.
*Haolam.* 37 vols. Cologne-Vilna-Odessa, etc.: 1907-1950.
*Otsar Hasifrut.* 6 vols. Jaroslaw-Cracow: E. Gräber, 1887-1902.
*Otsar Yisrael,* edited by J. D. Eisenstein. 10 vols. New York: 1907-1913.
    [Reprinted, Berlin-Vienna: 1924, London: 1935, New York: 1951, Jerusalem: 1970/71.]
*Otsar Yehude Sefarad.* Jerusalem: 1959-
*Perakim.* New York: American Hebrew Academy, 1956-
*Perakim.* Haifa: 1958-
*Pinkes far der Forshung fun der Yidisher Literatur un Prese.* New York: Congress for Jewish Culture, 1965-
*Hapoel Hatsa'ir.* 63 vols. Tel-Aviv: Mifleget Poale Erets-Yisrael, 1907-1970.
*Proceedings of the American Jewish Academy for Jewish Research.* Philadelphia: Jewish Publication Society of America, 1930-
*Publications of the American Jewish Historical Society.* 50 vols. Philadelphia: 1892-1961.
Raphael, Itzhak, *Rishonim Ve'acharonim.* Tel-Aviv: Tsiyoni, 1957.
Reines, Moses, *Dor Vechachamav.* Cracow: J. Fischer, 1890.
Reisen, Zalman, *Leksikon fun der Yudisher Literatur un Prese.* Warsaw: Central, 1914.
Reisen, Zalman, *Leksikon fun der Yidisher Literatur, Prese un Filologye.* 4 vols. Vilna: B. Kletzkin, 1926–29.
*Reshumot.* 6 vols. Odessa-Tel-Aviv: Dvir, 1918-1930.
*Revue des Études Juives.* 120 vols. Paris: Durlacher, etc., 1880-1961.
*Revue des Études Juives; Historia Judaica.* Paris: 1962-
Roth, Cecil, *Studies in Books and Booklore.* Westmead: Gregg International Publishers, 1972.
Schechter, Solomon, *Seminary Addresses.* Cincinnati: Ark, 1915. [Reprinted, New York: The Burning Bush Press, 1959.]
Schechter, Solomon, *Studies in Judaism.* Philadelphia: Jewish Publication Society of America, 1896. [Reprinted, Philadelphia: 1911.]
*Scritti in Memoria di Sally Mayer.* Jerusalem: Sally Mayer Foundation, 1956.
*Sefer Asaf,* edited by M. D. Casutto, J. Klausner, and J. Gutmann. Jerusalem: Mosad Harav Kuk, 1952/53.
*Sefer Hayovel . . . Ledoktor Binyamin Menasheh Levin Leyovlo Hachamishim,* Edited by Y. L. Maimon. Jerusalem: Mosad Harav Kuk, 1939.

*Sefer Hayovel shel Hadoar Limelot Lo Sheloshim Shanah,* edited by M. Ribalow. New York: Histadruth Ivrith of America, 1952.

*Sefer Klozner . . . Leyovel Hashishim,* edited by N. H. Tur-Sinai, and others. Tel-Aviv: Va'ad Hayovel, 1936/37.

*Sefer Margaliyot,* edited by I. Raphael. Jerusalem: Mosad Harav Kuk, 1973.

*Sefer Refa'el Mahler,* edited by S. Yeivin. Merchaviah: Sifriyat Poalim, 1974.

*Semitic Studies in Memory of Immanuel Löw,* edited by Alexander Scheiber. Budapest:1947.

*Hashilo'ach.* 46 vols. Berlin-Odessa, etc.: Achiasaf, 1896-1926.

Shunami, Shlomo, *Al Sifriyot Vesafranut.* Jerusalem: Rubin Mass, 1969.

Shunami, Shlomo, *Bibliography of Jewish Bibliographies.* Jerusalem: The University Press, 1936. Second Edition Enlarged, Jerusalem: Magnes Press, 1965. Supplement to Second Edition Enlarged, Jerusalem: Magnes Press, 1975.

*Sinai.* Jerusalem: Mosad Harav Kuk, 1937-

*Sinai, Sefer Yovel,* edited by Y. L. Maimon. Jerusalem: Mosad Harav Kuk, 1958.

*Soncino-Blätter.* 3 vols. Berlin: Soncino-Gesellschaft der Freunde des Jüdischen Buches, 1925-1930.

Steinschneider, Moritz, *Gesammelte Schriften,* edited by H. Malter and A. Marx. Berlin: Poppelauer, 1925.

Steinschneider, Moritz, *Jewish Literature from the Eighth to the Eighteenth Century,* translated by W. Spottiswoode. London: Longmans and Roberts, 1857. [Reprinted, New York: Hermon Press, 1965.]

*Studia Rosenthaliana.* Assen: Bibliotheca Rosenthaliana, 1967-

*Studies in Bibliography and Booklore.* Cincinnati: Library of Hebrew Union College- Jewish Institute of Religion, 1953-

*Studies in Jewish Bibliography and Related Subjects in Memory of Abraham Solomon Freidus.* New York: The Alexander Kohut Memorial Foundation, 1929.

*Studies in Jewish Bibliography, History, and Literature in Honor of I. Edward Kiev,* edited by C. Berlin. New York: Ktav Publishing House, 1971.

*Talpiyot.* 8 vols. New York: 1943-1961.

Tauber, Aryeh, *Mechkarim Bibliyografiyim.* Jerusalem: the University Press, 1932.

*Hatekufah.* 35 vols. Moscow-Warsaw, etc.: Stybel, 1918-1949.

*Hatoren.* 12 vols. New York: Achiever, 1913-1925.

*Hatsofeh Lechochmat Yisrael.* 15 vols. Budapest: 1911-1931.

*Di Tsukunft.* New York: Central Yiddish Culture Organization, 1892-

*The Universal Jewish Encyclopedia.* 10 vols. New York: 1939-1943.

*Vakhshtayn-Bukh; Zamlbukh tsum Ondenk fun Bernhard Vakhshtayn.* Vilna: Yivo, 1939.

*Ve'im Bigevurot . . . Minchah Lire'uven Mas,* edited by A. Even-Shoshan, and others. Jerusalem: Behotsa'at Yedidim, 1974.

*Vilner Zamlbukh.* 2 vols. Vilna: 1917-18.

*Visnshaftlekhe Yorbikher.* Moscow: Alruslendishe Visnshaftlekhe Geselshaft tsu Shtudirn di Yidishe Shprakh, Literatur un Geshikhte, 1929.

Weinreich, Max, *Bilder fun der Yidisher Literaturgeshikhte.* Vilna: Farlag Tomor, 1928.

*Yedi'ot Yad Vashem.* Jerusalem: Yad Vashem, 1954-

*Hayekev,* edited by L. Rabinovitch. St. Petersburg: Hamelits, 1894.

*Yad Lakore.* Tel-Aviv: Israel Library Association, 1946-

*Yidishe Dialogn,* edited by M. Livni. Paris: World Jewish Congress, 1968.

*Yidishe Kultur.* New York: Yiddisher Kultur Farband, 1938-

*Yivo Annual of Jewish Social Science.* New York: 1946-

*Yivo Bleter.* New York: 1931-

*Zeitschrift für die Geschichte der Juden.* Tel-Aviv: Olamenu, 1964-

*Zeitschrift für die Geschichte der Juden in Deutschland.* 5 vols. Braunschweig: 1887-1892.

*Zeitschrift für die Geschichte der Juden in Deutschland.* 8 vols. Berlin: Philo Verlag, 1929-1938.

*Zeitschrift für hebraeische Bibliographie.* 24 vols. Berlin-Frankfort: S. Calvary & Co.-J. Kauffmann, 1900-1921.

*Zikaron Leavraham Eliyahu . . . Lichevod Avraham Eliyahu Harkavi,* edited by Baron D. Günzburg and I. Markon. St. Petersburg: 1908. [Reprinted, Jerusalem: 1968/69.]

Zinberg, Israel, *Di Geshikhte fun der Literatur bay Yidn.* 9 vols. Vilna: Farlag Tomor, 1929-1966. [Reprinted, New York: Shklarski, 1943; Buenos-Aires: Congress for Jewish Culture, 1964-1970.] Hebrew translation, entitled *Toldot Sifrut Yisrael,* was published in Tel-Aviv and Merchavia by Sifriyat Poalim in 1955-1971. An English translation, entitled *A History of Jewish Literature,* is currently being published by Hebrew Union College Press and distributed by Ktav Publishing House.

Zunz, Leopold, *Gesammelte Schriften.* 3 vols. Berlin: L. Gerschel, 1875-76.

Zunz, Leopold, *Die Synagogale Poesie des Mittelalters.* Berlin: J. Springer, 1855. [Reprinted, Berlin: L. Lamm, 1919, and Frankfort, J. Kauffmann, 1920.]

Zunz, Leopold, *Zur Geschichte und Literatur.* Berlin: Veit und Comp., 1845. [Reprinted, Berlin: L. Lamm, 1919.]

Title page of the first organized list of Hebrew books, *De Abbreviaturis Hebraicis Liber* by Johannes Buxtorf, originally intended as an aid to Christian Hebraists and theologians. Franeker, J. Horreum, 1696.

JOHANNIS BUXTORFI
*D E*

# ABBREVIATURIS
## HEBRAICIS

*Liber novus & copiofus.*
*Cui accefferunt*

## OPERIS TALMUDICI

Brevis recenfio, cum ejufdem librorum & capitum Indice.

*Item*

### BIBLIOTHECA RABBINICA

*nova, cum Appendice , ordine*
*Alphabethico difpofita.*

EDITIONE hac ULTIMA.
Omnia caftigatiora & locupletiora.

*F R A N E Q U E R Æ,*

Apud JACOBUM HORREUM,
M. DC. XCVI.

ספר
שפתי ישינים
לפני נערים וזקנים׳
חכמים ונבונים· אלופים וגאונים:

Title page of *Siftei Yeshenim* the first Jewish bibliographical book in Hebrew by Shabba-tai ben Joseph Bass. Amsterdam, David de Castro Tartas, 1680.

# CATALOGUS

der ſeit vielen Jahren berühmten vollſtändigen

## Hebreiſchen Bibliothek

des ehemaligen Präger Ober-Rabbiners,

weiland Herrn David Oppenheimers

beſtehend

in Cabaliſtiſchen, Theologiſchen, Talmudiſchen, Phi-

loſophiſchen, Mathematiſchen, Mediciniſchen, und in andere Wiſſen-

ſchaften, einſchlagenden, theils gedruckten, theils auf Pergament

geſchriebene, ſehr alten rare und nicht mehr zu habenden

## Büchern.

Herausgegeben

von dem ißigen Beſißer

Iſaak Seligmann Berend Salomon

in Hamburg.

Hamburg,

gedruckt von Johann Michael Brauer.

1782.

ספר

## שם הגדולים

הוא מסדר סדר סמערכה שלשׁת עחסין משפחות סופרים שמות
דור נדור אלו שני חרות שלפניכו וסיו תולאותיו · פרטט וכתב
שם סגדולים מן סנאונים ועד דור אחרון הסמך ונראה בעלי
אוכרלין מחברי ספרים וסתניתי תיו · זמן זמנכ דוכתא דאיכיס
ושם כבודו וכבוד רכו לס"ס שכ"ו ויעם דור ל ש"ס מאל"ף עד תל"ו ·
יצין ופרח לכר כי רכ יודיע דרכיו סא נברה.וסא רסקא מאן כיסב
מר וסמר כתב אשר עמו אבכעותיו · כא סכתוכ ויחסו טועץ
כריא ושמר ס שמו ושם עירו מפי מוברים וספרים ילכו יוסקותיו
אככי סעירותיסא לנצרי כני ישראל בעיר אככי אדם
מעט כמתא שמאי

חיים יוסף דוד אזולאי ס"ט

## בליוורנו

בשנת    כי לוית חן הם    לפ"ק

## IN LIVORNO 1774.

Nella Stamperia di Gio. Falorni.

*Con Approvaʒione.*

# Chapter One

# General Hebraica Bibliographies

*Bibliographies not devoted to any specific form or topic in literature are designated as "general." In the Jewish field, all major bibliographies published up to the second half of the nineteenth century fall into this category.*

Early Stages. Johannes Buxtorf: *Bibliotheca Rabbinica.* Giulio Bartolocci: *Bibliotheca Magna Rabbinica.* Shabbethai Bass: *Sifte Yeshenim.* Johann Christoph Wolf: *Bibliotheca Hebraea.* Hermann Friedrich Köcher: *Nova Bibliotheca Hebraica.* Jehiel Heilprin: *Seder Mechabrim Veseder Sefarim.* Julius Fürst: *Bibliotheca Judaica.* Isaac Benjacob: *Otsar Hasefarim.* Menahem Mendel Slatkine: *Otsar Hasefarim Chelek Sheni.* Bernhard Friedberg: *Bet Eked Sefarim.* Mif'al Habibliyografyah Ha'ivrit.

## Early Stages

THE EARLIEST BIBLIOGRAPHICAL discussion in Jewish literature seems to have taken place in the Babylonian Talmud, where an attempt was made to establish the order of the books of the Prophets and the Writings, and their authorship.[1] Additional discussions are found, in several places in the Talmud, relating to the authorship of some books of the Bible, to the Canon, and to certain books of the Apocrypha.[2] Some bibliographical information is also transmitted in the geonic literature (sixth to eleventh centuries) and in medieval Jewish works.[3] But bibliography in the sense of listing works in a specific, thought-out order—whether in author or in title sequence—made its entrance into Jewish literature only in the earlier part of the seventeenth century.

2

The seventeenth century is in the annals of Jewish bibliography what the sixteenth century is in the annals of universal bibliography. It marks for both their respective first stages on the road to becoming modern disciplines. It was a Swiss scholar in the sixteenth century, Konrad Gesner (1516–1565),[4] who published the first universal list of books in classical languages, and with it he gave birth to modern bibliography; it was another Swiss scholar, Johannes Buxtorf, who, during the following century, published the first organized list of Hebrew books, and with it began the dawn of modern Jewish bibliography.

Konrad Gesner, the father of modern bibliography, was not yet fifty when he died, a victim of a plague that hit his city of birth, Zurich, while he served there as health officer. But in his relatively short life he also pioneered, besides bibliography, the sciences of modern biology, zoology, botany, geology, and mineralogy. His works in these areas are monumental, and with them he established a permanent place for himself in the history of modern science. No less monumental is his *Bibliotheca universalis* which was published in Zurich, in four volumes, over a period of ten years, beginning in 1545. On the title page of the first volume of his *Bibliotheca,* Gesner proposed to list works "in tribus linguis, latina, graeca et hebraica," and with it he extended the realm of universal bibliography to encompass Jewish literature.[5]

For knowledge of the Hebrew book, Gesner's *Bibliotheca* is of minor value. Only the fact that in its pages—perhaps for the first time in any bibliographical work—are listed some names and works by and about Jews merits its mention in a history of early Jewish bibliography.[6]

## Johannes Buxtorf: *Bibliotheca Rabbinica*

Four generations of the Buxtorf family were attracted to the Hebrew language and its literature;[7] but only the first two, a father and a son, left a permanent mark through their literary activities. Johannes Buxtorf, the father, was born in Westphalia in 1564, just one year before the death of Konrad Gesner. Although Gesner and Buxtorf had similar traits in that both devoted their lives to study and teaching and both were attracted to book collecting and writing, they were of different temperaments. Gesner strove to encompass the entire human experience, be it in classical studies, the natural sciences, or medicine. Buxtorf was satisfied to devote a lifetime to the mastering of just one area of human knowledge: Hebrew and its literature. Gesner introduced Hebrew into universal bibliography because to Gesner, the classicist, it was natural: Hebrew, a classical language, rightfully belonged in a universal bibliography of classical literature. Buxtorf, on the other hand, did not see it as simply as that; Buxtorf, the Semitist and Christian theologian, saw in Hebrew the language of the Scriptures, a means of proving the superiority of his religion. All the years that he spent in studying, translating, and composing books in the field of Hebrew language and literature had one purpose: to serve Christianity with the aid of Jewish sources.[8]

Johannes Buxtorf became fascinated with Hebrew during his student years at the German universities of Marburg and Herborn. He continued his studies later at the Swiss university of Basel and, after his graduation, he was appointed professor of Hebrew there. He remained in that position for the rest of his life, a period of thirty-seven years. His first appearance in the scholarly arena was with his *Juden Schul* (Basel, 1603), in which he made an effort to describe Jewish laws, customs, and ceremonies for the non-Jewish public. It was an effort that failed miserably, due to his biased and sometimes distorted manner of presentation.[9] A more serious effort was his *Praeceptiones grammaticae de lingua hebrea* (Basel, 1605). It was a sound contribution to the study of Hebrew grammar, and it led him to the field of Hebrew lexicography,[10] to the study of the biblical Masoretic text,[11] to the preparation of a new edition of the Hebrew Bible concordance by Isaac Nathan,[12] and to the editing and translating of various classical Hebrew texts, including a collection of Hebrew family letters with an appendix of letters by Maimonides and other famous medieval Jewish scholars.[13] For his translations of classic Hebrew texts Buxtorf has been called the "Christian Ibn Tibbon";[14] for his achievements in the field of Hebrew language and literature, we may call him the "Christian Eliyahu Bachur."[15] He died in Basel in 1629.

Among Buxtorf's lexicographical works, the volume *De abbreviaturis hebraicis* (Basel, 1613) deserves a place of honor.[16] Appended to it is another work called *Bibliotheca rabbinica*,[17] a little volume that lists 324 Hebrew works by title in alphabetical order, based on Buxtorf's extensive Hebrew book collection. It was the very first scientifically organized bibliography of Jewish literature.[18] Unlike Gesner's *Bibliotheca*, in which the bibliographic details on Jewish books are usually incomplete, Buxtorf's *Bibliotheca* in most cases furnishes full information. The *Bibliotheca rabbinica* listed both printed and handwritten Hebrew works, and the entries (with descriptive text in Latin) were, with some exceptions, in the following order:

Title (in Hebrew characters)
Transliteration and translation of title into Latin
Description and contents
Author (if not anonymous or a classical ancient Hebrew text)
Place and date of publication (for printed works)

Buxtorf's title arrangement in his *Bibliotheca* became standard practice in general Hebrew bibliography until recent years. There were two principal reasons for the popularity of the title arrangement. First, the complicated procedure of establishing the identities and correct forms of names for Hebrew authors was eliminated. Under the title arrangement, authors' names were copied from the title pages, and no effort was made for precise identification or for uniformity of names. Second, Hebrew works are usually better known by their titles than by their authors. Hebrew scholars, especially those of the traditional school, seldom paid attention to authors' names. They would be puzzled if asked who the authors were of the books they so often studied.[19] A Hebrew bibliography arranged by the names of the authors would have remained a closed book for most of the contemporary Hebrew scholars.

Buxtorf's pioneering work in Jewish bibliography, the *Bibliotheca rabbinica* (together with his *De abbreviaturis hebraicis*), survived four editions, the last of which was issued seventy-nine years after his death. Twenty-seven years after the publication of the first edition, Johannes Buxtorf, his son (1599–1664), prepared and published an enlarged and corrected second edition (Basel, 1640). He attached a thirty-nine page *Appendix,* compiled with the assistance of the Turkish-Jewish scholar Jacob Roman,[20] and added an author index. This edition, with a few minor changes, was reprinted fifty-six years later (Franequer, 1696). An enlarged and extended edition appeared twelve years later (Herborn Nassau, 1708).[21]

The role of the *Bibliotheca rabbinica* in the history of Jewish bibliography is manifold. It listed, for the first time in a single volume, hundreds of Hebrew works, both printed and handwritten, and registered them properly according to accepted rules of bibliography. For centuries it influenced the physiognomy of Hebrew bibliography by introducing the title arrangement. Its primary importance, however, is its generation of an entire chain of bibliographers, Christians and Jews, who widened and deepened this area of Jewish knowledge and established it as an independent branch of universal bibliography.

## Giulio Bartolocci: *Bibliotheca Magna Rabbinica*

Although Buxtorf's *Bibliotheca rabbinica* was the first bibliography devoted entirely to Jewish literature, it did encompass all areas of Jewish knowledge. But the 324 titles listed in the first edition and the more than 800 titles listed in the succeeding editions were only a fraction of the overall number of Hebrew titles in existence. At best, it was a first step on the road to an all-inclusive Jewish bibliography. Buxtorf's immediate successors in the field of Jewish bibliography, men like Cardinal Jean de la Pause Plantavit (1576–1651) who counted Leone da Modena (1571–1648) among his teachers of Hebrew,[22] and Johann Heinrich Hottinger (1620–1667), who introduced subject arrangement into Jewish bibliography,[23] did not move Jewish bibliography any further. Most of their efforts were spent on repeating the information already made available in the *Bibliotheca rabbinica,* including Buxtorf's errors, and sometimes adding their own.[24] There was a need for a bibliographer who would make it his goal to register and list, in one work, everything written by and about Jews. At this point Giulio Bartolocci entered the scene.

A priest by training, a teacher and librarian by profession, Bartolocci was born in Celleno, Italy, in 1613, the year that Buxtorf's *Bibliotheca rabbinica* first appeared. His interest in Hebrew language and literature began while he was studying for the priesthood, and he became well-versed in it thanks to the guidance of his teacher, a converted Jew, Giovanni Battista or Baptista (1588–1668 or 1671).[25] Battista had an interesting past. Born in the city of Safed in the Holy Land as Judah Jonah ben Isaac, he planned to enter the rabbinate. He traveled through Europe, visited the Jewish communities of Italy, stayed in Amsterdam and Hamburg, where he served—according to some sources—as a rabbi, and settled in Poland. There he embraced Christianity at the age of thirty-seven and adopted the name John Baptist. He was later expelled from Poland, whereupon he settled in Italy, first in Pisa as a teacher of Hebrew, later in Rome as professor at the Collegium Neophytorum and as associate librarian at the Bibliotheca Vaticana. There he worked out a plan for a new Hebrew bibliography, arranged chronologically according to the dates of the authors.

After Bartolocci completed his studies for the priesthood his interest in Hebrew studies continued, and in 1651 he was appointed professor of Hebrew and Rabbinics at the Collegium Neophytorum and Scriptor Hebraicus at the Bibliotheca Vaticana. There he joined his former teacher, Battista, as a colleague and co-worker. Battista, in the meantime, seems to have abandoned his plan for preparing a new Hebrew bibliography, and he turned over his accumulated material to Bartolocci. The Vatican Library, with its large collection of printed and handwritten volumes of Hebrew works, was an ideal place to bring such a project to fruition.[26] Bartolocci began working on an all-inclusive Hebrew bibliography, and he devoted the rest of his life preparing it.

The result of decades of intensive planning and research became visible in 1675, when Bartolocci published the first volume of his bibliography of Hebrew works in Rome. It was a bilingual bibliography, and it carried two titles, one in Hebrew and the other in Latin. In Hebrew it was entitled *Kiryat Sefer* (based on Joshua 15:15), a title that would later be adopted for several other Hebrew bibliographies, and in Latin it was called *Bibliotheca magna rabbinica*. Bartolocci's *Bibliotheca* was an impressive volume, externally as well as internally. Published in folio, on heavy paper, in attractive Hebrew and Roman typefaces, and printed in double columns, it was arranged alphabetically by the Hebrew forms of the authors' names, by topics, or by works. Each entry, with some exceptions, contained the following information:

|                *In Hebrew*                 |                *In Latin*                 |
| ------------------------------------------ | ----------------------------------------- |
| Author, topic, or work (if anonymous or if an ancient work) | Author, topic, or work (same as in the Hebrew) |
| Biographical data                          | Biographical data                         |
| Title                                      | Title (romanized and translated)          |
| Description of contents                    | Description of contents, with additional bibliographical data |
| Place and date of publication             | Place and date of publication (in the Hebrew and in the common reckoning) |
|                                            | Format                                    |
| Location of work (in case of manuscripts) | Location of works (for manuscripts, with the addition of information about the materials written upon: whether paper or vellum) |

The first volume of Bartolocci's *Bibliotheca* covered the first three letters of the Hebrew alphabet, *alef* through *gimel*. The second volume, published in Rome in 1678, covered the letters *dalet* through *tet,* and the third volume, issued there in 1684, was devoted entirely to the letter *yod.* Bartolocci died in 1687, on the threshold of completing his monumental work. He reached, in manuscript, the letter *shin,*[27] and the task of completing, editing, and preparing the final volume of the *Bibliotheca* for publication was turned over to his student, Carlo Giuseppi Imbonati (1650?–1697). Thus, the fourth and final volume of Bartolocci's *Bibliotheca*, prepared and completed by Imbonati, was published in Rome in 1693; it covered the letters *kaf* through *tav*. Imbonati later added a fifth volume as a supplement, that was published in Rome in 1694 under a Hebrew title, *Magen Vacherev Umilchamah*, followed by a Latin title, *Bibliotheca latino-hebraica*. Imbonati's *Bibliotheca* was the first of its kind, since it listed, in alphabetical order, more than 1300 works in Latin, on Jewish themes, written by non-Jewish writers. The emphasis in this bibliography was on theological works defending Christianity and attacking Judaism, as is indicated by the Hebrew title, "A shield, a sword, and war."

The massive four volumes of the *Bibliotheca magna rabbinica*—close to 3,500 pages, registering 1,960 entries, with Hebrew and Latin indexes of titles, cross-references, subjects, and names of authors and places— represented the first comprehensive Hebrew bibliography. Besides the treasures of the Vatican Library, Bartolocci utilized the collections of its subsidiary libraries and the information contained in the works of Buxtorf, Plantavit, and Hottinger, among others.[28] It seems that he relied heavily upon Buxtorf; even the Latin title of his work indicates a continuation of Buxtorf's effort: *Bibliotheca magna rabbinica*, an enlarged *Bibliotheca rabbinica*.

Had Bartolocci stayed within the bounds of bibliography, his work would probably have remained for a long time the most authoritative in this field. Unfortunately, he constantly overstepped such limits by including superfluous material.[29] He also exploited every opportunity to get involved in anti-Jewish polemics, and he was extremely careless in translating rabbinic texts.[30] Still, Bartolocci accomplished what he set out to do: to collect and to present in a single work all the printed and handwritten Hebrew works available in the libraries accessible to him or mentioned in preceding bibliographical, chronological, and historical works.[31] He also advanced the science of Jewish bibliography a step further by including in his entries additional information, such as biographical data, the format of codices,[32] their locations, and sometimes even the materials they were made of. The influence of Bartolocci's *Bibliotheca* was strongly felt among the succeeding generation of bibliographers.

A five-volume photo-offset edition of the *Bibliotheca magna rabbinica* together with the *Bibliotheca latino-hebraica* was published recently by Gregg Publishers (Farnborough, 1965–1968).

## Shabbethai Bass: *Sifte Yeshenim*

While Bartolocci was preparing the third volume of his *Bibliotheca* for publication, a scholar in Amsterdam completed and published the first Jewish bibliography compiled by a Jew. Shabbethai ben Joseph, the first Jewish bibliographer of note, was born in Kalish, Poland, in 1641, where his parents died in the massacre of 1655. He was educated in Prague, Bohemia, where he participated for a decade in the synagogue choir as a basso, from which he took his surname Bass.[33] During his stay in Prague, Shabbethai Bass was a clerk in a bookstore, where he acquired a working knowledge of Latin and, to a lesser degree, of Greek. At the bookstore he also acquired interests in publishing and his first notion about the science of bibliography. There he became aware of the need for an all-inclusive Jewish bibliography, and he began accumulating information for such a project. Bass's early steps as a bibliographer were not easy. He later remarked that to collect bibliographic data while in Prague he had "to search and investigate from house to house and from room to room, because there were not too many books housed together, not even in the synagogues." He further related that "sometimes, in order to locate a booklet," he had to go "several times and to search in various locations."[34]

Simultaneous with his beginning bibliographic research, Bass also ventured into the publishing field. The first result of his enterprise was a new edition of Moses ben Issachar Särtels' *Be'er Mosheh,* a popular Hebrew-Yiddish glossary to the Pentateuch and the Five Scrolls.[35] To it, Bass added an introduction, some notes on the rules of Hebrew grammar, and a poem in Yiddish. He published it in Prague in 1669. Soon afterward, the government closed down all Jewish printing shops in Prague, and Bass's publishing activities came to a sudden halt. He left Prague and began a long series of travels that took him to various parts of Poland, Germany, and Holland. During his sojourns, he distributed the book he had published, and also compiled material for three reference works that he planned to compose. The material he had begun to collect for a Jewish bibliography during his Prague years continued to grow constantly during his years of travel. Wherever he went, he visited private libraries as well as those of synagogues and educational institutions and recorded their holdings. At the same time he compiled material for a Jewish travel guide to Europe and for a super-commentary on Rashi's commentary on the Pentateuch.[36]

In 1679 Bass finally settled in Amsterdam, a city rich in collections of Hebrew books, private and communal. He accepted a position as a

proofreader in one of the several Jewish printing houses in that city. Some of
the rabbis, scholars, and wealthy book collectors befriended Bass and he
utilized their fine libraries of Hebrew books for his bibliography. A year
later he was able to complete and publish all three works: the travel guide,[37]
the supercommentary on Rashi,[38] and an all-inclusive Hebrew bibliography.

Buxtorf and Bartolocci designed their Hebraica bibliographies mainly
for the use of Christian Hebraists and theologians. Bass, on the other hand,
had in mind the Jewish reader exclusively. This is evident in the title of the
book, in its title page, in the approbations, and in the introductions. The
work appeared in Amsterdam in 1680 under the title *Sifte Yeshenim* (based
on Song of Songs 7:10), a name that did not at all reveal that it represented a
bibliographic work. This was customary with Jewish authors who believed
the title of a work should be related more to the name of its author than to
its contents.[39] Indeed, Bass explains that the Hebrew word *sifte* is consonan-
tally equivalent to his own name *Shabbethai,* since the letters *pe* and *bet* are
interchangeable.[40] Nor does the title page reveal anything of the contents of
the work. After stating that this is a work compiled by "Shabbethai
*Meshorer* Bass, of Prague, the brother of the saintly cabalist . . . Jacob
Strimers,"[41] the author refers the reader to the introduction. Only on the
verso of the title page, in a partially rhymed statement intended to en-
courage the reading of the introduction, comes a brief explanation of the
contents of the book. There is also very little revealed about the nature of
the book in the approbations of the rabbis. It is only after a careful reading
of the lenghty introduction, with the list of ten "benefits" that can be
derived from using the book, that its real nature comes to light.

Bass begins his introduction with a quotation from the cabalistic-ethical
work of Rabbi Isaiah Horowitz (1555–1630), *Shene Luchot Haberit* (known
as *Shelah*), to the effect that the ignorant can earn the same reward earned
by those who study the Torah, just by pronouncing the names of Hebrew
books, or the names of chapters of the Bible, the Talmud, the Midrash, and
other holy books. This Bass lists as the first "benefit" offered by his work.[42]
He later enumerates more rational arguments: for example, that his work
would help scholars learn what exists in their fields of interest; that it would
systematize the studying of Jewish sources; that it would help authors in giving names to their works; that it would inform scholars about the existence
of various editions of works and how to identify them.

In the tenth "benefit" Bass explains that he designed his work as a house
with doors and portals. Thus, he divided the *Sifte Yeshenim* into four sections:

a. a two-part subject index
b. a list of titles (body of the book)
c. an author index
d. a list of Judaica by non-Jewish writers

The two-part subject index preceding the body of the book (the "house") constitutes the "doors." The two sections following the body of the book are the "portals." In the "right-hand door" (first part of the subject index), he arranged the books of the Written Law, their commentaries, and all other related works, including grammars, dictionaries, concordances, cabala, liturgy, and poetry. In the "left-hand door" (second part of the subject index), he arranged the books of the Oral Law, their commentaries, and all related works, including science, philosophy, folklore, and medicine. The latter also contained a section of more than seventy works in Old Yiddish. In order to accommodate as many Hebrew books as possible into his scheme, Bass divided each "door" into ten "keys," and each "key" into further sections. The subject arrangement was artificial, and in a note at the end of the index (page 20b), he had to admit that he had failed to fit all the Hebrew books into this scheme.

He arranged the list of titles, the "house" which formed the body of the book, alphabetically and numbered the entries under each letter of the alphabet separately. The entries, with some exceptions, consist of the following:

Title
Author
Description (often with critical comment)
Place and (Hebrew) date of publication
Location (in case of manuscripts)
Format

Bass also indicated his sources for books known to him only by their titles but no longer extant, and he frequently employed cross-references. He listed about 2,200 titles, including approximately 265 duplications. More than 1,900 individual titles, therefore, were described, and, of these, approximately 1,100 were printed editions and about 825 were manuscripts or works not directly known to Bass.[43]

The author index was designated by Bass as the "major portal" (Sha'ar Bat Rabim). In it, he listed alphabetically all the authors referred to in the list of titles; Ashkenazic authors were entered by their second names, and

Italian and Sephardic authors by their first names.[44] For many of these names Bass also provided biographical data. At the end of this section he appended an alphabetical as well as a chronological list of tannaim, amoraim, saboraim, and geonim.

The final section of the book, which Bass called the "external portal" *(Sha'ar Hachitson)*, lists about 150 Judaica works written by non-Jewish scholars. Bass justified the inclusion of non-Hebrew works in his bibliography with the claim that this "will show the power of the Holy Tongue; that all nations make an effort to study and to write books in the Holy Tongue and to translate books from the Holy Tongue into other tongues."[45] Among the books listed in this section are the bibliographies of Buxtorf, Hottinger, and Plantavit, and Bartolocci's first volume. Bass thus gives us a glimpse of some of the sources he used in compiling, in planning the form of entries, and in arranging the subject and author indexes of his *Sifte Yeshenim.*[46]

Bass stayed on in Amsterdam for about five years, a period of time during which he acquainted himself thoroughly with the printing trade. He moved east to Dyhernfurth, near Breslau, where he established a printing and publishing shop. It was a successful business that required his total attention. He had family problems, however, and had to turn his printing shop over to his son. Bass moved to Breslau and devoted himself to the marketing of his publications. While he was still in Dyhernfurth, he had become the target of a group of Jesuits there, who denounced him to the authorities for spreading anti-Christian propaganda. They succeeded in having him and his son arrested a year after he settled in Breslau. Both were kept in jail for ten weeks before their case was heard. Once in court, they were vindicated and released. Bass died six years later, in 1718.

During all these years of hectic activity, Bass did not neglect his *Sifte Yeshenim.* In the hope of preparing a second, enlarged edition, he collected new material up to the last year of his life.[47] But he did not live to see a second edition, and his hope of seeing his Hebrew bibliography translated into other languages was never realized.[48] Nonetheless, Bass should have been satisfied to see, during the last years of his life, the role that his *Sifte Yeshenim* played in the preparation and compilation of a new and expanded bibliography of Hebrew literature which was published three years before his death.

A second edition of *Sifte Yeshenim,* edited and published by the printer Uri Zvi Rubinstein, of Lvov,[49] appeared in 1806 in Żołkiew, near Lvov, 126 years after the appearance of the first edition. The new edition contained some new material and corrections, and also a separate section (part two) consisting of close to 700 titles of Hebrew works that had appeared in print since the publication of the original *Sifte Yeshenim*. Rubinstein, however, demonstrated weak bibliographical abilities, and his effort is to be considered as a step backwards in the history of Jewish bibliography.

## Johann Christoph Wolf: *Bibliotheca Hebraea*

Jewish bibliography, the groundwork for which had been laid in the seventeenth century, began to flourish during the eighteenth century. At least two bibliographical efforts made during that century can be traced directly to the earlier work of Bartolocci and Bass. One was a monumental four-volume bibliography by a German Christian scholar, and the other a bibliographical appendix to a book on Jewish chronology by an East European Jewish scholar. While the appearance of the latter signaled the widening interest among Jewish scholars in this relatively new field of knowledge, the completion of the former came at a time when interest in Jewish studies among Christian scholars was waning. The author of the first, Johann Christoph Wolf, a professor of oriental languages and literature at the Hamburg gymnasium, could truly be considered the last of the group of great Christian bibliographers of Jewish literature. The author of the second, Rabbi Jehiel ben Solomon Heilprin, a rabbi and cabalist in the White Russian city of Minsk, was not a bibliographer at all; he acted primarily as a transmitter between Bass and future generations of Jewish bibliographers.

Born in 1683, Wolf became interested in the Hebrew language and its literature during his student years, and he wrote a history of Hebrew lexicography as a doctoral thesis.[50] His studies in Hebrew language and literature led him also to Karaite literature, and he later published a volume dealing with the texts of this branch of Hebrew literature.[51] But the crowning achievement of his literary activity was the publication of the *Bibliotheca hebraea*, the first volume of which appeared in Hamburg in 1715, three years before the death of Shabbethai Bass. It was an impressive volume of more than 1,200 pages, with 2,231 alphabetically registered author entries, preceded by a lengthy introduction dealing with such topics of Hebrew bibliography as dates, titles, authors' identities, printing places, and censorship, and followed by an index of Hebrew titles and by a list of cabalistic manuscripts prepared by Jacques Gaffarel (1601–1681).

The second volume of the *Bibliotheca hebraea* appeared in Hamburg in 1721. It contained a bibliographical history of the books of the Hebrew

Scriptures and the Apocrypha, a history of the Masorah and the Masoretes, a history of Jewish and Christian lexicographers and grammarians of the Hebrew language, a long essay on the Talmud, and a history of Hebrew printing. This was followed by a section called "Bibliotheca iudaica et antiiudaica," which listed anti-Jewish writings by classical writers, by Jewish apostates, and by Christians, and also Jewish apologetics and anti-Christian writings. The next section dealt with the Aramaic versions of the Hebrew Bible and with the Cabala, and the final section consisted of an alphabetical list of some 784 anonymous Hebrew works.

The third volume, published in Hamburg in 1727, contained additions and corrections to the 2,231 entries listed in the first volume and to the 784 anonymous works listed in the second volume. It also included an index of the Hebrew titles listed in all three volumes. The fourth volume, published in Hamburg, in 1733, consisted of additions to the various sections of the second volume, and included supplementary material to the additions of volume three. The volume concluded with indexes of authors, subjects, and titles. The entire four-volume work totalled more than 5,000 pages.

The publication of the *Bibliotheca hebraea* marked the beginning of a new era in Jewish bibliography. In preparing his work, Wolf made good use of the information accumulated by his predecessors, especially Bartolocci and Bass. He acknowledged his indebtedness to them in the introductions to the first and third volumes of the *Bibliotheca;* he considered his accomplishment as a continuation of their efforts. But he did not rely blindly on their information. He investigated every fact and detail in the works of his predecessors, submitted them to a critical reexamination in light of new sources, and incorporated the results in his entries. Wolf was fortunate in having access to one of the most important Hebraica collections of all times, the Oppenheimer Collection.[52] During the years he was preparing his *Bibliotheca,* Wolf made a number of trips to Hannover, where the Oppenheimer Collection was stored at that time, for the sole purpose of thoroughly examining its thousands of printed books and manuscripts. On the basis of these examinations, he offered in the *Bibliotheca,* especially in the third volume, thousands of corrections and additions to the biographical and bibliographical data accumulated by his predecessors, notably Bartolocci and Bass. An analytical description of the entries in the *Bibliotheca hebraea* will illustrate the labor Wolf invested in his work:

Author (in Hebrew characters)
Author (transcribed in Roman characters, with sources for origin of name)
Biographical data (sources are noted; errors in sources are corrected)

Title (in Hebrew characters)
Title (translated into Latin; biblical references given for titles with biblical
  connotations)
Contents
Place and date of publication (editions are listed; errors of predecessors
  are noted and corrected)
Format
Location (especially if available in the Oppenheimer Collection)

In his entries, Wolf made ample use of cross-references from various forms
of the name, especially when he dealt with authors who are known mainly
by their acronyms (e.g., Rambam, Rashi). He tried to achieve consistency
and uniformity of entry, an effort that sometimes bordered on the
ridiculous. In the first volume, for example, he listed such biblical personalities as Adam, Abraham, or Solomon as main entries, instead of refer-
ring the reader to the section on anonymous works and noting that some of
the cabalistic works attributed to them are later creations. Since Volume One
consisted of author entries only, he must have decided for the sake of uniformity of entry to list works of this type under their ascribed authors. Wolf's
work also suffered from an overabundance of material. This shows itself especially in the second and fourth volumes, where he included material unnecessary in a bibliographic work. The relevant information is lost there in a
sea of studies and essays on peripheral themes. Wolf himself was aware of
this shortcoming of his work; he considered about half of the material
superfluous for a bibliographic work, and he planned to remove the unnecessary studies and essays and publish them in a separate *Bibliotheca
hebraea realis*. He did not accomplish this separation before his death on
July 25, 1739.[53]

   The *Bibliotheca hebraea* (*hebraea* rather than *rabbinica*) was, as the name
suggests, intended to be a bibliography of everything written in Hebrew,
from the posttalmudic period up to the year 1700. Wolf approached his task
with "diligence, honesty, patience, and objectivity,"[54] and accomplished it
successfully. His was the only work on Jewish bibliography of such
magnitude to be begun and completed by a single author, and he was only
fifty-six years old at his death. The *Bibliotheca hebraea* later became the
basis for the greatest Jewish bibliography of the nineteenth century, Moritz
Steinschneider's *Catalogus* of the Hebraica collection in the Bodleian,[55] but,
in the meantime, it dominated the field of Jewish bibliography for about 150
years.

   The entire four-volume set of the *Bibliotheca hebraea* was reissued in
New York by the Johnson Reprint Corporation in 1967.

## Hermann Friedrich Köcher:
### Nova Bibliotheca Hebraica

An effort to supplement and update Wolf's *Bibliotheca hebraea* was made half a century after the publication of its last volume. Hermann Friedrich Köcher (1747–1792), a German scholar who earlier had written a number of works on Biblical themes,[56] published a two-volume work in Jena, in 1783–1784, under the pretentious title, *Nova bibliotheca hebraica*. He arranged his text similarly to Wolf's *Bibliotheca,* and he attempted to supplement every section of the *Bibliotheca*. It was an effort that produced poor results, from a bibliographical as well as from a scholarly point of view and was later described as a "backward step" in the development of Jewish bibliography.[57]

## Jehiel Heilprin:
### Seder Mechabrim Veseder Sefarim

The second contemporary of Shabbethai Bass, Rabbi Jehiel ben Solomon Heilprin (1660–1746), contributed very little to the science of Jewish bibliography. Heilprin composed a major work of Jewish chronology entitled *Seder Hadorot*[58] and included in it a section on Jewish authors and their Hebrew works. The section, called *Seder Mechabrim Veseder Sefarim,* was divided into two parts: one listed authors and the other listed titles. Each group was arranged alphabetically, and it copied verbatim from Shabbethai Bass's *Sifte Yeshenim* with the exception of minor additions of authors and titles overlooked by Bass, or some that appeared later. The only major changes were bibliographic omissions; in the author list Heilprin eliminated biographical data given by Bass, and in the title list he omitted places of publication. Otherwise he retained everything, including Bass's unique form of arranging the entries of authors based upon their origins, whether Ashkenazic or Sephardic.[59] Sometimes Heilprin included Bass's errors.[60]

Adding a bibliography section to his chronology seems to have been an afterthought for Heilprin. It might be that, as a cabalist, he was influenced by Shabbethai Bass's cabalistic arguments for composing his *Sifte Yeshenim*. In any case, the science of Jewish bibliography did not gain from Heilprin's efforts, but Jewish bibliography, as such, did. Heilprin's inclusion of a bibliography section in his great work gave Jewish bibliography status among Jewish scholars, who until that time might have looked down on it. This became a blessing for the further development of Jewish bibliography during the following decades.

## Julius Fürst: *Bibliotheca Judaica*

Imbonati in his supplementary volume to Bartolocci's *Bibliotheca*, Bass in his *Sifte Yeshenim*, Wolf in his *Bibliotheca*, as well as other early bibliographers in their works, added sections of Judaica to the Hebraica bibliographies they compiled. These were lists of carefully selected works dealing with specific subjects of Jewish studies, but none of them claimed completeness. Only one effort is known to have been made toward compiling a complete Jewish bibliography, registering both Hebraica and Judaica. The compiler of that bibliography was Julius Fürst, a prominent Jewish scholar and prolific writer of nineteenth-century Germany. Fürst, born in 1805[61] in the Poznań region of Poland, traveled to Berlin at the age of fifteen to enroll as a student at a local gymnasium. Five years later he entered the yeshiva of the renowned Rabbi Akiba Eger (1761–1837) in Poznań. He then attended the universities of Breslau and Halle, and in 1832 received his doctorate at the latter. He settled afterwards in Leipzig, and was appointed lecturer (1839) and then professor (1864) of Semitic languages at the university there. He died in 1873.

Fürst's literary activities were manifold. He reedited the Hebrew Bible concordance[62] and wrote many books, notably textbooks on the Aramaic language, dictionaries of the Hebrew and Aramaic languages, and histories of Jewish literature and Jewish sects. He also founded and edited a weekly scientific publication.[63] But one of the greatest achievements of his career was without doubt his three-volume bibliography of Hebraica and Judaica. Written in the German language and published in Leipzig during the years 1849 to 1863, it was entitled *Bibliotheca Judaica*, with the subtitle "Bibliographisches Handbuch der gesammten jüdischen Literatur mit Einschluss der Schriften über Juden und Judenthum und einer Geschichte der jüdischen Bibliographie." The words "der gesammten jüdischen Literatur" were later modified (on the title page of volume three) to read "umfassend die Druckwerke der jüdischen Literatur," reflecting more accurately the scope of the bibliography. A new edition of the first two volumes (letters A–H, I–M) appeared simultaneously with the publication of the third volume of the first edition (1863).

The *Bibliotheca Judaica* was a massive bibliography, consisting of more than 1,600 densely printed pages, with the entries arranged alphabetically by the names of the authors. The number of titles registered in this work has been estimated to have been as many as 40,000; of these, 18,000 were Hebraica (according to one estimate; another estimate places the number of Hebraica at 13,500).[64] An index of Hebrew titles was appended to volume three, and a history of Jewish bibliography, promised in the subtitle, appeared at the beginning of the same volume. It carried the heading "Zur Geschichte der jüdischen Bibliographie," and it occupied 104 pages. Fürst included the following information in each entry:

Author (with brief biographical data, often supplemented by footnotes)
Title (Hebrew titles were listed in Hebrew characters)
Description of contents
Place and date of publication
Format

Theoretically, the *Bibliotheca Judaica* was to have included all the Hebraica and Judaica printed up to and including the year 1840, but upon its publication it turned out to be full of lacunae. Thousands of titles that should have been included in the *Bibliotheca* were left out, as Fürst himself admitted in the introduction to volume three. Furthermore, Fürst was quite careless in accepting bibliographical information. For example, he personally examined, according to his admission,[65] only between 3,500 and 4,000 Hebraica titles, relying for the rest on the information of earlier bibliographers. The alphabetical arrangement of the main entries in the *Bibliotheca* also left much to be desired. In his eagerness to attach the name of an author or editor to each and every Hebrew work, he not only placed such biblical works as Proverbs, Ecclesiastes, and Song of Songs under the entry "Salomo b. David," and the book of Samuel under "Samuel b. Elkana," and the Talmud Yerushalmi under "Jochanan b. Napcha" (an arrangement he copied from some of his predecessors), but he also sometimes placed these and similar works under the names of their printers. Fürst was aware of the defects in his work, and he planned to issue supplementary volumes, which would list the books not registered in the *Bibliotheca*, and which would separate under a correct form entry all the Hebrew classical works arranged in the *Bibliotheca* under authors' names.[66] But this plan never materialized.

The *Bibliotheca Judaica* was the only effort ever made at compiling an all-inclusive bibliography of Hebraica and Judaica together. The enormity of the task surely frightened away those who might have followed in Fürst's footsteps. Despite its many defects, the *Bibliotheca Judaica* remains a useful tool of Jewish research even in our day, especially in the area of German Judaica.

A reprint edition of the *Bibliotheca Judaica* was issued in Hildesheim by G. Olms in 1960.


## Isaac Benjacob: *Otsar Hasefarim*

Two hundred years after the *Sifte Yeshenim* by Shabbethai Bass was printed, the second all-inclusive all-Hebrew bibliography appeared. In these two centuries, Jewish bibliography had made great strides toward establishing itself as an independent branch of Jewish scholarship. Johann Christoph Wolf and Hayyim Joseph David Azulai[67] in the eighteenth century, Leopold Zunz[68] and Moritz Steinschneider[69] in the nineteenth century, and the corps of Jewish scholars and bibliographers who followed in their footsteps were all instrumental in moving Jewish bibliography forward.

The nineteenth century, it should be noted, was the most fruitful century for Jewish bibliography. Catalogs of handwritten and printed Hebraica collections at the most important European libraries, compiled by Jewish scholars of high caliber, became available;[70] scholarly periodicals, devoted solely to the science of Jewish bibliography and edited by authorities in the field, began to appear;[71] and bibliographical consciousness began to penetrate Jewish literature and life. The first and only effort at a bibliography for the "gesammte Jüdische Literatur" was also made in the nineteenth century.[72] But it was not until the second half of that century that the hope of Jewish scholars and bibliographers of compiling a new all-Hebrew bibliography became a reality. Two men, a father and a son (assisted by a number of devoted scholars and bibliographers), should be credited with this accomplishment. The father, Isaac Benjacob, devoted "decades" of his life to compiling it; the son, Jacob Benjacob, devoted almost his entire life to publishing it, and afterwards to improving it.[73]

Isaac Benjacob was born in the year 1801 in a small town near the city of Vilna, in Lithuania. During his childhood his parents moved to Vilna, where he received his Jewish education. He also had a special tutor for Hebrew language and grammar and, at a young age, he began to write flowery Hebrew and to compose Hebrew poems, his poetic activity continuing even during his later years. He turned to business, and moved to the Latvian city of Riga. There he decided to specialize in the book trade, and he moved on to the center of book trading in those days, Leipzig. He stayed there for several years, during which time he published a number of Hebrew works, including his own *Michtamim Veshirim Shonim* (Leipzig, 1842).[74]

During those years he also published essays and poems in various Hebrew periodicals and worked diligently on the preparation of two dictionaries, one German-Hebrew and the other mishnaic-talmudic; they remain unpublished. He returned to Vilna and became involved in the civic and educational problems of the Jewish community,[75] but he did not neglect his publishing activities. Together with Abraham Dob Baer Lebensohn (Adam Hakohen) (1794–1878), he prepared and published a seventeen-volume set of the Hebrew Bible with a translation and commentaries in German,[76] and planned to issue a series of scientific editions of classical Hebrew works under the general title of *Kiryat Sefer Lechochmat Yisrael.*[77] Throughout these years, although occupied with a variety of activities, he concentrated his main efforts on compiling and publishing a new all-inclusive Hebraica bibliography. He died in 1863 before he could complete his work.

Isaac Benjacob probably began planning his Hebrew bibliography around the time that he began his book-dealing activities.[78] First he visualized it as an extension of Shabbethai Bass's *Sifte Yeshenim.*[79] Later, as the work progressed, he abandoned that idea and decided to start from the beginning.[80] While in Leipzig, he corresponded with and became aquainted with most of the well-known Jewish-German scholars, and they encouraged him in his bibliographical work. The most important and the most useful acquaintance he made during that time was Moritz Steinschneider.[81] Steinschneider became very fond of Benjacob and interested in his work, and he spent time and energy helping him with the preparation of his bibliographical entries. Benjacob considered his work as a definitive bibliography of Hebrew literature. He utilized every possible source of information, and he revised his manuscript three times[82] to make sure that the information was correctly transmitted. He sent the third version to his friend Steinschneider, to review and annotate it. After receiving Steinschneider's notes and remarks on the first eight letters of the alphabet, Benjacob began the final revision of his manuscript. He was able to prepare only the eight letters of the alphabet that he had received from Steinschneider, for he succumbed to a fatal illness in the midst of his efforts.[83]

Thirteen years after Isaac Benjacob's death, his son Jacob published an announcement in the Hebrew press of his intentions to edit and publish his father's Hebraica bibliography.[84] Jacob Benjacob was born in Vilna in 1858, and he was only five years old when he lost his father. Already in his early years he had become obsessed by the idea of publishing his father's most important work. He later became a successful businessman and an active member of the Jewish community of Vilna, participated in the early Zionist congresses, and was Theodor Herzl's host when the latter visited Vilna in 1903.[85] But his obsession with publishing and improving his father's bibliographical work stayed with him to his last days.

A year after Jacob Benjacob announced his intention of publishing his father's Hebraica bibliography, he submitted the manuscript to a printer. The printing took three years, and Jacob Benjacob used these years to revise the entire manuscript anew. He was assisted in this task by a number of scholars and bibliographers, but most of all by Steinschneider.[86] The complete text of Isaac Benjacob's bibliography was finally published in 1880 with the title *Otsar Hasefarim*. It lists, in alphabetical order by title, Hebrew (and a selection of Yiddish) works, published until the year 1863, printed as well as handwritten. A statement on the title page claims that the *Otsar* lists "up to 17,000" titles; in actuality, it registers only about 15,000, including some doubtful titles and duplications. The number of manuscripts included in the *Otsar* has been estimated at about 3,000.[87]

In the introduction to the *Otsar,* Jacob Benjacob listed "thirteen principles" upon which his father based the entries of his work:

Title
Author (including editor, copyist, annotator, and publisher)
Script (whether written in square Hebrew letters, Rashi characters, Ashkenazic or Sephardic cursives, etc.)
Language (Hebrew, Aramaic, mixed; grammatical Hebrew or slang)
Contents and description (additions by others are noted)
Interpretations and commentaries (printed or written together with the text)
Organization (parts, sections, chapters; how entitled)
Translations (from which work, language; into which script, language)
Place of publication
Date of publication
Format (changes that occurred in various editions)
Manuscripts: place and date of composing, location and call-number
Book without imprints (n. p., n. d.), or doubtful titles: opinions of bibliographers are cited, and sometimes decisions rendered; an effort is made to identify authors of anonymous works and to replace pen-names with real ones

These "thirteen principles," Benjacob's scheme for the entries of the *Otsar,* clearly reveal the advances Jewish bibliography had made during the two centuries since the publication of Shabbethai Bass's *Sifte Yeshenim.* An examination of the entries, however, shows a kinship with those of the *Sifte Yeshenim,* although the entries of the *Otsar* are more developed and of a better scholarly quality. The main distinction between the two related works is in the wealth of information and in the critical examination of the sources. Bass entered and registered any information, it seems, without questioning its reliability; Benjacob carefully examined all the sources at his disposal, and in cases of doubt he only presented the information and left the conclusions to the reader. Needless to say, every entry in the *Otsar* is fuller and more complete than its counterpart in the *Sifte Yeshenim* whose entries look anemic by comparison.[88] A comparison of the following entries illustrates the differences in information presented in the *Sifte Yeshenim* and the *Otsar:*

|          | *Sifte*        | *Otsar*         |
|----------|----------------|-----------------|
| Machzor  | 1½ columns     | 11 columns      |
| Talmud   | 3 columns      | 7½ columns      |
| Tanach   | 6½ columns     | 31½ columns     |
| Yosippon | 12 lines       | 2½ columns      |
| Zohar    | 24 lines       | 81 lines        |

Benjacob's *Otsar* was received enthusiastically by many scholars and bibliographers.[89] In addition to their praise and expressions of gratitude, some scholars and bibliographers began compiling and publishing corrections and additions to the *Otsar,* to be included in the supplementary volume promised by the publisher.[90] This second volume, according to the publisher, Jacob Benjacob, was to contain additions, corrections, and an author index.[91] Such a volume was never published, because within a short time the newly accumulated material outgrew the limits of the planned supplementary volume; the projected author index had to be enlarged to include additional names (joint authors, publishers, translators, etc.), and a subject index had to be compiled.[92] For these reasons, Jacob Benjacob abandoned the idea of a supplementary volume to the *Otsar,* and he began working on an entirely new and completely revised *Otsar Hasefarim.*[93]

He spent forty-five years of his life preparing the new edition and, when it was finally completed, the manuscript consisted of about 60,000 alphabetically arranged title entries in twelve volumes, with 20,000 additional slips for indexes. This new edition was to include, besides books in Hebrew, all books printed or written in Hebrew characters. The style of the entries differed in only a few details from the original (as outlined above), the major differences being the addition of the dates the works were written or translated, and the listing of reviews. There were to be indexes of authors (including translators and publishers), their family names and special surnames; countries, cities, etc.; printing places (in chronological order); and subjects.

The decades of effort invested in the new *Otsar* turned out to have been in vain. The *Otsar* was not destined to be published. When Jacob Benjacob reached the last stages of preparing the new *Otsar* for publication, he submitted a proposal for a subvention to the Polish Academy of Sciences in Cracow. The Academy agreed, in principle, to support the undertaking. The proposal was turned over to a committee to work out the details, and there the entire matter was laid to rest. This was in 1922. Benjacob died in 1926, and his son-in-law, Professor Moses Schorr (1874–1941),[94] inherited the manuscript. He tried for more than a decade to have it published. In 1928 he asked the Gesellschaft zur Förderung der Wissenschaft des Judentums in Berlin to take over the publication of the manuscript. The Gesellschaft agreed on condition that the project be financed jointly with the Central Conference of American Rabbis.[95] The Conference originally agreed to raise the sum of $6,000 for this purpose, but later, after learning that several years might be required to prepare the manuscript for print, withdrew its offer. In 1932 Schorr approached the Hebrew University and the Jewish National Library in Jerusalem. They rejected it for the above reasons, and also for lack of funds.[96] Other institutions were approached, but funds could not be found for such a project. Schorr finally decided to start printing the *Otsar* at his own expense, hoping that such a move would attract the needed support from individuals and institutions. During the years 1934 to 1935, he published a number of articles in Jewish periodicals about the state of the new *Otsar* and about his intentions.[97] But his efforts were fruitless, for nothing additional was published by Schorr about any progress made during the next few years.

The holocaust that engulfed Polish Jewry during World War II destroyed Jacob Benjacob's manuscript. When the war was over and Jewish scholars, survivors from European Jewry, began to arrive on the shores of the United States to organize their lives anew, one of the first Hebrew works to be reprinted was the original edition of Isaac Benjacob's *Otsar Hasefarim* (New York, n. d.; [i.e., 1944/45 or 1945/46]).[98]

## Menahem Mendel Slatkine:
### Otsar Hasefarim Chelek Sheni

A supplementary volume to Isaac Benjacob's *Otsar Hasefarim* was finally compiled and published in Tel Aviv in 1965 by a resident of Geneva. The compiler, Menahem Mendel Slatkine (1875–1965), a bookdealer by profession, had previously published two works related to Jewish bibliography: a two-volume study of Hebrew titles[99] and an analytical study of Shabbethai Bass's *Sifte Yeshenim*.[100] He became acquainted with Jacob Benjacob during World War I, and he followed with interest the developments concerning Benjacob's manuscript. After World War II, when he became convinced that the manuscript no longer existed, he decided to reconstruct some of the work done by Jacob Benjacob.[101] He concentrated his efforts in two directions: in annotating the entries of the *Otsar,* bringing them up to date with the aid of bibliographical tools published since 1863; and in preparing an index of authors, translators, commentators, and editors of the books listed in the *Otsar.*

He succeeded in annotating about one-third (over 4,000) of the entries, and he compiled an index. Of the 481 pages in his volume, two-thirds contained his annotations and one-third the index. The annotations included corrections of typographical or other kinds of errors; first editions overlooked by Benjacob; authorship of works, places and dates of publication questioned by Benjacob, but now established with certainty; works listed as manuscripts, but now available in printed editions; and information about the location of many manuscripts not furnished by Benjacob.[102]

Slatkine began this work late in life and had it printed shortly before his death. As a result, this work suffers from many inadequacies.[103] The hope of recreating Isaac Benjacob's *Otsar* in a new refined version, and of making it more accessible by providing indexes, was only partially fulfilled by Slatkine. His singular contribution is, no doubt, the index which opens the door a little wider to the most reliable and accurate Hebrew bibliography, the *Otsar Hasefarim.*[104]

### Bernhard Friedberg: *Bet Eked Sefarim*

While Jacob Benjacob, with the help of Moritz Steinschneider, was preparing the supplement volume to his father's Hebrew bibliography, a young man of seventeen became so excited by the *Otsar Hasefarim* that he decided to follow its example. That young man, Bernhard Friedberg, later related his experience in the following words:

> Thirty-five years ago, I came into possession of the work *Otsar Hasefarim* by Isaac Benjacob. I was attracted to it as if by a magnet, and I studied it diligently day and night.[105]

Born in Cracow, Poland, in 1876, Friedberg began his literary activities at an early age. His first work was published in 1895.[106] He later turned to business, first dealing in books and then in diamonds,[107] but he never neglected his writing. He wrote more than a dozen works, among them a four-volume work on the history of Hebrew printing in Europe,[108] and a massive, 844-page new and all-inclusive Hebraica bibliography entitled *Bet Eked Sefarim*.

In recapitulating the events that led him to compile his bibliography, Friedberg writes:

> Years went by. For business reasons, I had to visit almost all the most important libraries of Europe, where I discovered an abundance of printed books— in the hundreds and in the thousands—that Benjacob did not see. . . . I also found numerous errors in his statements. Since then, and until today, I decided to work constantly, to collect the clay and bricks to build the *Bet Eked Sefarim*.[109]

He goes on to claim to have rebuilt Benjacob's *Otsar* "from the foundation to the ceiling," and to have corrected its errors, a claim that is not substantiated by the facts.[110]

Printing of the *Bet Eked Sefarim* began in Antwerp (where Friedberg resided) in 1928, and it was completed there in 1931. In alphabetical order, the bibliography lists about 26,000 works in Hebrew, in Yiddish, and in various Jewish dialects, printed up to the year 1900. Friedberg structured the entries by title, as did Benjacob, but he added pagination, which is lacking in Benjacob's entries. He included a separate list of incunabula and books printed in limited editions, and he also provided three indexes:

> Subjects (which guides the reader to more than 100 topics)
> Authors (in which about 8,000 authors are registered)
> Places of printing (which lists 280 places where Hebrew printing was done from 1475 to 1900)

The last six pages of the *Bet Eked* listed several hundred duplicate entries in Benjacob's *Otsar*.[111]

Friedberg's effort was accepted with mixed feelings by Jewish scholars and bibliographers. They acknowledged his contribution to Jewish bibliography in extending the register of printed Hebraica up to the year 1900, and in making his bibliography more accessible to the user than Benjacob's *Otsar,* through the subject and author indexes. However, they also criticized him severely for the many gaps and errors in the *Bet Eked.*[112] Following Benjacob, with his complete mastery of the entire field of Jewish literature and masterful utilization of all available sources, Friedberg could not expect to receive many favorable comments. Compared to the *Otsar,* the *Bet Eked* seemed pale and dry, and it was a great disappointment to many scholars. But in the absence of anything better, it soon became a useful practical tool for bookdealers and bibliographers alike.

Friedberg survived the Nazi onslaught in his adopted country, Belgium. In 1946, at the age of seventy, he arrived in Israel and began preparing a new edition of his *Bet Eked.* The first volume of the new edition appeared in Tel Aviv in 1951, and five years later (1956), the fourth and final volume appeared. The four-volume set (1,420 pages) registered about 50,000 various editions of Hebraica works, printed up to the year 1950.[113] Friedberg also tried to correct some of the deficiencies pointed out by the reviewers of the first edition of *Bet Eked,* but since his work was done in great haste, he unfortunately entangled himself in new errors.[114] Nevertheless, the new *Bet Eked* became a standard work of Jewish bibliography, and soon was out of print. It is now the only all-inclusive Hebraica bibliography listing works printed from the beginning of printing through the first half of the twentieth century. Friedberg died in 1961.

Photographically reproduced reprints of the second edition of the *Bet Eked Sefarim* were recently issued in Israel (Jerusalem? in 1969 or 1970, and Tel Aviv in 1971).

An effort to supplement Friedberg's bibliography with Hebrew works published between 1950 and 1975 was recently made by M. Moriyah with the publication of *Bet Eked Sefarim Hechadash* (Kiryat Shemona, Safed, 1974—1976). The five volume work consists of almost 28,000 entries arranged by title. Volume 1, for *alef* and *bet* covers titles published through 1973 only.

## Mif'al Habibliyografyah Ha'ivrit

The deplorable situation in the field of Jewish bibliography—the lack of a complete and accurate register for Hebraica that would meet modern standards and requirements—has for a long time troubled many Jewish scholars, bibliographers, and librarians.[115] They felt that this basic bibliographic need had to be met by the present generation. The destruction of hundreds of thousands of Jewish books in Europe during World War II, and the liquidation of old established Jewish communities in Asia and Africa and their relocation in the State of Israel, resulted in a severe reduction of the number of extant copies of Hebrew titles. There was a clear possibility that titles now available in only a few copies would disappear entirely during the next generation. Some also expressed their concern about the constantly diminishing number of Hebrew bibliographers and book experts, a crisis that worsens with the passage of time. They feared that the next generation might lack the scholarly manpower for compiling a complete Hebraica bibliography.[116]

In the early 1950s, an Israeli scholar and bibliophile, Dr. Israel Mehlmann, therefore proposed to the Bialik Institute in Jerusalem, that it take the initiative in executing a plan for a scientific all-inclusive Hebraica bibliography.[117] The Bialik Institute accepted the proposal and invited several other Israeli institutions to participate in such an undertaking. After five years of negotiations, an agreement was signed in 1959 by the Hebrew University of Jerusalem, the Bialik Institute, the Rabbi Kook Institute, and the Ministry of Education and Culture of the State of Israel jointly to sponsor a project to prepare a complete register of printed Hebraica. Thus came into being the Mif'al Habibliyografyah Ha'ivrit (officially translated as the Institute for Hebrew Bibliography).[118]

In 1960 the Mif'al began its work on the premises of the Jewish National and University Library in Jerusalem. During that same year, the Editorial Council and the Editorial Staff of the Mif'al were also organized. They consisted of academicians, bibliographers, and bookmen.[119] One of the sponsoring institutions, the Rabbi Kook Institute, withdrew from the Mif'al a year later, but the other three decided to continue their support until the completion of the project.[120] When the Mif'al began its activities, members of the Editorial Council estimated that compiling the material would take eight to ten years, and that printing would require an additional five years. They also estimated that the bibliography would occupy twelve to thirteen volumes, of which two or three would be reserved for the various indexes.[121] As to the number of works that the bibliography would encompass, opinions varied between 80,000 and 150,000.[122]

The Mif'al, at the outset, adopted the following three "principles" of its purpose:

a. To register all books printed in the Hebrew language or in Hebrew characters, without exception. The cut-off date is to be 1960. The first stage of the effort will be devoted to Hebrew-language books; the second stage will concentrate on books in Hebrew characters. Each linguistic unit (i.e., Ladino, Yiddish, Judaeo-Arabic, etc.) will constitute a separate section.
b. To register books from actual copies at hand, and not on the basis of other lists ("unless not a single copy is known to be extant").
c. To compile a series of detailed indexes (title, subject, etc.) giving the user complete access to the information in the body of the bibliography.[123]

The Mif'al also established rules of entry, the most crucial of which were the following:

*Author.* Except for anonymous works, arrangement to be alphabetical by author's name in Hebrew with an Anglicized transcription, followed by brief biographical data.

*Title.* Title and all additional information to be copied directly from title page; superfluous facts that do not add to the identification of the work, to be left out. Information to be retained should include, besides the author's name, also his parents' names, place of residence, place of printing, printer or publisher, and year of publication. Works by the same author, or by another author, included in the same book, to be described in the same entry or in a note.

*Approbations.* To include exact name of approvers, their places of residence, and the dates of issuance.[124]

In 1963, after a few years of intensive work, the Mif'al issued a mimeographed volume (116 leaves) entitled *Choveret Ledugmah.* It consisted of the following five main-entry samples from the letter *alef:*

איבשיץ, אייזנשטיין, אלגאזי, ארחות צדיקים, אריסטו.

A refined and enlarged edition of the *Choveret Ledugmah* (48 pp.), with an added title in English, *Specimen Brochure,* was published in printed form a year later (1964). It included a sixth main-entry sample (אחד העם) besides the above-mentioned entries, an introduction by the chairman of the editorial staff, Professor Gershom Scholem, and the "rules of compilation" established by the Mif'al.[125] The latter two were printed in both Hebrew and English. Nothing has been issued since.

Jewish scholars, students of Jewish literature, bibliographers, and librarians will have to wait patiently for several more years for the appearance of the first volumes of this new, most promising, all-inclusive scientific Hebraica bibliography.[126]

## Chronological List of
## General Hebraica Bibliographies

### 1613

Buxtorf, Johannes (Germany, 1564—Switzerland, 1629).
Bibliotheca rabbinica nova, ordine alphabethico disposita. Basileae:
Typis C. Waldkirchi, impensis L. König, 1613.
Pp. 257—335. (Second part of his *De abbreviaturis hebraicis liber novus et copiosus*).

324 printed or handwritten Hebrew works. Titles in Hebrew, text in Latin.

*Order of entries:* Title, transliteration and translation of title, description and contents, author, place and date of publication (for printed works).

*Editions:* Basileae: Impensis Ludovici Regis, 1640 (enlarged and corrected by Johannes Buxtorf, the son), with "Appendix ad Bibliotheca rabbinica" (by Jacob Roman), and index of authors; Franequerae, Apud J. Horreum, 1696 (without significant changes); Herbornae Nassaviae, Stanno et sumtibus Ioan. Nicolai Andreae, 1708 (enlarged and brought up to date by Johann Adam Faber, Johann Heinrich Schramm, and Georg Christian Burcklin).

### 1675—1693

Bartolocci, Giulio (Italy, 1613—1687).
קרית ספר. Bibliotheca magna rabbinica de scriptoribus, et scriptis hebraicis, ordine alphabetico Hebraicè et Latinè digestis. Romae: ex typographia Sacrae congregationis de propaganda fide, 1675—1693.
4 vols. (ca. 3,500 pages). Folio format.

1,960 entries of printed and handwritten Hebrew works. Text in Hebrew and Latin. Indexes of titles, cross references, subjects, and names of authors and places in Hebrew and Latin.

*Order of entries:* In Hebrew: author, topic, or work (if anonymous or if ancient classic work); biographical data; title; description of contents; place and date of publication; location (if manuscript). In Latin: author, topic, or work; biographical data; title (romanized and translated); description of contents with additional bibliographical data;

place and date of publication (in the Hebrew as well as in the universal reckoning); format; location (for manuscripts, with addition of information, whether written on paper or on parchment).

*Editions:* Farborough: Gregg Publishers, 1965—1968 (photo-offset reprint). 4 vols. Folio format.

A disciple of Bartolocci edited Volume 4 and compiled a supplementary volume, as follows:

### (1694)

Imbonati, Carlo Giuseppe (Italy, 1650?—1696).

מגן וחרב ומלחמה. Bibliotheca latino-hebraica sive De scriptoribus latinis, qui ex diversis nationibus contra Iudaeos ... Romae: ex typographia Sacrae congregationis de propaganda fide, 1694.
    549 pages. Folio format.

More than 1,300 works in Latin by non-Jewish authors on Jewish (and anti-Jewish) themes. Subject index. Published as Volume 5 of Bartolocci's *Bibliotheca.*

*Editions:* Farborough: Gregg Publishers, 1968 (published as Volume 5 of Bartolocci's *Bibliotheca).*

### 1680

Bass, Shabbethai (Poland, 1641—Germany, 1718).
שפתי ישינים. Amsterdam: David Tartas, 1680.
    20 leaves, 92 pages, 93—108 leaves.

First Hebraica bibliography compiled by a Jewish scholar and written in Hebrew. About 2,200 printed and handwritten titles (minus approximately 265 duplications).

*Organization:* Four sections: two-part subject index (called "doors"); list of titles (the "house"); index of authors (the "major portal"); select list of Judaica by non-Jewish authors ("external portal").

*Order of entries:* Title, author, description (with occasional critical comment), place and Hebrew date of publication; location (of manuscripts), format.

*Editions:* Żołkiew: Mordecai Rubinstein, 1806. Edited by Uri Zvi Rubinstein, who added part two, consisting of 700 works that appeared since the publication of the first edition. Editor also introduced new material and corrections into first part. Inferior to original edition.

## 1715—1733

Wolf, Johann Christoph (Germany, 1683—1739).

Bibliotheca hebraea, sive, Notitia tum auctorum hebr. cujuscunque aetatis, tum scriptorum, quae vel hebraice primum exarata vel ab aliis conversa sunt, ad nostram aetatem deducta. Accedit in calce Jacobi Gaffarelli index codicum cabbalistic. mss. quibus Jo. Picus Mirandulanus comes, usus est. Hamburgi (etc.): Christian Liebezeit, 1715—1733.

4 vols. (more than 5,000 pages)

Based largely on Oppenheimer Collection (see Chapter 2 below).

*Organization:* Volume 1: 2,231 entries, index of titles, list of cabalistic works (compiled by J. Gaffarel). Volume 2: mainly devoted to long studies on biblical, talmudic, and linguistic topics, except for section listing apologetics and anti-Jewish works, and list of 784 anonymous Hebrew titles. Volumes 3 and 4 consist of additions and corrections to the preceding volumes, and include indexes of authors, subjects, and titles.

*Order of entries:* Author (in Hebrew characters, followed by romanized form with addition of sources for origin of name), biographical data, title (in Hebrew characters, followed by translation with references to origin of title), contents, place and date of publication, format, location (especially if available in Oppenheimer Collection).

*Editions:* New York: Johnson Reprint Corporation, 1967 (photo-offset reprint).

Supplement was compiled and published, as follows:

## (1783—1784)

Köcher, Hermann Friedrich (Germany 1747—1792).

Nova bibliotheca hebraica, secundum ordinem Bibliothecae hebraicae Io. Christoph Wolfii disposita, analecta literaria hujus operis sistens . . . Ienae: impensis haeredum C. H. Cunosis, 1783—1784.

2 vols.

Effort by Köcher considered "backward step" in history of Jewish bibliography.

## 1769

Heilprin, Jehiel (Russia, circa 1660−1746).

(סדר מחברים וסדר ספרים) שמות בעלי מחברים וכל הספרים . . .

Karlsruhe: Johann Friedrich Cornelius Stern, 1769.
Leaves (160)-180. Folio format (third part of his סדר הדורות).

Copied verbatim from Bass's *Sifte Yeshenim*, plus a few minor additions, and minus biographical data and places of publication.

*Organization:* Two sections: one listing authors; the other listing titles.

*Editions:* Reprinted numerous times in various editions; to be described in
    Volume Two of this work. The Hebrew title above in parenthesis is from the edition by Naphtali Maskileison (Warsaw, 1878−1882), the most reliable edition of the *Seder Hadorot.*

## 1849−1863

Fürst, Julius (Poland, 1805−Germany, 1873).
    Bibliotheca Judaica; bibliographisches Handbuch der gesammten jüdischen Literatur, mit Einschluss der Schriften über Juden und Judenthum und einer Geschichte der jüdischen Bibliographie. Leipzig: W. Engelmann, 1849−1863).
    3 vols. (more than 1,600 pages).

About 40,000 titles of printed Hebraica and Judaica (Hebraica estimated from 13,000 to 18,000). Cut-off date: 1840. Preceding Volume 3, history of Jewish bibliography; at end, index of Hebrew titles. The only Jewish bibliography listing Hebraica and Judaica in a single alphabet.

*Order of entries:* Author    (with    brief    biographical    data    often
    supplemented by footnotes), title (Hebrew titles in Hebrew characters), description and contents, place and date of publication, format.

*Editions:* Leipzig: Engelmann, 1863 (Volumes 1 and 2 only. In this edition
    as well as in Volume 3 of the first edition the subtitle was changed to read: "Bibliographisches Handbuch umfassend die Druckwerke der jüdischen Literatur, einschliesslich der über Juden und Judenthum veröffentlichten Schriften . . . "); Hildesheim: G. Olms, 1960 (photo-offset reprint).

## 1877—1880

Benjacob, Isaac (Russia, 1801—1863).
אוצר הספרים. Vilna: Romm, 1877—1880.
xxxii, 678 pages.

Originally planned as extension to Shabbethai Bass's *Sifte Yeshenim;* later developed into independent work. Edited and published by author's son, Jacob Benjacob, with assistance of several scholars, notably Moritz Steinschneider. Author revised manuscript three times. Despite statement on title page, actual number of titles only about 15,000. Titles also include Old Yiddish works. Cut-off date: 1863.

*Order of entries:* Title, author (including editor, copyist, annotator, and publisher), script (whether written in square Hebrew letters, Rashi characters, Ashkenazic or Sephardic cursives, etc.), language (whether in Hebrew, Aramaic, mixed, etc.), contents and description, interpretations and commentaries (if written or printed together with text), organization of work, translations, place and date of publication (manuscripts: place and date of composing, location, and call number), format.

*Editions:* New York, Hotsa'at Yerushalayim, n. d. (i.e., 1944/45 or 1945/46). (Photo-offset reprint.)

Supplementary volume was compiled and published, as follows:

### (1965)

Slatkine, Menahem Mendel (Russia, 1875—Switzerland, 1965).
אוצר הספרים חלק שני. Jerusalem: Kiryat Sepher, 1965.
481 pages.

Includes: annotations to about 4,000 entries in Benjacob's *Otsar;* corrections of errors (typographical or otherwise); editions of works omitted; places and dates of publication questioned by Benjacob but now established with certainty; manuscripts published since appearance of *Otsar;* locations of manuscripts not given by Benjacob; index of authors, translators, commentators, and editors listed in the *Otsar.*

## 1928—1931

Friedberg, Bernhard (Poland, 1876—Israel 1961).

בית עקד ספרים. Antwerp, 1928–1931.
4 leaves, 844 pages. Folio format.

26,000 printed Hebraica. Cut-off date: 1900.

*Organization:* Alphabetical list of titles; separate list of incunabula and
limited editions; indexes of subjects (over one hundred
topics), authors (about 8,000), places of printing (280 places); duplicate
entries in Benjacob's *Otsar.*

*Order of entries:* Similar to Benjacob's order of entries in the *Otsar,* with
omission of critical and bibliographical notes, and addi-
tion of pagination.

*Editions:* "Second edition, enlarged, improved and revised," Tel Aviv,
1951–1956. 4 vols. (1,420 pages). About 50,000 titles and editions. Cut-off date extended to: 1950; photographically reduced reprints issued in Israel, Jerusalem? 1969 or 1970 and Tel Aviv, 1971.

A supplement was compiled and published, as follows:

### (1974)

Moriyah, M.
בית עקד ספרים החדש, תש״י-תשל״ג. Kiryat Shemona, Safed, Hotsa'at
Machon Tsiyon, 1974–1976.
5 vols. Folio format.

More than 28,765 entries arranged by title. Lists Hebrew monographs
published during 1950–1975 (1973 for first two letters of the alphabet).

### 1963

Jerusalem. Mif'al Habibliyografyah Ha'ivrit.
חוברת לדוגמה .״. . הותקנו בידי נפתלי בן-מנחם ועמו חבר העובדים . . . . Jerusalem, 1963.
116 leaves (mimeographed).

Mif'al established in 1959. *Purpose:* to compile definitive Hebraica
bibliography. Estimated number of volumes to be published: twelve to thirteen (of which two or three will contain indexes). Publication of first volume
expected after 1975. Cut-off date to be 1960.

*Choveret Ledugmah* includes the following five sample entries: Eybeschütz,
Eisenstein, Algazi, Orchot tsadikim, Aristotle.

*Order of entries:* Author in Hebrew followed by romanization, biographical data, title (parents of author, residence), place of printing, printer, date of publication (Hebrew and universal, also acronym), pagination, format, approbations (names of approvers, their places of residence, dates of issuance), bibliographical notes.

*Editions:* Jerusalem, 1964 (48 pages), with addition of introduction, rules of compilation (in Hebrew and English; also English title page: *Specimen Brochure*), and a new entry: Achad Ha'am.

## JO. CHRISTOPHORI WOLFII,
Profesf. Publ. Lingvarum Orientt. & h. a,
Gymnafii Rectoris

# BIBLIOTHECA HEBRÆA,

*Sive*

## NOTITIA TVM AVCTORVM HEBR.
CVJVSCVNQVE ÆTATIS, TVM SCRIPTORVM,
QVÆ VEL HEBRAICE PRIMVM EXARATA VEL AB
ALIIS CONVERSA SVNT, AD NOSTRAM ÆTATEM
DEDVCTA.

Accedit in calce JACOBI GAFFARELLI
Index Codicum Cabbaliftic. MSS. quibus
Jo. Picus, Mirandulanus Comes, ufus eft,

*HAMBURGI & LIPSIÆ,*
Impenfis CHRISTIANI LIEBEZEIT
ANNO R. S. cɔ lɔcc xv.

Title page of volume 1 of *Bibliotheca Hebraea* by Johann Christoph Wolf, the last of the great Christian bibliographers of Jewish literature. 4 volumes, Hamburg, Impensis Christiani Liebezeit, 1715–1733.

# Chapter Two

# Catalogs of Hebraica Book Collections

*From the close to four hundred catalogs of printed and handwritten Hebraica and Judaica published during the last two hundred years, only the catalogs of collections housed in five European institutions substantially advanced the science of Jewish bibliography. Detailed descriptions of these catalogs, the achievements of the bibliographers who compiled them, and highlights of the lives of the collectors who brought them together will form the first part of this chapter.*

*The second part will briefly describe three Jewish book collections in the United States and their printed card catalogs. The separation was made in order to distinguish between the early scholarly catalogs, meant to assist not only the user of the specific book collection but also the scholar and student of Jewish literature in general, and library card catalogs, whose primary function is to serve as devices for locating books on library shelves.*

I

Bibliotheca Bodleiana. David Oppenheimer and the Oppenheimer Collection. Moritz Steinschneider: *Catalogus. . .Bodleiana*. Arthur Ernest Cowley: *Concise Catalogue*. Adolf Neubauer: *Catalogue of the Hebrew Manuscripts*. British Museum. Joseph Zedner: *Catalogue of the Hebrew Books*. Van Straalen's Supplement. George Margoliouth: *Catalogue of the Hebrew and Samaritan Manuscripts*. Leeser Rosenthal and the Bibliotheca Rosenthaliana. The Rosenthal—Roest *Catalog der Hebraica und Judaica*. Moses Aryeh Loeb Friedland and the Bibliotheca Friedlandiana. Samuel Wiener: *Kohelet Mosheh*. Bernhard Wachstein: *Katalog der Salo Cohn'schen Schenkungen*.

II

Printed Card Catalogs. New York Public Library: *Dictionary Catalog of the Jewish Collection.* Hebrew Union College—Jewish Institute of Religion, Cincinnati: *Dictionary Catalog of the Klau Library.* Harvard University Library: *Catalogue of Hebrew Books.*

## I. Catalogs of Hebraica Collections in European Institutions

### Bibliotheca Bodleiana

THE HISTORY of the magnificent Hebraica collections at most European libraries begins in the homes of devoted Jewish book collectors.[1] These bibliophiles, possessed by an irresistible drive to gather and to own printed Hebrew volumes and handwritten codices, spent fortunes in money, time, and energy to search, discover, and add choice works to their book holdings. Many years of their lives were devoted to the hobby of book hunting; they worked hard to satisfy this passion for books and, when they passed away, their heirs transferred these priceless possessions to public institutions for relatively insignificant compensation.

The migration of Hebrew books from private hands to public ownership turned out to be a blessing for Jewish scholarship. The movement of such collections into the library buildings of Western Europe began to accelerate during the first part of the nineteenth century, and bore fruit during the second half of that century in the form of precise, accurate, and scientific catalogs of these collections. Based on books at hand, carefully examined and thoroughly researched and investigated, these catalogs soon became the most reliable tools available for the Jewish scholar. First was the Bodleian Library at Oxford. Founded in the fifteenth century, the Bodleian received its first Hebrew books and manuscripts only two centuries later. But it took one more century to turn this library into a depository for the most important and magnificent Hebraica collection ever accumulated.[2] This was achieved with the acquisition of the Oppenheimer Collection in 1829.

# David Oppenheimer
## and the Oppenheimer Collection

David Oppenheimer, the man whose name became synonymous with great book collecting, was born in Worms, Germany, in 1664.[3] After studying for a number of years in the rabbinic schools (yeshivot) of several German communities (Friedberg, Metz, etc.), he was married at the age of seventeen. He continued his studies, and at the age of twenty-five (1689) he was appointed rabbi of the city of Nikolsburg and chief rabbi of Moravia. In 1702 Oppenheimer became rabbi of Prague. A decade later (1713) his jurisdiction also included one half of Bohemia, and it was extended five years later (1718) when he became *Landrabbiner* of all Bohemia.

In Nikolsburg as well as in Prague Oppenheimer devoted much time and energy to establishing and developing schools for the benefit of young scholars under his direction. He also spent a great deal of time in writing rabbinic commentaries, novellae, and responsa.[4] Oppenheimer was very active in the affairs of his community, and often had to travel long distances on community business. Despite his complaint that he "hardly has time to breathe,"[5] Oppenheimer found time for a hobby, a very expensive one, begun as a young man and continued during the rest of his life: book collecting.

Oppenheimer began collecting Hebraica works at an early age, and when he was twenty-four years old he prepared a catalog of his holdings, in which he listed 480 titles.[6] Rumor had it that the nucleus of his collection came from his uncle, Samuel Oppenheimer (1605?–1703), imperial court factor in Vienna, who received it from the emperor as an expression of thanks for services rendered during the war against the French. The books were reportedly plundered from Jews in France (or Turkey) by the emperor's army.[7] This version of the origin of the Oppenheimer Collection has been questioned by several scholars, and seems not to be supported by any evidence.[8] In fact, Oppenheimer purchased most of his books for a great deal of money. He attended the Leipzig book fairs to make contact with bookdealers and printers; he contracted with printers to have additional copies of their publications printed on special material (vellum or blue paper) for him. In the words of one of his biographers, "no place was too far and no price too high for him when it came to acquiring important books and manuscripts."[9] It is known, for example, that he paid the sum of 1,000 ducats for a copy of the Talmud that was especially printed for him on vellum.[10]

Unlike other bibliophiles who collect solely for their own benefit and pleasure, Oppenheimer wanted everybody to enjoy his treasures.[11] When he settled in Prague he learned that the censorship of Hebrew books in that city would make it impossible for him to display his books for public use. This made him decide to move his library to Hannover, to be displayed in the house of his father-in-law, Lefmann Berend Cohen.[12] The decision proved to be a wise one, for it saved his library from the fate that befell other Jewish book collections in Prague which were confiscated and burned a decade later (1714).[13] Oppenheimer traveled to Hannover from time to time to check and review his books, but most of the time they were cared for by librarians whom he hired for this purpose.[14]

Oppenheimer died in Prague in 1736, and the collection, consisting of about 4,500 printed volumes and 780 manuscripts, came into the ownership of his son Joseph.[15] Joseph died three years later (1739), and the next owner was his son-in-law, Hirschel Isaac Oppenheimer, rabbi of Hildesheim. He died twenty-one years later (ca. 1761), and the library passed to his widow, Gnendel Oppenheimer. She became involved in unfortunate business trans-actions and, in order to extricate herself from debts, she decided to put the collection up for sale at a public auction. She published a partial list of the books, consisting of 614 entries,[16] and turned to Moses Mendelssohn (1729–1786) for an evaluation of the entire collection. Mendelssohn es-timated the books to be worth between 50,000 and 60,000 Reichsthalers,[17] but the auction never took place, probably because of litigation against Op-penheimer's widow.

Around 1782 the collection again changed ownership, this time to a cousin of Gnendel Oppenheimer, Isaac Seligman Berend Salomon (Cohen), of Hamburg. He issued a new list of the books, and offered them for sale.[18] Since no acceptable offers of purchase were received, the books stayed in Hamburg with Salomon until his death. They were later packed in twenty-eight cases and placed in a Hamburg warehouse to await the outcome of litigation between the heirs. There they remained until 1826, when they were released by a court order. The cases were unpacked and the books displayed on the shelves of a Hamburg bookdealer. A catalog in Hebrew and Latin was prepared, and bids were invited.[19]

Since the days of Johann Christoph Wolf who first called the attention of the scholarly world to the Oppenheimer Collection (in his *Bibliotheca hebraea*), its fate attracted concern from many quarters as it passed from one hand to another until the time of its final disposition. Information and rumors about the status of the collection were exchanged from time to time among scholars in various countries, and communications appeared in a number of publications.[20] In 1872, after the publication of Berend Salomon's catalog of the collection, it was rumored that the owner demanded 100,000 Reichsthalers. An announcement in the *Frankfurter Journal* in 1785 stated that the price was 60,000 Reichsthalers. According to a letter written around that time, the Duke of Württemberg offered a large sum of money for the collection, but the owner insisted on 40,000 Reichsthalers. There were also rumors that the Empress Catherine of Russia and the king of Italy showed interest in the collection. An unsuccessful attempt was made in 1807 by a German lawyer to sell it to the notables of the Paris *Sanhedrin* assembled by Napoleon.[21]

An effort to acquire the books for the Westphalia gvernment was made in 1811 by a group of wealthy German Jews. The initiators succeeded in collecting promises for 4,000 Reichsthalers, but had to stop their activities because the Westphalian government collapsed. The same group later tried in vain to interest the Prussian government in purchasing it for only 6,000 Reichsthalers, payable in three annual installments. There was information in 1817 which indicated that the books could be purchased for 5,000 Reichsthalers, possibly even for 5,000 Mark. An appeal to Jews and Christians to save the books for the German universities was made that same year by a Christian scholar, Professor Anton Theodor Hartmann. Finally, in 1826, after the books were officially offered for sale, an effort was made by David Friedländer (1750–1834) to form a stock company that would secure the collection for Germany, and an appeal to the Königliche Bibliothek in Berlin was made by Leopold Zunz. The efforts failed; there was no interest in a Jewish book collection in Germany. The Bodleian Library entered the picture in 1829 and acquired the entire Oppenheimer Collection for the sum of 9,000 Thaler, perhaps the greatest bargain in the history of book purchasing.[22]

## Moritz Steinschneider: *Catalogus . . . Bodleiana*

Nineteen years after the Bodleian Library purchased the Oppenheimer Collection, the curators of that institution resolved to prepare and publish a catalog of the printed Hebraica books available on the shelves of their library. They selected for this task a young man of thirty-one, named Moritz Steinschneider. The curators of the Bodleian Library had no way of knowing that their decision to appoint a little-known young man for such a responsible project would open an entirely new chapter in the history of Jewish bibliography.

Moritz Steinschneider, who was to become the greatest Jewish bibliographer of all times, was born in Prossnitz, Moravia (now Prostĕgov, Czechoslovakia), in 1816.[23] Besides traditional Jewish schooling, as a young boy he also received instruction in music and dancing, and was thoroughly trained in French and in Italian. He studied for a while in the yeshiva at Nikolsburg (1830–1832), and then went to Prague to study secular subjects (1833–1835). While in Prague he also studied the Bible, the Talmud, and the Hebrew language. In 1836 he enrolled at the Vienna Polytechnic Institute, and attended lectures in Hebrew, Syriac, and Arabic at the Catholic Theological Faculty of the University of Vienna. After completing his studies (1839), he moved on to Leipzig to continue his studies in Arabic. He became friendly with Franz Delitzsch (1813–1890), and with him prepared for publication the work *Ets Chayim* by the fourteenth-century Karaite writer, Aaron ben Elijah (Leipzig, 1841). From Leipzig, Steinschneider continued to Berlin that same year and enrolled at the university there. Two years later (1841) he returned to Prague, first as a private tutor, and later as a teacher at a school for Jewish girls.

While in Prague, Steinschneider, together with David Cassel (1818–1893), began to work on a plan for publishing a Jewish encyclopedia. It did not materialize.[24] He returned to Berlin in 1845 and supported himself by giving private lessons and writing articles for periodicals. Soon he was invited by the editors of the German *Allgemeine Encyklopädie der Wissenschaften und Künste* (Ersch and Gruber) to prepare an article on Jewish literature. Steinschneider spent three years (1845–1847) writing this article, and when it was published three years later (1850), scholars and experts in the field of Jewish literature acclaimed it as a masterpiece of scholarly effort.[25] As a follow-up to his article on Jewish literature, he prepared an article, with David Cassel, entitled, "Jüdische Typographie und jüdischer Buchhandel," which was published in the same encyclopedia (1851).[26] These two accomplishments catapulted Steinschneider into the forefront of Jewish scholarship, and he remained there throughout the rest of his life.

Steinschneider's bibliographic activity had begun a decade earlier. During his first residency in Berlin (1841), he compiled an auction catalog anonymously for the Berlin bookdealer, A. Asher. In 1846, a year after his return to Berlin, Steinschneider was hired by Asher to go to Hamburg to examine the manuscript collection of the bibliographer and bibliophile, Heimann Joseph Michael.[27] Michael had died during that same year, and Asher had acquired his large collection of books and manuscripts. The deceased collector had begun to compile a catalog of his collection. He had completed the printed-book part of it, but the manuscript part had to be completed by his son. Asher wanted Steinschneider to compare the list with the actual manuscripts and to make sure that the descriptions were correct. As a result of his visit to Hamburg, Steinschneider produced a supplement to the manuscript part of the Michael catalog, including many corrections to the entries, and an index of authors. The catalog, together with Steinschneider's supplement and an introduction by Leopold Zunz, was published in Hamburg in 1848, under the title *Otsrot Chayim*. Asher was so impressed with Steinschneider's achievement, that later—after he had sold the Michael manuscripts to the Bodleian Library[28] and was asked to recommend a scholar to catalog the Bodleian printed Hebraica collection—he recommended Steinschneider for the job.

Steinschneider began cataloging the printed Hebraica at the Bodleian Library in 1848, and he completed it thirteen years later. He was able to do part of the work in Berlin with the help of the previously printed catalogs of the Oppenheimer Collection, but he also had to spend five summers (1850, 1851, 1853, 1855, 1858) in Oxford to compare his notes with the actual books. Printing of the catalog began in Berlin in 1852, and it dragged on until 1860, but a 105-page *Specimen* of five of the longest entries in the catalog appeared in 1857.[29] The complete work, under the title *Catalogus librorum hebraeorum in Bibliotheca Bodleiana* (Berlin, 1852–1860), consisted of 7,622 entries in 2,812 columns. The *Catalogus* was divided into three sections. The first section (4,162 entries) listed Hebrew classical and anonymous works, the second section (3,460 entries) registered authors and their works, and the third section consisted of the following indexes: printers, compositors, proofreaders, Maecenases, etc. (1,937 names)[30]; printing places of Hebrew books (119 locations); Hebrew works (5,208 titles); Hebrew Bibles (333 entries); and Hebrew place names (703 entries). Appended to the *Catalogus* was a 32-page *Conspectus* of the Hebrew manuscripts at the Bodleian Library (Berlin, 1857).[31]

The cut-off date of the *Catalogus* was 1732, the year that David Oppenheimer stopped collecting books, and also the year that Johann Christoph Wolf completed his *Bibliotheca hebraea*. Works printed up to 1732, but not available in the Oppenheimer Collection, were also registered by Steinschneider as were works published after 1732 if held by the Bodleian. The *Cat. Bodl.* (as the *Catalogus* is referred to by scholars) thus became the most complete register of Hebraica printed up to the year 1732. But the *Cat. Bodl.* was much more than a bibliographical record. Steinschneider, according to his own words, had put "one-fourth of his life and the greater part of his strength" into this work.[32] He invested in the catalog all his erudition and made it, in the words of one of his closest disciples, "*the* reference book on all questions of Jewish literature"; it became "an unrivaled tool for every serious scholar, and . . . the sound foundation of scholarly Hebrew bibliography."[33] Steinschneider organized the entries of the *Cat. Bodl.* in the following manner:

Author or main entry (in Roman characters)

Biographical data (in Latin). Alexander Marx describes this part in the following words: "After each name we find the most important information on the author and his unpublished works, and these notes become fuller and fuller as the work proceeds; new information gathered from hitherto inaccessible sources greatly enrich our knowledge. The wealth of learning, of originality, the combination of breadth and minuteness of research, evident in these notes on the biographies of the authors, is truly astounding."[34]

Title (in Hebrew characters)

Title translated and explained (in Latin). Marx: "The printed works of every author are enumerated with all the titles and editions that appeared before 1732, and later ones as far as they were found in the Library. Wherever necessary, bibliographical notes and references are added to every item, again frequently correcting earlier mistakes."[35]

Contents (in Latin)

Format

Place of publication (in Roman characters)

Printer or publisher (in Roman characters)

Date (Hebrew and universal; Hebrew dates in chronogram form were copied from title page)

The *Cat. Bodl.* not only established Steinschneider's fame as a scholar of the highest caliber, but also established his future style of writing: brief, concise, filled with common and uncommon abbreviations, making it difficult to read without special effort. He himself once admitted to a Hebrew writer that he wrote only for "three or four readers."[36] Still, he continued without interruption to write and publish books and articles for more than a half-century after the publication of the *Cat. Bodl.* Someone once calculated "that if one would put all the books and articles of Steinschneider one on top of the other, their height would considerably exceed that of their not very tall author."[37] The Hebrew writer Reuben Brainin (1862–1939) remembers that at the age of ninety Steinschneider was still collecting new material for his planned works, "as if he would have been sure that he would continue to live and work for another ninety years, at least."[38] This did not happen, and he passed away in 1907, at the age of ninety-one.[39]

Steinschneider was an enigma, full of contradictions. To some he appeared as a helpful, understanding teacher, to others as a strict, no-nonsense judge. He was modest, yet haughty; he was witty, and he was dry. Those who liked and revered him did so without reservation; those who hated and despised him did so without limit.[40] But he was the most diligent and productive Jewish scholar in modern times, and the results of his efforts will continue to serve Jewish scholarship for many generations to come.

Reprint editions of the *Cat. Bodl.* were issued in Berlin by Welt-Verlag in 1931, and in Hildesheim by Georg Olms in 1964.

## Arthur Ernest Cowley's *Concise Catalogue*

Steinschneider's catalog of the printed Hebraica in the Bodleian Library turned out to be "a bibliography rather than a catalog,"[41] and therefore did not serve the purpose for which it was intended. It was meant to serve as a tool of easy reference for the users and staff of the library. But the *Cat. Bodl.* listed many books that were not available at the Bodleian and omitted some that were; the text was written in a difficult Latin; and the entries did not include the shelf numbers.[42] Soon after the publication of the *Cat. Bodl.*, efforts were made to adapt the catalog to the needs of the Bodleian Library. Four such attempts are known to have been made, none of them successful. Finally, in 1916, the curators of the Bodleian Library accepted a proposal by Arthur Ernest Cowley (1861–1931) to compile an entirely new catalog based on Steinschneider's *Cat. Bodl.*

Cowley had come to the Bodleian Library in 1896 as an assistant to the librarian in charge of Hebrew manuscripts.[43] He brought with him a good grounding in the Hebrew language and in Jewish literature, and he participated in the preparation of a catalog of Hebrew manuscripts in the Bodleian Library.[44] He also edited and published several ancient Aramaic and Hebrew texts,[45] and taught Rabbinics at Oxford University. In 1899 he became librarian in charge of Hebrew manuscripts, and twenty years later (1919) he was appointed Bodleian Librarian.

Cowley began to work on compiling a new catalog of the Hebrew printed books at the Bodleian Library in 1916 and completed it in 1929. The new catalog appeared in Oxford in 1929 under the title *A Concise Catalogue of the Hebrew Printed Books in the Bodleian Library.* The work consisted of 816 pages, and it included "all Hebrew books that were in the Library in 1927." Books registered in the *Cat. Bodl.* which were not in possession of the library were excluded from Cowley's catalog. For purposes of inclusion in his catalog, Cowley defined a Hebrew book as "one printed entirely or mainly in Hebrew characters (whether in Hebrew, Arabic, German or any other language); an edition of a Hebrew work with notes in another language; a translation (with or without text) of such a work." This definition extended the borders of Hebraica to embrace works that ordinarily would not have been included in a bibliography of this type. On the other hand, Cowley excluded "European translations of the Bible or commentaries on it without text; European histories of the Jews or of Jewish literature; European grammars, lexicons or manuals of Hebrew."

The number of works listed in the *Concise Catalogue* is not easy to determine, since Cowley did not number the entries, but a reviewer has estimated it to be "over ten thousand."[46] The entries, as concise as possible, were arranged in the following order:

> Author or main entry (in Roman characters), followed by reference to
>   St[einschneider]
> Title (in Hebrew characters)
> Description of contents (in English)
> Place and date of publication
> Format
> Shelf number

Under many entries Cowley mentioned the author's contributions to specific Hebrew periodicals, and he sometimes listed biographical works about the author as well. Classic and anonymous works he entered under form or subject headings (e.g., Mishnah, Prayers, etc.), and titles within the entries for multititle authors he arranged chronologically—by date of publication (for contemporary authors) and alphabetically by title (for deceased ones). Cowley also used cross-references extensively between various forms of entry, and he appended an "Index of Hebrew Titles" at the end of the volume. This helped to make the handy catalog even more useful.

## Adolf Neubauer's *Catalogue of the Hebrew Manuscripts*

When Steinschneider began preparing his catalog of the Hebrew printed books at the Bodleian Library, it was understood that he would follow up this work with a similar catalog of the Hebrew manuscripts. Later, he was officially delegated this responsibility, and still later, in 1861, after he had completed his work on the *Cat. Bodl.,* he was requested by the Bodleian Librarian to "proceed with it [the preparation of the catalog of Hebrew manuscripts] with all the expedition you can."[47] For some unknown reason he did not so proceed, although he did publish a *Conspectus* in 1857 listing 500 manuscripts in the Bodleian Library, which was later appended to his *Cat. Bodl.*[48] The task of cataloging the Bodleian Hebrew manuscripts was thereupon entrusted to one of the most prolific Jewish scholars of the nineteenth century, Adolf Neubauer.[49]

Adolf Neubauer, the man who later became Bodley's assistant librarian and Oxford University's first Reader in rabbinic literature, was born in Hungary in 1831. He studied in Prague and Munich, and in 1857 he arrived in Paris to conduct research at the Bibliothèque Nationale. He then joined the Austrian consulate in Jerusalem as a member of its staff. There he became interested in the study of Hebrew manuscripts and began to publish the results of his research. In 1864 he went to St. Petersburg to examine the collection of Hebrew manuscripts brought together by the Karaite scholar Abraham Firkovich (1786–1874).[50] As a result of this visit, he published a German-Hebrew volume entitled *Aus der Petersburger Bibliothek* (Leipzig, 1866). Two years later appeared his French work, *La géographie du Talmud* (Paris, 1868; reprinted, Hildesheim, 1967) which earned him a prize from the Académie Française. During the same year he received his appointment to the Bodleian Library for the purpose of cataloging the Hebrew manuscripts there. Neubauer was appointed in 1873 to the post of Assistant Librarian of the Bodleian Library, and in 1884 he became Reader of Rabbinic Literature at Oxford. Owing to illness, he resigned the positions in 1899 and 1900 respectively. He lived for a short while in Vienna, then returned to England, this time to London, where he died in 1907.[51]

Neubauer arrived at Oxford in 1868 to prepare a catalog of the Hebrew manuscripts in the Bodleian Library, and eighteen years later the first volume of this catalog appeared. Entitled *Catalogue of the Hebrew Manuscripts in the Bodleian Library and in the College Libraries of Oxford* (Oxford, 1886), it listed 2,602 entries (in 1,132 columns, folio format), to which a portfolio containing forty facsimiles was appended. During the years preceding the publication of the *Catalogue* Neubauer had the opportunity to examine a number of catalogs of Hebrew manuscripts which were published during that period, and to develop his own style of cataloging this type of material. There were the catalogs of Hebrew manuscripts prepared by Steinschneider for the University of Leiden,[52] the Staatsbibliothek of Munich,[53] the Staats- und Universitätsbibliothek of Hamburg,[54] and the Preussische Staatsbibliothek of Berlin.[55] There were also the catalogs of Hebrew manuscripts in the Bibliothèque Nationale in Paris, compiled by Hirsch (Hermann) Zotenberg (born 1836);[56] the University Library at

Cambridge, compiled by Solomon Mayer Schiller-Szinessy (1820–1890);[57] and the Royal Library in St. Petersburg, prepared by Abraham Elijah Harkavy (1839–1919) and Hermann Leberecht Strack (1848–1922).[58]

Steinschneider's catalogs distinguished themselves by their lengthy treatment of every little detail;[59] Schiller-Szinessy filled his catalog with discourses, debates, and footnotes; Harkavy and Strack concentrated on the colophons of the manuscripts—to prove or disprove some of the statements therein;[60] and Zotenberg included in his entries only the bare facts of each manuscript, sometimes even overlooking or ignoring some. Neubauer's method, as described by him, was as follows:

> The descriptions of the mss. are as short as possible, without discursiveness and without references of other catalogues or to periodicals where similar mss. are described, unless strictly necessary. . . . Matter of historical or literary interest . . . has been indicated . . . although not always as full as many scholars could have desired. . . . Notice of variations from printed texts or from mss. in other libraries was out of the question—time and space would not allow of such minute statements.[61]

The Hebrew manuscripts collection at the Bodleian Library originated from about fourteen different collections acquired by that library up to the year 1886. Among them were 110 manuscripts from the Canonici collection, purchased in 1817; 780 from the Oppenheimer Collection, purchased in 1829;[62] and 862 from the Michael collection, purchased in 1848.[63] Neubauer grouped all the various collections together and arranged them by subjects (e.g., Bible, Talmud, liturgies, cabala, poetry, medicine, etc.). The text of the entries, except for the titles and colophons (when necessary), was in English.[64] Each entry included, besides the information available on the first page or colophon of the manuscript:

Description of contents
Description of script
Format
Description of material
Collation
Shelf number

The catalog was preceded by eight charts comparing the original numbers of the manuscripts in the various collections with the numbers given in the catalog, and it was concluded by indexes of (a) authors, translators, family names; (b) titles, subjects, and anonymous works; (c) scribes, owners, and witnesses of ownership; (d) censors; and (e) geographical names.

Volume 2 of the *Catalogue,* prepared jointly by Neubauer and Cowley (from column 32 on; by Cowley alone from column 226 on), appeared thirty years after the publication of Volume 1 (1906). It included all the Hebrew manuscripts acquired by the Bodleian Library up to the year 1906 and also a few that were overlooked in the first volume. The number of volumes described was 316, of which 166 were Genizah material consisting of about 2,675 fragments.[65] The total number of entries in both volumes now reached 2,918. Neubauer's method of description in the first volume was again employed, with some technical modifications, in this volume. Two indexes—a general index and a Hebrew-Arabic index—and a table of corrigenda and addenda to the entire *Catalogue* concluded the second volume. A third volume, planned by Cowley, never materialized.

## British Museum

The second most important collection of Hebraica in England is located in London at the British Museum, England's national library. When the British Museum opened its doors to the public in 1759 there were about half a million volumes on its shelves, among them only one Hebrew title, the editio princeps of the Talmud[66] which originally belonged to King Henry VIII but was presented to the museum by King George II. The museum received a gift during the same year of 180 volumes from a Jewish businessman, Solomon da Costa Atthias. The donor, an immigrant from Holland, accompanied his gift with a letter to the Trustees of the British Museum explaining his act as an expression of gratitude to the city of London, "in which he dwelt for fifty-four years in ease and quietness and safety."[67] According to one account, these books were originally intended to be presented to Charles II by the Jews of London. They were bound and marked with the royal cipher, but later were dispersed, after the king's sudden death, until da Costa collected them again.[68] According to another version, these books belonged to Charles II and were bound for him, as the royal cipher indicates, but he failed to pay for them. The booksellers refused to release the books until da Costa purchased them for the museum.[69]

Little progress was made in acquiring Hebrew books for the museum during the next 89 years, but in 1848 the museum acquired the printed books of the collection of Heimann Joseph Michael consisting of 4,420 volumes, and it immediately became one of the major depositories of Hebraica.[70] The

British Museum continued to acquire Hebraica, notably a sizable number of volumes from the library of the Italian-Jewish scholar, Joseph Almanzi (1801–1860).[71] By the end of the nineteenth-century, the British Museum was already in possession of more than 15,000 volumes of Hebraica.

## Joseph Zedner: *Catalogue of the Hebrew Books in the Library of the British Museum*

The bookdealer A. Asher, of Berlin, was indirectly responsible for the two greatest catalogs of Hebraica to be published in the nineteenth century. In 1848, he recommended Moritz Steinschneider to catalog the printed Hebraica at the Bodleian Library; Steinschneider was hired, and he produced the *Cat. Bodl.* Prior to that, in 1845, Asher had recommended Joseph Zedner to the post of Assistant at the Department of Printed Books of the British Museum; Zedner was hired, and he produced the *Catalogue of the Hebrew Books in the Library of the British Museum.*

Steinschneider and Zedner were extremely different from one another in every respect—in temperament, in intellectual background, and in working habits. Their differences are apparent in their catalogs. Steinschneider produced a bulky work, packed to the brim with bibliographic information, scholarly discoveries, and brilliant excursions; Zedner's catalog was modest, his entries concise, his scholarship unostentatious, and his methods accurate and simple.

Joseph Zedner was born in Glogau, in Lower Silesia (now Głogów, Poland), in 1804.[72] First he studied in the yeshiva of Rabbi Akiba Eger of Poznan—as did his contemporary, Julius Fürst[73]—and later he tried his hand at teaching in a Jewish school in Strelitz, in the province of Mecklenburg (now Russia). He then moved to Berlin to become a bookdealer, but instead wound up as a tutor in the family of the abovementioned bookdealer, Asher. When he accepted the position at the British Museum, he finally found his vocation. Zedner was forty-one years old when he began his work at the British Museum, and he stayed at his post for about twenty-four years. During these years, the Hebraica collection at the British Museum grew from about 600 titles to more than 10,000, thanks to Zedner's efforts. He resigned his post in 1869, due to ill health, and returned to Berlin, where he died in 1871.[74]

The *Catalogue of the Hebrew Books in the Library of the British Museum,* compiled by Joseph Zedner, was published in London in 1867. It consisted of 891 pages, in which "upwards of 10,000 bound volumes" of Hebraica were described. A list of the number of volumes in the fifteen major subject classes (printed in the Preface to the *Catalogue*) placed the categories of Bible, codes of law, and liturgies among the numerically strongest in the collection. Another list demonstrated the strength of the collection in first editions and rare volumes. It listed:

   65 works of the fifteenth century, mentioned by De Rossi[75]
237 works printed from 1500 to 1540, mentioned by De Rossi
   32 works printed from 1480 to 1540, not mentioned by De Rossi
   38 works of which no other copy or only 1 or 2 copies are known to exist

Besides works in the Hebrew language, Zedner also registered in the *Catalogue:*

1. Translations of postbiblical Hebrew works;
2. Works in the Arabic, Spanish, German, and other languages, printed with Hebrew characters;
3. Bibliographical works with special reference to postbiblical literature . . . also catalogues of Hebrew works and biographies of authors of Hebrew works.

The preface to the *Catalogue* included a detailed description of the rules of entry adopted for this work. Among them were: arrangement of entries to be alphabetical by the names of the authors; Jewish authors, up to the year 1700, to be entered under their first names; biblical names to be spelled according to the form used in the authorized English version of the Bible; foreign names to appear according to their spelling in the languages from which they are derived; ancient classical works to be arranged under form entries (e.g., Bible, Mishnah, liturgies, etc.); cross-references to be given from family names to first names, from forms of names used in other works to those used by Zedner, and from names of editors, translators, writers of marginal notes, and authors of collective works. Thus each entry consisted of the following:

Author or main entry (in Roman characters)
Title (in Hebrew characters. "The titles are copied from the books, the orthography of which is preserved, even in case of misprints. All irrelevant parts of the title are omitted, as also eulogies and honorable designations of the author.")
Description ("Where the title does not clearly state the contents of the work, explanations are added in English, and put between brackets.")

Place of printing (". . . places of printing are given as they appear in the book; when appearing only in Hebrew characters, they are followed by the English form between brackets.")

Date of publication ("The chronostic by which, in most cases, the date of Hebrew books is expressed, is copied only when contained in one or two entire words; in all other cases it is reduced to numerical letters, and the Christian era added between brackets. In works of which the date could not be ascertained, an approximate date has been supplied, followed by a note of interrogation.")

Format

The volume concluded with a list of addenda (consisting of books acquired during the printing of the *Catalogue,* especially from the Almanzi collection) and the following four indexes: surnames and nonbiblical first names; titles; Hebrew abbreviations; and places of printing.

In an estimate of Zedner, written more than three-quarters of a century after his death by a fellow librarian at the British Museum, we find the following interesting lines:

[The *Catalogue*] was a landmark in Hebrew bibliography. It combined the maximum of information with the minimum of space in a unique degree. It was here that Zedner's training as a bookseller stood him in such good stead. He was able to concentrate on the essentials and, unlike his other great contemporary in that field of knowledge, Moritz Steinschneider, knew what to omit. . . . The *Catalogue* was a monument at once of scholarship and lucid presentation, and has, in its own way, never been surpassed.[76]

The *Catalogue,* "in its original form," was reprinted in London in 1964. Added to this reprint edition were a brief list of corrigenda, published originally by Zedner in a bibliographical periodical,[77] and a small number of handwritten amendments in the title index.

## Van Straalen's Supplement

Twenty-five years after Zedner completed his work of compiling the Hebraica at the British Museum into a catalog, Zedner's successor, Samuel Van Straalen (1845–1902), completed his work of preparing a supplement to that catalog. Entitled *Catalogue of Hebrew Books in the British Museum Acquired during the Years 1868–1892* (London, 1894), it consisted of 532 pages (small folio format), in which 7,800 entries were registered. These entries include "some 4,650 . . . main titles . . . for the most part published within the last fifty years." The supplement volume also includes a Hebrew title index for both volumes. Van Straalen generally followed Zedner's example in arranging the entries of his supplement. He introduced only a few minor improvements, such as adding pagination and shelf numbers for each entry. But despite his effort to catalog his supplement with the same method and in the same manner as his predecessor, Van Straalen's end product did not measure up to its model. It lacked the precision and accuracy that had become the hallmark of Zedner's *Catalogue.*[78] Van Straalen later compiled another supplement, and also a subject index of the Heraica collection at the British Museum; both remained unpublished.[79]

## George Margoliouth's
### Catalogue of the Hebrew and Samaritan Manuscripts

In a discussion of the second volume of Adolf Neubauer's *Catalogue of the Hebrew Manuscripts* published in 1907,[80] the reviewer, while explaining the different methods employed by Steinschneider and Neubauer in cataloging Hebrew manuscripts, proposed "a third plan that might be adopted." This plan consisted of "first publishing a brief but carefully tabulated account of a collection of mss., and then proceeding to prepare a catalogue on a full scale." The author of that review, George Margoliouth (1853–1924), actually was describing his own method of cataloging collections of Hebrew manuscripts. A convert to Christianity and an ordained Anglican priest, Margoliouth was placed in charge of the Hebrew, Syriac, and Ethiopic manuscripts of the British Museum in 1891, and two years later he published a *Descriptive List of the Hebrew and Samaritan Mss. in the British Museum* (London, 1893). He devoted the next few decades to preparing a large and meticulously detailed *Catalogue of the Hebrew and Samaritan Manuscripts in the British Museum,* three volumes of which appeared between 1899 and 1915.

The history of the Hebrew and Samaritan manuscript collection at the British Museum began in the year 1700 with a gift by Sir Charles Cotton of one Samaritan manuscript and three Anglo-Jewish charters.[81] In 1753 the British Museum purchased the Harley collection, consisting of more than 130 manuscripts. Gifts and additional purchases brought the collection to about 200 manuscripts by 1840. During the years of Joseph Zedner's service, and with his advice, the museum acquired numerous individual manuscripts and also the celebrated Joseph Almanzi collection of 332 manuscripts

(1865).[82] Nearly 300 manuscripts were further acquired between the years 1877 and 1882 from the bookseller W. M. Shapira.[83] Genizah fragments began arriving at the museum in 1895, and the Moses Gaster collection was purchased in 1925.[84]

Margoliouth grouped together all the various Hebrew manuscripts at the British Museum and arranged them into broad subjects. Volume 1 of his *Catalogue* (London, 1899) described 339 biblical texts and commentaries. Volume 2 (London, 1905) described 393 manuscripts in the areas of (1) Midrash, (2) Talmud and halachah, and (3) liturgies. Volume 3, published in 3 parts (London, 1909–1915), described 474 manuscripts in the fields of cabala, ethics, philosophy, poetry, philology, science, etc., bringing the total number of entries in all three volumes to 1,206. The 65 Samaritan manuscripts intended for inclusion in Volume 3 were left out. The planned introduction to the history of the Hebrew manuscript collection and the indexes to the entire work were also omitted. The description of the manuscripts in each volume was  followed by (a) corresponding numerical lists of the old shelf numbers of the manuscripts and their numbers in Margoliouth's *Catalogue;* (b) brief lists of addenda and corrigenda; and (c) facsimiles of leaves of the most important manuscripts.

A final volume was published twenty years later (London, 1935). It was compiled by Jacob Leveen (born 1891 in Jerusalem), Librarian and later Keeper of the Department of Oriental Books and Manuscripts of the British Museum.[85] This fourth volume included the introduction left out by Margoliouth, four indexes (persons, titles, subjects, and places), additional and corrected headings, a supplementary list of manuscripts (159 entries), a numerical list of manuscripts and their corresponding numbers in the *Catalogue,* and addenda and corrigenda to all four volumes.

Volume 1 was arranged according to the order of the books of the Bible, each group arranged according to the dates of the codices, further subdivided by the different "schools of caligraphy." For the Bible commentaries, the dates of the authors were used as a guide. The same criterion was used in arranging the Talmud commentaries and legal compendia in Volume 2. Volume 3 was arranged according to shelf numbers, a practice which was noted disapprovingly by some bibliographers.[86] The entries in the *Catalogue* covered the entire range of information concerning the described manuscripts. They included the following:

Material (whether paper or vellum)
Size (in inches)
Collation

Number of lines per page
Physical condition (complete, defective, etc.)
Type of script
Date
Title or beginning sentence (in Hebrew characters)
Contents
Censors
Owners
Scribes
Colophon or other striking sentences (in Hebrew characters)
Bibliographical information

Margoliouth's *Catalogue* was an example of detailed description and clear presentation. Stress was laid on the identification and dating of materials, but above all there was an effort to be exact. Jacob Leveen, in the introduction to Volume 4 of the *Catalogue,* wrote about the work of his predecessor: " . . . the manuscripts were described with much scholarly care and with great minuteness and conscientiousness and on a scale hitherto unknown to catalogues of Hebrew manuscripts." Ismar Elbogen (1874–1943), in a review of Volume 2 of the *Catalogue,*[87] was impressed with "the copiousness . . . the exactness displayed . . . and the number, range, and reliability of the references." He felt that the *Catalogue* "deserves a place among the best works of this kind." And the British Museum's present Keeper of Oriental Printed Books and Manuscripts, in a "Preface to the reprinted edition" of Volume 1 of the *Catalogue,* writes enviously: "The generous descriptions given . . . belong to a more spacious and leisurely age when a cataloguer could describe his manuscripts in well nigh unlimited detail."

The first three volumes of Margoliouth's *Catalogue* appeared in a reprint edition in London in 1965.


## Leeser Rosenthal
### and the Bibliotheca Rosenthaliana

Almost all of the great private Hebraica and Judaica collections of the nineteenth century originated in Germany, and from there they were moved to permanent quarters in public institutions in other countries. No German institution or government was interested enough to acquire them for Germany. The last of these great collections, the Leeser Rosenthal collection, was offered upon the death of its owner to the government of Bismarck by his son as a gift to the Royal Library in Berlin; the offer was declined.

The owner, Leeser (Eliezer) Rosenthal, was born in Nasielsk, Poland, in 1794. He came to Germany at a young age as a teacher and later became a rabbi in one of the synagogues of Hamburg. His fascination with books on Jewish topics was so great that he spent his wife's entire dowry on purchasing such works. When he died in 1868, he left a collection of 32 Hebrew manuscripts and about 6,000 printed volumes among which were many incunabula and rare books.[88] He also left a catalog in manuscript, which he himself had prepared, of a large part of his Hebrew books.

After Germany refused to accept the books for the Royal Library, Rosenthal's children, who resided in Amsterdam, determined to bring the books to that city. His son, Baron George Rosenthal, decided to publish a scientific catalog of the entire collection, and he later offered the collection to the city of Amsterdam on the condition that it be kept at the university library as a separate unit, entitled the Bibliotheca Rosenthaliana. He also promised to make provision for the continuing expansion of the collection. The Municipal Council of Amsterdam accepted the offer during a meeting on July 21, 1880. The upkeep and expansion of the collection was assumed by the city of Amsterdam after World War I, and by 1936 the number of volumes in the collection reached 30,000. The Germans seized the Bibliotheca Rosenthaliana during World War II and transported it to Germany. A small number of volumes—the most valuable manuscripts and books—were hidden in Holland. The entire collection was retrieved from Germany after the war ("not undamaged") and returned to the university.[89]

## The Rosenthal-Roest
### Catalog der Hebraica und Judaica

When Leeser Rosenthal's son, Baron George Rosenthal, decided to publish a complete list of his father's collection of Hebraica and Judaica, he turned the task over to a man with great experience in this type of work, Meijer Marcus Roest. Born in 1821 in Amsterdam, Roest began his career as a teacher.[90] In 1855 he gave up teaching and accepted a position as compiler of Hebraica and Judaica catalogs for the Amsterdam bookseller and auctioneer Frederik Muller. He was also placed in charge of the Hebraica and Judaica department of the bookstore. The first catalog Roest compiled was published in 1857, and during the next several decades he became responsible for the publication of about twenty-five such catalogs.[91] Roest was a productive writer, and he edited and published a few Dutch-Jewish weeklies and also a scholarly quarterly.[92] A bibliography of his writings, published in 1967, lists 169 books and articles written during the years 1847 to 1886.[93] He was appointed the first Keeper of the Rosenthaliana after it was accepted by the city of Amsterdam, and he occupied this position until his death in 1889.

Roest began compiling the catalog of the Rosenthal collection in 1869, and printing commenced in Hannover in 1871. A year later, the printing company went out of business, and work on the catalog was interrupted for more than a year until it was resumed in Amsterdam.[94] The complete work, under the title *Catalog der Hebraica und Judaica aus der L. Rosenthal'schen Bibliothek,* was published in Amsterdam in 1875. It consisted of two volumes (1,727 pages), divided into two sections and a supplement. Section I listed, in alphabetical author arrangement, the printed Hebraica and Judaica, occupying the first 1,166 pages. Section II listed 32 manuscripts, followed by additions and corrections, and a Hebrew title index.[95] The supplement *(Anhang)* contained the partial Hebraica catalog to the collection, prepared by Leeser Rosenthal himself, and named by him *Yode'a Sefer.* This supplement listed 2,530 Hebrew works, arranged alphabetically by titles, published up to the year 1857.

Roest's descriptions are concise and exact, and are usually taken directly from the books.[96] Although he generally followed the technique so successfully employed by Joseph Zedner,[97] Roest's descriptions were more elaborate. Thus his entries included the following information:

Author or main entry (in Roman characters)
Title (in Hebrew characters)
Description and contents (in Hebrew, copied from title page)
Additional information (in German)
Place and Hebrew date of publication (in Hebrew characters; date in
  chronogram copied from title page)
Place and name of printer or publisher (in Roman characters)
Universal date
Format
Pagination
Approbations (with names of approvers, their places of residence, and dates of
  approval)
References to St[einschneider], Zedn[er], or *Anhang [Yode'a Sefer]*

Roest also edited Rosenthal's *Yode'a Sefer.* He corrected some inconsistencies in the alphabetization of the titles and here and there added remarks and notes. Rosenthal's descriptions, in contrast to Roest's, were lengthy and very detailed, with occasional references to the literature dealing with the author of a work. Opinions and short evaluations of the works are included in almost every entry, making each read like a miniature review.

For the Hebrew scholar the publication of the Rosenthal-Roest *Catalog* added one more reliable tool to the already existing catalogs of printed Hebraica by Steinschneider and Zedner. An East European Jewish bibliographer, some twenty years later, ruled that only three bibliographers belong in the pantheon of Jewish bibliography: Steinschneider, Zedner, and Roest.[98]

A reprint edition of the Rosenthal-Roest *Catalog* was issued in Amsterdam by N. V. Boekhandel & Antiquariaat B. M. Israël in 1966.

## Moses Aryeh Loeb Friedland
## and the Bibliotheca Friedlandiana

Private collectors of Hebraica and Judaica were as common in Eastern Europe as they were in Western Europe, but almost all of the collections created with such devotion by these bibliophiles were scattered and lost their identity with the death of their owners. Only a few survived and continued to carry the names of their original owners: those that were willed to public institutions with the provision that they be maintained as separate units. One such collector—perhaps the greatest of them all—was Moses Aryeh Loeb Friedland. Born in Dvinsk (Dünaburg), Latvia, in 1826, Friedland became the general army contractor of Russia, and was permitted to settle in St. Petersburg, a privilege granted to only a few select Jews.[99] He was later named an honorary citizen of St. Petersburg, and was several times presented with government medals.[100]

While in Petersburg, Friedland became interested in philanthropic activities, and he founded an orphanage and an old-age home there. He also involved himself in political and cultural activities on behalf of the Jews in Russia. But what made Friedland famous was the collection of books—the Bibliotheca Friedlandiana—that he first accumulated in his house and later presented to the Asiatic Museum of the Imperial Academy of Sciences in St. Petersburg. It consisted of more than 14,000 Hebraica titles, including about 300 volumes of manuscripts (close to 1,000 titles) and 32 incunabula.

Friedland built his collection from several other large collections accumulated by Jewish collectors in Russia.[101] He also acquired thousands of individual copies from bookdealers and private persons from all over the

world, and he hired a special librarian to catalog them. The announcement
of his decision to turn his library over to the Asiatic Museum was received
with great disappointment by the Jews of Russia. St. Petersburg was a
closed city to Jews, and Jewish scholars would have no access to the books,
so that Friedland's efforts would be wasted. Friedland received many
protests, and also advice about how to make his library most useful to
scholars. He ignored the protesters and letter-writers; he did not defend
himself, nor did he explain his action.[102]

There is only one known instance when Friedland explained the reasons
for his decision; he replied to a letter from a famous Russian rabbi, who had
suggested that Friedland transfer his library to Jerusalem, and had proposed
a complete program as to how such a library in Jerusalem should be established, organized, and run. In his response, Friedland acknowledged that
the rabbi's suggestion would have been worth consideration if it had come
earlier, before he publicly announced his intention to turn over his library to
the Asiatic Museum. Friedland then gave two reasons for his decision to offer his collection to the Asiatic Museum. First, he had witnessed the dispersion of other private Jewish libraries after the deaths of their owners, and he
had noticed an unwillingness by Jewish institutions in Russia to undertake
the responsibility for a collection such as his. Second, he felt that his gesture
would have a favorable effect on the attitude of the government toward the
Jewish community in Russia.[103]


## Samuel Wiener: *Kohelet Mosheh*

The Bibliotheca Friedlandiana was officially presented to the Asiatic
Museum in St. Petersburg on February 28, 1892. The museum added to it its
own collection of 10,000 Hebrew volumes, mostly depository copies of
Hebraica printed in Russia since 1811, and acquired from Friedland his
private librarian, Samuel Wiener.[104] Born in Borisov, White Russia, in 1860,
Wiener demonstrated bibliographic ability at a very young age. He was less
than thirteen years old when he prepared his first bibliographical lists,
registering the books in his father's library and those in the synagogue
libraries of his hometown. He later moved to Minsk and became a clerk in a
bookstore. From Minsk he moved on to St. Petersburg to become librarian
and book adviser to Friedland. He also became responsible for many of the
important book acquisitions made by his employer. Friedland later
entrusted him with the task of compiling a catalog of his collection, and

when he offered the books to the Asiatic Museum, one of the conditions he attached to the gift was that Wiener was to continue compiling the catalog under the auspices of the museum.

Part one of the catalog, listing printed works arranged by title, was named *Kohelet Mosheh Aryeh Leib Friedland.* It was issued in fascicles. Fascicle 1, consisting of 14 pages covering part of the letter *alef,* was published by Friedland in 1892. An enlarged edition of fascicle 1, consisting of 1010 entries covering the entire letter *alef,* was issued a year later (1893) by the Asiatic Museum, after it had accepted the collection. Fascicles 2 and 3, covering letters *bet* and *gimel—dalet,* appeared at two-year intervals (1895 and 1897). Friedland's death in 1899 slowed down the publication of the catalog,[105] and fascicles 4 and 5, covering letters *he—zayin* and *chet—tet,* appeared in 1902 and 1904 respectively. Fascicles 6 and 7, covering letters *yod* and *kaf,* were published about a decade and a half later (1918).[106] The upheavals that accompanied the Russian Revolution of 1918 forced Wiener to leave Russia. He settled in San Remo, Italy, where he died in 1929. The eighth and final fascicle, covering letter *lamed,* and edited by Joseph Bender, appeared in 1936.

The eight fascicles of Wiener's *Kohelet Mosheh,* consisting of 689 pages, registered 5,905 titles, which was less than half of the total number of titles in the original Friedland collection.[107] The cataloging was officially done under the supervision of Professor Daniel Chwolson (1819—1911; responsible for fascicles 1—6) and Academician Paul Kokovtsov (1861—1942; responsible for fascicles 7—8). In actuality, it was Wiener alone who executed the work. Wiener's method of cataloging was a model of completeness. He approached each title, regardless of importance, with the same thoroughness. He conscientiously registered in full each edition of the same work, indicating any small changes and differences that occurred in them. The entries, written entirely in Hebrew, were as precise as possible, based mostly on information extracted from the books themselves. They included:

Title
Author (frequently adding brief biographical information)
Contents (from title page, supplemented by information from introduction, table of contents, etc.)
Place of publication
Printer or publisher
Dates (Jewish and universal)
Format
Pagination
Type (square, cursive, etc.)

Approbations (including year of issuance)
References to: St[einschneider], Zedn[er], Roest, and [Van] Strln [Straalen]

In a eulogy on Wiener, one scholar and bibliographer praised his method of cataloging Hebrew books in the following words: "Wiener distinguished himself from all his predecessors by giving such clear and encompassing brief descriptions of the book and the author, that we do not have to see the book itself anymore."[108]

Although the *Kohelet Mosheh* was originally intended to register the books of the *Bibliotheca Friedlandiana,* Wiener included in it all the Hebrew books available at the Asiatic Museum (these were distinguished by an "A" next to the running-number). For the sake of bibliographical completeness in describing certain works available at the museum in many editions, Wiener even included editions known to him from other sources. For instance, the work *Bechinat Ha'olam* is represented in the catalog with 67 editions; the museum possessed only 46. This policy made the *Kohelet Mosheh* an even better tool in the field of Jewish bibliography.

The *Bibliotheca Friedlandiana* survived the stormy years of revolution and war, and it remained intact at the same institution, now known as the Leningrad Oriental Institute of the Academy of Science. It also remained inaccessible, as before, to the majority of the scholars most interested in its treasures.[109] But the incomplete catalog by Wiener (and Bender) is still considered a masterpiece of Hebrew bibliography, and it is still consulted and sought after.

A photographically reduced reprint edition of the eight fascicles of *Kohelet Mosheh* was published in Jerusalem in 1969. Fascicles 7 and 8 had been reprinted in Jerusalem once before by Wahrmann Books in 1963.

## Bernhard Wachstein:
### *Katalog der Salo Cohn'schen Schenkungen*

The last high-quality catalog of an important Hebraica collection was published about sixty years ago. This catalog had the distinction of being the only prominent scholarly catalog of a Hebraica collection owned by a Jewish institution, and it brought to a close a major chapter in the history of Jewish bibliography. The institution that housed the collection was the library of the Israelitische Kultusgemeinde in Vienna, and the bibliographer who compiled the catalog was Bernhard Wachstein.

Bernhard Wachstein was born in Tluste, Eastern Galicia, in 1868, and was considered a brilliant student of the Talmud at a young age.[110] He also studied secular subjects, and later enrolled as a student simultaneously at the Rabbinical Seminary and at the University of Vienna. He graduated in 1899 and, for a while, he planned to accept a rabbinical position, but then decided against it. He turned to librarianship, applied for a position at the National Library, and was rejected. The Israelitische Kultusgemeinde discovered him a few years later, in 1903, and hired him as librarian in charge of the Hebraica section of its Bibliothek. In 1906 he became assistant librarian, and soon afterwards he was appointed director of the library.

Wachstein stayed with the Bibliothek for more than thirty years, until his death in 1935. These were fruitful and beneficial years, not only for the institution he served but for Jewish studies in general. Under his directorship, the book collection at the Bibliothek grew to about 50,000 volumes, and the Bibliothek became one of the most important depositories of Jewish culture in Central Europe. During the same time, he compiled and published several important bibliographies based mainly on materials found in the Bibliothek;[111] he published a few monumental volumes dealing with the histories of the Jewish communities of Vienna[112] and Eisenstadt;[113] and he contributed immensely to the fields of Jewish folklore, genealogy, and many other areas of Jewish knowledge.[114] One of the most important bibliographies prepared by Wachstein was his *Katalog der Salo Cohn'schen Schenkungen*, with its Hebrew title *Minchat Shelomoh*.

In 1896, the Viennese Jewish philanthropist, Salo Cohn, acquired several hundred rare Hebraica volumes from the scholar and bibliophile, Solomon Joachim Halberstam (1832—1900),[115] and donated them to the Bibliothek in memory of his father. In 1909 he acquired a larger collection of rare Hebraica from the Chassidic bibliophile, Rabbi Nahum Ber Friedmann (1843—1883),[116] and donated it to the Bibliothek in memory of his mother. Wachstein compiled separate catalogs of these two collections and published them in two volumes under the general title of *Katalog der Salo Cohn'schen Schenkungen*. Volume 1 (Vienna, 1911) registered the Friedmann collection in 923 entries. The arrangement of the entries was alphabetical, by author, preceded by an introduction that included a geographical index of East European printers of Hebrew books, and followed by an index of Hebrew titles, and corrections and additions to the entries. Volume 2 (Vienna, 1914) registered the Halberstam collection in 415 entries. The arrangement of entries was the same as in Volume 1, preceded by an introduction that included a genealogical document relating to the Salo Cohn family, and followed by five indexes (Hebrew titles, Hebrew printers, places of Hebrew printing, chronological list of early Hebrew imprints dating from 1477 to 1540, and list of censors), and corrections and additions to the entries. The entries in Wachstein's *Katalog* included the following:

Author (in Roman characters)
Title (in Hebrew characters)
Description and contents (in Hebrew, extracted from the title page or from other places in the work itself)
Place of publication (in Hebrew as it appears on the title page, and in German)
Printer or publisher (in German)
Dates (Jewish, copying complete chronogram, and universal)
Pagination (only for Eastern and Palestinian imprints)
Format
Bibliographical notes (in German)
Approbations (only in Volume 2, and only those not listed by Roest or Wiener)
References to Wiener and other contemporary bibliographies (incunabula and early imprints, nearly 90 titles, were described with great detail, with references to Proctor, Hain, Freimann, and others)
Ownership inscriptions (copied in original form)
Marginal notes
Censors' signatures

In his introduction to Volume 1 of the *Katalog,* Wachstein described his system of cataloging as having a double goal, offering "a sufficient characteristic of the work, and a complete presentation of the biographical, genealogical, as well as of the typographical material." He accomplished it by extracting, most artfully, all the vital information from the complicated title pages and introductions of the Hebrew volumes. "He had the talent of presenting the maximum of contents with a minimum of words," wrote one scholar in his eulogy of Wachstein.[117] And a famous Hebrew bibliographer concluded that "his bibliographical works may serve as an example of how to compose works of this nature."[118]

Wachstein had planned to add more volumes to his *Katalog* which would register other interesting collections at the Bibliothek. He prepared various files for this purpose, but other projects as well as his health interfered with this plan. One of his last published bibliographical works was an additional index to the *Katalog,* entitled *Geographisches Register zu "Katalog der Salo Cohn'schen Schenkungen"* (Vienna, 1934). This register listed all the cities mentioned in the books included in the two-volume *Katalog,* arranged alphabetically by the Hebrew form of their names.[119]

The *Bibliothek* of the Israelitische Kultusgemeinde in Vienna was destroyed during the Nazi occupation of Austria prior to the outbreak of World War II, the books were scattered, and Wachstein's carefully prepared bibliographical files perished. All that survives of the Bibliothek is Bernhard Wachstein's printed *Katalog* and his other bibliographical works.

## II. Printed Card Catalogs

During the nineteenth century Europe was the site of almost all important Jewish book collections, but early in the twentieth century the United States began to overtake Europe in this area. By the mid-1960s there were at least half a dozen Jewish collections in the New World that could report having on their shelves 50,000 volumes or more.[120] Along with the growth of these cultural treasures, interest in Jewish scholarship also grew. The problem of furnishing bibliographic information concerning the holdings of major collections to interested parties became acute. Some information, mainly reflecting the holdings of the Library of Congress, and consisting largely of current publications, has become available in the printed card catalogs published by the Library of Congress since the 1940s. These are reproductions of catalog cards, assembled into three-column pages, and arranged either by author or by subject.[121] The bulk of the Hebraica and Judaica book collections in the United States are not included in these card catalogs. A major first step in the direction of correcting this situation was taken in 1960 with the publication of the card catalog of the Jewish collection in the New York Public Library.

## New York Public Library:
### *Dictionary Catalog of the Jewish Collection*

The Jewish Division of the New York Public Library was established in 1897 with a generous gift from Jacob Henry Schiff (1847–1920).[122] From a small beginning of about 2,000 volumes, the Jewish Division has grown during the first six decades of its existence to about 110,000 volumes. The first librarian of the Division was Abraham Solomon Freidus (1867–1923), who also developed a special classification system for the Jewish collection.[123] He was followed by Joshua Bloch (1890–1957).[124] These first two librarians were responsible for developing and shaping the collection into a major resource of Jewish knowledge.

G. K. Hall & Co. of Boston, pioneers in publishing card catalogs of specialized American libraries, were responsible for publishing the card catalog of the Jewish Division of the New York Public Library. Entitled *Dictionary Catalog of the Jewish Collection* (Boston, 1960), it reproduced 270,000 catalog cards in 14 folio-size volumes, representing holdings of about 100,000 books. Volumes 1–11 registered Hebraica and Judaica works, listed under author and subject entries in Roman characters. Volumes 12–13 listed Hebrew titles alphabetically, and Volume 14 included Yiddish and Ladino titles.

The catalog cards of the Jewish Division were not actually prepared and edited for the task of reproduction; they were left "as is." This resulted in some inconsistencies of entries and in defects in the quality of the reproduction, often making it impossible to decipher the added entries or similar information penciled in by hand on the cards. The arrangement of the Hebrew, Ladino, and Yiddish titles from left to right is an added difficulty for the user. But these are minor inconveniences compared to the truly great achievement of offering, for the first time, bibliographic access to such a large collection of Hebraica and Judaica accumulated under one roof.

The first supplement to the *Dictionary Catalog,* consisting of eight volumes, was also published by G. K. Hall in 1975. It reproduced about 114,000 cards of books added to the Jewish collection during 1961–1973, and it listed only books published up to 1971. Volumes 1–6 were arranged in the Roman alphabet, and Volumes 7–8, listing separately Hebrew, Yiddish, and Ladino works, were arranged in the Hebrew alphabet.

Additions to the Jewish collection are now listed regularly in the *Dictionary Catalog of the Research Libraries,* a computer-produced catalog published by the New York Public Library since 1972.


## Hebrew Union College—
## Jewish Institute of Religion, Cincinnati:
## *Dictionary Catalog of the Klau Library*

Four years after the publication of the card catalog of the Jewish collection at the New York Public Library, the same publishers, G. K. Hall & Co., issued a printed card catalog of an even larger Jewish book collection in the

United States. This time it was the catalog of the library of the Hebrew Union College-Jewish Institute of Religion in Cincinnati. Founded in 1875, HUC began to develop its library from a nucleus of 130 volumes. In a span of six years, the number of volumes grew to 8,000, and by the early 1960s it had reached about 175,000.[125] Responsible for this achievement were a group of distinguished scholars who served as librarians at this institution, notably Sigmund Mannheimer (1835–1909), the first librarian;[126] Judah Leon Magnes (1877–1948);[127] Max Schloesinger (1877–1944);[128] Adolph S. Oko (1883–1944);[129] and Herbert C. Zafren, the present librarian.

The card catalog of HUC–JIR appeared in 32 folio-size volumes entitled *Dictionary Catalog of the Klau Library* (Boston, 1964), and it registered 200,000 items, including those dealing with the "ancient Near East and other related fields." Volumes 1–27 registered Hebraica and Judaica works, listed under author and subject entries in Roman characters. Volumes 28–32 listed Hebraica titles alphabetically. The reproduction of the cards was superior to the preceding NYPL catalog, either as a result of advanced technology or the better quality of the originals. This enabled the reader to obtain almost complete information, except for some faded added entries and subject headings.[130]

## Harvard University Library:
### *Catalogue of Hebrew Books*

While NYPL and HUC–JIR decided to publish their holdings of Hebraica and Judaica in single sets of printed card catalogs, Harvard University Library decided to publish separate card catalogs of its "Judaica Collection," the first being a *Catalogue of Hebrew Books* (Cambridge, 1968).[131] Harvard's "Judaica Collection" is as old as Harvard College, but the development of the collection into a major resource began in 1929 with the acquisition of the 12,000-volume Deinard collection.[132] The Felix Friedmann collection of 15,000 volumes was purchased in 1951, and by the end of the 1960s the collection numbered approximately 100,000 volumes.[133] The development of the collection was the result of the devotion to Jewish literature by a number of Harvard-based Jewish scholars, especially Leo Wiener (1862–1930),[134] Lee Max Friedman (1871–1957),[135] Abraham Aaron Roback (1890–1965),[136] Harry Austryn Wolfson (1887–1975), and the present librarian of the collection, Charles Berlin.

The *Catalogue of Hebrew Books,* published by Harvard University Press, consisted of six volumes, and it reproduced 85,000 cards. Volumes 1—4 registered authors and subjects, arranged by the Roman alphabet, and Volumes 5—6 listed titles arranged by the Hebrew alphabet. The reproduction of the cards was very good, although they were reduced photographically to a much smaller size than the above-mentioned printed card catalogs. But many cards in the printed *Catalogue* did not represent actual holdings of the Harvard collection. These were Library of Congress cards—originally placed in the Harvard card catalog for reference purposes—that later found their way into the reproduced card catalog together with the regular cards.

Supplement I of the *Catalogue of Hebrew Books,* consisting of three volumes, was published in 1972. It reproduced about 40,000 cards, representing approximately 14,000 new titles added to the Harvard collection since the publication of the first six volumes in 1968. Volume 1 of the *Supplement* included a "classified listing" (arranged in call-number order), with an appendix, "Judaica in the Houghton Library,"[137] followed by a chronological index (of the Judaica). Volume 2 registered authors and selected subjects, and Volume 3 listed titles.

## Chronological List of Published Catalogs of Major Hebraica Book Collections

### 1852—1860

Oxford. University. Bodleian Library.

Catalogus librorum hebraeorum in bibliotheca Bodleiana; jussu curatorum digessit et notis instruxit M. Steinschneider. Berolini: typis A. Friedlaender, 1852—1860.

2 vols. (ca. 1,750 pages). Small folio format.

Based on Oppenheimer collection, acquired by the Bodleian Library in 1829, 7,622 entries (2,812 columns) of Hebraica printed up to 1732 (date when Oppenheimer stopped purchasing books). Works not in Bodleian also listed. Compiler invested in catalog "one fourth of his life and the greater part of his strength." Work called "unrivaled tool for every serious scholar . . . sound foundation of scholarly Hebrew bibliography." Also, "the Urim and Thummim (oracle) of every Jewish student."

*Organization:* Three sections. Section one: classical and anonymous works (4,162 entries); section two: authors (3,460 entries); section three: indexes (a. printers, compositors, proofreaders, Maecenases—1,937 names; b. printing places—119 locations; c. Hebrew titles—5,208 works; d. Hebrew Bibles—333 entries; e. Hebrew place names—703 entries). Appendix: Conspectus of Hebrew manuscripts in Bodleian (ca. 500 mss.).

*Order of entries.* Author (Roman characters); biographical data (Latin); title (Hebrew characters); title translated and explained (in Latin); contents (Latin); format; place of publication and name of printer (romanized); Hebrew and universal dates.

*Editions:* Berlin: Welt-Verlag, 1931; Hildesheim: Georg Olms, 1964 (photo-offset reprint).

### (1929)

Oxford. University. Bodleian Library.
A Concise Catalogue of the Hebrew Printed Books in the Bodleian Library. Oxford: Clarendon Press, 1929.
vii, 816 pages.

Compiled by Sir Arthur Ernest Cowley; "based upon M. Steinschneider's Catalogus librorum hebraeorum . . . " listed above. Estimated to include more than 10,000 works. Cut-off date: 1927. Includes index of Hebrew titles.

*Order of entries:* Author (Roman characters), followed by reference to St[einschneider]; title (Hebrew characters); description of contents (in English); place and date of publication; format; shelf number.

### 1867

British Museum. Dept. of Oriental Printed Books and Manuscripts.
Catalogue of the Hebrew Books in the Library of the British Museum. London: British Museum, 1867.
x, 891 pages.

Compiled by Joseph Zedner, and lists "upwards of 10,000 volumes." Catalog described as "landmark in Hebrew bibliography. It combined the maximum of information with the minimum of space."

*Organization:* Preface with statistical information and rules of entry; catalog; addenda of books acquired during printing; indexes: a. surnames and nonbiblical first names; b. titles; c. abbreviations; d. places of printing.

*Order of entries:* Author (Roman characters); title (Hebrew characters); description (English, if not stated on title page in Hebrew); place of printing (Hebrew and romanized); Hebrew and universal dates of publication; format.

*Editions:* London: British Museum, 1964 (photo-offset reprint with new preface, corrigenda originally published by Zedner in *HB* 10 (1870), and some manuscript amendments in title index).

A supplementary volume was published, as follows:

### (1894)

British Museum. Dept. of Oriental Printed Books and Manuscripts.
    Catalogue of Hebrew Books in the British Museum, Acquired during the Years 1868–1892. By S. Van Straalen. London: British Museum, 1894.
    vi, 532 pages. Small folio format.

7,800 entries. Index of Hebrew titles for both volumes.

*Order of entries:* Same as above, with addition of pagination and shelf-numbers (lacked Zedner's precision and accuracy).

### 1875

Rosenthal, Leeser (Poland, 1794–Germany, 1868). Collector.
    Catalog der Hebraica und Judaica aus der L. Rosenthal'schen Bibliothek.
    Bearb. von M. Roest. Amsterdam: J. Klausen, 1875.
    2 vols. (1,727 pages).

Circa 6,000 volumes, 32 manuscripts. Considered by contemporaries as perhaps the largest collection of this nature existing in Germany. Was later presented to city of Amsterdam, and came to be known as Bibliotheca Rosenthaliana.

*Organization:* Two sections with appendix. Section one: printed Hebraica and Judaica; section two: manuscripts. Appendix entitled *Yode'a Sefer,* contains descriptions of 2,530 Hebrew works (arranged by title), prepared in Hebrew by collector, edited by compiler. Cut-off date of appendix: 1857. Catalog preceded by introduction with outline of rules of entry.

*Order of entries:* Author (Roman characters); title (Hebrew characters); description and contents (from title page); additional information (in German); place and date of publication (Hebrew characters); place and name of printer (romanized); universal date; pagination; approbations; references to Steinschneider, Zedner, or *Anhang (Yode'a Sefer)*.

*Editions:* Amsterdam: N. V. Boekhandel & Antiquariaat B. M. Israël, 1966 (photo-offset reprint).

## 1886—1906

Oxford. University. Bodleian Library.
Catalogue of the Hebrew Manuscripts in the Bodleian Library and in the College Libraries of Oxford, Including Mss. in Other Languages, Which are Written with Hebrew Characters, or Relating to the Hebrew Language or Literature, and a Few Samaritan Mss. Compiled by Ad. Neubauer. Oxford, 1886—1906.
2 vols. + portfolio of 40 facsimiles. Small folio format.

Volume 2 compiled together with A. E. Cowley. 2,918 entries (describing 110 manuscripts from Canonici collection, 780 from Oppenheimer collection, 862 from Michael collection, and 2,675 Genizah fragments).

*Organization:* Volume 1: comparative charts of manuscripts in the various collections; 2,602 entries arranged by subjects; indexes: a. authors, translators, family names; b. titles, subjects, anonymous works; c. scribes, owners, witnesses of ownership; d. censors; e. geographical names. Volume 2: 316 entries; indexes: general, Hebrew-Arabic; corrigenda and addenda to both volumes.

*Order of entries:* Title and author (Hebrew characters); contents, scripts, format, material, collation, shelf number.

## 1893—1936

Akademiia Nauk SSSR. Institut Vostokovedeniia.
קהלת משה אריה ליב פרידלאנד. St. Petersburg, 1893—1936.
689 pages. Small folio format.

5,905 entries of printed Hebraica issued in eight fascicles. Compiled by Samuel Wiener under the supervision of Daniel Chwolson. Wiener was praised for "giving such clear and encompassing brief descriptions . . . that we do not have to see the book itself anymore." Some categories of books not available in the Friedlandiana were also listed.

*Organization:* Fascicle 1: letter *alef;* fascicle 2 (1895): letter *bet;* fascicle 3 (1897): letters *gimel—dalet;* fascicle 4 (1902): letters *he—zayin;* fascicle 5 (1904): letters *chet—tet;* fascicle 6 and 7 (1918): letters *yod* and *kaf;* fascicle 8 (1936, compiled by Joseph Bender): letter *lamed.*

*Order of entries:* Title; author (occasional brief biographical information); contents; place of publication; printer or publisher; dates (Jewish and universal); format; pagination; type; approbations; references to Steinschneider, Zedner, Roest, Van Straalen.

*Editions:* Fascicles 7—8, Jerusalem: Wahrmann Books, 1963; entire work, Jerusalem, 1969 (photographically reduced reprint edition).

### 1899—1935

British Museum. Dept. of Oriental Printed Books and Manuscripts.
   Catalogue of the Hebrew and Samaritan Manuscripts in the British Museum, by G. Margoliouth. London: British Museum, 1899—1935.
   4 vols. Folio format.

Volume 3 issued in three parts, 1909—1915; Volume 4 compiled by Jacob Leveen. 1,365 entries (describing, among others, 332 manuscripts from Almanzi collection, circa 300 manuscripts acquired from ill-fated bookseller Shapira, and sizable number of Genizah fragments). The descriptions were executed "with much scholarly care and with great minuteness and conscientiousness and on a scale hitherto unknown to catalogues of Hebrew manuscripts."

*Organization:* Volume 1: 339 biblical texts and commentaries; Volume 2: 393 manuscripts in areas of Midrash, Talmud, and Halachah, liturgies; Volume 3: 474 manuscripts in fields of cabala, ethics, philosophy, poetry, philology, science, etc. In each volume: a. corresponding numerical lists of manuscripts; b. addenda and corrigenda; c. facsimiles. Volume 4: introduction to history of collection; indexes (persons, titles, subjects, places); 159 new entries; numerical list of manuscripts, addenda and corrigenda to all volumes.

*Order of entries:* Description of material (paper or vellum); size, collation; number of lines per page; physical condition; type of script; date; title or beginning sentence; contents; censors; owners ;

scribes; colophon or other striking sentence; bibliographical information.

*Editions:* Volumes 1−3 only, London: British Museum, 1965 (photo-offset reprint).

## 1911−1914

Israelitische Kultusgemeinde, Vienna. Bibliothek.
   Katalog der Salo Cohn'schen Schenkungen, von Bernhard Wachstein.
Wien: Gilhofer & Ranschburg, 1911−1914.
   2 vols. Small-folio format.

Volume 1: Bücher aus der Sammlung des Rabbiners Nachum Ber Friedmann-Sadagora (923 entries); Volume 2: Bücher aus der Sammlung S. H. Halberstamm-Bielitz (415 entries). Wachstein presented the "maximum of contents with a minimum of words."

*Organization:* Volume 1: introduction with geographical index of Hebrew printing places in Eastern Europe, catalog, index of titles, corrections and additions. Volume 2: introduction with genealogical document relating to Salo Cohn family, catalog, five indexes: titles, printers, places of Hebrew printing, early Hebrew imprints (in chronological order) and censors, corrections and additions.

*Order of entries :* Author (Roman characters), title (Hebrew characters), description and contents (from title page), place of publication (Hebrew and German), printer or publisher (German), dates (Jewish and universal), pagination, format, bibliographical notes, approbations (in Volume 2 only, for works not listed by Roest or Wiener), references to Wiener and other contemporary bibliographers, ownership inscriptions, marginal notes, censors' signatures.

A supplement index was published, as follows:

## (1934)

Wachstein, Bernhard (Austria, 1868−1935).
   Geographisches Register zu "Katalog der Salo Cohn'schen Schenkungen," Wien, 1911, 1914. Wien, 1934.
   25 pages.

Lists cities mentioned in books registered in preceding two-volume *Katalog.* Arranged by Hebrew form of place names.

## 1960

New York. Public Library. Reference Dept.
Dictionary Catalog of the Jewish Collection. Boston: G. K. Hall, 1960.
14 vols. (12,120 pages). Large-folio format.

270,000 catalog cards, arranged in three columns; seven cards per column (represents holdings of circa 100,000 books).

*Organization:* Volumes 1–11: Hebraica and Judaica arranged by author and subject (in Roman characters); Volumes 12–13: Hebrew titles; Volume 14: Yiddish and Ladino titles.

*Supplements:* First Supplement. Boston: G. K. Hall, 1975. 8 vols. Folio format. 114,000 cards. Volumes 1–6: author and subject entries (in Roman characters); Volumes 7–8: Hebraica titles (Hebrew, Yiddish, Ladino).

## 1964

Hebrew Union College-Jewish Institute of Religion, Cincinnati. Library.
Dictionary Catalog of the Klau Library, Cincinnati. Boston: G. K. Hall, 1964.
32 vols. (ca. 18,000 pages). Large-folio format.

200,000 items, including "ancient Near East and other related fields." Cards arranged in same manner as preceding catalog.

*Organization:* Volumes 1–27: Hebraica and Judaica arranged by author and subject (in Roman characters); Volumes 28–32: Hebraica titles (Hebrew and Yiddish interfiled).

## 1968

Harvard University. Library.
Catalogue of Hebrew Books. Cambridge: Harvard University Press, 1968.
6 vols. Small folio.

85,000 cards, arranged in same manner as preceding catalogs.

*Organization:* Volumes 1–4: authors and subjects (in Roman characters); Volumes 5–6: Hebrew titles.

*Supplements:* Supplement I. Cambridge: Harvard University Press, 1972. 3 vols. Small folio. 40,000 cards (representing 14,000 new titles). Volume 1: classified listing (in call-number order), appendix, Judaica in the Houghton Library with chronological index. Volume 2: authors and selected subjects. Volume 3: titles.

*Chapter Three*

# Bio-Bibliographical Works

*Bio-bibliographies are works devoted to biographical as well
as to bibliographical knowledge. Since the line dividing
biographical from bio-bibliographical works is sometimes
very thin, only works that explicitly acknowledge this dual role
were selected for inclusion in this chapter. Other types of works
will be included among biographies, and will be discussed in
Volume Two of this work.*

*The chapter is divided into two parts. Part I deals with Azulai's
bio-bibliography, and with the bio-bibliographical works
evolved from Isaac Benjacob's standardized edition of Azulai.
Part II deals with independent bio-bibliographies.*

## I

Hayyim Joseph David Azulai: *Shem Hagedolim.* Aaron Walden:
*Shem Hagedolim Hechadash.* Solomon Hazan: *Hama'alot
Lishelomoh.* Moses Markovich: *Shem Hagedolim Hashelishi.* Zsig-
mond Schwartz: *Shem Hagedolim Me'erets Hagar.* Joseph Ben
Naim: *Malche Rabanan.*

## II

Giovanni Bernardo de Rossi: *Dizionario.* Mordecai Samuel
Ghirondi and Graziadio Nepi: *Toldot Gedole Yisrael Ugeone
Italyah.* Heimann Joseph Michael: *Or Hachayim.* Eleazar Kohn:
*Kinat Sofrim.* Simon Moses Chones: *Toldot Haposkim.*

I

## Hayyim Joseph David Azulai: *Shem Hagedolim*

A LMOST A CENTURY after the appearance of Shabbethai Bass's *Sifte Yeshenim*, less than half a century after the publication of the last volume of Johann Christoph Wolf's *Bibliotheca hebraea,* and only about five years after Jehiel Heilprin's *Seder Hadorot* came off the press, there appeared in Livorno (Leghorn), Italy, a booklet of 131 leaves, 83 of them consisting of bio-bibliographical material. The author of this little volume, Rabbi Hayyim Joseph David Azulai (known to Jewish scholars by the acronym of his name: Hida), was not a bibliographer in the formal sense of the term, and the entries in his bibliographic works were not structured according to any rules of entry, but the impact he made on the development of the science of Jewish bibliography has been felt up to our own day.

Azulai was one of the most unusual personalities of the eighteenth century. Born in Jerusalem in 1724,[1] he had shown great scholastic ability at a very young age, and when he reached the age of nine (or ten) he was accepted as a student at one of the prestigious rabbinic schools. He was barely twelve years old when he began to compose works and to deliver sermons. Several years later he began teaching in one of the Jerusalem yeshivot, and at the same time turned to the study of Cabala.

At the age of 30 he was chosen by the Hebron Jewish community as an emissary to European Jewry on their behalf. He left the Holy Land in the summer of 1753 and returned five years later. He traveled by caravan to Egypt, from Egypt by ship to Italy, and continued on to Germany, Holland, England, and France. From France he returned to Italy, to Livorno, where, in 1757, he issued his first published work.[2] He left Italy in the summer of 1757, and returned to Jerusalem via Turkey in the spring of 1758. Afterwards he served as a member of various rabbinical courts in Jerusalem and as a rabbi of the Jewish community of Egypt (1764–1769).

In the fall of 1772 he began his second trip to Europe. Again he traveled first to Egypt, from there he sailed to Tunisia and Italy, and continued to France, Holland, and back to Italy, where he settled in Livorno in the fall of 1778. One of his admirers established a place for him to study and to write his books, and he supported himself from the sale of his own books and also by selling antique books. His income was supplemented by gifts from admirers (some of them offering him a tithe of their profits) and by fees for preparing cabalistic amulets. He planned to spend his last years in the Holy Land, but death overtook him in Livorno in 1806, and his body was returned to Jerusalem, the city of his birth, about a century and a half later, in 1960.

Azulai's literary activity covered the entire field of Jewish knowledge. He was the author of 126 original works (82 of which remained unpublished).[3] His works included commentaries on the Bible and Talmud, sermons, ethical treatises, rabbinic dictionaries, responsa, law, and Cabala. During his travels he kept a diary in which he described the people he met, the events he witnessed, the customs he observed, the libraries he visited, and the books and codices he examined. This diary became a major source for the history of various Jewish communities in Europe during the eighteenth century.[4] Another work which he composed as a result of his travels became a classic in Jewish bibliography. This was his *Shem Hagedolim—Va'ad La-chachamim,* the first volume of which appeared in Livorno in 1774.

Azulai had a strong love for books and a special gift for identifying manuscripts. In addition to the many libraries that he visited, he also acquired many printed and handwritten Hebrew books for himself in the course of his travels, and he began to compile material about authors and books. His interest was solely in establishing the period during which the author flourished, when the work was composed (or published), by whom it was composed, and how authoritative the author was. For what purpose? He had noticed in rabbinic works that the scholars were often puzzled by contradictions they had discovered in the statements of authorities. Scholars sometimes had to use ingenuity in order to solve such "contradictions."

At the core of this problem, as Azulai saw it, was the fact that many rabbinic scholars had little biographical knowledge about the authors of the works they were studying; they were also deficient in bibliographical information, and they were not aware that some authors with identical names existed in different periods,[5] or that works with the same titles were composed by different authors.[6] They did not realize that some authors of equal stature sometimes lived in localities distant from one another, and therefore were not familiar with each others' works, or that sometimes a work by a greater authority appeared after the publication of a work by a lesser authority. Knowledge of these bio-bibliographical facts would have eliminated many unnecessary scholarly efforts to straighten out seeming contradictions in rabbinic literature. During his young years, Azulai had already prepared a pamphlet pointing out some of these problems encountered in rabbinic works.[7] Later, when he was able to examine and study the thousands of printed and handwritten books accumulated in public and private libraries in Europe, he returned to this topic, and his almost photographic memory and sharp mind enabled him to compose his four-volume Hebrew bio-bibliography, *Shem Hagedolim—Va'ad Lachachamim.*

Volume One (Livorno, 1774) was entitled *Shem Hagedolim* (cf. II Samuel 7:9), and it listed close to 400 entries of authors and works in alphabetical order dating from the geonic period up to (but not including) Azulai's own generation.[8] Appended to this work was a commentary by Azulai on *Pirke Avot,*[9] and addenda and corrigenda to both parts of the volume.

Volume Two (Livorno, 1786), also entitled *Shem Hagedolim,* listed close to 1,200 entries of authors and works. Appended to this volume were the author's addenda to three of his previously published works,[10] a minor Midrash published from a manuscript,[11] addenda to *Shem Hagedolim,* and a subject index to the entire volume.

Volume Three (Livorno, 1796), entitled *Va'ad Lachachamim* (based on *Avot,* 1:4),[12] listed close to 600 entries of authors and works. This was followed by a section of addenda and corrigenda, entitled *Bet Va'ad.* Appended to this volume was a collection of the author's responsa and novellae,[13] followed by more addenda and corrigenda to both works.

A second edition of Volume One of *Shem Hagedolim* was published in Livorno in 1798. Added to this volume and immediately following each letter of the alphabet, was the section called *Va'ad Lachachamim,* Volume Two, which listed about 350 additional entries of authors and works. The rest of the volume included Azulai's earlier mentioned commentary on *Pirke Avot,* and addenda and corrigenda to the entire volume. Several leaves of additional entries were published three years later (1801) as an appendix to a work by Azulai on the Minor Tractates of the Talmud.[14]

The four volumes of *Shem Hagedolim—Va'ad Lachachamim* (together with the various additions) gave biographical information on more than 1,300 authors and bibliographical data on more than 1,200 works.[15] Many of the works discussed by Azulai, especially many of the manuscripts, are no longer in existence, and the *Shem Hagedolim—Va'ad Lachachamim* is the only, or the major, source of information about them. The same is also true for the sources of biographical information on many of the authors discussed in this work. Azulai was very selective in preparing the bio-bibliographical entries for his work. He usually included authors and works that interested him or that he considered important; those he disliked, he ignored.[16] True to his main purpose, he devoted most of his attention to the codifiers and their works. His method was to examine earlier sources that discussed the same author or work, to accept or reject their statements, and to correct their errors with regard to the publication dates of some works and the periods of activity of some authors.[17] He employed scientific methods and arguments—internal and external evidence—in examining the assumed authorship of a work, and he often successfully proved or disproved it.[18] This procedure was entirely new in Hebrew historiography and bibliography, and it placed those two fields on a more scientific footing.

The *Shem Hagedolim—Va'ad Lachachamim,* as Azulai published it, was difficult to assess. Azulai compiled the material without any prearranged plan, and he scattered it over several volumes, each time beginning the alphabet anew, often repeating information already furnished previously, and sometimes making contradictory statements.[19] An effort to assist the user of the work was made in 1843−1847 when a new edition of all its volumes appeared in Krotoschin-Frankfort in three volumes. It included a biography of Azulai and notes on his work by several scholars,[20] but little effort was made to rearrange and unite the material.[21] This edition was even, in certain respects, inferior to the original editions.[22] Less than a decade later (1852) there appeared in Vilna an edition, prepared by Isaac Benjacob,[23] which gave the *Shem Hagedolim—Va'ad Lachachamim* a new face and permitted easy access to the material gathered there.

Benjacob compiled the materials of the various volumes of *Shem Hagedolim—Va'ad Lachachamim* and rearranged them into a two-part work. In the first part, which he called *Ma'arechet Gedolim,* he listed all the authors in alphabetical order that were dealt with by Azulai; in the second part, which he called *Ma'arechet Sefarim,* he listed all the works discussed by Azulai alphabetically.[24] The new arrangement enabled the reader to find the complete bio-biographical information offered by Azulai for a specific author or work under a single entry. Benjacob's editing of the text consisted of providing transitions here and there for the sake of continuity; removing repetitious entries, sentences, or references by Azulai to other parts of this work (no longer needed on account of the new arrangement); and adding cross-references (preceded by an asterisk) of authors or works not listed by Azulai under separate entries. From many entries, he removed extraneous material—not of a bio-bibliographical nature—and placed it at the end of the letter from which it was removed under a separate heading, *Kuntres Acharon.* Information relating to a specific author or work, but not of primary bio-bibliographical importance, he retained in place and distinguished from the rest of the material by printing it in a petite Rashi script. The work was preceded by a revised bio-bibliography of Azulai himself (published originally in the Krotoschin-Frankfort edition),[25] and concluded with several leaves of additions to the text (selected from the same edition),[26] and a short addenda and corrigenda.

Isaac Benjacob's edition of the *Shem Hagedolim—Va'ad Lachachamim* was reprinted numerous times (it went into about 20 editions), sometimes with modifications or additions, but the arrangement of authors in one part and works in the other was retained in all the various editions. A pirated edition (with omission of the bio-bibliographical essay on Azulai) was published in Lemberg in 1856. An edition with additions by Menahem Mendel Krengel was published in Cracow-Piotrków, 1905–1930 (under the title *Shem Hagedolim Hashalem*); reprinted with more additions by Henich Taub in New York (1958?), and, with an extra volume of additions to *Ma'arechet Gedolim* by Elazar Lipa Gartenhaus, in Brooklyn in 1958. With additions of text by Azulai and others, it was issued in Tel Aviv in 1959/60, and reprinted either in Tel Aviv of in Jerusalem several years later (1967?).[27]

## Aaron Walden: *Shem Hagedolim Hechadash*

Benjacob standardized Azulai's *Shem Hagedolim—Va'ad Lachachamim,* making it a basic source for Hebrew bio-bibliography. His edition of this work was also instrumental in influencing contemporary scholars to try their hand at this type of literature. The first work to be published as a result of Benjacob's edition of Azulai's bio-bibliographical work was Aaron Walden's *Shem Hagedolim Hechadash* (Warsaw, 1864). Born in Warsaw in 1838, and raised in a Chassidic family, Walden himself became an active Chassid by joining the elite group of followers of Rabbi Menahem Mendel of Kotsk (1788–1859).[28] He acquired a large amount of first-hand knowledge about the various Chassidic dynasties and their leaders, and he shared it with the readers of his work.[29]

As the name *Shem Hagedolim Hechadash* suggests, Walden intended his work as a continuation of Azulai's *Shem Hagedolim.* He stated it clearly in the subtitle: " . . . collection of names . . . of authors . . . of German, Polish, Russian, and Spanish scholars that flourished since the days of Hayyim Joseph David Azulai . . . and also some from previous generations."

Taking Benjacob's edition of Azulai's work as a prototype, Walden divided his work into two parts, one for authors and the other for titles, and he named these parts, as Benjacob did, *Ma'arechet Gedolim* and *Ma'arechet Sefarim.* In the first part he listed more than 1,500 biographies, and in the second part about 1,450 works.[30] But Walden possessed neither the erudition of Azulai nor his critical sense, nor did he have the editorial abilities of Benjacob, so that the relation between his work and Azulai's remained superficial. In the first part of his work he included the biographies of almost every important Chassidic leader from the time of Israel ben Eliezer

Ba'al Shem Tov (ca. 1700—1760), the founder of the movement, to his own day, and he filled up many pages just with Chassidic tales.[31] Many of the Chassidic leaders and scholars entered in the first part were not authors of works, so that the entries in the second part were not always related to the entries of the first part. Despite the statement on the title page, he included only a negligibly small number of Sephardic authors, and the bio-bibliographical information was mostly incomplete and often defective.[32]

With deficiencies such as these, Walden's *Shem Hagedolim* could not enjoy the reputation of Azulai's *Shem Hagedolim.* Oddly enough, however, because of the Chassidic material included in it the *Shem Hagedolim Hechadash* became attractive to many readers; it enjoyed a large circulation and was reprinted several times during the life of the author and later (Walden died in Kielce, Poland, in 1912). In the absence of more precise and scientific works in the field of Chassidism, the *Shem Hagedolim Hechadash* remains a useful source for Chassidic bio-bibliographical information.

The *Shem Hagedolim Hechadash* was reprinted in Warsaw in 1870. A new edition, with additions and corrections by the author's son, Joseph Aryeh Leib, was published in Warsaw in 1879; reprinted in Warsaw in 1881, and in Jerusalem in 1964/65. The first fascicle of a supplement compiled by another son, Moses Menahem (entitled *Yechabed Av;* cf. Malachi 1:6), was published in Piotrków in 1923 (reprinted in Warsaw in 1939 ?). A new edition of part one, supplemented by a list of rabbis who perished during the 1939—1945 Jewish holocaust years, compiled by Jehiel Zvi Klein, was published in New York in 1947/48.

## Solomon Hazan: *Hama'alot Lishelomoh*

The success of Walden's *Shem Hagedolim Hechadash* inspired other scholars to compose works of a similar bio-bibliographical nature. A number of efforts were begun to extend and to supplement the old (Azulai's) and the new (Walden's) *Shem Hagedolim.* Only a few of these scholars succeeded in publishing the complete, or partial, results of their efforts.

Eliezer Effrath, a resident of Kovno, Lithuania, published the first sixty-four pages of a planned two-part bio-bibliographical work on contemporary scholars and works in Vilna, in 1889, entitled *Dor Vedorshav* (cf. *Sanhedrin* 38b). He named the biographical part *Asefat Chachamim* and the bibliographical part *Asefat Sefarim,* but the section he published included only sixty-six biographies belonging to the letter *alef* (besides the thirty-nine pages of approbations and introductions).

Hayyim Braverman, a resident of Poland, began to publish additions to the works of both Azulai and Walden in Warsaw, in 1892, under the title *Anshe Shem* (cf. Numbers, 16:2). His ninety-six-page volume included (besides twenty-two pages of approbations and introductions) only biographical materials covering letters *alef* to middle of *lamed*.

In 1894, in Vilna, Levi Oftschynski (or Ovchinskii), another East European scholar, began publishing a bio-bibliographical supplement to the works of Azulai and Walden entitled *Nachalat Avot*. He planned to structure his work according to the model established by Isaac Benjacob (*Ma'arechet Gedolim* and *Ma'arechet Sefarim*), but he succeeded in publishing only the biographical part.

During the same year (1894) there appeared in Alexandria, Egypt, the first complete Hebrew bio-bibliographical work since Walden's *Shem Hagedolim Hechadash*. The name of this work was *Hama'alot Lishelomoh* (based on Psalms, 127:1) and it was written by Solomon Hazan. The author was born in Algeria around the end of the eighteenth century. He later moved to Damascus, and from there to Cairo where he became the head of a yeshiva. In 1832 he was appointed chief rabbi of Alexandria and, twenty-four years later (1856), he died while on a trip to Malta and was laid to rest there.[33] He left a number of manuscripts which were printed posthumously by his son. One of these was his bio-bibliographical work.

Hazan's *Hama'alot Lishelomoh,* designated as a companion volume to Azulai's *Shem Hagedolim,*[34] registered Azulai's contemporaries and the following generation of scholars, and their works.[35] The stress was on Sephardic scholars and works, and the method of presentation was similar to Azulai's. The arrangement was borrowed from Isaac Benjacob's edition of Azulai's *Shem Hagedolim,* but with a modification: each letter of the alphabet was divided into two sections. The first section, under the heading *Ma'arechet Gedolim,* listed scholars, and the second section, under the heading *Ma'arechet Sefarim,* listed works. The final four leaves of the volume listed, in chronological order, the last six chief rabbis of Alexandria, and their works.

A reprint edition of *Hama'alot Lishelomoh* was published in Israel (Jerusalem?) in 1967/68.

## Moses Markovich: *Shem Hagedolim Hashelishi*

The efforts to extend the work of Azulai and Walden which began in the nineteenth century continued well into the twentieth century. In 1910 there appeared in Vilna a volume entitled *Shem Hagedolim Hashelishi,* written by Moses Markovich (1855–1935). The volume was divided into a *Ma'arechet Gedolim* and a *Ma'arechet Sefarim,* the former consisting of 277 entries, up to the middle of the letter *alef* (Avraham Zakheim), and the latter consisting of 524 entries, stopping in the middle of Elef Hamagen.

Both parts of the *Shem Hagedolim Hashelishi* were preceded by numerous approbations of leading rabbis, among them the most recognized authorities of rabbinic scholarship.[36] All the approvers had great praise for the author and his work, and some expressed amazement that "a simple shoemaker" could compose such a work. A few even hinted that the author is "not used to holding a pen in his hands."[37] A few years later (1913) the author published three booklets on the history of three Lithuanian-Jewish communities[38] and, still later, an enlarged edition of his *Shem Hagedolim Hashelishi* (Keidani, 1932). Part one now consisted of 313 entries and part two of 630 entries, but none reached further than letter *alef.* On the title page of the new edition, the author wrote the following lines:

> . . . every sensible person should use me as an example. I am a simple man, a shoemaker, but I spent over forty years on this book, and I never tired of it. I was many times in need of bread, still I did not stop writing this book.

In the introduction, Markovich related biographical details of his life, his childhood, and his work. He was born in a small Lithuanian community, in the district of Raseiniai. When Markovich was eight and a half years old, his father died. He studied in a *cheder* in his hometown, and later in Raseiniai. His financial situation was so bad that he had to beg for food and, therefore, regularly showed up late at school until he was expelled. As a result, Markovich never learned to write at school—only to read.[39] An older brother came to his aid and trained him to become a shoemaker. He loved to buy books (mainly in Yiddish), and he read them eagerly; one day he acquired Azulai's *Shem Hagedolim* and, after reading it, he felt that he could compose such a work:

> . . . but I could not write even a single word, and the people in the city of Raseiniai were curious to know how I was going to accomplish the writing of such a work. . . . Daily I had to ask the youngsters who were studying in the Great Synagogue, to write a little for me, and they did it whenever I asked them. Some of them, when they saw how my writing was done, used to throw their pillows at me in jest. [It was customary at that time for students to sleep at the synagogue—Author.] I did not react to that, since I needed them . . . until my oldest son grew up, and began to write for me. And the people in the

city made fun of me . . . until they all saw that I had a big and heavy book, and they were amazed. . . .

Markovich had a phenomenal memory when it came to names and genealogies. The information he collected for his work came, not only from books, but also from newspapers, and he was successful in listing names and events which otherwise would have been lost. Unfortunately, when Markovich died most of his bio-bibliographical work remained unpublished, and it vanished during the years of the World War II holocaust.

### Zsigmond Schwartz: *Shem Hagedolim Me'erets Hagar*

The bio-bibliographical works of Azulai, and of those who followed in his footsteps, were not limited by geographical borders. Although each bio-bibliographer, including Azulai, understandably favored the localities they were best acquainted with, universality was their common objective. This would explain the high percentage of works in this category that remained incomplete; completeness was technically an unattainable goal; in addition, there were the financial difficulties inherent in publishing. The first bio-bibliographical work devoted to a single geographical area, and arranged along the lines of Isaac Benjacob's edition of the *Shem Hagedolim* (divided into *Ma'arechet Gedolim* and *Ma'arechet Sefarim*), was published in Hungary during the years 1913 to 1915.[40] The compiler, Zsigmond (Phinehas Zelig ha-Kohen) Schwartz, was born in Mád, Hungary, in 1877, and died during the holocaust years of World War II. He came from a rabbinic family, and was himself an ordained rabbi and an author and editor of several rabbinic works.[41] His bio-bibliographical work entitled *Shem Hagedolim Me'erets Hagar*[42] listed Hungarian rabbinical scholars, authors, and works, "from the earliest times to the present," and it was published in three parts.

Part one (Paks, 1913) consisted of more than 1,000 biographical entries *(Ma'arechet Gedolim),* covering letters *alef* through *lamed* (each letter divided into two sections, one for deceased scholars and the other for contemporaries), and it was supplemented by several pages of additions and corrections prepared by a brother of the compiler.[43]

Part two (Munkacs, 1914) listed about 700 biographical entries, covering letters *mem* through *shin,* concluding the biographical section. It was also supplemented, as was part one, by several pages of additions and corrections by the brother of the compiler.

Part three (Kisvarda, 1915) consisted of more than 700 bibliographical entries *(Ma'arechet Sefarim)*, supplemented by a 20-page fascicle entitled *Kuntres Acharon* (dated 1918). Schwartz later published two additional supplements to his bio-bibliography of Hungarian scholars and works, *Shem Hagedolim Hechadash (Me'erets Hagar)* (Kisvarda, 1935), and *Shem Hagedolim Hashelishi Me'erets Hagar* (Kisvarda, 1941). Both supplements listed names and addresses of rabbis, community leaders, and scholars.[44]

A reprint edition of the three parts of the *Shem Hagedolim Me'erets Hagar*, together with the supplements, under the title *Shem Hagedolim Ligedole Hungaryah* (cover title: *Shem Hagedolim Hashalem Migedole Hungaryah*), was published in New York, 1958/59.

## Joseph Ben Naim: *Malche Rabanan*

Another bio-bibliographical work devoted to a single geographical area was published in Jerusalem in 1931 under the title *Malche Rabanan* (based on *Nedarim,* 20b). The author and compiler of this work, Joseph Ben Naim, was born in Fez, Morocco, in 1882, and spent all his life there.[45] At a young age he began to collect material on the history of the Jews of North Africa. He visited the Jewish cemetery in Fez daily in search of manuscripts of former rabbis left in the Genizah. Often he searched in various yeshivot for old manuscripts or historical documents, and he acquired any Hebrew book that was offered to him. In this manner he accumulated one of the largest collections of Hebrew works in North Africa.[46] To his collection of books written by others, he added another collection: books that he himself wrote, thirty-four in all, covering a wide range of fields—commentaries on the Bible and Talmud, history, biography and bibliography, rabbinic responsa, zoological and botanical studies, precious stones mentioned in the Bible, and even poetry.[47] When he died in 1962, he had succeeded in publishing only five of his own works, among them his bio-bibliography of North African rabbis and scholars, entitled *Malche Rabanan.*

In the tradition of the various *Shem Hagedolim* (since Benjacob), Ben Naim also divided his *Malche Rabanan* into two parts. The first part was devoted to biography, and the second, which he named *Kevod Melachim,* to bibliography. He utilized for his bio-bibliography the works of Azulai, Hazan, and Benjacob's *Otsar Hasefarim,* and he properly credited them for the information he culled from their works. But most of Ben Naim's material came from local sources and documents, among them a great deal that never would have come to light if not for his untiring efforts.[48]

## II. Independent Bio-Bibliographies

### Giovanni Bernardo de Rossi: *Dizionario*

Both the first great Jewish bibliographer and the last great non-Jewish bibliographer of Jewish literature lived, flourished, wrote, and published their works in the same country, Italy. The former, Hayyim Joseph David Azulai, began to publish his bio-bibliographical works only a few years before the latter, Giovanni Bernardo de Rossi, began to publish his bibliographical volumes. No interrelation existed between the two; they drew their bibliographical nourishment from different sources. Azulai drew from Jewish sources exclusively; he may not even have been aware of the existence of other sources. De Rossi utilized mostly non-Jewish sources, although he was familiar with all the important Jewish sources, including Azulai's works.[49] One thing both had in common was the motivation that started them on the road to bibliographical activity: the need to prepare an auxiliary device for other work they were doing, although that work was in totally unrelated areas. Azulai began his bio-bibliography while working in the field of Jewish laws and customs; De Rossi, while preparing a *variae lectiones* of the text of the Hebrew Bible.

De Rossi, born in 1742 in a little northern Italian village, studied theology and Oriental languages at the University of Turin, and was appointed professor of Oriental languages at the University of Parma in 1769.[50] Soon thereafter he began compiling material on the variant readings of the text of the Hebrew Bible. For this purpose he started to acquire Hebrew Bible manuscripts and early printed books. He later enlarged the scope of his collection to include other types of Hebrew works. His book collecting awakened in him unusual bibliographical abilities, and the result was a number of bibliographical studies which he prepared and published.

Since the goal of his book collecting was his work on the text of the Bible,[51] he concentrated his bibliographical efforts in the area of early Hebrew printing. First came his study of the beginnings of Hebrew printing, together with a description of fifty Hebrew incunabula.[52] This was followed by studies of early Hebrew printing in Ferrara and Sabionetta.[53] Two additional works, on the history of Hebrew printing in the fifteenth and the first part of the sixteenth centuries, laid the groundwork for a scientific study of Hebrew incunabula and post-incunabula works.[54] He later published a bibliography of anti-Christian works by Jews;[55] a three-volume catalog of the Hebrew manuscripts in his collection,[56] and a list of the Hebrew printed books he acquired.[57] His last work in the field of Jewish bibliography appeared in 1808,[58] but his literary activity in other areas continued unabated until his death in 1831. He left more than forty printed works and more than eighty manuscripts he had written himself,[59] and his large collection of Hebrew books and manuscripts was presented to the Bibliotheca Palatina in Parma.

During the years when he was engaged in bibliographic work, De Rossi compiled a two-volume bio-bibliography called *Dizionario Storico degli Autori Ebrei e delle Loro Opere* (Parma, 1802). In his work he laid stress on authors and works connected with Bible studies, philosophy, and theology, but he also included authors and works dealing with Hebrew language, science, and, to a much lesser degree, Jewish law and customs. De Rossi drew his material mainly from Bartolocci and Wolf.[60] He collected the bio-bibliographical data available in their works and organized them into complete articles, supplementing and correcting them in the process. The organization of his entries was as follows:

Name (preferably surname, if available)
Nationality
Dates of birth and death
Profession
Important events in life of author
Most important works
Editions, translations, opinions, and criticism by other scholars

A German translation of De Rossi's *Dizionario* was published in Leipzig in 1839 under the title *Historisches Wörterbuch der jüdischen Schriftsteller und ihrer Werke*. The translator, C. H. Hamberger (d. 1847), changed the order of some entries, making it more difficult for the user to find some of the information. His translation also left much to be desired.[61] Still, the lack of anything similar in the German language made this edition popular, and it was reprinted soon thereafter (Bautzen, 1839 or 1840). The difficulty of locating information in this edition was solved in 1846 with the publication by Heimann Jolowicz (1816–1875) of *Ausführliches Sach- und Namen-*

*register zu de Rossi's "Historischem Wörterbuch der jüdischen Schriftsteller und ihrer Werke"* (Leipzig, 1846). A reprint edition of Hamberger's translation, together with Jolowicz's index, was published in Amsterdam by Philo Press in 1967.

An English translation, prepared by Mayer Sulzberger (1843–1923), was printed in installments in an American Jewish periodical during the 1860s,[62] but was not published in book form.

## Mordecai Samuel Ghirondi and Graziadio Nepi: *Toldot Gedole Yisrael Ugeone Italyah*

Jewish bio-bibliography continued to thrive in Italy. Inspired by Azulai's *Shem Hagedolim—Va'ad Lachachamim,* a number of Italian Jewish scholars began to collect supplementary material, concentrating largely on authors and• works of Italian origin. Among these scholars was Graziadio (Chananeel) Nepi, one of the most prominent rabbis in Italy. Born in Ferrara circa 1759,[63] Nepi became a rabbi and physician in his hometown and soon gained a reputation as a great talmudic scholar. On account of his scholarship, he was elected as a delegate to the Paris *Sanhedrin* convened by Napoleon I in 1806.[64] In 1822, he accepted a rabbinic position in Cento, where he died in 1836.[65] Nepi left three works in manuscript: a collection of rabbinic responsa, a volume of sermons, and an incomplete bio-bibliography entitled *Zecher Tsadikim Liverachah* (based on Proverbs 10:7).

Another Italian-Jewish scholar who was inspired by Azulai's bio-bibliographical work was Mordecai Samuel Ghirondi. Born in Padua in 1799, he began to write books at a very young age.[66] He attended the rabbinical school in Padua, and in 1824 was nominated to a teaching position there. Five years later (1829) he was appointed assistant rabbi of Padua, and two years later he became the chief rabbi. He died at the age of fifty-two (1852) in Padua.

Ghirondi was a very industrious person. He spent his days in "community activities, studying with students, and in charitable work," his nights were devoted to writing. He wrote more than thirty books, but only a few were published.[67] Among the books that he left were two incomplete works to which he had devoted much time and patience. One was a bio-bibliography entitled *Toldot Gedole Yisrael,*[68] he had compiled ; the other was a copy of Nepi's unpublished *Zecher Tsadikim Liverachah,* to which he had written additions and corrections. Ghirondi's son, Ephraim Raphael, decided to publish both works together since they complemented one another. The combined Ghirondi-Nepi bio-bibliography appeared in Trieste in 1853 under the title *Toldot Gedole Yisrael Ugeone Italyah.*

The bio-bibliographies by Ghirondi and Nepi were printed on facing pages, Ghirondi's *Toldot Gedole Yisrael* on the right-hand page, and Nepi's *Zecher Tsadikim Liverachah* on the left-hand page. Ghirondi's work listed 831 entries, two-thirds of which had never before appeared in any similar work, and Nepi's work listed 507 entries.[69]

An index of surnames in the Ghirondi-Nepi bio-bibliography, compiled by Leopold Löwenstein (1843—1924),[70] was published in 1914 in a German Jewish bibliographical periodical,[71] under the heading *Register zu Nepi-Ghirondi Toldot Gedole Yisrael.* With the appearance of the Löwenstein index, the 370-page Ghirondi-Nepi volume became a very useful tool in the field of Hebrew bio-bibliography.

A reprint edition of *Toldot Gedole Yisrael,* together with a companion volume containing the Löwenstein index, excerpts from a manuscript of *Zecher Tsadikim Liverachah,* and a reprint of a catalog of the Nepi book collection, was published in Israel (Jerusalem?) 1967/68.

## Heimann Joseph Michael: *Or Hachayim*

A contemporary of Ghirondi was Heimann (Hayyim) Joseph Michael, a businessman and bibliophile in the city of Hamburg. There was, to a certain degree, a parallel between Ghirondi's and Michael's lives. Both were born during the last decade of the eighteenth century, and both died while they were still in their early fifties; both had extensive book collections, and both left incomplete bio-bibliographies that were published posthumously by their sons.

Michael was born in Hamburg in 1792, and he died there fifty-four years later (1846). Like Ghirondi, he devoted his days to professional activity and his nights to study and writing. His writing activities included correspondence with scholars who turned to him with bibliographic problems. Among these were the pillars of Jewish scholarship in the nineteenth century, Leopold Zunz (1794—1886) and Salomon Judah Löb Rapoport (1790—1867). Zunz visited Michael's home in Hamburg, and he spent some time in his library. He was so impressed with it that he expressed the wish to leave Berlin and settle in Hamburg, just to be close to this great book collection. In a letter to Michael, he wrote the following interesting lines:

> Would I have known a trade, even the one of a clerk, that would leave me one-third or one-half of the day free, and would earn me at least 25 marks a week, I would move there [to Hamburg] since I am satisfied with a little, and God will take care of the rest.[72]

Michael was the type of book collector who knew the contents of his books thoroughly, and he often shared with Zunz the information he acquired while examining works that he had purchased. From time to time he also informed Zunz of new purchases of rare books and manuscripts. His correspondence with Rapoport was of a similar nature.[73] The letters addressed to Michael, especially by Zunz, sometimes demanded much attention. In one letter, for example, he was asked by Zunz to prepare a list for him of the printers and proofreaders of Hebrew books published in Prague before 1560.[74]

Despite his occupation with business, with studying his books, and with an involved correspondence, Michael also occupied himself with preparing a catalog of his Hebraica collection and a "bibliographical and literary-historical dictionary of rabbinic writings."[75] Shortly after Michael's death, his son Michael Heimann completed the catalog and published it with an index and notes to the manuscripts by Steinschneider and an introduction by Zunz.[76] But his bio-bibliographical work had to wait forty-five years for publication; it finally appeared in Frankfurt a.M. in 1891 under the title *Or Hachayim* (based on Psalms 56:14; Job 33:30).[77]

The *Or Hachayim* was edited by Eliezer Loeb (1837—1892), chief rabbi of Altona, and Abraham Berliner (1833—1915), renowned Hebrew scholar and bibliographer. Loeb added many footnotes to the text and also some informative notes and references incorporated in the text itself and distinguished by brackets. Due to ill health, Loeb was forced to stop at page 547, and Berliner edited the final 70 pages adding several leaves of notes and corrections at the end.

The entire work consisted of 1,230 alphabetically arranged entries of early Hebrew authors and their works; each entry was divided into two parts. In the first part, Michael offered all possible biographical information about the author which he had collected bit by bit from approbations to books, from rabbinic responsa, and from other sources, and had masterfully welded together into a complete biographical unit. He made good use of information already culled by Zaccuto, Azulai, and other bio-bibliographers and historiographers, pointing out, in many instances, errors or doubtful information in their statements. In the second part of each entry, Michael listed the author's works, whether printed or not printed. Here, too, he made good use of information presented by his predecessors, correcting in the process some of their errors. His own collection of printed and handwritten books was of great assistance to him in compiling the material and in solving many bibliographical difficulties.

The main shortcomings of this bio-bibliographical work—the lack of an index of titles, the incompleteness of a number of entries, and the like—are the result of Michael's death before he was able to prepare his work for publication. "In spite of its incompleteness and all the progress made in the last eighty years," wrote Alexander Marx about half a century after the publication of *Or Hachayim*,[78] "Michael's book still remains one of our indispensible tools." This sentiment is echoed by Naftali Ben-Menahem a quarter of a century later in an introduction to a new edition of the *Or Hachayim*, published in Jerusalem.

Michael's *Or Hachayim* was reprinted in 1965 in Jerusalem by Mosad Harav Kuk,[79] and in New York by Hermon Press.

## Eleazar Kohn: *Kinat Sofrim*

A year after the publication of Michael's *Or Hachayim,* a new bio-bibliography entitled *Kinat Sofrim* appeared in Lemberg. The author, Eleazar Kohn (born 1864),[80] a *shochet* by profession, arranged his work in chronological order according to the dates of death of the authors, beginning with Rav Saadiah Gaon (892?–942) and ending with Solomon Ganzfried (1804–1886), author of *Kitsur Shulchan Aruch.* This arrangement made it difficult to locate the names of authors. A chronological index of names preceding the work was of no great help in this respect.

The entries were divided into two parts: text and footnotes. The text listed the name of the author, brief biographical data, and titles of works, without bibliographical detail. The footnotes, occupying at least two-thirds of the work, furnished elaborate biographical and bibliographical information. Each entry thus included the following:

Name of author
Genealogical information (including names of teachers, students, and associates)
Place and date of birth
Place of residence and activities engaged in

Date of death and places of death and burial (cause of death if author died in unnatural way)
Geographic description of localities
Literary activities (books, glosses, letters; printed and in manuscript)
Titles and contents of works (including places and dates of publication, and changes of titles that occur in different editions)

Although Kohn utilized most of the bio-bibliographical sources already discussed, he added ample information from sources not used by his predecessors. He also demonstrated a critical sense in the presentation of the material. This quality made the *Kinat Sofrim* a worthwhile addition to the already existing literature of Hebrew bio-bibliography.


## Simon Moses Chones: *Toldot Haposkim*

The last Hebrew bio-bibliographical work of note appeared in Warsaw in 1910. Limited in scope and structured differently from its forerunners, it became a relatively popular work and enjoyed several editions. The author, Simon Moses Chones, a native of Vilna and a proofreader by profession, had previously published and annotated Abraham ben Elijah's bibliographic index to the Midrashic literature.[81] His bio-bibliographic work was designed to deal only with works of the codifiers of Jewish law, and he called it, accordingly, *Toldot Haposkim.*

Chones arranged his work alphabetically by the titles of codes, commentaries to codes, or just halachic works. An author index at the end of the volume indicated under which work to search for the author. But there was no consistency in this arrangement, and some entries were by authors. Some authors were entered under their honorary titles and some under the acronyms of their names. Some responsa works were entered under *She'elot Uteshuvot,* and some were listed under their titles or authors. The alphabetization of the entries was also faulty in many instances, and in later editions personalities "that are not among the interpreters of the law" were also incorporated into the work "on account of their greatness and prominence."[82]

Chones compiled the material from all the obvious sources and presented it in a popular form.[83] He devoted little space to description of the works, but rather concentrated on the biographies of the authors, for which he quite often intermingled fact with legend.

A second and revised edition of the *Toldot Haposkim* was published in

Warsaw in 1922. A third edition, with additions, was published there in 1929, and reprinted in a photographically reduced format in New York in 1946.

## Chronological List of
## Azulai's Bio-Bibliographical Works

### 1774

Azulai, Hayyim Joseph David (Holy Land, 1724—Italy, 1806). שם הגדולים. Livorno: Nella Stamperia di Gio. Falorni, 1774. 131, (1) leaves.

About 400 entries of authors and works, from geonic period up to (but not including) Azulai's generation.

*Organization:* Leaves 1—83: *Shem Hagedolim;* leaves 84—128: *Chasde Avot* (commentary on *Pirke Avot*); leaves 129—131: addenda and corrigenda to both parts of volume.

### 1786

שם הגדולים חלק שני. Livorno: A. I. Castello & E. Sadun, 1786. 104 leaves.

About 1,200 new entries.

*Organization:* Leaves 1—87a: *Shem Hagedolim Chelek Sheni;* leaves 87b— 96: *Pe'at Harosh* (additions to his *Rosh David, Ledavid Emet* and *Simchat Haregel*); leaves 97—99: *Midrash Temurah;* leaves 100—104: addenda to *Shem Hagedolim* and subject index to entire volume.

### 1796

ועד לחכמים. Livorno: E. Sadun, 1796. 54, 72 leaves.

About 600 new entries.

*Organization:* Leaves 1—48a: *Va'ad Lachachamim;* leaves 48b—54: *Bet Va'ad* (additions to *Va'ad Lachachamim*); leaves 1—69a (second numbering): *Tuv Ayin* (responsa and novellae); leaves 69b—70a: more additions to *Va'ad Lachachamim;* leaves 70b—72: *Simat Ayin* (addenda and corrigenda to *Tuv Ayin*).

## 1798

שם הגדולים ח"א . . . ועד לחכמים ח"ב. Livorno: E. Sadun, 1798.
(2) pages, 144 leaves.

About 350 additional entries to *Va'ad Lachachamim.*

*Organization:* Leaves 1—89a: second edition of *Shem Hagedolim,* part one; each letter of the alphabet followed by a section called *Va'ad Lachachamim,* part two; leaves 89b—134: second enlarged edition of *Chasde Avot* (with additions, indicated by design of a hand, called *Rashe Avot*); leaves 135—143a: *Shulchan Bamidbar* (addenda and corrigenda to *Shem Hagedolim, Va'ad Lachachamim,* and *Chasde Avot*); leaves 143b—144: index of sources.

## 1801

לקוטים . . . לקונט' שם הגדולים ועד לחכמים. Livorno: E. Sadun, 1801.
Leaves 202—208 (in his *Kikar La'aden*).

## 1843—1847

שם הגדולים. Krotoschin (Krotoszyn): B. L. Monasch, 1843; Frankfurt a. M.: J. F. Bach, 1844—(1847).
3 volumes.

First effort to bring together all volumes of *Shem Hagedolim* and *Va'ad Lachachamim.* Considered inferior to original editions. Numerous typographical errors.

*Organization:* Volume 1 (Krotoschin, 1843; (6), 173 pages): approbation by Meir Malbim; introduction of publisher; *Shem Hagedolim* Vol. 1, based on 1774 edition. Volume 2 (Frankfurt a. M., 1844; 101 pages): *Va'ad Lachachamim* Vol. 1, with additions *Bet Va'ad* inserted in each letter of the alphabet. Volume 3 (Frankfurt a. M., 1847; xvi, 283 pages): introduction by publisher; biography of Azulai by Eliakim Carmoly; *Shem Hagedolim* Vol. 2 and *Va'ad Lachachamim* Vol. 2, with Azulai's addenda arranged after each letter of the alphabet; noted by Aaron Fuld, Raphael Kirchheim, and Eliakim Carmoly (some notes interpolated in text).

**1852**

ספרי שם הגדולים, ועד לחכמים...שתי מערכות; א. מערכת גדולים, ב. מערכת
ספרים...ערוך ומסודר...על־ידי יצחק אייזיק בן־יעקב. Vilna: Romm, 1852.
2 volumes (xiv pages, 92 leaves; 174 [2] pages).

More than 1,300 author entries; more than 1,200 title entries. Materials from Azulai's various volumes of *Shem Hagedolim* and *Va'ad Lachachamim,* with his addenda and corrigenda, rearranged into a two-part work; cross-references added; extraneous material placed at end of entry; material of secondary importance printed in petite script.

*Organization:* Volume 1: introduction by editor; bio-bibliographical essay of Azulai by Carmoly (published originally in preceding edition; revised by editor); *Ma'arechet Gedolim*—list of authors. Volume 2: *Ma'arechet Sefarim*—list of works; notes by Aaron Fuld (from preceding edition) and by editor; addenda and corrigenda.

*Editions:* Isaac Benjacob's arrangement retained in all future (about twenty) editions. **Reprinted without changes:** Lemberg: Gedruckt bei E. Winiarz, 1856 (pirated edition); Vienna: Verlag von J. Schlesinger's Buchhandlung, 1864; Ramat-Gan: Ortsel, Chevrah Lehadpasah, 1954; Jerusalem, 1953/54 and 1969/70. **Reprinted without Benjacob's name:** Jozefow: Defus Shlomo Ubaruch Zetser, 1868; Warsaw: Bidefus Yitschak Goldman, 1876; Warsaw: Bidefus Lewin-Epstein, 1902 (reprinted by Ceilingold, 1909/10 and 1920/21). **Reprinted with additions:** Podgorze: Bidefus shel Shaul Chananiah Daitsher, 1905; Piotrkow: Bidefus David Kopelman, 1930, under title: *Shem Hagedolim Hashalem* (additions by Menahem Mendel Krengel); reprinted, Warsaw: Defus Sikora Umilner, 1930; with additional notes by Enoch Henich of Sasow, New York: Grossman, 1958? with additional notes by Zadok Hakohen Rabinowitz and Mordecai Samuel Ghirondi and extra volume of additions to *Ma'arechet Gedolim* by Elazar Lipa Gartenhaus, Brooklyn: Hotsa'at Torah Or, 1958. **Reprinted with additional texts:** Tel Aviv, 1959/60; Jerusalem? 1967? (photo-offset of Warsaw, 1867 edition). Additional texts included: *He'elem Davar* by Azulai, *Shivche Harav Chida,* and *Igeret Rav Sherira Gaon.*

## Chronological List of Bio-Bibliographies
## Evolved From Benjacob's Edition
## of Azulai's Shem Hagedolim

### 1864

Walden, Aaron (Poland, 1838–1912).
שם הגדולים החדש . . . שתי מערכות; א. מערכת גדולים, ב. מערכת ספרים. Warsaw:
Published by the author, 1864.
2 parts in one volume.

Part one: more than 1,500 author entries; part two: 1,540 (or 1,600) title entries. Lack of critical sense; information incomplete and sometimes defective. Useful source for Chassidic bio-bibliography.

*Editions:* Warsaw, Behotsa'at Aharon Mints, 1870; with additions and corrections by Joseph Aryeh Leib Walden, the author's son, Warsaw, 1879; reprinted, Warsaw, 1881, Jerusalem, 1964/65. First fascicle of supplement by Moses Menachem Walden, another son of the author, under title *Yechabed Av,* Piotrków, 1923; reprinted, Warsaw, 1939? New edition of part one, with list of rabbis who perished during World War II, compiled by Jechiel Zvi Klein, New York, 1947/48.

### 1894

Hazan, Solomon (Algeria, end of 18th cent.–Malta 1856).
המעלות לשלמה. הוא שם הגדולים מהדורא תנינא . . . שתי מערכות: מערכת גדולים . . .
מערכת ספרים . . . Alexandria: Bidefus shel Chayim Mizrachi, 1894.
116 leaves.

Method of presentation similar to Azulai. Stress on Sephardic scholars and works. Each letter of alphabet divided into two sections: one for authors *(Ma'arechet Gedolim),* the other for works *(Ma'arechet Sefarim).* At end, list of chief rabbis of Alexandria.

*Editions:* Jerusalem? 1967/68.

### 1910

Markovich, Moses (Lithuania, 1855–1935).
שם הגדולים השלישי. Vilna: S. F.·Garber, 1910.
2 parts in one volume (48; 64 pages).

Part one *(Ma'arechet Gedolim):* 277 entries in letter *alef* up to entry: Avraham Zakheim. Part two *(Ma'arechet Sefarim):* 524 entries in letter *alef* up to entry: Elef Hamagen. Includes also material from newspapers and magazines.

*Editions:* Keidani, 1932 (part one: 313 entries; part two: 630 entries).

## 1913–1915

Schwartz, Zsigmond (Hungary, 1877–1944?).

שם הגדולים מארץ הגר ... שתי מערכות: א) מערכת גדולים, ב) מערכת ספרים ... . Paks: Rosenbaum, 1913; Munkács: Kohn & Fried, 1914; Kisvárda: Klein, 1915. 3 parts (69, 52, 40 leaves).

More than 1,700 biographical and more than 700 bibliographical entries.

*Organization:* Part one: *Ma'arechet Gedolim,* letters *alef—lamed* (each letter divided into two sections: one for deceased and the other for contemporary scholars), followed by section *Avne Tsedek* (additions and corrections by Abraham Judah Schwartz, a brother of the author). Part two: *Ma'arechet Gedolim,* letters *mem—shin* (arranged as above), followed by more additions and corrections by brother of author, and by index of cities. Part three: *Ma'arechet Sefarim,* supplemented by a *Kuntres Acharon* (dated 1918). Additional biographies published later in *Shem Hagedolim Hechadash Me'erets Hagar* (Kisvárda, 1935) and in *Shem Hagedolim Hashelishi Me'erets Hagar* (Kisvárda, 1941).

*Editions:* New York: "Yerushalayim," 1958, together with all supplements, under title *Shem Hagedolim Ligedole Hungaryah* (cover title *Shem Hagedolim Hashalem Migedole Hungaryah*).

## 1931

Ben Naim, Joseph (Morocco, 1882–1962).

מלכי רבנן: והוא סידרא דרבנן ...(כבוד מלכים ... שמות הספרים ...). Jerusalem: Bidefus Hama'arav, 1931.

2 parts in one volume (7, 126, 4, 23 leaves).

Material culled from works of Azulai, Hazan, and Benjacob, and also from original sources and local documents. Part one: biographies of North African rabbis and scholars. Part two: bibliography of works by North African rabbis and scholars.

## Chronological List of
## Independent Bio-Bibliographies

### 1802

Rossi, Giovanni Bernardo de (Italy, 1769–1831).
Dizionario Storico degli Autori Ebrei e delle Loro Opere. Parma: Dalla Reale Stamperia, 1802.
2 parts (viii, 192; 170 pages).

Utilized works of Bartolocci and Wolf; with many additions and corrections. Part one: letters A–K; part two: letters L–Z.

*Order of entries:* Name (surname, if available); nationality; dates of birth and death; profession; major events in life of author; most important works; editions, translations, opinions, and criticism by other scholars.

*Editions:* Translation into German by C. H. Hamberger under title *Historisches Wörterbuch der jüdischen Schriftsteller und ihrer Werke* (Leipzig: L. Fort, 1839); second edition, Bautzen: J. U. Reichel, (1839?). Heimann Jolowicz compiled an *Ausführliches Sach- und Namenregister* (Leipzig: H. Hunger, 1846). Hamberger's translation together with Jolowicz's index was reprinted in Amsterdam by Philo Press in 1967. English translation by Mayer Sulzberger, printed in *Occident* (Philadelphia, 1867–1869).

### 1853

Ghirondi, Mordecai Samuel (Italy, 1799–1852); Nepi, Graziadio (Italy 1759–1836).
תולדות גדולי ישראל וגאוני איטליאה. Trieste: Tipografia Marenigh, 1853.
376 pages.

831 + 507 entries.

*Organization:* Ghirondi's *Toldot Gedole Yisrael* printed on right-side page; Nepi's *Zekher Tsadikim Liverachah* on left-side page.

*Editions:* Jerusalem? 1967/68.

*Index* prepared by Leopold Löwenstein published in *ZfHB* 17 (1914); also published as a separate (Frankfort, 1915); reprinted, Jerusalem? 1967/68 (reprint includes also excerpts from a manuscript copy of *Zecher Tsadikim* and a catalog of Nepi Collection).

## 1891

Michael, Heimann Joseph (Germany, 1792–1846).
אור החיים. Frankfurt a. M.: J. Kaufmann, 1891.
viii, 617 pages.

1,230 entries. Edited by Eliezer Loeb (up to page 547) and Abraham Berliner (from page 547).

*Organization:* Each entry divided into two parts: part one—biography; part two—bibliography. Volume begins with introduction (in German) by Berliner, and concludes with Berliner's annotations and corrections.

*Editions:* Jerusalem: Mosad Harav Kuk, 1965 (introduction by N. Ben-Menahem; Berliner's introduction translated into Hebrew; annotations by S. J. Halberstam); New York: Hermon Press, 1965.

## 1892

Kohn, Eleazar (Poland, 1864–    ).
קנת סופרים. Lemberg: Verlag von L. Margosches, 1892.
(10), 125 leaves.

*Organization:* Entries arranged chronologically, beginning with Saadiah Gaon and ending with Solomon Ganzfried; each entry divided into two parts: text and footnotes. The text contains brief information; the footnotes elaborate. Entries preceded by introduction and index, and followed by annotations and additions.

## 1910

Chones, Simon Moses (Russia, 19th cent.–Poland, first half of 20th century).
תולדות (הגאונים) הפוסקים. Warsaw: F. Baumritter, 1910.
635 pages.

Compiled from popular works, with main emphasis on the biographical part, where fact and legend are intermingled. Bibliographical part inadequate and faulty.

*Organization:* Entries arranged alphabetically under titles of codes, commentaries of codes, or other type of halachic works, followed by index of names.

*Editions:* Second revised edition, Warsaw: Ceilingold, 1922; third edition, Warsaw: Kahana, 1929; reprinted in a photographically reduced format, New York, 1946.

*Chapter Four*

# Subject Bibliographies
# of Hebraica Literature

*The number of Hebraica subject bibliographies runs into the thousands, but for the history of Jewish bibliography only a few are of real interest. From these few, four key works have been selected for discussion in this chapter. Two are in the field of modern Hebrew literature, one is limited to Jewish literature in print, and the fourth concentrates on traditional Hebrew literature that came into being during the span of a millennium.*

*A section on translations from world literature into Hebrew and Yiddish is included for the sake of completeness in the discussion of the development of Hebraica bibliography.*

\*William Zeitlin: *Bibliotheca Hebraica.* Chaim David Lippe: *Bibliographisches Lexicon.* Benzion Dinur and Abraham Yaari: *Hasifrut Hayafah Be'ivrit.* Translations into Hebrew and Yiddish. Menachem Mendel Kasher and Jacob Ber Mandelbaum: *Sare Ha'elef.*

## William Zeitlin:
### Bibliotheca Hebraica Post-Mendelssohniana

ONE YEAR AFTER the publication of Isaac Benjacob's *Otsar Hasefarim* there appeared in St. Petersburg the first fascicle of a bibliography devoted to modern Hebrew literature. In its format and in its scientific registration of a specific part of Hebrew literature, this work represented a "first" in Hebraica bibliography, and it paved the way for future scientific Hebraica bibliographies. The compiler, William (Ze'ev) Zeitlin, was born in the city of Gomel (Homel), Russia, around the middle of the nineteenth century.[1] He received a traditional and also a secular education in his hometown, and in the early 1870s he enrolled in the school of medicine at the University of Königsberg. He soon withdrew and moved to the faculty of philosophy. He later continued his studies in Berlin, Geneva, and Paris. Around 1890 he settled in Leipzig, where he died thirty years later (1921), lonely and forsaken.[2]

Zeitlin began his writing career with biographical and historical articles in the Hebrew press. He also wrote poetry. His first article was a biography of the former head of the rabbinical school and censor of Hebrew publications in Warsaw, Jacob Tugendhold (1791–1871).[3] He soon turned his full attention to compiling material for a bibliography of modern Hebrew literature from the time of Moses Mendelssohn (1729–1786), i.e., the beginning of the German Haskalah. By-products of Zeitlin's effort were a number of subject bibliographies, which appeared in various publications. These included a list of Hebrew periodicals[4] and a bibliography of Zionist works.[5] He also published a list of pseudonyms of modern Hebrew writers.[6] But the first results of his main effort became visible in 1881 when he published the first fascicle of his *Bibliotheca Hebraica post-Mendelssohniana* in St. Petersburg. The fascicle consisted of 80 pages, entries arranged alphabetically by the names of the authors, ending with the name Hurwitz. Works were registered that appeared up to the year 1880. A decade later (1891) Zeitlin began publishing a "second, revised and enlarged edition" of his bibliography, and completed it in 1895.

Zeitlin's new *Bibliotheca* registered works that appeared up to the year 1890. The bibliography was published in two parts, and it carried an added Hebrew title, *Kiryat Sefer*.[7] Part one (Leipzig, 1891) covered letters A–M, and part two letters N–Z. To this were added a list of anonymous works (arranged by title), a list of commemorative publications issued by Jewish communities or organizations (arranged alphabetically by place of publication), a supplement of more than forty entries to letters B–M, additamenta and corrigenda, and two indexes: one of Hebrew titles and the other of authors and translators. The entire work consisted of 548 pages, and it listed more than 3,500 Hebrew titles. The entries in the new edition followed the arrangement of the previous edition: alphabetical according to the names of the authors, but within each entry, the titles were arranged chronologically.

Zeitlin spent 20 years preparing his *Bibliotheca*. He used the works of Fürst and Benjacob, he searched in the bookstores of Vilna and Warsaw, he consulted reference tools in the libraries of Königsberg, Berlin, Geneva, Paris, St. Petersburg, and Kiev, and the results of all these efforts are to be found in his work. Besides listing authors' names and the titles of independent works in his entries, he included biographical information and articles in periodicals, and introductions to works. In some instances he also registered authors and works that preceded the Mendelssohnian era, such as scientific editions of medieval works. He produced an almost complete record of the post-Mendelssohnian Hebrew literature, and established the *Bibliotheca's* reputation as a reliable and basic work in its field that has lasted to our own day.

Although Zeitlin prepared the entries for the *Bibliotheca* in as concise a form as possible, he managed to include in each entry the following details:

Author (in Roman characters)
Biographical data (with occasional reference to sources)
Title (in Hebrew characters)
Title transliterated and translated (in German)
Description and contents (in German)
Place and date of publication
Format
Pagination
Occasional additional bio-bibliographical information and helpful notes

During the years of World War I, Zeitlin compiled a supplementary volume to the *Bibliotheca* in which he registered works that appeared during the years 1890–1915.[8] After Zeitlin's death, this volume was offered to a publisher in Leipzig, but he did not accept it for publication and it was lost during the years of World War II.[9] A suggestion that Zeitlin's *Bibliotheca* be translated into Hebrew, with the inclusion of works printed up to the 1940s, was made during the late 1940s at a conference of Hebrew bibliographers in Israel.[10] It remained a suggestion.

## Chaim David Lippe: *Bibliographisches Lexicon*

Eighteen eighty-one, the year William Zeitlin published the first edition of his *Bibliotheca* in St. Petersburg, was also the year of the publication of another bibliography that appeared in Vienna. Although the two bibliographies were compiled independently—and with entirely different objectives—they were similar in some respects. Both used German as their language, both were limited in scope, and both offered biographical data on the authors. There was also a similarity in the arrangement of the entries and in the structures of the works. But they were poles apart in their objectives. Zeitlin planned his *Bibliotheca* as a scientific tool for the benefit of the "theologian, philologist, and historian of [Jewish] culture and literature," and he strove to compile as complete a record of the post-Mendelssohnian Hebrew literature as was humanly possible. Chaim David Lippe, the compiler of the other bibliography, did not make any pretense at scholarly achievement.[11] His goal was a practical one: to develop an auxiliary tool for the failing Jewish book trade.

Lippe was born in 1823 in Stanislawów, Galicia (now the Ukrainian SSR).[12] He received an intensive education in Jewish and secular studies, and acquired expertise in a number of languages. He served as a cantor and as a teacher of religion and languages in Czernowitz, Bukovina (1849–1852), and in Eperies, Hungary (1852–1873). While in Hungary, he published articles dealing with equal rights for Jews, and also a pamphlet about religious conflicts within the Hungarian Jewish community.[13] He later moved to Vienna and engaged in the Jewish book trade.

In 1874 Lippe began his bibliographical activities with the publication of a bibliographical monthly entitled *Der Sammler*.[14] After entering the book trade, he observed various ills plaguing the market. He diagnosed them as the result of a lack of communication among dealers and between dealers and customers. His monthly publication, he hoped, would bridge the gap in communication and would contribute towards developing a healthy Jewish book market. When the monthly ceased to appear (after the third issue), Lippe devoted himself to preparing a handbook that would serve the Jewish bookdealer and customer alike. The idea was to include complete information in the handbook on all books of Jewish interest available on the market, and also to list the names and addresses of potential buyers.

Years of hard work in searching, compiling, and organizing began to bear fruit in 1879 with the publication of fascicle 1 of Lippe's planned handbook, and it came to a (temporary) conclusion in 1881, with the publication of fascicle 7-8 of the 704-page volume. The title of the handbook was *Bibliographisches Lexicon der gesammten jüdischen Literatur der Gegenwart und Adress-Anzeiger,* and it carried a separate title page in Hebrew with the heading *Asaf Hamazkir* (based on II Kings 18: 18, 37). Lippe seems to have used Julius Fürst's *Bibliotheca Judaica* as a prototype for his *Lexicon.* This is evident not only from the phrasing of the title page, but also from the internal organization of his work: the adding of biographical data to the names of authors and the listing of Hebraica and Judaica in a single alphabetical arrangement.[15]

Lippe's *Lexicon* listed about 10,000 names and addresses of "rabbis, preachers, teachers, cantors, writers, and friends and supporters of Jewish literature in the Old and New World," and it registered 1,156 Hebraica and several thousand Judaica titles available on the market. The *Lexicon* listed, in a single alphabet in Roman characters, the names of prospective book buyers together with names of authors. The entries of the prospective book buyers included:

Name
Profession (rabbi, cantor, teacher, etc.)
Organization associated with
Address

The author entries, although concise (with a few exceptions),[16] included the following details:

Author
Biographical data (in German; occasionally also author's address)
Title (Hebraica titles in Hebrew characters)
Translation of title and complete description of contents (in German)
Place and date of publication
Format
Pagination
Price
Name (often also address) of publisher or dealer

The last fascicle of the *Lexicon* included a large section of additions and corrections; a list of 97 Jewish periodicals (in about a dozen languages), with subscription prices and addresses of publishers or agents; an index of Hebrew titles; and a list of cities. The final pages listed publications that appeared during the printing of the *Lexicon* and corrigenda to the text.

When Lippe published his complete *Lexicon* in 1881, he announced on the flyleaf of the work that he was planning to issue annual supplement volumes beginning with December of the same year. This plan was partially realized only a few years later with the publication of three fascicles of a volume two published in Vienna during the years 1887–1889. Altogether, the volume contained 288 pages and ended at the name Steinberg, due to a severe illness that befell the compiler.

Lippe returned to his plan ten years later, at the age of 76, with the publication of Volume 1 of a new series of his *Bibliographisches Lexicon* (Vienna, 1899). The new, 500-page volume also carried a separate Hebrew title page with the heading *Asaf Hamazkir Hechadash,* and it listed close to 900 Hebraica and more than 2,000 Judaica titles published since the appearance of the earlier volumes. The number of addresses in the new volume was somewhat lower than in the preceding volumes since the entries were limited only to "rabbis, theologians, and writers," but the Judaica titles were augmented with the inclusion of works on Jewish themes by non-Jewish authors.[17] The new volume, like the first one, also contained a large section of additions and corrections, an enlarged list of periodicals (146 entries), an index of Hebrew titles, and a list of cities.

The publication of Volume 1 of the new *Lexicon* was Lippe's last publishing activity. He died a year later, in 1900, at the age of 77. The bibliographical volumes Lippe published—not intended for scholars and researchers, not meant to become tools for bibliographers—are now, contrary to Lippe's own expectations, major sources for the history of Jewish literature in the nineteenth century.

Benzion Dinur and Abraham Yaari:
*Hasifrut Hayafa Be'ivrit*

In their bibliographical works William Zeitlin and Chaim David Lippe registered Hebraica that had appeared in print during a set period of time. Acceptance into these bibliographies was decided, not on the basis of content, but rather on the basis of title-page imprint. Although Zeitlin intended his *Bibliotheca* to become *the* bibliography of modern Hebrew literature, he included many works that definitely did not belong in this category, but did carry the magic imprint certifying them as "post-Mendelssohniana." Lippe's *Lexicon,* intended to reflect the existing book market, indiscriminately registered everything "current." Perhaps no need was felt for a bibliography devoted only to purely Hebrew literature.

The situation changed more than a quarter of a century later, during the second half of the 1920s. The Balfour Declaration issued by the British government in 1917, granting the establishment of a Jewish national home in Palestine, helped to increase the influx of Jews to that country. They became instrumental in establishing new educational and cultural institutions, and in transforming the venerable holy tongue into a modern living language. In Jerusalem, a Hebrew University was established (with Hebrew as a language of instruction), in which modern Hebrew literature became a subject for academic studies in a special department. There was now a need for a bibliographic tool to assist the scholar, the student, and the reader of modern Hebrew literature.

Benzion Dinur (1884–1973), an educator and historian, who later served as minister of education and culture of the State of Israel (1951–1955), was the first to realize the need for a bibliography of modern Hebrew literature. For a number of years he compiled material for such a work, and then turned it over to the Jewish National and University Library of the Hebrew University in Jerusalem for publication.

Abraham Yaari (1899–1966), a young librarian at the Jewish National Library who later became a prominent and highly productive Jewish bibliographer, edited and completed Dinur's material. He compared the entries with the actual books available at the National Library; he added new sections to the division of the material; he augmented the sections devised by Dinur with listings of recent publications and new editions of earlier printed works, and he prepared the bibliography for publication. The National Library published the work in Jerusalem, in 1927—as the first in a series of subject catalogs of books available at the library—under the title *Hasifrut Hayafa Be'ivrit*.[18]

The Dinur-Yaari bibliography registered original Hebrew belles-lettres as well as translations into Hebrew from other literatures, and it covered the years 1729 to 1926. The year 1729 was chosen by the compilers as the starting date, since they considered the appearance of the first work of poetry by Moses Hayyim Luzzatto (1707–1746) as the beginning of the era of modern Hebrew literature.[19] The bibliography consisted of 3,388 entries (3,221 titles) divided into the following twelve sections:

Miscellaneous
Collective works; periodicals
Poetry from Luzzatto to Judah Loeb Gordon (1729–1884)
Gordon's poetical works
Poetry since Gordon (1885–1926)

Bialik's poetical works
Occasional poems
Dramatic works
Novels, short stories
Essays, literary criticism
Juvenile literature
Juvenile periodicals

The arrangement of works within each section was alphabetical by authors' names; periodicals and anonymous works were listed by title. The arrangement of works under each author was alphabetical by title. Each entry was registered on the basis of the title page, and information not available on the title page was added in brackets. The entries included detailed pagination, and the contents of volumes of collected works were carefully listed. Additions and corrections and indexes of authors and titles concluded the volume.

Additions to *Hasifrut Hayafa Be'ivrit* were published by Abraham Yaari (282 entries) and Israel David Beth-Halevy (84 entries) during the years 1929/30–1930/31 in a bibliographical periodical issued by the National Library.[20]

## Translations into Hebrew and Yiddish

The Dinur-Yaari bibliography, which also included modern works translated from other languages into Hebrew, may have been instrumental in the publication of a number of lists of translations of modern works into Hebrew and Yiddish. The first of such lists was compiled by Israel Schapiro (1882–1957), head of the Hebraic Section of the Library of Congress, under the Hebrew-English title: *Otsar Targumim Ivrim Misifrut Ha'anglit. Bibliography of Hebrew Translations of English Literature* (New York, 1929).[21] The list registered 259 titles of translated belles-lettres and scientific works available at the Library of Congress. The entries, based on Library of Congress catalog cards, were arranged alphabetically by the names of the authors, and they included the following information:

Author (in Roman characters)
Biographical data (usually dates of birth and death of author)
Original title (in Roman characters)
Translated title with name of translator (in Hebrew characters)

Place of publication (in Hebrew and in the vernacular)
Date of publication (Hebrew and universal)
Pagination
Format (in centimeters)
Occasional notes (in English)

Schapiro's list was updated twenty years later (1950) by Jacob Israel Dien-stag (born 1912), a librarian at Yeshiva University in New York. Published in a Jewish-American bibliographical annual in New York[22] under the title "Tirgumim Ivriyim Misifrut Anglit-Yehudit," the list includes 108 entries divided into five sections. The entries are in Hebrew, with the name of the author and title in Roman characters at the bottom of each entry, followed by an author index in Roman characters.

Schapiro also compiled and published a list entitled *Otsar Targumim Ivrim Misifrut Hagermanit. Bibliography of Hebrew Translations of German Works* (New York, 1934). This list includes 538 titles, arranged and entered in the same manner as the earlier one. Both lists are followed by indexes of authors (in Roman characters) and titles (in Hebrew characters).

Yehuda Aryeh Klausner (born 1910), a librarian at the Jewish National Library in Jerusalem, compiled a list of Hebrew translations from ancient literatures and published it in a Hebrew bibliographical periodical in Tel Aviv under the title "Sifrut Hatirgumim Ha'ivrit."[23]

Leah Goldberg (1911—1970), a well-known Hebrew poetess and profes-sor of comparative literature at the Hebrew University in Jerusalem, delivered a series of lectures for librarians in 1951 on translations of belles-lettres from world literature into Hebrew.

Reuben Levi (1888—1965), a bibliographer and organizer of libraries in Israel, compiled a list of Hebrew translations from world literature based on Leah Goldberg's lectures, and published it together with a summary of her lectures, under the title *Sifrut Yafah Olamit Betirgumeha Le'ivrit* (Tel Aviv, 1951). The list was divided into five sections (ancient literature, modern literature, drama, poetry, novels, and short stories), and it concluded with an index of authors and an index of titles.[24]

Hayyim Leaf-Lipshitz (born 1914), an instructor of Hebrew literature at Teachers Institute of Yeshiva University in New York and an editor of Hebrew publications, published a list of Hebrew translations from Yiddish in *The Jewish Book Annual* in 1949 under the title "Hasifrut Haidit Betirgum Ivri."[25] Yudel Mark (born 1897), a Yiddish scholar and lexicographer, reciprocated in the same publication (about forty pages later) with a review of Yiddish translations from Hebrew rabbinic texts, entitled "Der Drang tsu di Alte Kvaln."[26] Several years later, Mayer Horowitz (born 1913), a Yiddish writer, journalist, and librarian, published in the same annual a "Bibliografye fun Yidishe Iberzetsungen fun der Englisher Literatur."[27] The list registered only translations that had appeared in book form, and it was divided into four sections: fiction, dramatic works, poetry, and juvenile literature. The entries were bilingual:

| *In English* | *In Yiddish* |
|---|---|
| Author (with dates of birth and death) | Author's surname |
| Title | Title |
| | Translator |
| | Place of publication |
| | Publisher |
| | Date of publication |
| | Pagination |

## Menachem Mendel Kasher and Jacob Ber Mandelbaum: *Sare Ha'elef*

The publication of *Hasifrut Hayafah Be'ivrit* was the result of a joint effort by a scholar and a librarian-bibliographer. A similar partnership resulted in 1959 in the publication of another important bibliography of Hebrew literature. This time it was a bibliography of printed Hebrew works of authors who flourished during the years 500 to 1500 C.E. The plan for such a work originated with a scholar of great renown, Menachem Mendel Kasher, while editing an encyclopedia of rabbinic interpretations on the Pentateuch.

Born in Warsaw, in 1895, Kasher was ordained as a rabbi at the youthful age of eighteen (1913).[28] For a number of years he was active in the field of Jewish education, both in Poland (since 1915) and in Palestine, where he settled in 1925. He wrote and edited numerous works and articles, but since 1937 his main effort was concentrated on editing and publishing (with notes and supplements) a talmudic-midrashic encyclopedia of the Pentateuch, entitled *Torah Shelemah*.[29] In the course of his work on *Torah Shelemah* Kasher became aware of the lack of an adequate bibliographic tool for posttalmudic Hebrew literature.[30] He discussed the matter with various bibliographers, and was encouraged to start compiling material for such a work. He later met Jacob Ber Mandelbaum (born 1912), a bibliographer and librarian at Yeshiva University Library in New York, who was willing

to join him in an effort to bring the compiling and editing task to a conclusion. The joint effort came to a climax in 1959 in New York with the
publication of a volume entitled *Sare Ha'elef* (based on Exodus 18:21, 25, et
passim).

*Sare Ha'elef* listed about 1,500 printed works by authors who flourished
during the first millennium after the completion of the Babylonian Talmud,
i.e., from the year 500 C.E. to the days of Rabbi Joseph Caro (1488–1575),
author of the most popular Jewish code of law, the *Shulchan Aruch.*[31] It
registered, not only independent volumes, but also works that appeared in
periodicals, festschriften, etc., and it was divided into seven main sections.
Kasher compiled and annotated sections one, four, five, and six, and
Mandelbaum, sections two, three and seven. The division of the sections
was as follows:

Section one:    a. Tannaitic Midrashim and Talmuds; b. Later Midrashim;
              c. Minor Midrashim, individual sections or fragments

Section two:    a. Commentaries on the Pentateuch; b. Collections and frag-
              ments

Section three:    a. Commentaries on the Prophets and Writings; b. Collections
              and fragments

Section four:    a. Talmudic methodology and definitions of terms; b. Commen-
              taries on the Mishnah, Tosefta, and Talmuds

Section five:    a. Geonic responsa; b. Responsa by the early codifiers

Section six:    Codes of law

Section seven: Miscellaneous (among others: liturgy, history, ethics, philosophy,
              cabala, science)

The first section was preceded by six introductory entries listing sources
dealing with editions of the Bible, commentaries on the *Targumim,* and
Hebrew editions of the Apocrypha, pseudo-Apocrypha, and Dead Sea
scrolls. The entries were entirely in Hebrew, and they occasionally included
references to sources relating to the author or the work. The arrangement
within each section (with the exception of sections one and four) was
alphabetical by the titles of the works, and no effort was made to give
pagination or to detail various editions of a specific work. Section seven was
followed by addenda and corrigenda, and five indexes (titles; authors;
talmudic volumes; topical list for section seven; works mentioned in annotations) concluded the volume.

An effort to supplement *Sare Ha'elef* with works published between
1959 and 1967 was made in 1967 by Israel Ta-Shema with a thirty-page

pamphlet entitled: *Sifre Rishonim; Sifre Halachah* (Jerusalem, 1967).[32] A complete supplement, prepared by Mandelbaum and edited by Kasher, listing works published between 1959 and 1966 and adding notes and corrections to the main work, was published in Jerusalem in 1970 under the title "Kuntres Hashlamah" (in *Sefer Adam-Noach*).[33]

## Chronological List of Major Hebraica Subject Bibliographies

### 1881−1891/95

Zeitlin, William (Russia, ca. 1850−Germany, 1921).
  Bibliotheca Hebraica post-Mendelssohniana. Bibliographisches Handbuch der neuhebräischen Literatur seit Beginn der Mendelssohn'schen Epoche bis zum Jahre 1880. Lfg. I. Petersburg, 1881.
  80 pages.

Arranged by names of authors. Published up to the name Hurwitz.

Complete work published, as follows:

קרית ספר. Bibliotheca Hebraica post-Mendelssohniana. Bibliographisches Handbuch der neuhebräischen Literatur seit Beginn der Mendelssohn'schen Epoche bis zum Jahre 1890 . . . Zweite Neu Bearbeitete und Erweiterte Aufl. Leipzig: K.F. Koehler's Antiquarium, 1891−1895.
  iv, 548 pages.

More than 3,500 titles. Listed also, articles in periodicals and introductions to works, and registered scientific editions of medieval Hebrew writers published since Mendelssohn.

*Organization:* Bibliography, A−Z; list of anonymous works; commemorative publications; supplement; additamenta and corrigenda; two indexes: Hebrew titles, authors and translators.

*Order of entries:* Author (Roman characters); biographical data; title (Hebrew characters); title transliterated and translated (in German); description of contents (in German); place and date of publication; format; pagination; additional bio-bibliographical data and helpful notes.

## 1881—1899

Lippe, Chaim David (Austria, 1823—1900).

Bibliographisches Lexicon der gesammten jüdischen Literatur der Gegenwart und Adress-Anzeiger . . . nebst bibliographisch genauer Angabe sämmtlicher von jüdischen Autoren der Gegenwart publicirten, speciell die jüdische Literatur betreffenden Schriftwerke und Zeitschriften . . . für Buchhändler, Rabbinen, Gemeinden und Freunde der jüdischen Literatur. Wien: Verlag von D. Löwy, 1881—1889.

2 vols. (704, 288 pages).

About 10,000 names and addresses of authors and of prospective book buyers; several thousand Hebraica and Judaica titles, all arranged in a single alphabet. Added title page in Hebrew: *Asaf Hamazkir.*

*Organization:* Volume 1 (issued in seven fascicles, 1879—1881): bibliography and addresses; list of periodicals (subscription prices and addresses of publishers or agents); index of Hebrew titles; list of cities; works published during printing of volume; corrigenda. Volume 2 (issued in three fascicles, 1887—1889): ended at the name Steinberg.

*Order of Entries:* Author (Roman characters); biographical data (in German; occasionally, author's address); title (Hebraica titles, in Hebrew characters); translation of title and description of contents (in German); place and date of publication; format; pagination; price; name (often also address) of publisher or dealer.

Volume 1 of a new series was published, as follows:

Bibliographisches Lexicon der gesammten jüdischen und theologisch-rabbinischen Literatur der Gegenwart mit Einchluss der Schriften über Juden und Judenthum . . . Neue Serie: Bd. I. Wien: C. D. Lippe, 1899.

xxxii, 496 pages.

About 3,000 Hebraica and Judaica works published since the appearance of first volumes. Included also works of Jewish interest by non-Jewish authors. Added title page in Hebrew: *Asaf Hamazkir Hechadash.*

## 1927

Jerusalem. Hebrew University. Jewish National and University Library.

הספרות היפה בעברית (המקורית והמתורגמת). Jerusalem: Jewish National and University Library, 1927.

viii, 330 pages.

Compiled by Benzion Dinur and Abraham Yaari. Hebrew belles lettres from 1729 to 1926. 3,388 entries (3,221 titles). Lists also translations into Hebrew.

*Organization:* Topical arrangement in following sections: Miscellaneous, collective works, periodicals; poetry from Luzzatto to J. L. Gordon; Gordon's poetry; poetry since Gordon; Bialik's poetry; occasional poems; drama; novels, short stories; essays, literary criticism; juvenile literature; juvenile periodicals. Additions and corrections; indexes of authors and titles.

*Order of entries:* Author; title; description; place of publication; date; pagination (bibliographical information based on title page; additional information added in brackets). Contents of collected works carefully detailed.

*Supplements:* Yaari, Abraham. *Miluim.* Jerusalem, 1929. Reprinted from *KS* 6 (1929/30): 119−138, 277−290. 282 entries. Index of titles.

Beth-Halevy, Israel David. *Nosafot.* Jerusalem, 1930/31. Reprinted from *KS* 7 (1930/31): 282−289. 84 entries. Index of titles.

### 1959

Kasher, Menachem Mendel (Poland 1895−          ); Mandelbaum, Jacob Ber (Poland 1912−          )

שרי האלף. New York: Machon Torah Shelemah, 1959.
15, 455 pages.

About 1,500 printed works by authors who flourished from 500 to 1500 C. E. Besides independent volumes, also registered those published in periodicals, festschriften, etc.

*Organization:* Topical arrangement in following sections: postbiblical literature; commentaries on the Pentateuch; commentaries on the Prophets and Writings; commentaries on the Talmud; responsa; the codes; miscellaneous. Addenda and corrigenda. Indexes of titles; authors; talmudic volumes; topical list for sections of miscellaneous; works mentioned in annotations.

*Supplements:* Ta-Shema, Israel. *Sifre Rishonim; Sifre Halachah.* Jerusalem: Merkaz Harav, 1967. 30 pages.

177 entries of rabbinic works by ancient authors published during 1959—1967. Indexes of authors and editors. Essay by S. Z. Havlin on modern editions of ancient Hebrew texts.

Mandelbaum, Jacob Ber. "Kuntres Hashlamah." In *Sefer Adam-Noach,* pp. (213)—295. Jerusalem, 1969.

Lists books published during 1959—1966 with corrections to main work.

## Chronological List of Translations into Hebrew and Yiddish

### 1929

Schapiro, Israel (Poland, 1882—Israel, 1957).
אוצר תרגומים עברים מספרות האנגלית. Bibliography of Hebrew Translations of English Literature. New York, 1929.
43 pages. Reprinted from *Studies in Jewish Bibliography and Related Subjects, in Memory of Abraham Solomon Freidus.* New York, 1929.

259 titles. Lists works available at Library of Congress; entries according to rules of Library of Congress. Indexes of authors and titles.

*Supplements:* Dienstag, Israel Jacob. "Tirgumim Ivriyim Misifrut Anglit-Yehudit." *JBA* 8 (1949/50): Hebrew section, pp. 35–47.
108 entries in topical arrangement. Index of authors.

### 1934

Schapiro, Israel (Poland, 1882—Israel, 1957)
אוצר תרגומים עברים מספרות הגרמנית. Bibliography of Hebrew Translations of German Works. New York: Bloch Publishing Company, 1934.
79 pages.

538 titles with indexes of authors and titles.

### 1944

Klausner, Yehudah Aryeh (Russia, 1910—    )
ספרות התרגומים העברית. *Yad Lakore* no. 5/6 (1944), pp. 11—22.

Bibliographical essay on translations into Hebrew of ancient belles lettres. Based on author's lectures at the Hebrew University, Jerusalem.

## 1949

Leaf-Lipshitz, Hayyim (Russia, 1914—     )

הספרות האידית בתרגום עברי. *JBA* 7 (1948/49), Hebrew section, pp. 18—27.

## 1951

Goldberg, Leah (Lithuania, 1911—Israel, 1970).

ספרות יפה עולמית בתרגומיה לעברית. Tel Aviv: Hamerkaz Letarbut, 1951. 164 pages.

Bibliography was compiled by Reuben Levi, based on lectures by Goldberg. Divided into five sections, with indexes of authors and titles.

## 1953

Horowitz, Mayer (Russia, 1913—     )

ביבליאגראפיע פון יידישע איבערזעצונגען פון דער ענגלישער ליטעראטור. *JBA* 11 (1952/53), pp. 136–153.

Lists only translations that appeared in book form. Divided into four sections. Entries are bilingual.

*Chapter Five*

# Judaica Bibliographies

*Although works of Jewish interest written in non-Hebrew
characters outnumber the works written in Hebrew characters,
bibliographically they have not fared well. Not even one all-
inclusive Judaica bibliography has ever been published. The
discussion of the development of Judaica bibliography will,
therefore, occupy only one chapter of this volume, and will
describe several key Judaica catalogs and subject bibliographies
published since the 1930s.*

*To round out the discussion, a segment of this chapter will be
devoted to translations from Hebrew and Yiddish.*

Aron Freimann. Stadtbibliothek Frankfurt am Main: *Katalog der
Judaica und Hebraica.* Bibliotheca Rosenthaliana: *Systematische
Catalogus van de Judaica.* Volkmar Eichstädt: *Bibliographie zur
Geschichte der Judenfrage.* Wiener Library: *German Jewry.* Leo
Baeck Institute: *Katalog.* Ludwig Rosenberger: *Judaica.* Harvard
University Library: *Judaica* and *Judaica in the Houghton Library.*
Translations from Hebrew and Yiddish.

## Aron Freimann

THE UNDERLYING RELIGIOUS significance of the Hebrew language and its script attracted a number of prominent Christian and Jewish scholars to Jewish bibliography.[1] They concentrated almost entirely on registering works in Hebrew characters—Hebraica. Only a few attempts were made to compile records of the literature written by and about Jews in all the languages of civilization—Judaica. Most notable in this respect are the works of Carlo Giuseppe Imbonati, who compiled a bibliography of more than 1,300 Latin works on Jewish themes;[2] Julius Fürst, who compiled a Hebraica-Judaica bibliography in which he listed more than 20,000 Judaica titles;[3] Chaim David Lippe, who published several volumes of Hebraica-Judaica available in print, in which he listed several thousand "current" Judaica titles;[4] and Meyer Kayserling (1829–1905), who compiled a bibliography of works by and about Jews written in Spanish and Portuguese.[5] An effort at compiling and publishing a general, all-inclusive Judaica bibliography ended unsuccessfully due to lack of interest. The bibliographer who attempted to prepare such a work was Aron Freimann.

Born in the Poznan region of Germany (now Poland) in 1871,[6] Freimann first received a traditional Jewish education in his hometown, and later moved to Berlin to attend the university and the Rabbiner Seminar.[7] At the University of Berlin he studied such subjects as history and Oriental languages, but he preferred bibliography, and he devoted himself to the study of library science. He was graduated in 1896, and a year later he accepted the position of Wissenschaftlicher Hilfsarbeiterrat at the Frankfurt am Main Stadtbibliothek. In 1904 he became librarian of the theology department of that library, in charge of the Hebraica and Judaica section. He remained in this position for about thirty years, when he was forced to retire by the Nazi regime in 1933. During the years of his service at the Frankfurt Stadtbibliothek he developed the Jewish collection there as the "richest collection on the European continent of printed Hebraica and Judaica."[8] For this accomplishment he was awarded, in 1919, the title of professor. Freimann emigrated to the United States in 1938, where he served as a consultant in bibliography at the New York Public Library's Jewish Division from 1939 to 1945. He died in 1948.

Beside his bibliographic activities, Freimann was involved in community and literary activities. Among others, he served as board member (1918), vice-president (1928), and president (shortly before leaving Germany) of the Organization of Jews in Germany. He participated in reviving the publication society Mekize Nirdamim;[9] he was among the editors of a scientific periodical[10] and of an encyclopedia[11] devoted to the history of the Jews in Germany. He edited a volume of documents dealing with the Shabbatean movement,[12] a scientific edition of Azulai's diary of travels,[13] and co-edited several festschriften and memorial volumes.[14] He also wrote a number of works about Jewish communities in Germany.[15]

Freimann's contributions to the field of Jewish bibliography were even more impressive. For more than twenty years he edited a bibliographical Jewish periodical,[16] and he published hundreds of essays and studies covering every phase of Jewish bibliography.[17] In 1924 he began to publish a *Thesaurus* of Hebrew cradle-books,[18] and during his last years in New York he prepared and issued *A Gazetteer of Hebrew Printing.*[19] Freimann's catalog of Hebrew manuscripts was published posthumously,[20] but a "Bibliotheca Judaica" that he worked on for "more than thirty years" remained unpublished.[21] The planned Bibliotheca would have contained "a complete record of all printed Judaica." When he died he left "several large boxes of slips, frequently written on both sides, which contain an almost complete record of all publications in this field."[22]

## Stadtbibliothek Frankfurt am Main:
### *Katalog der Judaica und Hebraica*

But Freimann did leave a "record" of printed Judaica, although an incomplete one. This was a catalog of Judaica available at the Frankfurt Stadtbibliothek, published sixteen years before his death, which has now become a standard bibliography of Judaica. Around the turn of the century Freimann was entrusted with the task of compiling a complete record of the library holdings in the areas of Hebraica and Judaica.[23] The plan called for the publication of a two-volume catalog, one listing Judaica and the other Hebraica. The first volume appeared in Frankfurt a.M. in 1932 under the title *Katalog der Judaica und Hebraica.* The second volume was never published. The Hebraica and Judaica collection at the Frankfurter Stadtbibliothek included a number of important private collections of Jewish scholars such as Isaak Markus Jost (1793–1860), Nehemiah Brüll (1843–1891),[24] Abraham Berliner (1833–1915), Abraham Merzbacher (1812–1885), and others. The Judaica collection at the Stadtbibliothek was, as a result, one of the finest of this nature ever accumulated. During World War II the collection was partially destroyed, and the *Katalog* prepared by Freimann ceased to be a record of a specific collection and became the only

Judaica bibliography of its scope ever compiled and published.

The *Katalog,* consisting of 646 pages (besides the introduction and table of contents), registered more than 10,000 Judaica works printed up to the year 1930, and it was divided into the following ten major categories:

General works (includes also: encyclopedias; bibliographies, collective works; periodicals; catalogs; history of printing; biographies)
Language and literature (includes also biblical and postbiblical literature)
Geography and history
Philosophy and cabala
Education
Art
Law
Sociology
Natural sciences
Theology (includes also homiletics and liturgy)

The register of works was followed by an index of authors, titles, and subjects. The entries were detailed, especially those describing serials and multi-volume works, but they did not include pagination. Cross-references appeared only in the index, and books belonging to more than one category were usually listed only once. Works with Hebrew titles were registered in Hebrew characters with translations in parentheses, and information not available on a title-page was furnished in brackets. A by-product of the *Katalog* was Freimann's effort to establish the identities of writers of anonymous works; he also succeeded in decoding a large number of pseudonyms.

The *Katalog,* with the addition of an introduction by Annie Fraenkel, was reprinted in Graz, Austria, by the Akademische Druck- u. Verlagsanstalt in 1968.[25]

## Bibliotheca Rosenthaliana:
### *Systematische Catalogus van de Judaica*

The publication of the Judaica catalog of the Frankfurt a.M. Stadtbibliothek was a factor in the decision of another institution also to start publishing its Judaica catalog. The institution was the Amsterdam University Library, which housed the Bibliotheca Rosenthaliana (discussed earlier in this work).[26] During the second half of the 1930s the Rosenthaliana had grown to about 30,000 volumes and had become one of the largest Jewish book collections on the European continent. Since the original collection, especially the Hebraica part of it, was thoroughly cataloged prior to its presentation to the city of Amsterdam,[27] the University Library decided to follow the example of the Frankfurt a.M. Stadtbibliothek, and to publish a Judaica catalog as the first part of the entire Rosenthaliana collection.[28]

Publication commenced in Amsterdam in 1936 with the appearance of part one of the *Systematische Catalogus van de Judaica der Bibliotheca Rosenthaliana*. Parts two to five appeared annually up to 1940. When World War II engulfed the Netherlands, all activities at the Rosenthaliana had to cease. The German invaders seized tle collection, put it under seal, and later shipped it to Germany. They also seized the librarian, L. Hirschel, and the assistant, R. M. Hillesum, together with their families, and deported them to a death camp. After the war ended, the books were recovered and returned to Amsterdam—"not undamaged"—but the librarian and the assistant never came back. It took nearly two decades to reorganize the work on the catalog, and in 1964 part six appeared. Part nine, the final part, was published in 1966, bringing the total number of pages for the entire catalog to 1,233. The approximate number of works registered was over 10,000.

The entries as well as the classification of the *Systematische Catalogus* were very similar to the entries and classification of Freimann's *Katalog*, although here and there alterations and extensions were made. Thus the work was divided into the following six major categories:

Books on general subjects
Language
Literature
Theology
History
Miscellanea (includes also geography; sociology; education; law; sciences; psychology; philosophy; and cabala)

A one-volume reprint edition of parts 1–5 appeared in Amsterdam, published by Menno Herzberger & Co., 1965.

The publication of a supplement to the *Systematische Catalogus* became a necessity even before the main body of the *Catalogus* was completed in print. This was due to acquisitions made by the Bibliotheca Rosenthaliana during the post-war years. The first installment of such a supplement, entitled *Supplement I/1*, was published in Amsterdam in 1971. The supplement introduced a few innovations, such as cross-references, and the inclusion of Hebraica publications printed with an added title page, introduction, or summary in a European language.

Volkmar Eichstädt:
*Bibliographie zur Geschichte der Judenfrage*

The king of Moab hired Balaam, the prophet, to pronounce a curse on his foes, the Israelites. The pronouncements turned into blessings, and came to be regarded as among the finest examples of ancient Hebrew poetry. In order to prove their anti-Jewish theories, the Nazis hired a number of scholars and pseudoscholars in the 1930s to conduct "research" relating to Jewish history and literature. In the fall of 1935 they inaugurated the Reichsinstitut für Geschichte des neueun Deutschlands under the leadership of Walter Frank, an historian turned Nazi.[29] This Reichsinstitut paid a major part of its attention to the *Judenfrage,* and between 1937 and 1944 published eight volumes of anti-Jewish "research."[30] Despite its clear tendency to lend a scientific seal of approval to the theories and actions of the Nazi regime, some of the historical research done at the Reichsinstitut turned out to be of permanent value.

Among the early projects ordered by Frank was the preparation of a bibliography of works available in German libraries that dealt with the Jewish question. For this purpose, Frank first proposed to establish a large Judaica book collection at the Reichsinstitut, and he tried to acquire the collection of the Frankfurt am Main Stadtbibliothek. When he failed, he decided to go ahead with the bibliographical project.[31] Volkmar Eichstädt, a librarian at the Preussische Staatsbibliothek, was hired for this task in 1936—the year that the Bibliotheca Rosenthaliana in Amsterdam began publishing its *Systematische Catalogus*—and two years later the first volume of the project appeared. Entitled *Bibliographie zur Geschichte der Judenfrage* (Hamburg, 1938), it registered in its 267 pages more than 3,000 entries of German Judaica printed between the years 1750 and 1848.[32] The compilation of the material was based on the holdings of the Preussische Staatsbibliothek in Berlin, the Bayerische Staatsbibliothek in Munich, the Stadtbibliothek of Frankfurt a.M., and a number of smaller German institutional libraries, and could be considered—for the areas it covered—as a union catalog of German Judaica holdings in the principal libraries of Germany during the 1930s.

Eichstädt listed in his bibliography "not only books and pamphlets, but also articles in newspapers and periodicals, and chapters from sociological, theological, and historical works." The entries contained complete bibliographical information, often annotated, and the material was divided into eighteen main sections. The first eight sections were arranged chronologically in the following manner:

1750—1780 (Lessing, Michaelis, Voltaire, and the Lavater-Mendelssohn controversy)
1781—1792 (French Revolution)
1792—1806 (Fichte, Kant, Friedländer; beginning of antisemitic movement)
1806—1815 (Napoleon's policies towards the Jews; efforts for Jewish emancipation)
1815—1819 (development of antisemitic movement)
1820—1830 (post-Napoleonic era)
1830—1840 (continued efforts for Jewish emancipation)
1840—1848 (the Jewish question)

The next four sections dealt with efforts for Jewish emancipation in the following German regions:

South German states
North German states
Prussia
Austria

The final six sections dealt with the following topics:

German laws pertaining to Jews
Religion and history of the Jews (Wissenschaft des Judentums; books on Mendelssohn; Jewish biographies)
Missionary activities among Jews
The Jewish Reform movement
Jews in German belles lettres (Heine, Börne, etc.)
Miscellaneous (including favored anti-Jewish topics among the Nazis: Jewish criminality, mixed marriages, Judaism and Freemasonry, the Rothschilds, etc.)

The volume concluded with a list of newspapers quoted in the bibliography, and a general index.

Eichstädt's *Bibliographie zur Geschichte der Judenfrage* is a unique work not because of the circumstances of its compilation and production, but mainly because it is the only Judaica bibliography not compiled as a catalog of a specific collection. Eichstädt compiled two more volumes that would have brought his bibliography up to the year 1934; they were lost during the first chaotic years of post-war Germany.[33]

A reprint edition of Eichstädt's *Bibliographie* was issued in Westmead, England, by Gregg International Publishers in 1969.

## Wiener Library: *German Jewry*

While Walter Frank was making plans for the establishment of a large library of Judaica books to be used for anti-Jewish purposes by his Reichsinstitut and Volkmar Eichstädt was compiling his Judaica bibliography for the same purposes, a group of Jewish refugees from Nazi Germany began to lay plans for establishing a center to collect books and documents relating to the Nazi regime and to the situation of the Jews under its rule. In 1934 they founded a Jewish Central Information Office in Amsterdam under the directorship of Alfred Wiener (1885–1964). In 1939 this office was moved to London and became known as the Wiener Library.

Before, during, and after World War II, the Wiener Library was busy collecting material on Germany and German Jews, and in 1949 it began to publish lists of specific groups of books in its possession. The first list registered books dealing with the situation in Germany under the Nazi regime.[34] The second list concentrated on books dealing with the situation in Germany during the pre-Hitler years.[35] A third volume, consisting almost entirely of German Judaica, was entitled *German Jewry, Its History, Life, and Culture* (London, 1958). Edited by Ilse R. Wolff, the 279-page volume listed, in a topical arrangement, 3,434 entries of works published up to the year 1945.[36] The books included in this bibliography covered "not only the Jews of Germany . . . but equally the German-speaking, and often German-educated, Jews of Austria, Czechoslovakia, and Switzerland." The volume thus becomes an important reference tool for the history of the Jewish communities of Central Europe.

The material in *German Jewry* was divided into the following nine main sections:

> Reference books (encyclopaedias, biographical handbooks, statistics, bibliographies, and catalogs)
> History (subdivided by periods, social and cultural, economic, legal, and regional)
> Jewish life and thought (includes also religion, education, institutions and organizations)
> Integration, assimilation, Zionism
> Biography
> Participation in cultural life
> Participation in economic and political life
> Antisemitism
> Periodicals

The volume concluded with an index of authors and main entries.

## Leo Baeck Institute: *Katalog*

Another institution founded by German Jews, similar in nature to the Wiener Library but much broader in scope, was the Leo Baeck Institute. Created in 1955 by the Council of Jews from Germany, it concentrated on "collecting material and sponsoring research into the history of the Jewish community in Germany and in other German-speaking countries."[37] The Institute set up three centers—in Jerusalem, London, and New York— assigning a different task to each center. The New York center was given "the task of collecting the published and unpublished documentation of German-speaking Jewry." As a result the New York center was successful in collecting important amounts "of published and unpublished material . . . constituting perhaps the most significant documentation of the history of German-speaking Jewry in the Western world."[38]

In 1959 the three Leo Baeck centers began to publish a series of volumes jointly under the title *Schriftenreihe wissenschaftlicher Abhandlungen.* Volume twenty-two of this series (Tübingen, 1970) consisted of *Katalog Band I* of the New York center's library and archive. Edited by Max Kreutzberger (with the assistance of Irmgard Foerg), the *Katalog*—the first in a planned series of seven—registered, in its over 600 pages, close to 4,000 entries of (mostly) German Judaica. Preceded by a lengthy introduction by the editor on the nature and development of German-Jewish scholarship, and adorned by 23 facsimiles, the register was divided into the following three main sections:

> German-speaking Jewish communities (3,014 entries arranged alphabetically by the names of the localities; larger communities subdivided by period, organization, etc.; includes documents of governments and Jewish organizations, pamphlets, and broadsides)
>
> Newspapers, periodicals, yearbooks, almanacs, and calendars (854 entries divided into two subsections, each one further subdivided into several smaller subsections)
>
> Autobiographies and memoirs (450 unpublished manuscripts, dating, with a few exceptions, from the early nineteenth century to the holocaust years of the Nazi regime)

The bibliographical data in all three sections of the *Katalog* were quite complete, and the entries were often annotated with useful information. Each entry in section three included biographical information on the author of the manuscript and a brief digest of the contents of the autobiography or memoir. An index of authors, titles, places, and topics (and a list of works published by the Leo Baeck Institute during the years 1956—1969/70) concluded the volume.

## Ludwig Rosenberger: *Judaica*

The Nazi-inspired and Nazi-produced Judaica bibliography by Eichstädt, the Judaica catalogs of the Wiener Library, and the New York Leo Baeck Institute (which came into being as a consequence of Nazi outrages) concentrated almost entirely on German Judaica. Eichstädt concentrated on German Judaica because the purpose of his bibliography was to serve the Nazi scholars with material available in German libraries; the Wiener Library and the Leo Baeck Institute concentrated on collecting German Judaica because their goals were to document the historical events connected with Germany and the German-speaking Jewries. Different in scope and in nature is a catalog of a private collection published in Cincinnati in 1971 under the title *Judaica: A Short-Title Catalog of Books, Pamphlets, and Manuscripts Relating to the Political, Social, and Cultural History of the Jews and to the Jewish Question in the Library of Ludwig Rosenberger, Chicago, Illinois.*

Ludwig Rosenberger (born 1904 in Munich) began to collect books dealing with Jewish history and the Jewish question while still a young man in his native country.[39] He acquired books in languages he could read and study easily, and he built his Judaica collection around subjects in which he was specifically interested. Rosenberger himself compiled and classified the catalog of his collection, Herbert C. Zafren edited the material, and the Hebrew Union College Press published it in a limited edition of 450 copies (as Volume Two of its Bibliographica Judaica series).

The 495-page volume registers more than 16,000 entries, and it is divided into more than 200 sections and subsections. The catalog begins with reference works, followed by independent topics (such as art, drama and poetry, sociology, economics, general Judaica), and continues with history, historians, and Jews in various countries, subdivided by events and personalities. This is followed by a section on Zionism, territorialism, socialism (including works on Karl Marx, Leon Trotsky, and a number of Soviet leaders of Jewish descent), the Jewish question (including works dealing with ritual-murder cases), *Protocols of the Elders of Zion,* converts and conversionism, intermarriage, and Nazism (including Judaica published under the Nazis, anti-Nazi literature, and Nuremberg-trial records).

The *Judaica* catalog was illustrated with 116 facsimiles of rare books and autographs (inserted in three groups), and the last two leaves included an "Alphabetical index to the section headings." The publication of a "detailed index" was postponed for sometime "in the future" when a supplement to the catalog would be issued.

Rosenberger's *Judaica* represented an unusual Jewish book collection in private possession. It was unusual not only because of the large number of rare items it included, twenty-five incunabula among them, but also because of the emphasis its owner placed on areas usually neglected by other collectors of Judaica. What is most unusual is the publication of the catalog itself: the only Judaica catalog of a private collection of this magnitude ever to be published.

A 55-page supplement of Rosenberger's *Judaica* was issued in Cincinnati in 1974 by the Hebrew Union College Press (as Volume Four of its Bibliographica Judaica series).

## Harvard University Library: *Judaica* and *Judaica in the Houghton Library*

The major Judaica catalogs—from Freimann to Rosenberger—were dominated by the German language. They reflected the actual state of affairs in the field of published Judaica, and also the special interest of the collectors and the compilers. The tragic events in Europe during the years of the Nazi regime resulted in, among other things, a partial transplantation of Jewish intellectual activities into the English-speaking countries. The current annual output of English-language Judaica—which far outdistances Judaica publications in other languages—is the best testimony to the success of the transplantation process. This changed situation is also demonstrated in the most recent catalog of Judaica issued by Harvard University Library.

The published card catalogs of the Jewish collections at the New York Public Library in 1960 and the Hebrew Union College Library in Cincinnati in 1964 may have been instrumental in the publication of Harvard University's *Catalogue of Hebrew Books* in 1968.[40] While the former institutions reproduced the cards of both Hebraica and Judaica in a single alphabetical arrangement, Harvard reproduced only the cards of the Hebrew books and promised to publish separate catalogs for Yiddish and Judaica. The publication by Harvard University Library of a volume entitled *Judaica* (Cambridge, 1971) partially fulfilled this promise.

Harvard's *Judaica* catalog was produced as Volume 39 in the Widener Library Shelflist series. Widener Library houses Harvard's main research collection, including the Judaica materials. Early in the 1960s, Harvard University Library began to computerize the shelflist and classification schedules at Widener and to produce computer generated lists of library holdings, hence the Shelflist series. Computerization of records enables manipulation for the sake of obtaining various types of information. Some benefits of this manipulation process were offered in the *Judaica* catalog. The 302-page volume was divided into four sections, preceded by prefaces and statistical summaries. The summaries consisted of:

Analysis of shelflist entries by language (26 languages, with English and German leading in the number of entries: English—4,360, German—2,499)
Count of titles (9,074)
Count of volumes (11,800)

The four sections contained the following:

Classification schedules (accompanied by notes and explanations)
Classified listing by call number (divided into monographs, class Jud, and periodicals, class PJud; both sections together formed a kind of subject guide to the entire collection)
Chronological listing (from 1470 to 1971; the section offered a glimpse of the growth of English Judaica during the last few decades; chronological arrangement could be useful for a variety of purposes, such as collection development, quantity of publication, intellectual interests and cultural trends at any given year, etc.)
Author and title listing

The entries in all sections were cut to the bare essentials: author, short title, place and date of publication. Some of the errors, inconsistencies, and deficiencies of the shelflist—which is normally used only as an inventory record and as a tool for assigning call numbers—were transferred to the catalog. And these were multiplied by human error, because most computerization is done by personnel with little bibliographic training. Nonetheless, Harvard's *Judaica* volume was a new concept in Judaica catalog printing, and the benefits it offered surely outweighed the deficiencies.[41]

Houghton Library is Harvard University Library's rare-book department. Its rare books holdings also include rare Judaica. One thousand seven hundred twenty-five items of Houghton's Judaica were included in sections three and four of Harvard's *Judaica* volume. The original catalog cards for these items, together with an additional 600 titles, were reproduced in 1972 as an appendix to volume one of Harvard University Library's *Catalogue of Hebrew Books: Supplement I,* entitled *Judaica in the Houghton Library.*[42] It was also published as a separate volume. The approximately 2,300 titles in this catalog represented works cataloged at Houghton since 1957, and it constituted "only a part of that library's Judaica holdings." For the 1,725 items listed in the *Judaica* volume, *Judaica in the Houghton Library* provided computer-generated indexes by date, place of publication, and title.

The New York Public Library's Jewish collection card catalog registered about 100,000 volumes, 60 percent of them Judaica. The Hebrew Union College card catalog registered about 200,000 items, 70 percent of them Judaica, ancient Near East, and other related material. The Harvard catalogs registered only about 11,000 titles, but the production of the catalogs as separate registers, in a manner new to the users of this type of literature, makes them a most valuable addition to Judaica bibliography.

## Translations from Hebrew and Yiddish

The events of the last three decades—the destruction of European Jewry, the establishment of the State of Israel, and the cultural and intellectual maturation of the English-speaking Jewries, especially in the United States— resulted, in the English-speaking countries, in an ever-growing interest in the Hebrew literature that is blooming in the State of Israel, and in a curiosity about Yiddish literature that once flourished in Eastern Europe. In a bibliographical survey by Maurice T. Galpert of "Modern Hebrew Literature in English Translation," published about a year after the establishment of the State of Israel,[43] the author had little more to review than the translations of Bialik, Tchernichovsky, Agnon, and the anthologies of Leo W. Schwarz.[44] Less than a decade later, Jacob Kabakoff, in a survey of "Israeli Literature in English Garb,"[45] could already enumerate and review a much longer list of translated Hebrew works. The number of Hebrew works—novels, short stories, poems, essays, etc.—translated into English kept growing at a fast pace, and in one more decade it enabled the publication of a 110-page *Bibliography of Modern Hebrew Literature in English Translation* (Jerusalem, 1968), compiled by Yohai Goell.

Goell included independent works in his *Bibliography* as well as works that appeared in anthologies and periodicals. He registered more than 3,400 entries, representing an estimated 7,500 references to books and periodicals, covering translations that had appeared in print "from the beginning of the penultimate decade of the 19th century" to December 31, 1965. The material was compiled at the Jewish National and University Library in Jerusalem, and it was based "almost solely" upon the holdings of that institution. This resulted in some gaps in the *Bibliography,* because many publications, especially early English-Jewish periodicals, were unobtainable at the Jerusalem library.

Goell arranged the work into the following sections:

General anthologies
Poetry
Prose
Drama
Essays, criticism, and miscellaneous[46]
Children's literature—poetry
Children's literature—prose
Addenda

The entries were concise but bibliographically complete, and included the following information:

Author (or editor if work appeared in an anthology)
Title
Translator
Place of publication ⎫
Publisher ⎬ for books and anthologies
Date of publication ⎭

Name of publication ⎫
Number of volume ⎬ for periodicals
Date of publication ⎭
Page numbers

The volume concluded with indexes of authors, translators, periodicals (containing only those "of which all or most of the available issues were checked"), and authors and titles in the original Hebrew (incomplete due to difficulties in identifying some translated works).

The immigration to Israel of large segments of French-speaking and French-reading Jews (mostly from North Africa), and the renaissance of Jewish cultural life in France during the postwar years, necessitated the translation of Hebrew works into French. A bibliography of Hebrew works translated into French during the years 1940–1965 was issued in Jerusalem in 1966 by the Department for Cultural Contacts of the Ministry of Foreign Affairs of the State of Israel. Prepared by Ruth Tronik and Tania Manzur and entitled *Sifrut Ivrit Meturgemet Letsarfatit; Reshimah Bibliografit, 1940–1965* (with an added title in French: *Bibliographie d'Ouvrages Hébraïques Traduits en Français, 1940–1965*), it lists works that appeared as independent volumes or as parts of anthologies. The 17-leaf pamphlet (printed on one side of the leaf in two columns) registers seventy entries in the areas of literature (including children's literature), philosophy, and biography. The entries are complete, and they also include the original titles in Hebrew. Two author indexes, one in Hebrew and the other in Roman characters, conclude the volume.

Seven years after the publication of Yohai Goell's *Bibliography of Modern Hebrew Literature in English Translation*, his 117-page *Bibliography of Modern Hebrew Literature in Translation* (Tel Aviv, 1975) appeared. Published by the Institute for the Translation of Hebrew Literature, the new volume listed, "with very few exceptions," only translations that had appeared in separate volumes published since 1917. The volume includes more than 600 entries alphabetically divided into twenty-five languages; each group is subdivided according to the classification scheme prepared by Goell for his earlier volume (see above). Two appendixes ("Monographs on Modern Hebrew Literature" and "Chronological List of Translations"), an index of Hebrew authors, and an index to translators, editors, and authors of monographs, conclude the volume.

The revival of interest in Yiddish during the last decades, especially in the United States, brought with it demands for a bibliography of Yiddish literature.[47] The demands have not been met, but, for the benefit of the English reader, lists of Yiddish works in English translation began to make their appearance. The translation of Yiddish works into English had its beginning in 1898 with the publication in Boston of Leo Wiener's translation of a volume of poetry by a Jewish-American Yiddish poet.[48] Up to World War II another sixty to seventy Yiddish works became available in English translation. This growth was reflected in the list of "Books on and Translations from the Yiddish Literature Available in English" that was appended to Abraham Roback's *The Story of Yiddish Literature* (New York, 1940),[49] and in Shlomo Noble's bibliographical survey of "Modern Yiddish Literature in English Translation" that was published eight years later.[50]

The post-World War II years witnessed a great upsurge in the publication of English translations from Yiddish literature. During the last three decades there were almost three times as many translations published as had been published during the half century preceding 1945. This recent development is reflected in a list compiled by Dina Abramowicz, librarian of the Yivo Institute for Jewish Research in New York, entitled *Yiddish Literature in English Translation; Books Published 1945–1967* (New York, 1968). The thirty-five-page list registers more than 200 items arranged according to the names of the authors. Each entry includes complete bibliographical information extracted from the title page, plus pagination and, whenever available, the original Yiddish title in transliteration. An index of subjects concludes the volume.

A second edition of *Yiddish Literature in English Translation,* together with a "Supplementary List of Translations for the Period Ending April, 1968," was published in New York in 1968 (c. 1969).

---

A general, all-inclusive Judaica bibliography is still a dream of many scholars and students in the area of Jewish studies. Some of the groundwork has been done, mostly by a few individuals; the completion of the work requires a joint effort. Dov Sadan (born 1902) issued such a challenge while addressing a conference of Israeli librarians:

> Our first demand is a complete bibliography of our literature. The beginning of such a work—a complete Hebrew bibliography—is now being prepared between the walls of the National Library. Just as it is a must to hasten the work [on the Hebrew bibliography] for the benefit of this generation, so it is mandatory to extend it to include a complete *Jewish* bibliography, that is to say that it should include works written in Jewish languages, and also in foreign languages, that constitute part of our literature. . . . [51]

Since it is now doubtful whether the work done on the Hebrew bibliography will be completed in time to benefit the present generation,[52] it is doubly doubtful that Sadan's challenge will be taken up by the Mif'al Habibliyografyah in Jerusalem.

# Chronological List of
# Judaica Bibliographies and Catalogs

## 1932

Frankfurt am Main. Stadtbibliothek.
 Katalog der Judaica und Hebraica. Erster Band: Judaica. Frankfurt am
Main: Druck von M. Lehrberger & Co., 1932.
 xii, 646 pages.

More than 10,000 titles. Compiled by Aron Freimann. Cut-off date: 1930.

*Organization:* Subject arrangement in ten major categories: general works,
            language and literature, geography and history, philosophy
and cabala, education, art, law, sociology, natural sciences, theology. Index
of authors, titles, subjects, and cross-references.

*Editions:* Reprinted, with the addition of an introduction by Annie
            Fraenkel, Graz: Akademische Druck- u. Verlagsanstalt, 1968.

## 1936—1966

Amsterdam. Bibliotheca Rosenthaliana.
 Systematische Catalogus van de Judaica der Bibliotheca Rosenthaliana.
Amsterdam: International Antiquariat Menno Herzberger, 1936—1966.
 9 parts (1,233 pages).

More than 10,000 titles. Parts 1—5 compiled by L. Hirschel and M. S. Hillesum; parts 6—9 by L. Fuks and co-workers.

*Organization:* Similar to preceding catalog, but divided into six major
            categories: general, language, literature, theology, history,
miscellanea (geography, sociology, education, law, science, psychology,
philosophy and cabala).

*Editions:* Photo-offset edition of parts 1—5, Amsterdam: Menno
            Herzberger & Co., 1965.

*Supplements:* Supplement I/1, the first of several to be published
            periodically, Amsterdam: A. L. van Gendt & Co., 1971.

**1938**

Eichstädt, Volkmar.
Bibliographie zur Geschichte der Judenfrage. Hamburg: Hanseatische Verlagsanstalt, 1938.
x, 267 pages.

More than 3,000 entries, covering works printed between 1750 and 1848. Compiled for use by Nazi scholars at Reichsinstitut für Geschichte des neuen Deutschlands. Bibliography based on material available at German institutions. Registered also articles in newspapers and periodicals, or sections from related works. Only Judaica bibliography not compiled as catalog of a specific collection.

*Organization:* Chronological and topical arrangement divided into eighteen main groups: 1750−1780, 1781−1792, 1792−1806, 1806−1815, 1815−1819, 1820−1830, 1830−1840, 1840−1848; efforts for Jewish emancipation in: south German states, north German states, Prussia, Austria; laws pertaining to Jews; religion and history of Jews; missionary activities among Jews; Jewish Reform movement; Jews in German literature; miscellaneous. List of periodicals quoted in bibliography; general index.

*Editions:* Reprinted, Westmead, England: Gregg International Publishers, 1969.

**1958**

Wiener Library, London.
German Jewry, Its History, Life and Culture. London: published for the Wiener Library by Vallentine, Mitchell, 1958.
279 pages.

3,434 entries. Compiled by Ilse R. Wolff. Cut-off date: 1945. Covered also books on "German-speaking, and often German-educated, Jews of Austria, Czechoslovakia and Switzerland."

*Organization:* Nine main sections: reference books, history, Jewish life and thought, integration-assimilation-Zionism, biography, participation in cultural life, participation in economic and political life, antisemitism, periodicals. Index of authors and main entries.

*Supplements* are published annually in the *Year Book* of the Leo Baeck Institute.

## 1970

Leo Baeck Institute of Jews from Germany.
  Katalog. Hrsg. von Max Kreutzberger unter Mitarbeit von Irmgard
Foerg. Tübingen: J. C. B. Mohr (Paul Siebeck), 1970.
  xli, 623 pages; 23 facsimiles.

First volume in planned series of seven. Close to 4000 entries.

*Organization:* Lengthy introduction by editor on nature and development
              of German-Jewish scholarship. Register of works divided
into three main sections: German-speaking Jewish communities (3,014
entries); periodica (854 entries); autobiographies and memoirs (450 unpublished manuscripts). Index of authors, titles, places, and topics.

## 1971

Rosenberger, Ludwig (Germany, 1904–   ).
  Judaica; a short-title catalogue of the books, pamphlets, and manuscripts
relating to the political, social, and cultural history of the Jews and to the
Jewish question in the library of Ludwig Rosenberger, Chicago, Illinois.
Cincinnati: Hebrew Union College Press, 1971.
  495 pages; 116 facsimiles.

16,000 entries. Compiled by owner, edited by Herbert C. Zafren. Limited
edition of 450 copies.

*Organization:* Divided into more than 200 sections and subsections (among
              others: reference works, art, drama and poetry, sociology,
economics, general Judaica, history and historians, Jews in various
countries, Zionism-socialism-antisemitism, Nazism, etc.). Alphabetical index of section headings.

*Supplements:* Cincinnati: Hebrew Union College Press, 1974. 55 pages.

## 1971

Harvard University Library.
  Judaica. Cambridge: Harvard University Press, 1971.
  302 pages.

9,074 titles (11,800 volumes). Computer-generated lists manipulated from
computerized shelflist and classification schedules. Brief descriptions.

*Organization:* Prefaces and statistical summaries; classification schedules; classified listing by call number; chronological listing; author and title listing.

### 1972

Harvard University. Library.
   Judaica in the Houghton Library. Cambridge: Harvard University Press, 1972.
   193 pages (in its *Catalogue of Hebrew Books: Supplement I,* Vol. 1).

About 2,300 titles of rare Judaica, 1,725 of which were previously listed briefly in above-mentioned volume, *Judaica,* now registered here with complete descriptions from reproduced original catalog cards, supplemented with computer-generated indexes by date, place of publication, and title.

## Chronological List of
## Translations from Hebrew and Yiddish

### 1966

Israel. Misrad Ha-huts.
   ספרות עברית מתורגמת לצרפתית. Jerusalem, 1966.
   17 leaves.

70 entries, covering publications of monographs in the areas of literature, philosophy, and biography, for the years 1940-1965. Entries include original Hebrew titles. Author indexes in Hebrew and in Roman characters.

### 1968

Abramowicz, Dina.
   Yiddish Literature in English Translation. New York: Yivo Institute for Jewish Research, 1968.
   35 leaves.

Lists more than 200 books published during the years 1945—1967. Entries include original Yiddish titles in transliteration. Index of subjects.

*Editions:* Second edition, with addition of "Supplementary List of Translations for the Period Ending April 1968," New York, 1968 (c. 1969).

## 1968

Goell, Yohai.
Bibliography of Modern Hebrew Literature in English Translation. Jerusalem, Executive of the World Zionist Organization, Youth and Hechalutz Dept.; Jerusalem, New York, Israel Universities Press, 1968.
   vii, 110, 22 pages.

More than 3,400 entries (about 7,500 references to books and periodicals), "from the beginning of the penultimate decade of the nineteenth century" to December 31, 1965. "Based . . . almost solely upon the holdings of the Jewish National and University Library in Jerusalem."

*Organization:* General anthologies; poetry; prose; drama; essays, criticism, and miscellaneous; children's literature—poetry; children's literature—prose; addenda. Indexes of authors, translators, periodicals, authors and titles in Hebrew.

*Order of entries:* Author, title, translator, place of publication, publisher, date of publication. If published in periodical: name of publication, number of volume, date of publication, page numbers.

## 1975

Goell, Yohai.
Bibliography of Modern Hebrew Literature in Translation. Tel Aviv: The Institute for the Translation of Hebrew Literature, 1975.
   117 pages.

More than 600 entries of separate works published since 1917. Alphabetically divided into twenty-five languages.

*Organization:* Each linguistic group subdivided into: general anthologies, poetry, prose, drama, essays and miscellaneous, children's literature; list of monographs on modern Hebrew literature; chronological list of translations; index of Hebrew authors; index of translators, editors, and authors of monographs.

*Order of entries:* Same as in Goell's earlier volume.

# Chapter Six

# Bibliographical Periodicals

*Bibliographical periodicals devoted to the study of the Hebrew book as well as to offering information on current and retrospective books of Jewish interest on a global scale will be discussed in the first part of this chapter. Book-trade periodicals will be discussed next, followed by periodicals designed to cover publications of Jewish interest in a specific country. The final discussion will concentrate on periodicals published to serve the bibliographer, student, and scholar with personal and subject bibliographies and with essays and studies on all phases of the Jewish book.*

I

*Hamazkir-Hebräische Bibliographie. Central-Anzeiger für jüdische Litteratur. Zeitschrift für hebräische Bibliographie. Yerushalayim. Kiryat Sefer* (Warsaw). *Qirjath-Zepher* (!) and *Bibliography of Hebraica and Judaica.* Bibliographical Periodicals in Yiddish. *En Hakore. Soncino Blätter. Kiryat Sefer* (Jerusalem).

II

*Hame'asef—Der Sammler. Bloch's Book Bulletin. Das jüdische Buch* and *Bibliographie des jüdischen Buches. Hamodi'a. Alim. Megilat Sefer. Hed Hasefer* and *Tachazit Hasefer. Olam Hasefer* and *Hasefer Beyisrael. Israel Book Publishers' Quarterly, Israel Book Publishers' Bulletin,* and *Israel Book World.* Collective Catalogs. *Judaica Book Guide* and *Judaica Book News. M. B. S. Reference Catalogue.*

.

III

*Sefer Hashanah Lebiblioyografyah Yehudit Bepolanyah. Jewish Book Annual. Katalog farn Khoydesh fun Yidishn Bukh. Dapim, Yad Lakore, En Hakore,* and again *Yad Lakore. Kuntres Bibliyografi. Shenaton Hamemshalah* and *Reshimat Sifre Chovah. Megilat Hasefer. Accessions List: Israel.*

IV

*Journal of Jewish Bibliography. Studies in Bibliography and Booklore. Areshet. Hasefer, Tagim,* and *Ale Sefer.*

# I. Bibliographical Periodicals
## Dealing with Current and Retrospective Books

### *Hamazkir—Hebräische Bibliographie*

BIBLIOGRAPHY in its early stages was mainly concerned with registering manuscripts and retrospective printed material. As printing became common and publishing began to accelerate, the attention of bibliographers gradually turned to current publications. At the end of the eighteenth and during the early nineteenth centuries, magazines in Germany and in other European countries introduced sections devoted to literary news and book reviews. The next step was the appearance of periodicals devoted entirely to books. Some of these periodicals dealt with current books, others with retrospective, and still others divided their pages between both.[1]

Jewish bibliography went through a similar process. The growing attention to current Jewish publications became visible in the first half of the nineteenth century, when several major German-Jewish magazines introduced special sections devoted to book reviews and literary news items.[2] Next came a periodic publication devoted entirely to Jewish books.

It was the foresightedness of the Berlin bookdealer A. Asher (1800–1853) which was greatly responsible for the bibliographic careers of Moritz Steinschneider and Joseph Zedner,[3] and it was the foresightedness of his successors in the firm which was responsible for the launching of the first Jewish bibliographical periodical. Tailored to the specific peculiarities of the Jewish literary field, but modeled after the already existing periodicals of this nature in the German literary field, A. Asher & Co. began publishing a periodical early in 1858, entitled *Hamazkir—Hebräische Bibliographie; Blätter für neuere und ältere Literatur des Judenthums,* edited by Moritz Steinschneider.[4]

Published as a bimonthly, *Hamazkir—HB* was divided into two main sections:

I. Current ("Gegenwart")
II. Retrospective ("Vergangenheit")[5]

Section one included:

News item about books published or about to be published (culled from newspapers and private communications)
List of current publications (divided into periodicals and monographs; each group subdivided into Hebraica and Judaica)
List of articles of Jewish interest printed in (mostly non-Jewish) magazines
Catalogs and news about book collections
Miscellaneous notes (mostly necrology)

The news items about books, based on private communications, were arranged alphabetically by places of publication; the rest, by the names of the authors. The periodicals and monographic Hebraica in the list of current publications were arranged alphabetically by their titles;[6] monographic Judaica, by the names of the authors. The magazine articles were arranged alphabetically by the titles of the magazines, and the catalogs and news about collections were arranged either by places or by the names of institutions, collectors, or publishers.

The entries in all groups (except in the first) contained complete bibliographic information and were accompanied by the editor's comments, reviews, or summaries. Most detailed were the entries in the list of current publications; they included the following:

| Periodcals | Monographs | |
| --- | --- | --- |
| | *Hebraica* | *Judaica* |

*In Hebrew:*

| | | |
| --- | --- | --- |
| Title (Hebraica titles in Hebrew characters and in transliteration and translation) | Title | Author |
| | Author | Title |
| Description (usually from subtitle) | Description (culled from title page) | Description (culled from title page) |
| Editor or publisher (including his occupation) | | |
| Volume or issue number | | |
| Frequency | | |
| Format and number of sheets per issue or per volume; occasional pagination | | |
| Place of publication | Place of publication | Place of publication |
| | Printer or publisher | Printer or publisher |
| Date of publication (Hebrew and universal dates for Hebraica publications) | Date of Publication | Date of publication |
| | Format | Pagination |
| Subscription price | | Price |

*In German:*

| | | |
| --- | --- | --- |
| | Title (transliterated and translated) | |
| | Author | |
| | Description | |
| | Format | |
| | Place of publication | |
| | Printer or publisher | |
| | Hebrew and universal dates | |
| | Pagination | |
| | Price | |
| Commentary, review, or summary (frequently accompanied by bibliographical footnotes) | Commentary, review, or summary | Commentary, review, or summary |

Section two included studies of retrospective Hebraica; descriptions of rare Hebrew printed works, incunabula, manuscripts; contributions to the history of Hebrew printing and the Jewish book trade; personal and subject bibliographies and miscellaneous bibliographical notes.

In the "Programm" printed at the beginning of the first issue, the editor stated that the purpose of the publication is to serve as a "Repertorium" of the literature relating to Judaism, for the benefit "of scholarship as well as for the book trade." Every work that has Jews or Judaism as its theme, whether written by Jews or non-Jews, "belongs here."[7] The editor also contemplated the annual publication of a review of Jewish literary activity, "especially in the areas of science and art." About his attitude to current publications, he wrote: "Our policy with regards to current literature, generally speaking, is not to criticize but to report. Our purpose is to acquaint the public as early as possible with the most recent publications . . ."

Steinschneider's temperament was not made to abide by the rules that he himself had laid down, and already in the first issue he severely criticized a number of new publications.[8] He repeatedly did this in issue after issue, sometimes becoming quite personal. Especially biting and personal were his attacks on the historians Isaac Marcus Jost (1793–1860)[9] and Heinrich Grätz (1817–1891)[10]; but he let his sharpest arrows fly against Eliakim Carmoly (1802–1875)[11] and Julius Fürst (1805–1873).[12] "His criticism," Shimom Bernfeld wrote some years later, "distinguished itself by its severity. It was evident from his writing that he enjoyed criticizing severly both the works and the authors."[13] Whether this is true or not is a matter for interpretation, but one thing is clear: Steinschneider's comments and reviews in *Hamazkir—HB* created a strong resentment against him among most of his contemporaries, and when publication was suspended at the end of 1865 with Volume 8, many scholars breathed easier.[14]

On the first page of the November–December 1865 issue of *Hamazkir— HB,* the editor printed a "Final Statement" ("Schlusswort") that he could not continue his work due to other obligations. He had hoped that other scholars would take over his burden; but since this had not materialized the present issue would be the last to be published, although he would try to publish yearbooks to fill the gap. The promised yearbooks were not published, but three years later (January–February 1869) *Hamazkir—HB* reappeared. The editor was the same, but the publisher was different.

The format of the renewed periodical, now published by Julius Benzian, did not differ from the earlier published volumes, except that in the first few issues an effort was made to catch up with the registration of works that had appeared during the years when publication of *Hamazkir—HB* was suspended. This effort was instrumental in reducing Steinschneider's famous "comments" to a minimum. There was also more evidence of assistance by other scholars, and each issue included "Mittheilungen aus den Antiquariat von Julius Benzian."[15]

The renewed *Hamazkir—HB* continued to appear for more than a decade reaching twenty-one volumes (126 numbers; the last issue dated November–December 1881/82).[16] During that time the editor renewed his sharp and biting attacks and reviews. His pet targets were the same personalities and ideas that he had previously fought, and to these he now added the developing Jewish nationalism and the movement to colonize the Holy Land. His last attack (in the final issue) was the following comment on the epoch-making work by Leo Pinsker, *Autoemancipation* (Berlin, 1882):

> Based on the assumption that the antipathy against the Jews cannot be overcome (!), therefore a Jewish state has to be established. ... This kind of propaganda for the colonization of Palestine is more dangerous than antisemitism, and it is high time to protest against it.

"It was symbolic, " wrote G. Kressel,[17] "that during that year the publication of *Hamazkir* ceased. The year that marked a turning point in our history (the publication of Pinsker's work) also marked the end of the organ that served as a shelter for the old school that was opposed to the new spirit."

A reprint edition of *Hamazkir—HB* was published in Hildesheim by G. Olms in 1972.

## Central-Anzeiger für jüdische Litteratur

Eight years after *Hamazkir—HB* ceased appearing, a new bibliographical periodical was launched. The editor of the new publication was Nehemia Brüll. He was born in Moravia in 1843, studied at the Vienna Israelitisch-Theologische Lehranstalt and at the Vienna University, and served as a Reform rabbi in Bisenz, Moravia, and in Frankfort. He became disappointed in the rabbinate and, in the 1880s, resigned his position and turned to creative scholarship. Between 1874 and 1890 he edited and published ten volumes entitled *Jahrbücher für jüdische Geschichte und Litteratur* written largely by himself. The volumes contained long studies in the areas of Bible, Talmud, and history, and short reviews of new publications. Each volume consisted of about two hundred pages, with two-thirds of the material devoted to reviews, so that the total number of reviews in the ten volumes reached an impressive 183.[18]

In 1890 Brüll's *Jahrbücher* was superseded by his own bibliographical periodical entitled *Central-Anzeiger für jüdische Litteratur; Blätter für neuere und ältere Litteratur des Judentums.* Published in Frankfort by H. L. Brömer, Brüll's *Central-Anzeiger* was designed as a continuation of Steinschneider's *Hamazkir—HB.* It was in fact a complete imitation of it, with one exception: it did not attack "everybody and everything" as *Hamazkir—HB* did. The notes and comments following the entries contained a more balanced attitude toward most of the new publications, usually restricting themselves to detailed descriptions and conventional criticism.

The first number of the *Central-Anzeiger* appeared early in 1890, and a year later (February 1891) Brüll died, after issuing only three more numbers of his planned bimonthly. At the request of the publisher and as a tribute to a deceased friend, Moritz Steinschneider undertook to edit a double number 5–6 (September–December 1890) in order to complete the volume. Since Brüll did not leave a sufficient amount of material to fill out the entire issue, Steinschneider wrote several large comments and reviews of new works and added a list of more than one hundred Hebraica titles that appeared during the eight-year period from the time that *Hamazkir—HB* ceased publication until the time that the *Central-Anzeiger* took over. The list—certainly incomplete— was prepared by one of Steinschneider's students (Poznanski), and it was based on Steinschneider's private library. The arrangement of the list was alphabetical by title—a sign of the haste with which it was compiled. The issue appeared in June 1891, and it was Steinschneider's last effort as an editor.

## Zeitschrift für hebräische Bibliographie

A five-year gap in registering current Jewish publications occurred after the death of Nehemia Brüll and his *Central-Anzeiger.* Early in 1896 the *Zeitschrift für hebräische Bibliographie* made its appearance in Berlin, and with it began a new era in this important branch of Jewish bibliography. Presented as a continuation of *Hamazkir—HB* (in the "Programm" printed on the first page of the first issue), the *Zeitschrift* adopted not only the name of its prototype (*Hebräische Bibliographie)* but also its external appearance and internal format. The periodical was divided into two major sections, each one subdivided in the same, or in a similar, order as *Hamazkir—HB.*[19] The entries in section I contained all the components essential for scientific bibliographic reporting, and they were frequently followed by comments, reviews, and summaries. Like its predecessor, *Hamazkir—HB,* the *Zeitschrift* was published bimonthly, and it was connected with a publisher, S. Calvary & Co.

Still, these similarities were all on the surface, and a number of basic differences existed between the two periodicals. There was a more objective treatment of current publications in the *Zeitschrift* than there had been in *Hamazkir—HB.* The merciless pronouncements against target authors disliked by the editor that had been practiced in *Hamazkir—HB* disappeared entirely from the pages of the *Zeitschrift.* There was also a complete change of attitude towards the national movement—the renaissance of Hebrew language and literature and the colonization of the Holy Land—two national goals particularly abhorred by Steinschneider.

G. Kressel, who saw a certain symbolism in the fact that *Hamazkir—HB* ceased to exist in the year that Pinsker published his *Autoemancipation* (1882), also found it symbolic that the new bibliographical periodical, the heir to *Hamazkir—HB,* came to life in the year that Theodor Herzl published his *Judenstaat* (1896). Wrote Kressel:

> Zionism, which at that time gathered under its wings the distant and the estranged, was also the spirit that dominated the pages of the renewed bibliographical periodical.... There was more attention there to Achad Ha'am, to Herzl, to *Luchot Achiasaf,* to the poems of Bialik, and all this not long after the days when modern Hebrew literature was treated with rude attacks by Steinschneider in *Hamazkir....*[20]

Credit for these basic changes belongs to the editor of the first volumes of the *Zeitschrift,* Heinrich Brody (1868–1942).[21] Brody, born in Ungvar, now Uzhgorod, Hungary, studied in the yeshivot of his native country, at the Berlin Rabbiner Seminar, and at the Berlin University, and he specialized in the study of medieval Hebrew literature. In the early 1890s Brody began publishing articles in the Hebrew press as well as separate studies in Hebrew and German. His main efforts were directed at preparing scientific editions and studies of medieval Hebrew poetry in Spain.[22] In 1898 Brody became rabbi in Náchod, Bohemia, and seven years later (1905) he moved to Prague to take over the directorship of the Hebrew school (Talmud Torah) there. In 1912 he was appointed chief rabbi of Prague, and eighteen years later (1930) he exchanged his post for the directorship of the Berlin-based Research Institute for Hebrew Poetry (also known as Hamachon Lecheker Hashirah Ha'ivrit, established by Zalman Schocken [1877–1959]). In 1934, as a result of the Nazi ascent to power in Germany, he relocated in the Holy Land, together with the Research Institute which he headed for the rest of his life.

When Brody launched the *Zeitschrift,* he added to the title the legend "with the assistance of well-known scholars," and in the first issue he listed a number of scholars who had promised to participate. Among them were Wilhelm Bacher, Abraham Berliner, Solomon Joachim Halberstam, David Kaufmann, Adolf Neubauer, Martin Schreiner, and Moritz Stein-schneider—the cream of Jewish scholars in the nineteenth century. But three years later, after he took over his rabbinic position in Náchod, Brody realized that even this assistance would not be enough to ensure a regular continuation of the periodical, and he began to search for a coeditor. The last issue of Volume 3 (November—December 1898) closed with an announcement that "in order to create the necessary conditions for a regular appearance of our periodical, we decided to suspend publication temporarily." Publication resumed a year later (January—February 1900) in Frankfort, with Aron Freimann as coeditor and J. Kauffmann as publisher.[23] The long interruption in publication was explained on the front page as "partially due to the editor's . . . appointment as rabbi of Náchod, and partially due to the change of publishers."

The change of publishers and the coopting of an editor had no visible effect on the *Zeitschrift* and its policies which remained the same even later, when Brody dropped out (beginning with the November—December issue of 1905) and Freimann remained the sole editor. Publication was again suspended in 1912—without explanation but probably because of financial difficulties—with Volume 15, and when it was resumed in 1913, a legend on the volume title page stated, "Subsidized by the Zunz-Stiftung and the Gesellschaft zur Förderung der Wissenschaft des Judentums." This statement was later modified to read: "The Zunz-Stiftung contributed towards the printing of this work, without taking any responsibility for its contents."

The *Zeitschrift* continued publication during all the years of World War I, but finally collapsed during the years of the economic crisis that followed it. The last issue, consisting of 64 pages and constituting Volume 23, nos. 1—12, was published in 1920. A Volume 24 was prepared and printed in a few issues but was not published.[24]

## Yerushalayim

Jewish bibliographical periodicals that came into being during the second half of the nineteenth century, although they dealt with the Hebrew language and literature, used the German language as a means of communication with their readers. All the descriptions, reviews, comments, and studies, except Hebraica titles and occasional quotations, were in German. This was the language of scholars and of the book trade, and the editors, it seems, did not think that the, at that time, underdeveloped Hebrew language could perform the same function. But a Jewish publisher in Cracow was of a different opinion and, in 1900, the year in which the *Zeitschrift* came back to life after being suspended, he began publishing the first bibliographical periodical in Hebrew. It was an interesting experiment that failed, not because of the inadequacy of Hebrew, but because of the periodical's amateurish nature.

Jonas Kreppel, the editor and publisher of this first bibliographical periodical in Hebrew, was an interesting personality himself; he was unusually talented in many areas, but he was no bibliographer. Born in 1874 in Drohobycz, Galicia, Kreppel was considered a prodigy, and he planned to become a rabbi.[25] At the age of fourteen, he gave up his rabbinic aspirations, turned to secular studies, and wound up as a typesetter in the local printing shop of Aaron Hirsch Zupnik (1843–1917).[26] Zupnik himself, besides being a printer, had literary ambitions. He wrote a number of books and edited and published newspapers and magazines in German, Hebrew, and Yiddish.[27] Zupnik's printing shop turned out to be ideal for Kreppel. Besides learning how to set type, Kreppel learned the art of journalism, the ability to write fluently on any subject. His entry into the writing profession was accomplished without the loss of a single drop of ink, since he composed his articles for Zupnik's publications straight out of the type composing box.[28]

In 1896 Kreppel became the editor of one of Zupnik's publications.[29] Two years later he married the daughter of Josef Fischer, a well-known Hebrew printer in Cracow. He moved to Cracow, took charge of his father-in-law's shop, and began publishing newspapers in German, Hebrew, and Yiddish,[30] at the same time also contributing articles to various other publications. He wrote on everything under the sun: problems of the day, science, short stories, book reviews, feuilletons, etc.

During World War I, after the Russians entered Galicia, Kreppel escaped to Vienna. There he established and edited several newspapers in German, and also wrote and published a number of works in that language. One of his works,[31] issued while the war was still in progress, earned him an important position at the Austrian foreign ministry and the title "Regierungsrat." During the 1920s, Kreppel published several major works in German, among them two reference works,[32] and also wrote and published about one hundred booklets of folk stories in Yiddish.[33] He tried in vain to be appointed consul in Palestine[34] and remained at the foreign ministry until the Nazi Anschluss (1938). He was deported to Dachau and killed by the Nazis.

One of Kreppel's first publications after he had settled in Cracow was the Hebrew bibliographical periodical *Yerushalayim*.[35] He planned this periodical as a bimonthly, and in the subtitle he described it as "a review of Jewish literature in all languages." A German subtitle also read: "Literarische Revue." The word bibliography was not mentioned at all, but a short statement "To the readers" promised to review and impartially describe the new publications. The plan was to combine literary criticism and bibliography into one periodical. Each issue was thus divided into two sections: (1) reviews of current publications; (2) list of current publications.

Section one consisted of some larger and smaller articles and reviews and some simple descriptions of new books, and it was divided into a few subsections, such as monographs, periodicals, belles lettres, etc. Section two was divided into three groups: Hebrew, Yiddish, and Judaica; it listed only books not dealt with in the review section.

Five numbers in four issues (152 pages) of *Yerushalayim* appeared during 1900–1901, and then came a long interruption. Seven years later an additional issue appeared, dated July–August 1908 and designated as "second year no. 1–2." It consisted of 32 pages in semifolio format and was planned as a monthly. Its subtitle now clearly stated: "Yarchon Sifruti-Bibliyografi,"[36] and the German subtitle read: "Literarisch-bibliographische Revue." Kreppel was again the editor, but "Verlag Koheleth" was named as the publisher. "Koheleth" was described as a company of shareholders with the aim of "assisting the development of Jewish literature by publishing books, magazines, and scientific and popular periodicals," and it was probably founded and owned by Kreppel. The table of contents indicated the following eight sections:

General literary review
Periodicals
Literature
Current publications
Catalogs
Literary chronicle
Review of general literature in German
Advertisements

The editorial statement "To the readers" promised that *Yerushalayim* would become a "literary-bibliographical treasury" that would represent a "complete and encompassing view of the development of our literature in all languages." It was a promise that could not be kept, since this was the last issue published. Many years later, already a Regierungsrat in Vienna, Kreppel turned again to book reviews and bibliography, and published *Das Buch,* a bimonthly "Literarisch-bibliographische Revue" that dealt mainly with general German works, but also devoted some space to Judaica.[37]

In an evaluation of Kreppel and his *Yerushalayim,* written forty years after its appearance,[38] Eliezer Raphael Malachi (born 1895) called this periodical "a bibliographical curio" which "did not make any impression when it was published; it was almost not mentioned in the contemporary periodicals." Malachi explained the attitude of contemporary Hebrew scholars to *Yerushalayim* with the fact that Kreppel "did not possess bibliographical ability, and he also did not prove himself as a critic; the daily Hebrew press had much better book reviews. . . ." The second volume of *Yerushalayim,* according to Malachi, was even worse than the first. True, the style was more modern, but in the reviews Kreppel "represents himself as an expert for each and every subject, and he pronounces his verdicts with the voice of final authority." Since Kreppel "was not a bibliographer, and as a writer he did not prove himself," his pretentious voice became repulsive.

In contrast to the first volume of *Yerushalayim* which, with its modest voice, was ignored by almost everyone, the second volume, with its loud noise, did attract some special attention. Samuel Josef Agnon (1888–1967), who was later to become the first Nobel Laureate for Hebrew literature, wrote a review in a Tel Aviv periodical[39] in which he wondered that "a man who likes the name 'Yerushalayim' so strongly . . . would not even mention the (periodical) *Ha'omer* that appears in the city of Jerusalem."[40] Much stronger words were used by Micha Joseph Bin Gorion[-Berdichevsky] (1865–1921):

There is nothing hidden from the editor of this all-inclusive periodical. He judges arrogantly works of prose and poetry, astronomy and arithmetic, natural sciences and philosophy; he judges in matters of science of Judaism and history of literature, Torah and languages, ethics and good manners . . . and not only things written in Hebrew or Yiddish . . . but also things written in languages of the various nations: in all the living languages. And this "know-it-all" . . . is not Moses ben Maimon, or Moses (Moritz) Steinschneider, but a simple Jew, who until now . . . was hidden somewhere, and now appeared in his entire glory with his broad knowledge, and who signs his name as Yonah (Jonas) Kreppel. . . .[41]

Malachi felt that Kreppel's pretentious tone and arrogance in the second volume of *Yerushalayim* had "irritated" Berdichevsky and provoked his outburst, but there is room to believe that what really provoked Berdichevsky was an unfavorable review of four of his books in the first volume of *Yerushalayim*.[42] It is probably as the rabbinic saying goes, "Here found the creditor a chance to collect his debt."[43]

## *Kiryat Sefer* (Warsaw)

Berdichevsky, in the very place where he so unceremoniously attacked Kreppel and his bibliographical periodical *Yerushalayim*, discussed another bibliographical periodical and its publisher:

> There was in Warsaw some time ago a bookseller; he used to sell Haskalah works—which he cherished—for high prices. His name was Scheinfinkel. He tried to publish a bibliographical periodical under the title *Kiryat Sefer*. It had value and plan, although it was far from scholarship and science. At least, he did not squeeze himself into territory that was not his. He satisfied himself with registering the books, their titles, and contents, systematically and precisely . . . and when literary items and comments were included, they were not by the publisher, but . . . by . . . scholars. . . .

Benjamin Zvi Scheinfinkel began publishing his *Kiryat Sefer* in Warsaw in 1903,[44] and a year later, when it reached issue number six, publication ceased. All six issues together constituted about 96 pages, and they contained:

Feature articles
Lists of current Hebraica
Communications
Advertisements (by the publisher and other dealers)

In the second issue, Scheinfinkel listed sixteen scholars who had promised to donate their services to the periodical, among them Heinrich Brody, Simon Moses Chones, and Samuel Wiener, but only a few of those listed actually participated. The first two issues featured a history of Jewish bibliography;[45] the next three issues reviewed the short stories of the Russian-Jewish writer, Semen Solomonovich Iushkevich (1868–1927); the last issue dealt with the modern novel. Letters by Jewish scholars addressed to Jacob Reifmann (1818–1894) were featured in each issue. The bibliographical section, entitled *Ma'arechet Sefarim*, was divided by subject, and it listed current publications in great detail, including the prices and addresses of authors or dealers. Communications by Hebrew bibliographers and scholars appeared in several issues.

## *Qirjath-Zepher [!]* and *Bibliography of Hebraica and Judaica*

The first two bibliographical periodicals in Hebrew—*Yerushalayim* and *Kiryat Sefer*—may have inspired the Leipzig bookdealer, M.W. Kaufmann, to issue similar publications for German Judaica. In 1904 he published a sixteen-page pamphlet under the Hebrew title *Kiryat Sefer* (awkwardly transcribed:*Qirjath-Zepher*), with a subtitle, "Bibliographischer Vierteljahres-Bericht für die Interessenten der jüdischen Literatur u. Religionswissenschaft." Ten years later (1914), he published a larger pamphlet (38 pages) entitled *Bibliographischer Vierteljahres-Bericht für die jüdische Literatur.* It carried about 40 book reviews written by a number of scholars, and a classified list of 94 current Judaica publications, under the heading "Neuerscheinungen vom. 1. Januar bis zum 31. März 1914." Although the 1904 pamphlet was designated as "no. 1—2," and the 1914 pamphlet was described as "first year, no. 1," no other issues were published.

Nineteen hundred four was also the year in which the registration of current Jewish publications was begun in the British Isles. Israel Abrahams (1858—1925), coeditor of the London *Jewish Quarterly Review,* compiled and published lists of current Hebraica and Judaica in that periodical. The lists appeared in Volumes 17 (1905) and 18 (1906), but were later discontinued. They were also issued in two separate annual pamphlets under the title *Bibliography of Hebraica and Judaica,* and they covered publications from autumn 1904 to the end of 1906. The entries were arranged alphabetically by author, and they included the following information:

Author
Title
Description
Place of publication
Publisher
Pagination
Price

## Bibliographical Periodicals in Yiddish

During the years preceding World War I and immediately thereafter, the activity of publishing Jewish bibliographical periodicals and registering current books was extended eastward towards Lithuania and Russia. It was an effort that mainly concerned a single branch of Jewish literature, that of Yiddish. In 1911, Abraham Hirsch Kotik (1867 or 8—1933),[46] a writer and teacher, published the first bibliographical periodical in Yiddish in Bialystok, Poland. Entitled *Der Idisher Bibliograf,* and described as a "periodical for bibliography, librarianship, and science," the 24 pages of the first (and last) issue contained, besides the introductory material, an article on Jewish folk music, a list of current plays, a list of current Yiddish textbooks, an article on librarianship, and book news.

Kotik's publication had the distinction of being the first bibliographical periodical in the Yiddish language, but it left no impression on the future development of Jewish bibliography in Yiddish. Instead, another publication, which was devoted only partially to bibliography, became instrumental in establishing Jewish bibliography in Yiddish. It was *Der Pinkes,* edited by Samuel Niger (1883—1955) and published in Vilna in 1913 as the first volume of a "yearbook for the history of Yiddish literature and language, folklore, criticism, and bibliography." Published in folio format, *Der Pinkes* included, in its section for criticism and bibliography, reviews and descriptions of new works, a list of Yiddish newspapers and periodicals published in various countries during 1912 (compiled by Zalman Reisen), a list of Yiddish works published in Russia during 1912, and a statistical review of the Yiddish book market for the same year (compiled by Moses Shalit). A supplement to this volume was a bibliography of Yiddish philology consisting of more than 500 entries (compiled by Ber Borochov). The outbreak of the war a year later interfered with the publication of additional volumes of the yearbook, but a reprint edition was published in 1923.[47]

Vilna was also the place where two bibliographical periodicals in Yiddish were launched a year later (1914), but the outbreak of World War I was once again the cause of their discontinuation. The first, entitled *Yohrbukh far Yudishe Biblioteken,* was published early in 1914; the second, entitled *Der Yudishe Bibliotekar,* was planned as a quarterly, and it appeared in April of the same year. Both were edited by Abraham Kirzhnitz (born 1888), and they came into being as a result of the liberalized policies of the Russian government with regard to legalizing established Jewish libraries.[48] The *Yohrbukh* was divided into five chapters, three of them devoted entirely to libraries and librarianship. The remaining two chapters were partially devoted to bibliography, and they included:

Brief lists of current Hebrew, Russian Judaica, and Yiddish works (topically arranged)

Lists of "confiscated books" to be removed from library shelves (1906 to April 1913)

Addresses of Jewish libraries in Russia

Addresses and subscription prices of Jewish periodicals

Addresses of Jewish bookdealers

*Der Yudishe Bibliotekar* was divided more evenly between material dealing with libraries and librarianship, and bibliography. The lists of current books were similar to those published in the *Yohrbukh,* but they were enhanced by the addition of a section of short reviews of new publications. The list of "confiscated books" covered the period from April 1913 to April 1914.[49]

The end of World War I, and the ensuing revolutions in Russia, opened up wide possibilities for Yiddish literature. A group of Yiddish activists, associated largely with the Jewish socialist organization Der Algemeyner Yidisher Arbeterbund—shortened into "Der Bund,"[50] profited from the new situation in 1918 by establishing a publishing house for Yiddish literature—"Kultur-Lige"—in Kiev in the Ukraine. A year later the group launched a bibliographical periodical entitled *Bikher Velt; Kritish-Bibliografisher Zhurnal.* Edited by Nachman Meisel (1887—1966) and A. Litvak (1874—1932), *Bikher Velt* included essays on Yiddish literature, reviews of new publications, literary news, and lists of current Yiddish books. Besides the necessary bibliographical data, the entries in the lists of current books included the price and number of copies printed. The first issue of *Bikher Velt* appeared in January 1919, and the third and last (no. 4—5) came out in August of the same year.

*Bikher Velt* was discontinued due to the changing political environment in Russia and the decision of the ruling Bolshevik party to dismantle all other political parties. The Kultur-Lige was closed down, and many of its founders decided to leave the country and moved on to Poland. The editors of *Bikher Velt* were among those who left Russia, and in 1921 they reached Warsaw where they reorganized and reestablished the Kultur-Lige.[51] In January 1922, they renewed the publication of *Bikher Velt* as a bimonthly bibliographical magazine.[52]

Published in folio size, *Bikher Velt* generally continued the format of its predecessor, but, as publication progressed, its scope was gradually enlarged. The first section of each issue was occupied by essays about Yiddish writers and Yiddish literature. Next came a section of reviews, followed by bibliographies of retrospective and current Yiddish publications and literary news items. The final section was usually devoted to obituaries and librarianship. A new feature was added with issue number six (November—December 1922): it consisted of quotations of the most striking sentences from reviews of new Yiddish works that had appeared in Yiddish periodicals in various countries.

The publication of *Bikher Velt* was interrupted after the appearance of issue number 1—2 of Volume 3 (January—April 1924), and it was resumed four years later, in April 1928, with its reappearance as a monthly magazine in quarto format. The renewed *Bikher Velt* continued to present the same features, but there was now less stress on bibliography and more on essays. Two new features were added to the revived periodical: "Notes" about Jewish literature (of a journalistic, and sometimes polemical, nature) and excerpts from letters by readers, expressing their opinions about new books. The last issue appeared in July 1929.

*Bikher Velt* contributed greatly to the systematic registration of Yiddish literature and to arousing bibliographical consciousness in Yiddish-speaking circles. Its contribution was no less important to the entire field of Jewish bibliography.[53] *Bikher Velt* was the only Jewish periodical to attract under one roof, Jewish scholars, Yiddish writers, and Yiddish readers. The gap left by its demise was partially filled by new bibliographical periodicals in Yiddish, and also by some nonbibliographical Yiddish periodicals that began to register current Yiddish books.

One of the new bibliographical periodicals in Yiddish was *Bikher Nayes,* a monthly "devoted to the Yiddish book" that appeared intermittently in Warsaw from August 1926 to July 1939. It was probably published originally as a temporary substitute for the suspended *Bikher Velt,* and it contained book reviews and lists of current Yiddish books.

An attempt to publish a Yiddish bibliographical periodical of a more scholarly nature was made in Kharkov, in the Ukraine, in 1930, with the appearance of Volume 1 of the *Bibliologisher Zamlbukh* (546 pages). The volume was published under the auspices of the Institute for Yiddish Culture of the Ukrainian Academy of Science, and it was edited by J. Liberberg. The material included, among other subjects,

> studies on the history of the Jewish printing presses in Russia
> studies on the history of the Jewish press in Russia
> bibliographical studies and book reviews
> bibliographies (Lenin in Yiddish; additions to the Peretz bibliography)
> statistical study of Yiddish book production in the Soviet Union from 1917 to 1921, and a list of books published during the same period[54]

A second volume of the *Bibliologisher Zamlbukh* never appeared, and many of the contributors to the first volume met their end in the jails of the Soviet Union, among them its editor, J. Liberberg.

Another Soviet publication was *Dos Yidishe Bukh in Sovetnfarband,* published in Minsk, in White Russia, by the Jewish Section of the Lenin Library and Bibliographical Institute during the years 1933—1936. Four issues of this periodical appeared, in which 1900 titles of Yiddish books published in the Soviet Union from 1932 through 1935 were registered.[55] One more Soviet publication was launched in Moscow in 1934 under the title *Sovetishe Yidishe Bikher Nayes.* It listed in its first issue about 130 titles, but was not continued.[56]

The latest endeavor to publish lists of current Yiddish books was begun in January 1965 by the New York-based Cyco Publishing House and Book Distribution Center (the spiritual heir of the Kultur Lige) with the occasional issuing of price lists entitled *Bikher Velt Byuletin.* A cut of the title of the Warsaw edition of *Bikher Velt* served as the title for the new *Byuletin.* The same cut was also used by Cyco for its *Bibliografishe Reshime fun Yidishe Bikher* (compiled by Isser Goldberg and published during 1964—1965) and *Dos Yidishe Bukh, di Yidishe Prese* (compiled by the above and published in New York in 1966).

## En Hakore

In 1922, when *Bikher Velt* began its Warsaw appearance, it was the only Jewish bibliographical periodical in existence. The *Zeitschrift für hebräische Bibliographie,* which had appeared with short interruptions during the span of a quarter of a century, had died of neglect two years earlier. The gap it left was not filled by *Bikher Velt,* which was concerned only with Yiddish literature (an area of little concern to the *Zeitschrift* while it was still alive). But in 1923 an attempt was made in Berlin to replace the *Zeitschrift* in the area of Hebraica literature with a quarterly "for critique and bibliography" entitled *En Hakore* (cf. Judges 15:19). The new periodical was edited by David Arye Friedman, assisted by Zvi Woislawski (both 1889—1957), and it was similar in format as well as in content to the early volumes of the Warsaw *Bikher Velt* which may have served the editors as the prototype for their publication.

Only two issues of *En Hakore* appeared (no. 1, dated January—March 1923, and no. 2/3, dated April—September 1923), and they included the following sections:

Essays devoted to a literary personality (issue no. 1: David Frishman; issue no. 2/3; Hayyim Nahman Bialik)

Essays about writers and books

Bio-bibliographies of Hebrew writers (compiled by Zechariah Fishman;[57] bio-bibliographies of the following writers were published: David Frishman, Saul Hurwitz, Reuben Brainin, Hayyim Nahman Bialik, Judah Loeb Gordon)

Reviews of current books

Literary news items; books to be published

List of current books (issue no. 1 covered the year 1922, and issue no. 2/3 covered 1923 with additions to 1922)

Several months after the publication of the second and last issue of *En Hakore,* another bibliographical periodical began to appear in Jerusalem in Hebrew which took over the systematic registration of Hebraica published in the Holy Land and in the Diaspora. This eliminated the need to continue publication of another periodical of the same nature.[58]

## Soncino Blätter

What *En Hakore* attempted to do for Hebraica after the demise of the *Zeitschrift,* another Berlin publication attempted to do for Judaica two years later. It was the *Soncino Blätter,* published by the Soncino Gesellschaft der Freunde des jüdischen Buches. Founded in Berlin in 1924 by a group of Jewish bibliophiles,[59] the Gesellschaft adopted the name of the Italian-Jewish family of printers of the fifteenth and sixteenth centuries who flourished in Soncino (in the duchy of Milan) and in other places, and who distinguished themselves by producing some of the most beautiful examples of early Hebrew printing.[60] The aim of the Gesellschaft was to publish "exemplary" editions of Jewish works, in the belief that the external appearance of Jewish books is as important as their contents, and that "the Jewish book should represent the quality of Jewish intellectual creations even in its external form."[61] True to this slogan, the Gesellschaft, in the second year of its existence, embarked on a publishing program that produced a number of outstanding examples of typographical craftsmanship.[62]

Hand in hand with the publication of "exemplary" editions, the Gesellschaft also began publishing the *Soncino Blätter,* in 1925, as a "contribution to the knowledge of the Jewish book." The *Blätter,* edited by Herrmann Meyer, appeared in folio format and was set in impressive type befitting a publication for bibliophiles. Three volumes appeared between 1925 and 1930, and, among other subjects, they included:

Essays and studies dealing with Jewish books, book collections, book production, and the history of Hebrew printing (among the participants: Jewish writers, thinkers, scholars, historians, and bibliographers, such as Arnold Zweig and Max Brod; Martin Buber and Hugo Bergmann; Ludwig Blau, Samuel Krauss, Heinrich Brody and Elia S. Artom; Majer Balaban, Moses Schorr, and Ismar Elbogen; Aron Freimann, Arthur Zacharias Schwarz, Alexander Marx, and Bernhard Wachstein)

Personal bibliographies (in Volume 1: Simon Dubnow; in Volume 3: Heinrich Brody)[63]

Notes about books; news items about book exhibits and book societies (some of a specific Jewish nature and some of a general nature, but of special interest to bibliophiles)

Book reviews

Lists of current Judaica (list in Volume 1 covered the years 1920–1925; it was compiled by the editor, and was partially based on the private collections of the members of the editorial board of the *Blätter;* list in Volume 2 covered the years 1926–1927, and it also included some Hebraica publications; there was no list of current publications in Volume 3)

The lists of current Judaica in the *Soncino Blätter* included close to 1,500 entries; each entry consisting of the following:

Author
Title
Place and date of publication
Publisher
Pagination
Format
Description of binding
Occasional critical notes

## *Kiryat Sefer* (Jerusalem)

The three volumes of the *Soncino Blätter* brought to a close the German period in Jewish bibliography.[64] The center of gravity of Jewish scholarship in the 1930s moved from Germany, either voluntarily or as a consequence of political upheaval. Palestine on the one hand, and the United States on the other, became the new centers of attraction for Jewish scholarship. The formal inauguration of the Hebrew University, the first Jewish university in modern times, was held in Jerusalem in 1925; this was the occasion for presenting to the university the collection of the Jewish National Library (which had been under the jurisdiction of the Zionist Organization since 1920) and naming it the Jewish National and University Library. The National Library had originally been formed from the collection of the Jerusalem B'nai B'rith and from the gifts of Dr. Joseph Chazanowicz (1844–1919), of Bialystok.[65] It began to grow rapidly during the first half of the 1920s, and it was felt that its merging with the university would be a blessing for both institutions.

Even before the National Library officially became part of the university, its director, Shmuel Hugo Bergmann (1883–1975), who later served as the first rector of the University, began publishing a bibliographical quarterly in Jerusalem in Hebrew, entitled *Kiryat Sefer*.[66] The new periodical, edited by a group of scholars and bibliographers associated with both the Hebrew University and the National Library,[67] was intended to serve the academic community with information about current publications of Hebraica and Judaica, and also with studies dealing with various phases of the Jewish book, printed as well as handwritten. In a statement of purpose, printed on the first page of the first issue (April 1924), the editors made it clear that the periodical was not meant to serve the "reading public at large," but was "aimed towards the professional scholars who are interested in specific research . . . in new developments in their fields, in studies of biographies of authors, and in the publication of manuscripts. . . ."[68]

In line with the stated aim, *Kiryat Sefer* was divided into five sections:

Bibliography of current publications (subdivided into books published in Palestine and books of Jewish interest published in the Diaspora)
Manuscript texts and archival materials ("From the Library treasures")
Bibliographical studies and research
Brief bibliographical comments
News items about the development of the National Library

A sixth section, entitled *Betoch Kitve Et*, was added twenty years later (beginning with Volume 21, 1944/45). It listed "the contents of periodicals in Jewish studies, in Hebrew and in other languages, and also individual essays of Jewish interest from general periodicals." Belles lettres and other nonscholarly materials were excluded from this section.

The lists of current publications in *Kiryat Sefer* were arranged by subject; the entries were complete and exact, and they were occasionally accompanied by annotations, comments, and reviews written by experts in specific fields. Volume indexes, listing authors and titles in the Hebrew, Roman, Arabic, and Cyrillic alphabets, were issued annually. Cumulative indexes, listing the studies and reviews, were issued in 1939 (covering Volumes 1—15), 1950 (covering Volumes 16—25), and 1960 (covering Volumes 26—35). An enlarged index to the first forty volumes was issued in 1967 under the title *Maftechot Lema'amarim, Lehe'arot Uledivre Bikoret.* It included lists of:

Studies
Reviews
Reviewers
Names and topics
Personal bibliographies
Manuscripts described or published
Supplements issued[69]

*Kiryat Sefer* was modeled entirely upon *Hamazkir—HB* and the *Zeitschrift für hebräische Bibliographie.* This resulted in a variety of structural weaknesses. G. Kressel, on the occasion of the appearance of Volume 20 of *Kiryat Sefer,* complained that "it does not satisfy the bibliographical demands of the wide public," and that "the reader . . . does not feel that anything has changed in the spirit and purpose that ruled during the days of *Hamazkir.*"[70] Earlier, on the occasion of the appearance of Volume 5 of *Kiryat Sefer,* S. Eisenstadt pointed out the lack of proportion and the presence of subjectivity in the reviews: "an expert criticizes his colleague out of personal envy and intentionally underscores each negligible defect in his work. . . ."[71] Five years later, on the occasion of the appearance of Volume 10 of *Kiryat Sefer,* Eisenstadt pointed out additional defects in the periodical, such as the incompleteness of the information with regard to the development of the National Library:

. . . Only books and manuscripts received as gifts are mentioned here . . . mostly without bibliographic details. Acquisitions by purchase or by exchange are not listed. There is no information on the size and development of the serials department.[72]

With regard to the section listing current books, he again found a lack of proportion in the treatment of the works: "Some important books are registered without any additional information or comment, and some second- and third-rate books are reviewed on several pages." Eisenstadt also felt that the lists of current books should not be limited to Hebrew literature and Jewish studies only, but should include the general sciences.

On the other hand, Abraham Yaari, who was also one of the coeditors of

*Kiryat Sefer,* on the same occasion stressed the basic difference between *Kiryat Sefer* and its predecessors (*Hamazkir—HB* and *ZfHB*):

> Their attention was turned mainly towards the past, and this resulted, even unknowingly, in contempt for the present. Even to chassidic and rabbinic books, which were printed in thousands of copies during the last generations, no proper attention was paid, and, of course, not to modern literature.[73]

But *Kiryat Sefer* introduced "for the first time complete equality" between the past and the present:

> A report of any Jewish economic institution appears here next to a historical study by a scholar; a work of modern Hebrew literature is registered next to a text from the Genizah in broken lines. There is also, for the first time, complete equality for the various Jewish dialects.

*Kiryat Sefer* has recently completed half a century of uninterrupted publication, a unique feat for a Jewish bibliographical periodical. Some of the weaknesses detected in the earlier volumes and pointed out by the reviewers were later overcome and corrected. A number of improvements were instituted. The contributions of *Kiryat Sefer* to the field of Jewish bibliography have been immense, and its coverage of current Jewish publications became almost complete. But no *basic* changes have taken place during all these years. The statement that laid down the policy of the periodical in the first issue is still valid, and the initial structure, which was copied from the German-language bibliographical periodicals *Hamazkir—HB* and *Zeitschrift für hebräische Bibliographie,* is still the backbone of *Kiryat Sefer.*

# II. Book-Trade Periodicals

## Hame'asef—Der Sammler

The publication of Steinschneider's *Hamazkir—Hebräische Bibliographie* in 1858 served as an inspiration for the publication of another Jewish bibliographical periodical in 1874. Chaim David Lippe, a cantor-teacher turned bookdealer,[74] convinced his partners in the Buchhandlung der

Brüder Winter in Vienna to publish such a periodical under his editorship. Encouraged by the resentment in many circles against Steinschneider's attacks in *Hamazkir—HB,* and hoping that his venture would help to stabilize the ailing Jewish book market, Lippe launched the first issue of his periodical in August 1874. Borrowing the idea of a Hebrew-German title for his publication from Steinschneider's *Hamazkir—HB* Lippe named his periodical *Hame'asef—Der Sammler.*[75]

The Hebrew-German title was the only idea Lippe borrowed from Steinschneider while preparing his periodical. Unlike *Hamazkir—HB,* which was devoted largely to scholarly bibliographical studies, Lippe planned his *Hame'asef—Der Sammler* as a Jewish version of the "*Börsenblatt* and similar periodicals." This was to be the first Jewish book-trade periodical, and was to be devoted solely to the task of bringing together the bookseller with the potential book buyer.[76] Accordingly, the new periodical included the following:

> Lists of current publications (each entry containing: author, title, contents, place, date, price)
> Books to be published (with advance reviews)
> Lists of retrospective books available from or wanted by the publishers
> Lists of Jewish bookdealers in various cities
> Lists of periodicals available on subscription from the publishers

*Hame'asef—Der Sammler* was projected as a monthly, but only three numbers were issued (totalling 52 pages). It seems that Lippe's partners were not ready to invest much in the venture, and perhaps the response was not too encouraging. Lippe himself later blamed the inexperience of one of his partners for the discontinuance of the periodical.[77] He felt that it was a mistake to have stopped publishing it. Later, when he became financially independent, Lippe revived the idea of a Jewish book trade periodical by publishing a *Bibliographisches Lexicon.*[78]

## Bloch's Book Bulletin

More than half a century separated the publication of the first Jewish book-trade periodical from the next. During that half century a new center for Jewish scholarship began to develop and take shape in the United States. The end of World War I and the collapse of the Russian and German regimes contributed to an influx of Jewish intellectuals and scholars in

North America. Their presence soon became visible in an increasing volume of published Hebraica and Judaica.

During the first postwar decade, this new Jewish population center showed little bibliographical activity,[79] but in 1929 two attempts were made by Jewish bookdealers in New York to launch bibliographical periodicals as an aid to the book trade. One succeeded in issuing only two pamphlets, and the other continued publication with interruption for about forty years. The one that failed was published by Reznick, Menschel and Company, and it was entitled *Olam Hasefarim;* "a quarterly for bibliography and information on current books." The other, which had the distinction of becoming the first Jewish bibliographical periodical in the English language, was published monthly by the oldest Jewish bookstore in the United States, the Bloch Publishing Company.

Founded in Cincinnati in 1854, the Bloch Publishing Company moved to New York in 1901, and there it developed an extensive Jewish book trade. In February 1929 the first issue of *Bloch's Book Bulletin,* a handy booklet in octavo, appeared, featuring:

> Notes and news dealing with current Jewish publications
> Bibliographies and price lists of current and retrospective Hebraica and Judaica (English, French, and German)

Additional issues followed, new features were added, and existing ones were extended. In time, the *Bulletin* became the only source of reliable information about the Jewish book market and Jewish publication activities. To reflect the *Bulletin's* growing coverage of Hebraica publications, a Hebrew title page—*Iton Bibliyografi*—was added with issue number 5 (November 1929). The names of the editors began to appear on the title page with issue number 43 (January–February 1937). Up to and including issue number 106 (May–July 1953), the *Bulletin* was edited jointly by Anna Fisch and Solomon Kerstein; later, by Kerstein alone.

During the 1960s the *Bulletin* began to appear only semiannually and annually, and "due to increased production and distribution cost" its mailing was restricted, in the summer of 1966, to "active accounts" and "requests only." The last issue (no. 166/67) appeared in winter, 1969.


## Das Jüdische Buch and
## Bibliographie des Jüdischen Buches

The publication of *Bloch's Book Bulletin* served as a signal for other bookdealers, in other countries, to launch publications of a similar nature. In April 1931 the Frankfort bookdealer Joel Sänger issued the first number of *Das jüdische Buch; eine bibliographische Monatsschrift*. It consisted of sixteen mimeographed leaves, listing current Judaica. A second issue was never published, but instead Sänger followed up the first, three years later, with a *Bibliographie des jüdischen Buches,* a quarterly publication of which only four issues appeared (Heft 1−3/4, 1933−1934; Jahrgang II, Heft 1−2, 1935). The four issues together listed more than 1,200 Judaica titles. A planned fifth issue (Jahrgang II, Heft 3−4), with an index to both volumes, did not materialize.

## Hamodi'a

Also in 1931 there began to appear a Hebrew bibliographical publication, issued in Lvov, Poland, by the bookstore of Reuben Margulies (1889—1971). A prolific scholar and a renowned bibliographer, Margulies devoted many years of his life to the Jewish book trade, first in his hometown of Lvov and then in Tel Aviv. He later served as director of the Rambam Library in Tel Aviv.[80] In November 1931, Margulies published the first number of *Hamodi'a*, "a monthly for bibliography, book reviews, and booklore." During the next three years (1932−1934) an additional thirteen numbers appeared; and in 1935, after Margulies transferred his bookstore to Tel Aviv the first issue of a new series appeared. Six more issues were published at irregular intervals during the next three years (1935−1936; 1938).

*Hamodi'a* consisted of sixteen-page pamphlets, devoted almost entirely to listing Hebraica books available at Margulies's bookstore. Here and there appeared a study or a review, but these were exceptions. The lists were arranged alphabetically by title, current and retrospective, in a single alphabet and, since most entries did not include dates of publication, it was impossible to distinguish the old from the new. Bibliographically it was a great disappointment, and, of the three functions of the publication described in its subtitle, only the first was partially realized.

## Alim

In contradistinction to *Hamodi'a* stands another dealer's periodical in Hebrew, published in Vienna by the bibliographer and bookdealer, David Fränkel (born 1876). Entitled *Alim Lebibliyografyah Vekorot Yisrael,* it was published as a quarterly for almost four years. The first issue (Jahrg. I, Heft 1) appeared in June 1934, and the last (Jahrg. III, Heft 3) was published in February 1938. *Alim* featured:

> Lists of current Hebraica (arranged by title; each entry containing: title, author, description, pagination, place and date of publication, format, price)
> Bibliographical and historical studies and comments
> Lists of retrospective Hebraica available at Fränkel's bookstore (arranged by title, with complete bibliographical information)
> Lists of current Judaica (arranged by author, with complete bibliographical information)

The editor and publisher himself participated heavily with bibliographical studies and comments, and by attaching interesting bibliographical footnotes to the lists of current Hebraica. These footnotes served a dual purpose: to give additional information about authors and works included in the listings, and to call the attention of the reader to other works by the same author or to works of a similar nature by other authors which are available at the Fränkel bookstore. Other contributors of studies and comments were such scholars and bibliographers as Elkan Adler, Simcha Assaf, Simon Bernstein,[81] Joshua Bloch, Aron Freimann, A. M. Habermann, Michael Higger, Guido Kisch, Samuel Krauss, Jacob Mann, and Isaac Rivkind.

## Megilat Sefer

One of the last of this type of publication by individual Jewish bookdealers was issued in Jerusalem during the years 1934–1939. It appeared under the title *Megilat Sefer,* with an added English title, *Bulletin of New Books,* and it was published by Rubin Mass, previously a Jewish bookdealer in Berlin.[82] *Megilat Sefer* registered current books only, in subject arrangement. Five issues were published, with an average of between 150 to 200 entries in each issue.

## Hed Hasefer and Tachazit Hasefer

In 1939, the last year in which *Megilat Sefer* appeared, the United Hebrew Book Publishers of Palestine came into being. This group, consisting of thir-

teen founding members, considered one of its goals to be the establishment
of a trade periodical for the benefit of Hebrew book sellers and book buyers
in Palestine and in other countries. The outbreak of World War II, with its
damaging effect on the book trade, gave impetus for such a project, and in
1941 the group, with the assistance of the Bialik Institute,[83] published a
periodical entitled *Hed Hasefer.*

*Hed Hasefer* consisted of three sections:

> Notes concerning books (including a topically arranged list of Hebrew books
> published in Palestine from September 1939 through July 1941, and reports on
> publishing activities in the land)
> Reviews and evaluations of current Hebrew books
> Literary supplement (consisting of poems and essays extracted from current
> works) and advertisements by publishers

*Hed Hasefer* did not continue, and for several years the Hebrew Book
Publishers were content to issue occasional book bulletins for the use of
their members.[84] In 1946 they began publishing collective catalogs,[85] and a
year later they attempted to publish an English-Hebrew periodical entitled
*Palestine Book News* jointly with the Foreign Trade Institute, but abandoned it after issuing several numbers. Another unsuccessful effort at establishing a Hebrew book-trade periodical was made five years later by a
private company in Tel Aviv, the Bernstein-Cohen (formerly: A. Karmi)
Literary Agency. Entitled *Tachazit Hasefer* (subhead: "Israel's Monthly of
the Book Trade"), the new publication made its appearance in August 1953,
and ceased with the third issue in October of the same year. *Tachazit
Hasefer* was a handy publication that included the following features:

> Reports on developments in the Hebrew book trade
> Literary news items (divided into domestic and foreign)
> List of books published during the preceding month
> List of books to be published during the current month
> Miscellaneous articles relating to books and book publishing

## *Olam Hasefer* and *Hasefer Beyisrael*

The features established in *Tachazit Hasefer* were adopted several months
later by a new periodical launched by the Hebrew Book Publishers. Entitled
*Olam Hasefer,* the new periodical began publication in April 1954, and it

continued at irregular intervals for about four years; the last issue (no. 16; i.e., no. 14) was dated October 1958.

After an interruption of about one year, the same group (now known as the Book Publishers Association of Israel) began publishing another Hebrew book-trade periodical, entitled *Hasefer Beyisrael,* with an English title page, *Book News from Israel.* The first issue appeared in December 1959, and its internal structure was similar to the defunct *Tachazit Hasefer* and *Olam Hasefer,* but it differed greatly externally. The tastefully designed covers and layout made it much more attractive than its predecessors, and may have been an important factor in its continuing publication. Contributing to the outer attractiveness of each issue of *Hasefer Beyisrael* were special cover illustrations of bibliographical significance—such as scenes from illuminated Hebrew manuscripts, Hebrew printers' marks, and Jewish ex-libris.[86]

## *Israel Book Publishers' Quarterly,*
## *Israel Book Publishers' Bulletin*
## and *Israel Book World*

Encouraged by the success of its *Hasefer Beyisrael,* the association launched an English version of that periodical one year later under the title *The Israel Book Publishers' Quarterly.* After the first two issues (nos. 1−2/3, December 1960-December 1961), the title was changed to *Israel Book Publishers' Bulletin.* The change of name did not alter the fate of this periodical, and after three more numbers were issued during a four-year period (no. 4, April 1963; no. 5, December 1966; no. 6, March 1967), publication was discontinued.

It was only three years later that a book-trade periodical in the English language began to appear in Israel on a regular basis. Entitled *Israel Book World* (reminiscent of the Hebrew title *Olam Hasefer*), it was published in Jerusalem by the Israel Book and Printing Center of the Israel Export Institute, and it was edited by Israel Soifer. The "Statement of Purpose" that appeared in the first issue (August 1970) announced its "aim of providing timely information about printing and publishing in Israel, . . ." to inform its readers "about recently published books and about forthcoming projects," and to "record Israel's resources in authors and authorities, in translators and editors, in graphic artists and illustrators, in publishers, printers, and booksellers." Accordingly, *Israel Book World* was divided into three main sections:

Feature articles about new publications, book market events, book production
and distribution statistics, etc.
News items and reports relating to publishing activities in Israel ("The Publishing
Picture")
Information on printing facilities in Israel ("Printing Services")

There were also smaller sections, such as:

Information about new and forthcoming publications ("Publishers' Showcase,"
arranged alphabetically by the names of the publishers)
Description of new periodicals ("Periodical Parade," with addresses of publishers
and prices of subscriptions)
Obituaries of literary personalities
Brief notices about people involved in literary and publishing activities ("Per-
sonal/Personnel")

## Collective Book-Publishers' Catalogs

Efforts to acquaint the potential Hebrew book buyer with current publications also brought to the fore the question of how to make him aware of the
existence of other noncurrent Hebrew materials. The United Hebrew Book
Publishers tried to tackle this problem in 1946 by proposing to issue collective catalogs and collective subject lists of members periodically. Indeed, a
volume entitled *Reshimat Hasefarim Umafteach* was issued in Tel Aviv in
1946. It was a loose-leaf binder, consisting of about twenty individual
catalogs published by members during the years 1943–1945, and preceded
by a topically arranged index to guide the user to the various catalogs. The
group of catalogs together registered more than three thousand works,
representing the bulk of Hebrew literature published in Palestine since the
end of World War I.

*Reshimat Hasefarim* was supplemented a year later with a *Mafteach
Lakatalogim* (Tel Aviv, 1947). This was a two-part, author-title index,
providing for each entry the name of the publisher and the price. The index
was preceded by a list of names and addresses of the member publishers.
The political and economic changes that took place in the following year
with the establishment of the State of Israel prevented the Hebrew Book
Publishers from continuing the regular publication of additional collective
catalogs. In the early 1950s the Association established an office in New York,
and on that occasion it published a thirty-four-page *Katalog Me'uchad* (Tel
Aviv, 1951). It was a topically arranged pamphlet that represented a selec-

tion from the more than 4,000 books in print and available from the member publishers. A more complete catalog could not be published "due to the paper shortage" in Israel.

The inability of the Hebrew Book Publishers to continue the regular publication of collective catalogs opened the door for an individual entrepreneur—Jacob Bar-David of the Bar-David Literary Agency—to enter the field and, in 1957, he issued a volume in Tel Aviv entitled *Katalog Hasefer Hayisra'eli—Israel Book Catalog*. The volume consisted of four sections:

Book catalogs of more than 50 Israeli publishers (arranged in alphabetical order by the name of the publishers)
Index of titles
Index of authors
Index of subjects

The publication of Bar-David's *Katalog* brought to life the Book Publishers Association of Israel (formerly the United Hebrew Book Publishers), and in 1959 an extended edition of the *Mafteach Lakatalogim* appeared under the title *Mafteach Kelali Lekatalogim* (Tel Aviv, 1959). The new volume registered authors and titles originally listed in catalogs issued by members of the Association up to 1958. The entries were brief, giving only author, title (or vice-versa), publisher, and page number of the particular catalog.

During the same year, 1959, Volume 2 of Bar-David's *Katalog* appeared, covering 1958/59. Volume 3 was published in 1960, and Volume 4 in 1961. Volume 4 was the largest, including catalogs from more than seventy publishers, and it was also the last, for in the same year the Book Publishers Association issued a bulky volume entitled *Katalog Sefarim Kelali*, the first in a series of volumes to be published at regular intervals.

The Association's *Katalog* incorporated the features of the *Reshimat Hasefarim Umafteach*, published in 1946, and the Bar-David *Katalog*. Thus, it included:

Original catalogs of Association members only
Index of titles (on colored paper)
Index of authors
Index of subjects (much broader than in Bar-David's *Katalog;* on colored paper)

Volume 2, even bulkier than the first volume, was issued in 1964—1965. Volume 3 appeared in 1968, with a few improvements. The dealers' catalogs were reset in a uniform type, and each catalog was preceded by a brief account of the history and aims of the company. The resetting of the catalogs made the volume less bulky and much easier to handle. Volume 4 was published in 1969, and Volume 5, produced with the help of a computer, was issued in 1973. This volume registered about 15,000 titles from the lists of more than 100 publishers (74 Association members and 28 nonmembers), and it was edited by Zvi Shteiner. The material here was also divided into four groups, but in reverse order, placing the publishers' lists as the last group. It was this last group that contained the most important bibliographical details in the entire volume. These included the following:

Title
Author
Occasional description
Indication whether original work or translation
Original language of work
Language translated from
Translator
Illustrator
Number of volumes or pages
Price

## Judaica Book Guide and Judaica Book News

While the publishers in Israel were busy finding ways and means to promote the Hebrew book, their counterparts, the Judaica dealers in the United States, did very little for the promotion of English-language Judaica. It is true that in October 1946 a *Jewish Book Guild News* came into being, published in New York by the Jewish Book Guild of America, a sort of a Jewish Book-of-the-Month-Club, but this publication featured mainly those books which the Guild offered to its members, making its coverage of other Judaica works very limited. Only in September 1967 did a trade publication devoted entirely to English-language Judaica make its appearance in the United States. Entitled *Judaica Book Guide,* and published as a quarterly by the Jonathan David Company of New York, it featured:

News items of literary significance ("Of Books and Authors")
Annotated list of current Judaica ("The Quarterly Record")
Reviews
List of books scheduled for publication

*Judaica Book Guide* appeared for about two years (last issue: June 1969?), and it was replaced in the fall of 1970 by *Judaica Book News,* published semiannually by Bookazine Company, of New York. The new publication included:

    News items of literary significance
    Feature articles relating to books
    Lists of new and forthcoming books
    Indexes to advertised books (title index, author index, and advertisers index)
    List of best sellers

## M. B. S. Reference Catalogue

Menorah Book Service of London compiled and published a *Reference Catalogue of Books of Jewish Interest in English Available in Print* in 1968. Volume 2 appeared in 1970, listing more than 2,700 titles classified into about 50 categories, and supplemented by author and title indexes.

# III. Bibliographical Periodicals Covering Specific Countries

## Sefer Hashanah
### Lebibliyografyah Yehudit Bepolanyah

The coverage of current publications by the various Jewish bibliographical periodicals, with the exception of trade periodicals, was intended to be universal. That was an unattainable ideal; in fact, the periodicals did not completely cover the publications of even a single country. *Kiryat Sefer,* the organ of the Jewish National and University Library in Jerusalem, was the first Jewish bibliographical periodical to introduce a separate listing for the publications of one specific country—Palestine-Israel—having as its goal to cover a geographic area as fully as possible.

    A similar goal was adopted in 1936 by the Warsaw Society of Friends of the Hebrew University in Jerusalem, when it launched a bibliographical annual to register works of Jewish interest published in Poland. Entitled *Sefer Hashanah Lebibliyografyah Yehudit Bepolanyah* (Warsaw, 1936), with separate title pages in Polish and Yiddish and edited by Edward Isaac Jacob Poznanski (1902–1974),[87] it covered works in Hebrew, Polish, and Yiddish, published during 1934.[88] The annual was divided into three sections: Hebrew (142 entries), Yiddish (330 entries), and Polish (163 entries), and it offered complete bibliographical information for each entry. The changing world situation and the departure of the editor for Palestine prevented the publication of additional volumes.

## Jewish Book Annual

The idea of providing bibliographical coverage of the Jewish book output in a single country was also adopted in the United States. It began with the publication of Jewish book lists for the celebration of Jewish Book Week which were compiled by Fanny Goldstein, a librarian at the Boston Public Library, who had also originated the idea of the Book Week. The Jewish Book Week celebrations later developed on a national scale, and in 1940 a National Committee for Jewish Book Week was formed to assist local groups in planning their programs. In 1942 the National Committee began publishing a *Jewish Book Week Annual,* and in 1943—after the National Committee became the Jewish Book Council and Jewish Book Week was replaced by Jewish Book Month—the title was changed to *Jewish Book Annual.*

The first ten volumes of the *Jewish Book Annual* (1942–1951/52) were divided into three linguistic sections: English, Hebrew, and Yiddish, each having separate title pages and independent material. Each section included bibliographical and literary essays, reviews, surveys, and occasional bibliographies of current publications. This format was changed with Volume 11 (1952/53), when the linguistic division was abolished and a single pagination and a unified table of contents were established. The final shape of *Jewish Book Annual* was established with Volume 13 (1955/56), when the material in each volume was divided into three major groups:

Bibliographical essays and studies (in all three languages)
Literary anniversaries of authors (short biographical articles and evaluations in all three languages; occasional personal bibliographies; calendar of anniversaries)

Bibliographies of current publications (began to appear regularly with volume nine); divided into Judaica (American Jewish nonfiction books; American Jewish fiction books; American books on Zionism and Israel; American Jewish juvenile literature; Judaica published in England), Hebrew (American Hebrew books; selection of Hebrew books published in Israel), Yiddish (American Yiddish books; recently extended to cover universal output)

The *Jewish Book Annual* thus became an essential tool for information on current Jewish book publication in the United States. Cumulative indexes published in Volumes 11 (1952/53), 20 (1962/63), and 25 (1967/68) assist the user in gaining easy access to the material accumulated in the first twenty-five volumes of the *Jewish Book Annual*.

## *Katalog farn Khoydesh fun Yidishn Bukh*

The idea of a Jewish Book Month also attracted attention beyond the borders of the United States,[89] and in Argentina it was adopted, with some modifications, by the representative body of Argentinian Jews, the Asociación Mutual Israelita Argentina. As part of their annual Book Month activities, the Asociación began in 1947 to sponsor a central Jewish book fair. By 1961 the fair had reached such proportions that the organizers decided to publish an annual *Katalog farn Khoydesh fun Yidishn Bukh,* in which potential book buyers would find all the necessary information about the fair. The *Katalog* was thus divided into the following sections:

Yiddish (with subsection of children's books)
Hebrew (with subsections of children's and rabbinic books)
Spanish Judaica
Foreign Judaica (mostly German and English; began with 1962 volume)
Jewish playing records (began with 1963 volume)

The entries were arranged alphabetically by the names of the authors (a topical arrangement of all sections was instituted with the 1969 issue), and they included:

Author
Title
Place and date of publication (beginning with 1962 volume)
Publisher (beginning with 1962 volume)
Pagination (beginning with 1966 volume)
Price (including discounts)

## *Dapim, Yad Lakore, En Hakore*
## and again *Yad Lakore*

The need for bibliographical periodicals designed to serve the librarian and the general reader became acute in Palestine in the early 1940s. The reason for this urgency was the establishment of numerous new libraries by various Jewish organizations and communities. *Kiryat Sefer,* published by the Jewish National and University Library, was not designed to offer up-to-date bibliographic information to the general Hebrew reader or librarian, and it remained an isolated bibliographical periodical for the benefit of a few.

An effort to fill this bibliographic gap was made in July 1942 by the cultural department (section for libraries) of the representative body of the Jewish community in Palestine, the Va'ad Le'umi, when it began to publish a periodical in Jerusalem entitled *Dapim Liyedi'at Hasefer Vehasafranut.* Edited by Haim Bar-Dayan (born 1899) and described as an aid "for those who are active in public libraries," it continued as a quarterly "nontrade" publication until October 1943. All together, five issues appeared (July, October 1942; February, June, October 1943), in which the following was included:

> Lists of current publications (with prices)
> Special bibliographies
> Book reviews
> Articles and information on books, libraries, and librarianship

Even before the final issue of *Dapim* was published, a substitute periodical came into being and took over the function of the soon to be defunct *Dapim,* appearing in Tel Aviv in August 1943 under the title *Yad Lakore, Lasafran, Lamoreh, Lamadrich Ulefe'ile Tarbut.* Published jointly by the Histadrut and Hakibuts Hame'uchad and edited by Shlomo Derech, *Yad Lakore* was a continuation of a periodical by the same title that had been published by Hakibuts Hame'uchad in En Charod from the summer of 1938 to the winter of 1941. A total of four issues had appeared of the original *Yad Lakore,* and they contained short lists of current publications and book reviews mainly of kibbutz interest. The new *Yad Lakore* extended its coverage (beginning with the December 1943 issue) to the entire field of current Hebrew books published in Palestine. It thus featured:

> Articles and news items dealing with libraries and librarianship
> Book reviews

Personal and subject bibliographies
Lists of current Hebrew publications

The new *Yad Lakore* was planned as a bimonthly, but only six numbers in four issues were published, the last one (no. 5−6) being dated August 1944. The bibliographical gap thus created was soon filled by an annual publication entitled *En Hakore,* reminiscent of a periodical with the same title published more than twenty years earlier in Berlin. The new periodical, edited by Emanuel Bin Gorion (born 1903) and published by Bet Michah Yosef, a Tel Aviv city library established in memory of his father, Micha Joseph Bin Gorion (Berdichevsky), listed current Palestinian Hebrew imprints only. *En Hakore* appeared for a period of three years (1944/45− 1946/47), further publication being unnecessary after the appearance of a new periodical, again called *Yad Lakore.*

The new *Yad Lakore* (with an added English title *The Reader's Aid*) was launched in Tel Aviv, again jointly by the Histadrut and Hakibuts Hame'uchad, in May−June 1946. First it was published as a bimonthly, later (beginning with Volume 2) as a quarterly. The subtitle of the first two volumes was similar to the one that preceded it; this was later changed several times.[90] The constant changes in the subtitle may have been a reflection of the unstable condition of the new periodical, and the frequent turnover of its editors and publishers.[91] This probably also affected the publication schedule of the periodical to the extent that during the first two decades of its existence only eight volumes were published.[92] Relatively regular publication began with Volume 8, number 2 (March 1967).

The changes of editors and publishers also affected the structure of the periodical. Volume 1 was divided into three main sections:

Essays and studies about books and libraries
Bibliographies (personal and subject) and lists of current Hebrew books
Book reviews

In Volume 2 the book review section dwindled greatly, and the lists of current books were expanded, resulting in a special 120-page supplement.[93] The lists were discontinued with Volume 3, and the book reviews began to pick up again with Volume 6. The contents of the essays and studies also went through a certain transformation. The first volumes devoted more space to the history of Hebrew bibliography and bibliographers[94] and to personal bibliographies of modern Hebrew authors; the later volumes, although continuing to include personal and subject bibliographies, concentrated more on articles of a professional nature, including practical librarianship.

*Yad Lakore* today is becoming an *aid* for the librarians of public libraries in Israel. The *kore,* the average reader, would find it of little help.

## Kuntres Bibliyografi

One year after the appearance of the first issue of *Yad Lakore,* its future publisher, the Department of Libraries of the Histadrut, began to issue a bimonthly mimeographed bibliographical publication which listed current books. Published consecutively under such titles as *Yad Lasafran, Hasafran,* and *Alim Lasafran,* this publication appeared during a span of three years, from May 1947 to March 1950, and was discontinued because in April of that year the Department of Libraries took over publication of *Yad Lakore* in which a special section was devoted to the listing of current books. But the publisher felt that, to meet the need for quick information about new books, a more frequent publication was in order than the quarterly *Yad Lakore.* This feeling was also shared by the United Hebrew Book Publishers (later known as Book Publishers' Association of Israel). Consequently, both joined in issuing a monthly list of current Hebrew publications, entitled *Kuntres Bibliyografi.*[95]

The new publication began to appear in Tel Aviv in April 1951,[96] and was compiled and edited by Reuben Levi (1888–1965). Levi had previously prepared the lists of current books for *Yad Lakore,* but the publication of the *Kuntres* made their continuance in *Yad Lakore* superfluous, so they were discontinued. Levi compiled and edited the first fifteen volumes of the *Kuntres,* and after his death the work was continued by Samuel Lachower, who compiled and edited Volumes 16 (1965/66) to 20 (1969/70). The *Kuntres* ceased publication with number 11/12 of Volume 20, dated July–September 1970.

*Kuntres Bibliyografi* was published as a monthly, and it registered books and periodicals in a topical arrangement. The entries were complete, and they offered detailed bibliographical information, including tables of contents and frequent bibliographical annotations. Volume indexes, listing authors, editors, publishers, and titles, were issued annually.

## Shenaton Hamemshalah
## and Reshimat Sifre Chovah

While the publication of *Kuntres Bibliyografi* was still in the planning stages, an annual Israel government publication, *Shenaton Hamemshalah,* introduced a listing of Hebrew books published in Israel. Beginning with the volume for the year 1950/51, these lists appeared regularly in each volume of the *Shenaton.*[97] They were arranged by broad subjects, and the entries included the most essential bibliographical information.

An attempt to register the entire book production of Israel officially was made a few years later by the Israel State Archives and Library. Encouraged by the depository copies it had begun to receive as a result of a law that went into effect in 1953, in June 1954 the State Archives and Library began publishing a bimonthly entitled *Reshimat Sifre Chovah Shenitkablu Beganzach Hamedinah Vehasifriyah.* An added title in English read *List of Books Deposited in the State Archives and Library.* The publication continued to June 1957 (Volume 2, number 6), and it was partially replaced by a list issued periodically by the library of the Keneset.[98]

The published issues of *Reshimat Sifre Chovah* were divided into three sections:

List of works (consisting of reproduced catalog cards arranged by author)
List of publishers (and under the name of each publisher, the list of books he published)
List of titles

## Megilat Hasefer

The bibliographical periodicals published in Israel during the 1940s and 1950s were mainly intended to supply the Hebrew reader in Israel with book information. A bibliographical Hebrew periodical with a distinct orientation towards the potential Hebrew reader outside Israel began publication in Jerusalem in 1957. Entitled *Megilat Hasefer,* it was edited by A. M. Habermann and published by the World Hebrew Union, with the assistance of the Department for Education and Culture in the Diaspora of the World Zionist Organization. Its English subtitle described it as a "quarterly devoted to new Hebrew books." Only three issues were published during a period of one year (spring, summer 1957; spring 1958), and it ceased thereafter.

*Megilat Hasefer* contained the following features:

Articles and news items about books and libraries
Reviews of modern Hebrew works published in Israel
Lists of current publications
Lists of forthcoming publications

Each issue also contained a special additional list of Hebrew works. Issue one included a list of a basic Hebrew book collection of fifty titles; issue two listed a selection of Hebrew periodicals published in and outside Israel; and issue three featured children's books in Hebrew and a selection of available Hebrew dictionaries and lists of terminologies.

## Accessions List: Israel

Another publication, produced in Israel but meant to serve Hebraists, Judaists, and librarians in countries other than Israel, came into being in the 1960s. This publication was the result of a book-buying program conducted by the United States under the terms of Public Law 480. The law, officially designated as the Agricultural Trade Development and Assistance Act and also known as the Food for Peace program, was passed by Congress in 1954. Under its terms, underdeveloped countries were permitted to acquire American surplus food and pay for it in their own currencies; the accumulated currencies were to be spent in the purchasing countries on economic and cultural activities. The law was amended in 1958[99] to authorize the Librarian of Congress to establish book-purchasing programs in the countries benefiting from Public Law 480; the books acquired with the accumulated local currencies were also to be distributed to American libraries other than the Library of Congress. Since Israel was one of the benefiting countries, the Library of Congress opened an American Libraries Book Procurement Center in Tel Aviv early in 1964 and began book acquisition activities.[100]

Initially, twelve American research libraries participated in the program (this number later grew to twenty-five), and the Book Procurement Center in Tel Aviv, as an extra service to these libraries, prepared preliminary catalog slips for each item acquired and mailed them to the participant libraries together with the books. These slips were assembled to produce a monthly record of purchasing activities, entitled *Accession List: Israel*. Each issue of the list was divided into two sections:

Monographs (with a subsection of nonbook materials, such as maps, etc.)
Serials

The entries were prepared according to the rules of the American Library Association. Hebrew works, or works in Hebrew characters, were given main entries in Roman characters, with the title and the rest of the title page

information in Hebrew. Annotations and additional bibliographical information were given in English. Titles in Hebrew characters were also
romanized to assist American library personnel not versed in the Hebrew
alphabet in their matching and identification activities. Author indexes were
issued at the end of the calendar year, and an *Annual Cumulated List of
Serials* was issued at the beginning of each fiscal year (July).

During the span of a decade, and especially after the demise of *Kuntres
Bibliyografi*, the *Accession List: Israel* performed a double function: to serve
as an aid to the librarians and users of American libraries participating in
the PL 480 program, and to serve as a bibliographical register and a major
source of information on current Israeli publications.[101] The PL 480 book
acquisitions program in Israel ended in 1973 due to the drying up of Israeli
lira deposits in American accounts, and the final issue (Volume 10, number
4) of *Accession List: Israel*—which had been launched in April 1964—was
dated January—April 1973.[102]

# IV. Periodicals Serving Scholars,
# Students and Bibliographers

## *Journal of Jewish Bibliography*

Several years before the *Jewish Book Annual* was launched in New York by
the National Committee for Jewish Book Week,[103] a scholar and bibliographer in the same city began to publish an English-language Jewish
bibliographical periodical of a different nature, perhaps the first of its kind
in the field of Jewish bibliography. It was the *Journal of Jewish Bibliography*,
a quarterly established and edited by Joshua Bloch (1890—1957), head of
the Jewish Division of the New York Public Library, "in collaboration with
eminent scholars." In the first issue, dated October 1938, the editor
described "the purpose of the *Journal* . . . to serve as a repository of
bibliographical information and other matters pertaining to Jewish
booklore . . . to fill a gap, created by the discontinuance of such publications as the *Zeitschrift für hebräische Bibliographie*, and the *Soncino Blätter*."

The *Journal*, in fact, tried to fill the gap only partially, since a major function of the above-mentioned bibliographical periodicals was the listing of current publications, something that the *Journal* did not intend to do. Even *Soncino Blätter,* which may have served as the prototype for the *Journal,* included lists of current books. The policy of the *Journal* was to list "only those publications which are sent to the editorial office. . . ." But in the area of Jewish bibliographic studies and research, the *Journal* surely filled a gap. The *Journal* seems to have been the first Jewish bibliographical periodical devoted solely to bibliographic studies, essays, and reviews. Although the *Journal* was oriented toward the reader of English, some of its materials were also in German and Hebrew. Among the participants were bibliographers and scholars such as Israel Davidson, Ismar Elbogen, Aron Freimann, Michael Higger, Raphael Mahler, Alexander Marx, Isaac Rivkind, Cecil Roth, Isaiah Sonne, and Solomon Zeitlin.

Fifteen issues of the *Journal of Jewish Bibliography* were published from October 1938 to July 1943 (Volumes 1−4, number 3). The decision to cease publication might have been influenced, among other reasons, by the emergence of the *Jewish Book Annual.*

## Studies in Bibliography and Booklore

A decade after Bloch's *Journal* ceased publication, another Jewish bibliographical periodical made its appearance in Cincinnati, Ohio; it was similar in nature and structure to the *Journal* but more sophisticated and advanced. *Studies in Bibliography and Booklore* (reminiscent of the title of a book by the renowned Alexander Marx[104]), which was published by the library of the Hebrew Union College-Jewish Institute of Religion and edited by its director, Herbert C. Zafren (born 1925), made its first appearance in June 1953. The purpose of the publication, it was stated, was to reintroduce "the study of the *Book* into the realm of scientific research," a task begun originally by Bartolocci, Wolf, and Steinschneider, who "believed that books attain scientific dignity only through association with the life of the author or through literary evaluation."

True to its stated aims, the new periodical concentrated on publishing studies, special bibliographies, and, to a lesser degree, reviews. The studies, written in English, German, and Hebrew, dealt with various aspects of the Jewish book, and the special bibliographies were devoted to historical and literary topics. For example, "A Catalogue of the Hebrew Books Printed in the 15th Century Now in the Library of the Hebrew Union College," by

Moses Marx, was printed in Volume 1 (1953/54); "Judaica—Napoleonica:
A Bibliography of Books, Pamphlets, and Printed Documents, 1801—
1815," by Zosa Szajkowski, was printed in Volume 2 (1955/56); "A Supplementary Falasha Bibliography," by Wolf Leslau, appeared in Volume 3
(1957/58); and "The Khazars: An Annotated Bibliography," by Bernard D.
Weinryb, was published in Volume 6 (1962—64). Volume 7 (1965) was
devoted entirely to "The Haggadah: Past and Present," and part of Volume
8 (1968) dealt with Judeo-Persian studies. Among the participants with
studies and occasional comments were the following bibliographers and
scholars: Abraham Duker, Philip Friedman, A. M. Habermann, Lawrence
Marwick, James Parkes, Joseph Reider, Isaac Rivkind, Judah Rosenthal,
Cecil Roth, Alexander Scheiber, Isaiah Sonne, and Abraham Yaari.

## Areshet

The publication in the United States of the English-language *Studies in
Bibliography and Booklore* preceded by five years the publication in Israel of
a similar periodical in Hebrew. Published by the Rabbi Kook Institute in
Jerusalem[105] and edited by Naftali Ben-Menahem (1911—1974) and Itzhak
Raphael (born 1914), the new periodical made its appearance in 1958 under
the title *Areshet* ("an annual of Hebrew booklore").[106] It was a bulky volume
that included:

> Bibliographical essays, studies, and notes
> Histories of Hebrew printing presses
> Special bibliographies
> Obituaries for writers who passed away during the preceding year (dropped in
> Volume 5)
> List of publications by the Institute for preceding year (dropped with Volume 4)

*Areshet* attracted many well-known Hebrew scholars and bibliographers,
and the material published in its first five volumes is most impressive. For
example, "The Parenzo Printers in Venice," by A. M. Habermann,
"Hebrew Printing in Izmir," by A. Yaari, "The Monash Printing House at
Krotoschin," by A. Posner, "Hebrew Periodicals in Hungary," by N. Katzburg, and "Seventy Years of Rabbinic Periodicals in Transylvania," by Y.
Y. Kohen, were printed in Volume 1 (1958). J. I. Dienstag published, in
Volumes 2 (1960), 3 (1961), and 4 (1966), a series of bibliographies on works
by Maimonides *(Be'ur Milot Hahigayon: Igeret Teman; Sefer Hamitsvot);* I.

Raphael published, in Volumes 2 and 3, a bibliography of *Shivche Habesht;* and J. Rosenthal published, in the same volumes, a bibliography of anti-Christian polemics. Volume 2 also contained S. Weingarten's index to *Magyar Zsidó Szemle* (1884–1948). M. Benayahu's bibliography of *Shivche Ha'ari* was printed in Volumes 3 and 4, and his and I. Mehlmann's studies of the Hebrew printing presses in Safed and Venice appeared in the same volumes. In Volume 4 also appeared the Hebrew translation of Steinschneider's *Vorlesungen über die Kunde hebräischer Handschriften,* with notes and additions by Habermann.[107] Volume 5 (1972) included, among others, Habermann's bibliography of *Masechet Purim,* Y. Y. Kohen's index of nineteenth-century rabbinic responsa from Transylvania, and J. Hacker's bibliography of nineteenth-century Hebrew imprints from Constantinople.

Other participants in *Areshet* included: N. Allony, S. Bernstein, E. D. Goldschmidt, A. J. Katsh, G. Kressel, A. R. Malachi, R. Margulies (bibliographical references to rabbinic works, published in Volumes 1, 2, 4), A. Mirsky, T. Preshel, Y. Ratzabi, A. Scheiber, J. Schirmann, M. H. Schmelczer, and H. Yalon.

## Hasefer, Tagim and Ale Sefer

*Areshet,* although published by an organization devoted to the study and dissemination of rabbinic literature,[108] also included material of a nonrabbinic nature, and even admitted participants with a secular point of view. Its obituary section—published in the first four volumes—included names of religious as well as nonreligious authors. A bibliographical periodical devoted solely to Jewish religious literature was first published in Jerusalem four years before the appearance of the first volume of *Areshet.* Entitled *Hasefer,* it was published by the Jerusalem-based Central Torah Library in Israel and was edited by its librarian, Zvi Harkavy (born 1908). This periodical, which made its first appearance in May 1954, included:

Bibliographical essays
Special bibliographies
News items about books and libraries

The essays included a history of the Romm printers and publishers of Vilna;[109] the special bibliographies consisted of a bibliography of Talmud commentaries, compiled by Reuben Margulies,[110] and a list of current religious Hebraica published in Israel, compiled by Isser Frenkel;[111] and the news items concentrated mostly on religious books and libraries in Israel.

Five issues (nine numbers) of *Hasefer* appeared between 1954 and 1961, the final issue having the title *Kuntres Hasefer Hatorani*. Eight years later, the Center of Torah Libraries in Bene Berak began publishing another bibliographical periodical, also devoted exclusively to Jewish religious literature. Entitled *Tagim* and edited by Meir Wunder, the new periodical was first published in 1969. Its purpose, as described in the foreword, was "to publish essays in the Torah spirit . . ." concentrating on "rabbinic bibliography, exploration of the Hebrew book, biographies of authors and Torah scholars, histories of (Hebrew) printing presses and libraries, book reviews. . . ." Volume 2 of *Tagim* was published in 1971, and Volumes 3-4 in 1972. Volumes 2-4 were edited by Yehoshua Markowitz.

*Ale Sefer,* a new bibliographical periodical of a more scholarly nature, edited by Israel Ta-Shema and published by the Department of Bibliography and Librarianship of Bar-Ilan University, made its appearance in Ramat-Gan in June 1975. The first issue consisted of studies in Jewish bibliography and Hebrew printing by well-known bibliographers and scholars.

## Retrospective Jewish Bibliographical Periodicals*

| Title | Editors or Publishers | Places of Publication | Dates of Publication | Volumes, Numbers, or Pages | Frequency | Category** |
|---|---|---|---|---|---|---|
| Accessions List: Israel | Library of Congress | Tel Aviv | 1964–1973 | Vols. 1–10, no. 4 | Monthly | III |
| Alim | D. Fränkel | Vienna | 1934–1938 | Vols. 1–3, Heft 3 | Quarterly | II |
| Bibliografishe Reshime fun Yidishe Bikher | I. Goldberg | New York | 1964–1965 | 2 issues | Annual | I |
| Bibliologisher Zamlbukh | J. Liberberg | Kharkov | 1930 | Vol. 1 | Annual? | I |
| Bibliographie des jüdischen Buches | J. Sänger | Frankfort | 1933–1935 | Vols. 1–2, Heft 1–2 (546 pages) | Quarterly | II |
| Bibliographischer Vierteljahresbericht für die jüdische Literatur | M. W. Kaufmann | Leipzig | 1914 | Vol. 1, no. 1 (38 pages) | Quarterly | I |
| Bibliography of Hebraica and Judaica | I. Abrahams | London | 1905–1906 | 2 issues (41, 46 pages) | Annual | I |
| Bikher Nayes | Kultur Lige | Warsaw | 1926–1939 | nos. 1–4/5 (3 issues) | Monthly; irregular | I |
| Bikher Velt (1) | Kultur Lige | Kiev | 1919 | | Quarterly | i |
| Bikher Velt (2) | Kultur Lige | Warsaw | 1922–1924; 1928–1929 | Vol. 1–3; Vol. 1–2 | Bi-monthly; monthly | I |
| Bikher Velt Byuletin | Cyco Lige | New York | 1965–? | | Irregular | I |
| Bloch's Book Bulletin | Bloch Pub. Co. | New York | 1929–1969 | nos. 1–166/67 | Monthly; irregular | II |
| Central-Anzeiger für jüdische Litteratur | N. Brüll; M. Stein-schneider | Frankfort | 1890–1891 | Vol. 1 (5 issues) | Bimonthly | I |
| Dapim | H. Bar-Dayan | Jerusalem | 1942–1943 | 5 issues | Quarterly | III |
| En Hakore (1) | D. A. Friedman; Z. Woislawski | Berlin | 1923 | nos. 1–2/3 | Quarterly | I |
| En Hakore (2) | E. Bin Gorion | Tel Aviv | 1944/45-1946/47 | Vols. 1–3 | Annual | III |

\* Includes some publications partially devoted to Jewish bibliography.

\*\* See categories at the beginning of Chapter Six.

## Retrospective Jewish Bibliographical Periodicals (cont.)

| Title | Publisher/Editor | Place | Dates | Extent | Frequency | |
|---|---|---|---|---|---|---|
| *Hebräische Bibliographie*; see, *Hamazkir-Hebräische Bibliographie* | | | | | | |
| *Hed Hasefer* | United Heb. Book Pub. | Tel Aviv | 1941 | 72, [24] pages | | II |
| *Der Idisher Bibliograf* | A. H. Kotik | Bialystok | 1911 | 24 pages | | I |
| Israel Book Catalog; see, *Katalog Hasefer Hayisra'eli* | | | | | | |
| *Israel Book Publishers' Quarterly* (from no. 4: Bulletin) | Book Pub. Ass'n. Israel | Tel Aviv | 1960–1967 | nos. 1–6 (5 issues) | Irregular | II |
| *Journal of Jewish Bibliography* | J. Bloch | New York | 1938–1943 | Vols. 1–4, no. 3 (15 issues) | Quarterly | IV |
| *Judaica Book Guide* | Jonathan David Co. | New York | 1967–1969? | Vols. 1–3, no. 1? | Quarterly; semiannual | II |
| *Das jüdische Buch* | J. Sänger | Frankfurt | 1931 | no. 1 (15 leaves) | | II |
| *Katalog Hasefer Hayisra'eli* | J. Bar-David | Tel Aviv | 1957–1961 | Vols. 1–4 | Annual | II |
| *Katalog Me'uchad* | United Heb. Book Pub. | Tel Aviv | 1951 | 34 pages | | II |
| *Kiryat Sefer* | Z. Scheinfinkel | Warsaw | 1903–1904 | nos. 1–6 (96 pages) | Quarterly | I |
| *Kuntres Bibliyografi* | R. Levi; S. Lachower | Tel Aviv | 1951–1970 | Vols. 1–20 | Monthly | III |
| *Mafteach Kelali Lakatalogim* | Book Pub. Ass'n. Israel | Tel Aviv | 1959 | | | II |
| *Mafteach Lakatalogim* | Book Pub. Ass'n. Israel | Tel Aviv | 1947 | 147 pages | | II |
| *Hamazkir—Hebräische Bibliographie* | M. Steinschneider | Berlin | 1858–1865; 1869–1881/2 | Vols. 1–21 (126 nos.) | Bimonthly | I |
| *Hame'asef—Der Sammler* | C. D. Lippe | Vienna | 1874 | nos. 1–3 (52 pages) | Monthly | II |
| *Megilat Hasefer* | A. M. Habermann | Jerusalem | 1957–1958 | nos. 1–3 | Quarterly | III |
| *Megilat Sefer* | Rubin Mass | Jerusalem | 1934–1939 | nos. 1–5 | Irregular | II |
| *Hamodi'a* | R. Margulies | Lvov; Tel Aviv | 1931–1934; 1935–1938 | nos. 1–14; nos. 1–7 | Irregular | II |

# Retrospective Jewish Bibliographical Periodicals (cont.)

| Title | Editor/Publisher | Place | Dates | Issues | Frequency | |
|---|---|---|---|---|---|---|
| *Olam Hasefarim* | Reznick, Menschel | New York | 1929 | 2 issues | Quarterly | II |
| *Olam Hasefer* | Hebrew Book Publishers | Tel Aviv | 1954–1958 | nos. 1–14 | Irregular | II |
| *Der Pinkes* | Sh. Niger | Vilna | 1913 (re-printed 1923) | Vol. 1 | Annual | I |
| *Qirjath-Zepher* (1) | M. W. Kaufmann | Leipzig | 1904 | 16 pages | Quarterly | I |
| *Reshimat Hasefarim Umafte'ach* | Hebrew Book Publishers | Tel Aviv | 1946 | Various pagings | | II |
| *Reshimat Sifre Chovah* | Israel State Archives & Library | Tel Aviv | 1954–1957 | Vols. 1–2, no. 6 | Bimonthly | III |
| *Der Sammler; see, Hame'asef—Der Sammler Hasef* | | | | | | |
| *Sefer Hashanah Lebibliyografyah Yehudit Bepolanyah* | Z. Harkavy | Jerusalem | 1954–1961 | Nos. 1–9 (5 issues) | Irregular | IV |
| *Soncino Blätter* | E.I.J. Poznanski | Warsaw | 1936 | Vol. 1 | Annual | III |
| *Sovetishe Yidishe Bikher Nayes* | H. Meyer | Berlin | 1925–1930 | Vols. 1–3 | Irregular | I |
| *Tachazit Hasefer* | A. Karmi | Moscow | 1934 | No. 1 | Monthly | I |
| *Yad Lakore* (1) | Hakibuts Hame'uchad | Tel Aviv | 1953 | Nos. 1–3 | Irregular | I |
| *Yad Lakore* (2) | Histadrut-Kibuts Me'uchad | Tel Aviv | 1938–1941 | Nos. 1–6 (4 issues) | Bimonthly | III |
| *Yerushalayim* | J. Kreppel | Cracow | 1900–1901; 1908 | Nos. 1–5 (4 issues); no. 1–2 (1 issue) | Bimonthly; monthly | I |
| *Dos Yidishe Bukh in Sovetnfarband* | Lenin Lib., Jew. Sec. | Minsk | 1933–1936 | 4 issues | Annual | I |
| *Yohrbukh far Yudishe Biblioteken* | A. Kirzhnitz | Vilna | 1914 | 147 pages | Annual | I |
| *Der Yudishe Bibliotekar* | A. Kirzhnitz | Vilna | 1914 | 4 issues | Quarterly | I |
| *Zeitschrift für hebräische Bibliographie* | H. Brody; A. Freimann | Berlin; Frankfort | 1896–1920 | Vols. 1–23 | Bimonthly; irregular | I |

## Current Jewish Bibliographical Periodicals*

| Title | Editors or Publishers | Places of Publication | Beginning Date of Publication | Frequency | Category** |
|---|---|---|---|---|---|
| Ale Sefer | Bar-Ilan University | Ramat-Gan | 1975 | Irregular | IV |
| Areshet | I. Raphael; N. Ben-Menahem | Jerusalem | 1958 | Annual; irregular | IV |
| Israel Book World | Israel Export Institute | Jerusalem | 1970 | Quarterly | II |
| Jewish Book Annual | Jewish Book Council | New York | 1942 | Annual | III |
| Judaica Book News | Bookazine Co. | New York | 1970 | Semiannual | II |
| Katalog farn Khoydesh fun Yidishn Bukh | Asoc. Mutual Israelita Argentina | Buenos Aires | 1961 | Annual; irregular | III |
| Katalog Sefarim Kelali | Book Pub. Ass'n. Israel | Tel Aviv | 1961 | Biannual; irregular | II |
| Kiryat Sefer | Jewish Nat'l. & Univ. Libr. | Jerusalem | 1924 | Quarterly | I |
| MBS Reference Catalogue | Menorah Book Service | London | 1968 | Biannual; irregular | II |
| Hasefer Beyisrael | Book Pub. Ass'n. Israel | Tel Aviv | 1959 | Monthly | II |
| Shenaton Hamemshalah | Gov't. of Israel | Tel Aviv | 1949 (bibliographic section began with vol. for 1950/51) | Annual | III |
| Studies in Bibliography and Booklore | Herbert C. Zafren | Cincinnati | 1953 | Biannual; irregular | IV |
| Tagim | Center of Torah Libr. | Bene Berak | 1969 | Annual; irregular | IV |
| Yad Lakore | Histadrut (etc.) | Tel Aviv | 1946 | Bimonthly; irregular | III |

\* Includes some publications partially devoted to Jewish bibliography.
\*\* See categories at the beginning of Chapter Six.

# Chapter Seven

# Indexes to Jewish Periodicals and Monographs

*The indexes selected for discussion in this chapter are divided into four groups. Group I discusses indexes that cover everything (or almost everything) of Jewish intellectual interest available in Jewish and non-Jewish periodicals. Group II concentrates on indexes concerned with culling from periodicals material dealing with Jewish life and culture in specific countries. Group III lists indexes of large runs of individual Jewish periodicals; and Group IV turns to indexes of Jewish monographic works: Festschriften and classic rabbinic books.*

*The four groups together should offer an up-to-date view of the achievements—and lack of achievement—in this vital branch of Jewish research literature, although the material offered here is far from exhaustive.*

I

Moïse Schwab: *Répertoire des Articles Relatifs à l'Histoire et à la Littérature Juives. Hasid's Index to Periodicals and Booklist.* Salo Wittmayer Baron: *Bibliography of Jewish Social Studies. Index to Jewish Periodicals. Reshimat Ma'amarim Bemada'e Hayahadut. Me'ir Enayim* and *Me'ir Letsiyon. Bibliografishe Yorbikher fun Yivo.*

## II

Moritz Stern: *Quellenkunde zur Geschichte der deutschen Juden. Sistematicheski Ukazatel' Literatury o Evreiakh.* Majer Balaban: *Bibliografia Historii Żydów w Polsce i w Krajach Ościennych.* Peter Thomsen: *Die Palästina-Literatur. Palestine and Zionism. Die hebräische Publizistik in Wien.* Jacob Rader Marcus: *An Index to Scientific Articles on American Jewish History.*

## III

From Tables of Contents to Indexes: *Monatsschrift für Geschichte und Wissenschaft des Judentums. Revue des Études Juives. Jewish Quarterly Review. Hashilo'ach. Hatekufah. Gilyonot. Ha'achdut. Kuntres* and *Hapoel Hatsair. Mibifnim. Niv Hakevutsah.* Miscellaneous indexes to Hebraica and Judaica periodicals.

## IV

Marcus-Bilgray: *An Index to Jewish Festschriften.* Charles Berlin: *Index to Festschriften in Jewish Studies.* Indexes to the Talmud and Midrash. Indexes to *Mishneh Torah* and *Shulchan Aruch.* Indexes to Responsa Literature. Indexes to Cabalistic and Chassidic works. Lists of Approbations and Subscriptions.

# I. General Jewish Indexes to Periodicals

## Moïse Schwab:
### *Répertoire des Articles Relatifs à l'Histoire et à la Littérature Juives*

A YALE UNIVERSITY student in the 1840s by the name of William Frederick Poole noticed that the old sets of periodicals in the library were seldom used by students. After making some inquiries, he discovered that few of the students had any idea of the contents of the old sets, and he decided to analyze and index some of them. His ventures turned out most successfully and resulted in the *Index to Periodical Literature* (New York, 1853). With the help of cooperating libraries—each one indexing a number of allotted titles—this *Index* had expanded some thirty years later to include 470 American and English periodicals published since 1802. The total number of articles indexed during that period was about 590,000. It was later supplemented by annual and five-year cumulations, and it was continued under different titles until 1910, when it was finally replaced by the more advanced Wilson indexing system.[1]

Indexing of periodicals on a regular basis, and on a large scale, was also adopted by a number of European countries during the second half of the nineteenth century, with France among the first to introduce the practice.[2] It was also in France that the first effort to produce an all-inclusive Jewish index of periodicals was made at the end of the nineteenth century.

The compiler of the first all-inclusive Jewish index of periodicals was Moïse Schwab. Born in Paris in 1839, Schwab studied in a yeshivah in Strassburg, and later (1858–1867) served as secretary to the Jewish scholar and orientalist, Salomon Munk (1803–1867).[3] He received his doctoral degree from the University of Jena a year later (1868) and was afterwards appointed as librarian at the Bibliothèque Nationale in Paris. Schwab was a highly productive author, and besides the hundreds of articles and essays he published, he also wrote a large number of important works,[4] among them a French translation of the Jerusalem Talmud,[5] and the *Répertoire des Articles Relatifs à l'histoire et à la Littérature Juives, Parus dans les Périodiques, de 1783 à 1898.*[6]

Part one of Schwab's *Répertoire* appeared in Paris in 1899. It was a lithographed reproduction of a handwritten copy,[7] and it included:

A list of indexed periodicals (94 titles)
An index of articles (arranged by the names of the authors)

Part two–three—also lithographed from a manuscript—was published in 1900, and it contained:

A list of subjects (Table des matières)
A list of Hebrew titles (Mots hébreux)

Three years later (1903) Schwab issued a *Supplément*—again in lithograph—that contained the following:

List of additional indexed periodicals (34 titles)
Index of articles (arranged by author)
List of initials and pseudonyms of Hebrew authors
List of subjects
List of Hebrew titles
Errata to the 1899 edition
Additions

The publication of the *Répertoire* was received enthusiastically by scholars and bibliographers. But, although they praised Schwab's reliability in citing titles and references, they also pointed out some shortcomings with regard to his transcriptions and identifications of authors.[8] For example, Julius Fürst was interfiled with a rabbi in Mannheim of that name; Zacharias Frankel with P. F. Frankl; and Max Grunwald with Moritz Grünwald. Some authors were listed twice under different forms of their names. To take another example, the compiler did not know that Simon Bachrach (father of Professor William Bacher) and Simon Bacher were the same, and that so were Emanuel Baumgarten and Mendel Baumgarten. There were also simple misreadings of Hebrew names, such as Buber instead of Bacher. Another shortcoming was the omission of English, American, and Ladino periodicals. In this connection it was suggested[9] that a collective indexing effort be organized to assist the compiler in his work.[10]

Schwab was also criticized for being inconsistent in his selections of material, especially in the areas of Bible studies and theology. As a general rule, he excluded belles lettres, polemics, apologetics, contemporary problems, etc. But even in these areas of exclusion there was a lack of consistency. A major deficiency, of course, was the reproduction of the work from a handwritten copy, which made it quite difficult to be used. Some pages were reproduced in an entirely unreadable state.

Schwab worked for a number of years in preparing an expanded and improved edition, and in 1914 he began printing it. World War I interrupted his work and, by the time the war was over, Schwab had died (1918). The work was finally published in 1923 under the supervision of Professor Braun and Dr. Wilhelm Freyhan. The new volume, entitle *Répertoire des Articles Relatifs à l'Histoire et à la Littérature Juives, Parus dans les Périodiques, de 1665 à 1900,* and dated Paris, 1914–1923, was an improved edition in every respect. Besides the physical improvement—printing from type—the new volume incorporated new material. The starting date for periodicals to be indexed was moved back from 1783 to 1665, and several Festschriften were included among the volumes indexed.[11]

But many of the shortcomings noticed in the first volumes still plagued this volume. Names were wrongly transcribed or identified, some were listed under several forms, and some were interfiled with names of a similar sound, e.g., Kotban instead of Kasswan; Arnstein instead of Ornstein; Banhord instead of Bonhard. Abramowicz, Schalom Jakob, was also listed as Abramowicz, Schalom, and Mendeli libraire; Benjacob, Issac, also appeared as Benjacob, S. A.; Benseb, J. L. was also listed separately under Krakau, Juda Löb; Chajes, H. P., was interfiled with Chajes, Hirsch; and Flam, Jacob, with Flam, Markus. The 35 entries under Kohn, Mose Löb, belonged to about five different authors.[12] Among the shortcomings should also be included the absence of a list of the titles indexed, and the lack of lists of subjects and Hebrew titles, available in the earlier editions. Thus the new volume included the following:

Index of articles (arranged by author)
List of authors' initials in Roman characters
List of authors' initials and pseudonyms in Hebrew characters
Additions and corrections to the earlier editions (as suggested, among others, by Alexander Marx, Samuel Poznanski, and William (Zeitlin)

The Paris 1914–1923 edition of Schwab's *Répertoire* was reprinted in New York in 1971 by Ktav Publishing House, under the title, *Index of Articles Relative to Jewish History and Literature Published in Periodicals from 1665 to 1900.* The reprint edition included the following additions: an introduction and list of abbreviations (i.e., list of indexed periodicals and Festschriften) by Zosa Szajkowski, a reproduction of part two–three of the first edition, and a list of corrections by Bernhard Wachstein.[13]

## Hasid's Index to Periodicals and Booklist

The compiler of the first Jewish index of periodicals and, later, the proponents of compiling such indexes continuously, saw the importance of an index either as a useful tool for accomplished scholars or as an inventory of national and cultural achievement.[14] Jewish literature in those days was considered to be the dominion solely of experts.[15] Jewish studies at public institutions were almost nonexistent, and interest in Jewish topics was slight among the laity as well.

This situation began to change rapidly in the 1930s, especially in the United States. It was reflected in the publication of *Hasid's Index to Periodicals and Booklist* launched in New York in April 1932 by the Hasid Publishing Company, with the aim of meeting "the needs of rabbis, teachers, social workers, communal leaders, and of libraries and educational institutions for a concise bibliography of current periodical literature and of new books on subjects of Jewish interest."

*Hasid's Index* was a monthly cumulative and annotated index, arranged by subject. It covered books and periodicals in English, German, Hebrew, and Yiddish published since January 1932. The name of the compiler, Harry S. Linfield (born 1889) together with an "advisory board," began to appear in issue number three (June 1932). Issue number three also introduced several improvements, such as broader coverage, better annotations, and more diversified subjects. Issue number five in August 1932, introduced a separate Table of authors, Subjects and Selected Titles. This was changed later (Vol. 2, no. 4, April 1933) to two lists: one for subjects and one for authors. The next issue (July 1937) dropped the list of subjects, and signaled the beginning of irregular appearance of the *Index.*[16]

Publishing responsibility for *Hasid's Index* was assumed by the Jewish Statistical Bureau of New York—the organization directed by Linfield—beginning with Volume 1, number 8, November 1933, with Hasid Publishing Company remaining the distributor. Each published issue now covered about 200 articles in periodicals, studies in collected works, and books. The last issue appeared in February 1937 (Vol. 6, nos. 1–2). A retrospective *Hasid's Index to Periodicals and Booklist* to cover the years 1921–1931 was in preparation, but it was never published.[17]

# Salo Wittmayer Baron:
## Bibliography of Jewish Social Studies

The interest in Jewish matters that began to develop in the United States during the first part of the 1930s grew steadily during the second half of that decade. Colleges and universities introduced new programs of Jewish interest and extended their existing programs in this area.[18] By 1940 a sizable student body devoted to Jewish studies and research already existed. To assist these students "in their research and reading" was "the primary purpose" of the *Bibliography of Jewish Social Studies, 1938–1939,* compiled and edited by Salo Wittmayer Baron (born 1895), professor of Jewish history at Columbia University and the author of numerous works and studies, among them a monumental multivolume history of the Jewish people.[19]

Baron's *Bibliography* was published originally in *Jewish Social Studies.*[20] It was reissued in 1941 as a separate volume with additions and an index. Baron defined the term "social" in his *Bibliography* "in its widest sense," in effect including almost everything published in 1938–1939 of Jewish interest. "A little more, it has been felt, would do much less harm in a bibliography than a little less." By the same token, he also extended the term "studies" to include "publications on contemporary affairs, written by politicians and publicists . . . even though they can hardly be considered 'studies' in the technical sense." But there was selectivity as well. Jewish dailies and weeklies, "as a rule," were not indexed and, from non-Jewish periodicals, mainly "scholarly publications" and occasionally "significant publicist essays bearing upon the contemporary scene" were selected. Another kind of selectivity was the involuntary result of oversight or the nonavailability of materials in New York libraries. "Perhaps one-quarter of all the entries . . . were not available for inspection and checking."

The *Bibliography* consisted of 4,231 entries covering the years 1938 and 1939, and "for the sake of completeness" it also covered a limited number of books published during 1937 and 1940. Arrangement was by subject, divided into two major sections: one listed material dealing with almost every phase of Jewish life and thought, and the other was devoted exclusively to materials dealing with Jewish history in general, and Jews in various countries in particular. Thus, the first section was divided into the following twenty-six main groups (each one assigned a different letter of the alphabet, A to Z):

Encyclopedias, general periodicals, and jubilee volumes
Bibliography, library service, and typography

Biography
Religion
Judaism and other religions
Law
Philosophy (including ethics and homiletics)
Cabala and Chassidism
Science
Folklore and daily life
Archaeology (including the history of writing and numismatics)
Art and music
Language
Literature
Jews and Judaism in general literature
Anthropology and race problems
Antisemitism
Apologetics and defense of Jewish rights
The Jewish question
Zionism and anti-Zionism
Socialism and labor movements
Community organization
Education
Economic Life
Migration and the refugee problem
Population and demography

The second section was divided into the following sixteen groups (each one assigned a double letter of the alphabet, AA to PP):

History (general, ancient, medieval, modern, current)
Palestine
United States
Canada
Latin America
The British Empire (except Canada and India)
France
Germany
Austria, Czechoslovakia, and Hungary
Italy
U.S.S.R.
Poland (including Galicia and Vilna)
Balkan States
Other European States
Africa (except South Africa)
Asia (except Palestine)

Although Baron intended his *Bibliography* to serve principally as an aid to students (he stressed "practicability . . . rather than compliance with strict bibliographical standards"), he included complete bibliographical information in the entries as follows:

Author

Title

Title translated (titles of books and articles in French, German, Italian, and Spanish, in vernacular only, since "scholarly English readers" would manage to grasp the meaning; titles of books in Dutch, Hebrew, Polish, Yiddish, and other languages, in vernacular and in English translation; articles or essays in the same languages, in English translation only, followed by name of the original language in parentheses)

|           *Books*           |          *Articles, essays*          |
|-----------------------------|--------------------------------------|
| Place of publication        | Name of publication                  |
| Publisher                   | Number of volume or issue            |
| Date of publication         | Date (month and year)                |
| Pagination                  | Page numbers                         |

Brief descriptions and bibliographical notes followed many entries, particularly those with ambiguous or meaningless titles, and cross-references were used liberally. More than 800 entries were added to the 1941 reissue of the *Bibliography,* and an Index of Authors, Editors, and Biographical Subjects completed the volume.[21]

## Index to Jewish Periodicals

Baron planned to make his *Bibliography* a regular feature on a biennial basis, in the periodical in which it was first published. His plan never materialized, but twenty-three years later a publication was launched that tried to offer regular bibliographical guidance, although on a much smaller scale, to materials of Jewish interest available in current periodicals. Similar in appearance to *Hasid's Index* but limited in coverage to a select number of Jewish periodicals, the new publication appeared in Cleveland in 1964 under the title *Index to Jewish Periodicals.* The arrangement was in dictionary style, and it included a broad range of topics of Jewish interest. Volume 1, edited by Marion Gans, Miriam Leikind, and Bess Rosenthal, indexed forty-four "American and Anglo-Jewish journals of general and scholarly interest" published from June 1963 to May 1964. An attempt was made in Volume 3 (nos. 1−2) to index three Hebrew periodicals *(Kiryat Sefer, Tarbits, Tsiyon)*, but that effort was never repeated. The *Index*, consequently, is designed exclusively for the English reader and thus serves the needs of a limited audience.

With Volume 2, the *Index* began to appear semi-annually, indexing in each issue between forty and fifty publications. The most distinctive feature of the *Index* is its broad coverage of book reviews. Miriam Leikind edited Volumes 2−10, nos. 1−2, and, beginning with Volume 10, nos. 3−4, she worked with Jean H. Foxman and Bess Rosenthal. The *Index* is published by the Cleveland College of Jewish Studies Press, with the financial assistance of charitable Jewish foundations.

## Reshimat Ma'amarim Bemada'e Hayahadut

While the responsibility for indexing Jewish material in English periodicals was assumed partially by the *Index to Jewish Periodicals,* articles and essays in Hebrew, Yiddish, and other languages remained beyond bibliographical control. The most logical place for launching such a project would have been the State of Israel. Indeed, even before the State of Israel was formed, voices of Jewish scholars and librarians were heard demanding the establishment of a national bibliographical institute that would also register the articles, essays, and studies in periodicals, in addition to books current and retrospective.[22] When such an institute was finally created years later, the indexing of periodicals was not even mentioned in its program of activities.[23] True, an effort to meet these demands was made in 1944 by *Kiryat Sefer* with the addition of a section which listed current issues of periodicals with their contents.[24] This was of limited benefit because the material in the indexed periodicals was not registered individually under separate entries, and no cumulations were prepared. The coverage was also incomplete, since belles lettres and contemporary problems were excluded.[25] Although this new section in *Kiryat Sefer* did not satisfy the need for a Jewish index of periodicals, it served nonetheless—twenty-five years later—as the basis for compiling a long-awaited and urgently needed annual entitled *Reshimat Ma'amarim Bemada'e Hayahadut,* with an English title, *Index of Articles on Jewish Studies.*

*Reshimat Ma'amarim* made its first appearance in Jerusalem in 1969. It was edited by Issachar Joel (born 1900), assistant director of the Jewish National and University Library at Jerusalem, and was issued by the editorial board of *Kiryat Sefer* with the assistance of the Department of Education and Culture in the Diaspora of the World Zionist Organization. Issue one, covering 492 periodicals (81 in Hebrew, 9 in Yiddish) and 26 anthologies published during the year 1966, consisted of 2,349 entries. The arrangement was by subject, divided into the following twelve main sections:[26]

Bibliography
Jewish studies (including institutes)
Old Testament
Apocrypha; Dead Sea scrolls
Mishnah, Talmud, Midrash, halacha
Spiritual trends in Judaism
Liturgy; the Jewish year and its customs
Literature
Language
Jewish history
Jewish cultural life
Palestine; Zionism; State of Israel

The subject scheme, with the exception of a few innovations, was based on the one developed by *Kiryat Sefer* for the registration of current publications, and the entries themselves were based on the materials listed in the Periodicals section of that bibliographical quarterly. This, and the fact that the actual technical work of putting the material together was performed by the staff of *Kiryat Sefer,* factually established *Reshimat Ma'amarim* as an annual extension of, or supplement to, *Kiryat Sefer,* adopting all the weaknesses and defects inherent in that work. This was revealed in the inadequacy of the scheme (in comparison to the one developed by Baron) and in the inconsistency of the inner arrangement of the sections and subsections.[27]

Issue two, covering publications for the year 1967 (with additions to 1966), and consisting of 2,947 entries, was published in 1970. The subject scheme was enlarged in this issue by adding to it such topics as Jewish law and labor, Socialism, and was improved by a number of other alterations.[28] Issue three, covering 1968 (with additions to 1966/67), and consisting of 2,687 entries, was published in 1971; issue four, covering 1969 (with additions to 1966/68), and consisting of 2,927 entries, was published in 1972; issue five, covering 1970 (with additions to 1966/69), and consisting of 3,389 entries, was published in 1973; and issue six-seven, covering 1971–1972 (with additions to 1966/70), and consisting of 6,343 entries, was published in 1974. Issues eight and nine, covering 1973 and 1974 (with additions to previous years), and consisting of 3,490 and 2,528 entries respectively, were published in 1975.

*Reshimat Ma'amarim* is now an established basic research tool for current Jewish studies. Its coverage is constantly expanding, and it already surpasses anything previously attempted in this area. Each issue includes, besides the entries arranged according to the subject scheme, the following useful features:

List of indexed periodicals and anthologies
Index of subjects (limited to names: persons, places, books, etc.; expanded with issue four to include topics not listed in the subject scheme)
Index of authors of Hebrew articles
Index of authors of non-Hebrew articles
List of abbreviations (printed on folded leaves)

Additional evidence of the permanence of *Reshimat Ma'amarim* was the decision made in 1975 by the editorial board of *Kiryat Sefer* to discontinue publishing the section "Betoch Kitve-Et" in *Kiryat Sefer* (beginning with Vol. 50) and, instead, to publish *Reshimat Ma'amarim* more frequently, i.e., semiannually.

## Me'ir Enanyim and Me'ir Letsiyon

In 1968, while *Reshimat Ma'amarim* was still in preparation, there appeared in Bene Berak, Israel, the first volume of another index which in time came to complement *Reshimat Ma'amarim.* Entitled *Me'ir Enayim* (based on Psalms 19:9) and edited by Meir Wunder (who, in the tradition of rabbinic authors, attached his personal name to the title of his work[29]), the new index covered Jewish material of a religious nature that was published, during the Hebrew year 5727 (1966/67), in about 25 Hebrew periodicals in Israel and the United States. The editor originally began compiling indexes of religious topics published in periodicals for reference purposes while serving as librarian at the Religious Council Library in Ramat-Gan. On the advice of friends, he decided to prepare such indexes on a regular basis and to make them available to the public in the form of annual volumes.

Volume 1 of *Me'ir Enayim,* consisting of 917 annotated entries, was

published by the Center of Torah Libraries. It was divided into the following four sections:

  List of articles (arranged alphabetically by the names of the writers)
  List of book reviews (arranged by the names of the authors of the books
    reviewed)
  Obituaries
  Index of names, titles, topics

Volume 2, consisting of 1,052 annotated entries, was published in 1969. It
indexed forty-one Hebrew periodicals published during 1967/68, and it
listed material extracted from an additional eighteen periodicals issued during the same period. The material in this volume was arranged by subject,
and it was divided into the following fifteen main sections:

  Bible
  Mishnah, Talmud
  Novellae
  Codes, halachah (with summaries of decisions by rabbinical courts in Israel)
  Liturgy and religious poetry
  Ethics; meditations; cabala; Chassidism
  Jewish history
  Palestine
  State of Israel
  Jewish law (with summaries of decisions by Israel state courts)
  Six-Day War
  Education and teaching
  Bibliography and librarianship
  Book reviews
  Biographies of Jewish religious personalities (past and present)

Volume 3, consisting of 1,100 annotated entries, was published in 1972. It
indexed sixty Hebrew periodicals—with selections from additional
publications—published during 1968/69. The subject arrangement was
somewhat changed in this volume,[30] and a few extra features were added.[31]
Volume 3 was the last of the *Me'ir Enayim* series, which was replaced a year
later by a new publication devoted to indexing only material dealing with
practical halachic problems.

    The new publication, again edited by Meir Wunder and entitled *Me'ir
Letsiyon,* was launched in Jerusalem in 1973 by the New York-based
Research Institute of Religious Jewry. The experience gained through the

publication of the three volumes of *Me'ir Enayim* convinced the editor of the importance of concentrating his efforts in the area of practical Jewish law, an area completely neglected in other bibliographic tools.[32] The publishers of *Me'ir Letsiyon* thus plan to issue additional volumes at two- to three-year intervals.

Volume 1 of *Me'ir Letsiyon,* consisting of 770 annotated entries (each entry including a brief summary of the verdict), completely indexed thirty-two Hebrew periodicals and partially indexed thirty-eight others, all published during 1969/70—1970/71. Arrangement was according to the order of the books of the *Shulchan Aruch,* followed by a section on modern halachic problems. Three indexes (periodicals, topics, names) concluded the volume.

Since some fifty percent of the material registered in *Me'ir Enayim* and most of the material included in *Me'ir Letsiyon* are not covered by *Reshimat Ma'amarim,* the *Me'ir Enayim* and *Me'ir Letsiyon* indexes constitute important companion volumes to the *Reshimat Ma'amarim* index.

## Bibliografishe Yorbikher fun Yivo

Most of the indexes discussed above were not limited to the coverage of Jewish periodicals in any specific language; they strove to include as many languages as possible; even the *Index of Jewish Periodicals* at one time tried to cover some Hebrew publications.[33] But there were also a few attempts to concentrate on indexing materials of Jewish interest available in periodicals of a specific language, namely English, Hebrew, or Yiddish.

Albert M. Hyamson (1875—1954) compiled "A Bibliography of All Books and Articles on Subjects of Jewish Interest Published in the English Language During the Past Year" in 1904. It covered "all British and American publications of Jewish interest that have appeared since November 1, 1903." It registered "books . . . newspaper and magazine articles," and it excluded "sermons . . . leading articles appearing in Jewish periodicals . . . fiction . . . short stories. . . . " The index was published in an Anglo-Jewish periodical[34] and included 719 entries; it was divided into lists of authors, subjects, and obituaries.

William Zeitlin, under the entries for some authors in his *Bibliotheca hebraica,*[35] had included their articles published in Hebrew periodicals. Later attempts to compile exclusive indexes of Hebrew periodicals, however remained largely in the planning stages. Benzion Dinur (1884—1973) began to compile an index of articles in the early 1920s "from all the Hebrew news-papers and periodicals, from the past to the present," to be arranged by author, title and subject.[36] Samuel Isaac Feigin (1893–1950) advanced a proposal, in the late 1920s, to establish an international index of Hebrew periodicals.[37] Neither of the projects materialized as a publication.

Around the same time, in 1928, in Warsaw, the first volume appeared of a planned annual index of books and periodicals in Yiddish, an area greatly neglected in other bibliographical works and projects. The volume, com-piled and published by the Bibliographical Center of the Yiddish Scientific Institute (Yivo) in Vilna, and accordingly entitled *Bibliografishe Yorbikher fun Yivo,* consisted of about 12,000 entries of Yiddish books and periodicals published during 1926.[38] The material was divided into seven main sections:

List of periodicals (arranged alphabetically by countries)
List of one-time publications
Index of articles (under heading: "Science, literature and art;" arranged in a modified Dewey decimal classification order)
List of periodicals launched in 1927
List of books published in 1927
List of periodicals in Hebrew and in European languages available at the Yivo Bibliographical Center
Index of names

The Yiddish Scientific Institute had been founded by a group of Yiddish scholars and supporters of the Yiddish language and literature at a con-ference in Berlin in 1925. The publication of the *Yorbikher* only three years later was a great accomplishment for its Bibliographical Center. But the haste with which the work was done resulted in a number of defects, some of them noticed by the members of the Center themselves,[39] and some pointed out by others.[40] The main weaknesses were in the adaptation of the decimal system to this specific type of material, and in the gaps left in the coverage of some books and periodicals. The lack of a subject index and the inadequate registration and interpretation of some of the material constituted ad-ditional defects. Balanced against the defects was the solid achievement of having compiled into one volume such an enormous number of Yiddish entries. The compilers were convinced that they could improve the coverage and the quality of the work in future volumes. The text for a second volume, covering 1927, was compiled and turned over to the printer. It was set in type but never published, probably due to lack of funds.[41]

# II. Indexes Devoted to Jewish History and Culture in Specific Countries

## Moritz Stern:
### Quellenkunde zur Geschichte der deutschen Juden

Carl August Hugo Burkhardt, an archivist in Weimar, Germany, sent a bibliography to the editors of a Jewish-German magazine issued in Braunschweig in the late 1880s. He registered material published in German periodicals dealing with German Jewish history. Since Burkhardt did not include any material from German Jewish periodicals in his bibliography, the editor assigned Moritz Stern (1864–1939), who later served as librarian of the Jewish community library in Berlin, to complete the bibliography. After reshaping and augmenting Burkhardt's bibliography with material from German Jewish periodicals, Stern published it in 1888 in the Braunschweig magazine with the title, "Aus der Zeitschriften-Literatur zur Geschichte der Juden in Deutschland: Verzeichnis von Abhandlungen und Notizen."[42] The bibliography consisted of 1,159 entries divided into two parts:

General German Jewish history
History of German Jewish communities (arranged by the names of the communities)

Several years later, Stern published a revised and enlarged edition of the same bibliography as a separate volume with the title: *Quellenkunde zur Geschichte der deutschen Juden, Band I: Die Zeitschriftenliteratur* (Kiel, 1892). The revised bibliography consisted of 1,419 entries arranged in the same manner as in the earlier edition, but also including an index of places.

### Sistematicheskii Ukazatel' Literatury o Evreiakh

In 1892, the year in which Moritz Stern published his *Quellenkunde,* a similar volume devoted to the history of the Jews in Russia and in the world appeared in St. Petersburg. *Sistematicheskii Ukazatel' Literatury o Evreiakh na Russkom Iazyke* was published by the Mefitse Haskalah society; it consisted of 9,579 entries, covering books and articles in periodicals published in Russia from 1708 through 1889. The material was divided into the following two parts:

> History of the Jews in Russia
> Jews in the world

Part one was subdivided into the following eleven chapters (with further subdivisions in each chapter):

> General Jewish history in Russia
> The social-political situation
> Organization of community life and internal problems
> Religious customs and issues
> Ethnography of Jewish settlement in Russia
> Enlightenment
> Russian-Jewish literature
> The economic situation
> Emigration movement
> General views and polemics on the Jewish problem
> Jews in Russian belles lettres

Part two was subdivided into the following seven chapters (with further subdivisions in each chapter):

> General essays on the Jews, their fate and peculiarity
> Ancient Jewish history
> Religion
> Mosaic-Talmudic law
> Literature
> History and contemporary Jewish situation in foreign countries
> Jews in translated belles lettres

The 568-page volume concluded with an index of authors, reviewers, translators, etc., and an index of subjects.

The *Ukazatel'* first appeared as a supplement to the Russian-Jewish periodical *Voskhod,* and a year later (1893) it reappeared as an independent monograph. A reprint edition was published in Cambridge, England, by the Oriental Research Partners, 1973.[43] Supplementary volumes, though planned, never materialized.[44]

## Majer Balaban: *Bibliografia Historii Żydów w Polsce i w Krajach Ościennych*

What Mefitse Haskalah did for the history of Russian Jewry, Professor Majer Balaban (1877–1942) planned to do for the history of Polish Jewry.[45] In 1908 he compiled, and published in a Polish periodical,[46] a bibliography of the literature dealing with the history of the Jews in Poland, printed during the years 1899–1907. In 1911 he published a similar list in another Polish periodical[47] covering material printed during the years 1907–1911. Three decades later he issued part one of his *Bibliografia Historii Żydów w Polsce i w Krajach Ościennych za Lata 1900–1930* (Warsaw, 1939). Published as Volume 10 of the writings of the Institute for Judaistic Studies in Warsaw, part one of Balaban's *Bibliografia* registered books and periodical articles in Hebrew, Polish, Yiddish, and other languages. The total number of entries was 2,948, arranged by subject and divided into eight chapters.

Balaban planned to extend the work to twenty-five chapters, and to add an index of personal names and place names. The outbreak of World War II prevented its further publication, and when Balaban died in the Warsaw ghetto in 1942, the project died with him.

## Peter Thomsen: *Die Palästina-Literatur*

During the same year that Balaban began publishing bibliographical material on the history of the Jews in Poland, a new bibliographical index appeared that was also devoted mainly to a single country but with a much wider range. Compiled by Peter Thomsen (1875–1954)[48] and entitled *Systematische Bibliographie der Palästina-Literatur,* the new index appeared in Leipzig in 1908 with the assistance of the Deutscher Verein zur Erforschung Palästinas. Between 1878 and 1894 the Verein had published annual surveys of literature dealing with Palestine in its *Zeitschrift*[49]. Thomsen picked up where the *Zeitschrift* left off, and his index registered books and articles published during the years 1895–1904. The material consisted of 2,915 entries, arranged in seven main groups:

General works
History (with subdivision for Jewish history)
Historical geography and topography

Archaeology
New archaeological discoveries
Modern Palestine (with subdivision for Zionism and Jewish colonization of
Palestine)
Geography

The volume also included an index of authors and selected topics.

For his volume Thomsen indexed around 350 periodicals, and he included works and articles in various languages—English, German, Hebrew,
and Russian, among others. Although his subject scheme was highly
elaborate and covered every phase and area of old and new Palestine (and to
a lesser extent Syria and Lebanon), Thomsen repeated the listings of certain
entries under several topics. This approach elicited a favorable response
from scholars, who felt that it should be applied on an even larger scale.[50] In
1911 Thomsen published a second edition of his *Systematische Bibliographie*
under a new title, *Die Palästina-Literatur,* a title that was used for all the
subsequent Palestine indexes prepared by Thomsen.

Volume 2 of *Die Palästina-Literatur,* covering the years 1905—1909, was
also published in 1911. The title page listed a number of collaborators,
among them William Zeitlin[51] who was responsible for compiling the
Hebrew and Zionist literature. Zeitlin's efforts are evident in the large
number of entries accumulated under the subdivision of Zionism and Jewish
colonization. The title page also credited the following four bodies with
financing the publication of the volume: Deutscher Verein zur Erforschung
Palästinas, Palestine Exploration Fund, Zionistische Kommision zur Erforschung Palästinas, and Die Gesellschaft zur Förderung der Wissenschaft
des Judentums. This volume included about 3,755 entries, and there were
several improvements over the first. The sections Archaeology and New
Archaeological Discoveries were combined into one, more subdivisions
were added, and a larger number of topics were included in the index of
authors and selected topics.

Volume 3, covering the years 1910—1914 and consisting of 4,148 entries,
was published in 1916, and Volume 4, covering the years 1915—1924 and
consisting of 8,437 entries, was published in 1927. William Zeitlin, who was
responsible for indexing Hebrew and Zionist literature, died in 1921; his
place in this volume was taken by Samuel Klein (1886—1940). Zeitlin had
prepared slips for part of the material to be included in this volume, but they
were lost after his death. This was a loss for the subsection dealing with
Zionism, since Klein concentrated mainly on Hebrew literature.[52]

Volume 5, covering the years 1925—1934 and consisting of 11,252 entries was published during 1936—1938. From this volume, the materials dealing with Bible, Zionism, and Jewish literature in general were removed, first because of the phenomenal growth of literature dealing with Palestine, and also because *Kiryat Sefer* covered these subjects. However, since *Kiryat Sefer* did not include periodical articles in its coverage, the decision to exclude these areas from Volume 5 resulted in a net loss to scholarship.

World War II interrupted further publication of *Die Palästina-Literatur* and, a decade after the war had ended, Thomsen died at the age of seventy-nine. He left three volumes in manuscript—volumes 6, 7, and A—which were published posthumously by his friends and followers. Volume 6, covering the years 1935—1939 and consisting of 9,189 entries, was published in 1956; and Volume 7, covering the years 1940—1945 and consisting of 11,506 entries, was published during 1969—1972.

The third volume left by Thomsen—volume A—was an index of the materials published during the years 1878—1894. It consisted of 12,818 entries and was published in Berlin from 1957 to 1960. The publication of volume A closed the gap that had existed in Palestine bibliography between the work of Reinhold Röhricht (1842—1905)—who, in his *Bibliotheca Geographica Palestinae* (Berlin, 1890; reprinted, Jerusalem, 1963), listed works in chronological order dealing with Palestine from the year 333 to the year 1878—and the first volume of Thomsen's *Die Palästina-Literatur,* that began with the year 1895.

Efforts by Thomsen's followers to continue his project of indexing material dealing with Palestine did not materialize.

## Palestine and Zionism

Names of people as well as of books are sometimes misleading and, in regard to books, the user at least is sometimes happy to be misled. A case in point is Salo Wittmayer Baron's *Bibliography of Jewish Social Studies,* which included much more than the title suggested.[53] Nobody complained. Similar was the case of another bibliographic index that was launched in New York one year after Peter Thomsen stopped compiling his *Palästina-Literatur.* Entitled *Palestine and Zionism: An Author and Subject Index to Books, Pamphlets and Periodicals* and published by the Zionist Archives and Library in New York,[54] the new publication began to appear in January 1946 as a bimonthly index with annual cumulations.

The second half of the 1940s and the early part of the 1950s were years when the terms Palestine, Zionism, Jews, and Israel became synonymous in many minds. These were also years when the demand increased for complete and accurate information about everything connected with Jews. The editors of the new index met these needs by interpreting the words Palestine and Zionism in such a manner as to make it possible to include almost everything pertaining to contemporary Jewish life. The users presumably did not mind being "misled" by this broad interpretation.

*Palestine and Zionism* was divided into two parts:

Periodical index (preceded by a list of indexed publications)
Book and pamphlet list (followed by a list of publishers)

The entries in both sections were arranged in alphabetical order, dictionary style. Since the printing was done by the H. W. Wilson Company, the printers and publishers of the Wilson indexes,[55] *Palestine and Zionism* benefited greatly, not only from adapting the Wilson indexing system, but also from the typographical expertise and organizational experience of that company.

*Palestine and Zionism* indexed annually more than 400 Jewish and general periodicals and collective works. Daily newspapers were excluded, and only works received by the library were listed in part two. Both parts included materials in English, Hebrew, Yiddish, and other languages. Hebrew and Yiddish authors were entered in English transliteration, and titles in the same languages were entered in English translation.

Volumes 1–3 (January 1946–December 1948) were edited by Sophie A. Udin; they were followed by a three-year cumulation (New York, 1949). Beginning with Volume 4 (January –December 1949), editing was assumed by Sylvia Landress. The index now added titles to its dictionary arrangement, and the subtitle was amended accordingly to read: "Author, Title, and Subject Index." The publication of this periodicals index, the most comprehensive and professionally executed of its kind in the Jewish field, was brough to a close with Volume 11 (1956).

## Die hebräische Publizistik in Wien

Different in scope and in purpose from the bibliographical indexes discussed earlier was an index published in Vienna in 1930. Its scope was limited by language, time, and place, and its purpose was of an historical literary nature. Entitled *Die hebräische Publizistik in Wien*,[56] and compiled by three Austrian-Jewish scholars, it indexed about fifteen Hebrew periodicals that appeared in Vienna between 1820 and 1889. The work was divided into three parts:

Index of nine periodicals that appeared during the years 1820–1865
Index of two periodicals that appeared during 1865–1889
Index of four periodicals that appeared during 1868–1877

Part one, compiled by Bernhard Wachstein,[57] dealt with the Hebrew periodicals established by the followers of the Mendelssohnian school whose aim was to attract people to the idea of Enlightenment.[58] Part two, compiled by Israel Taglicht (1862–1943),[59] dealt with talmudic-rabbinic periodicals, in which a new, scientific approach—a consequence of the Enlightenment movement—is evident.[60] Part three, compiled by Alexander Kristianpoller (1884–1942),[61] dealt with periodicals that started out with the idea of Enlightenment but left it, and turned to Jewish national ideas.[62]

All three parts were preceded by detailed introductions in which the authors described the ideas that had come to the fore during the period in which the periodicals and the people involved in them had flourished. The largest and most elaborate introduction was by Wachstein (about eighty-five pages), describing the forces that were active in Hebrew literature from the days of the Enlightenment movement to the days of Perez Smolenskin (1842–1885).[63] He examined the various periodicals, issue by issue, evaluated each writer, and summarized the contributions made by these periodicals to Hebrew literature.

The entries in each part were arranged alphabetically by the name of the author and included the following information:

Author (in Roman characters)
Biographical data (in German, with bibliographical annotations; compilers invested great erudition and effort in obtaining data, contacting, in many instances, the birth or death places of the authors to obtain reliable information)
Title (in Hebrew characters, arranged in chronological order)
Description (in German, sometimes annotated)
Title of periodical (in abbreviated Roman characters)
Volume number
Pages

Each part also included separate sections for:

Anonymous articles and essays (in which an effort was made to identify the authors)

Articles and essays signed by pseudonyms, initials, anagrams (not included in part two)

Edited texts of earlier authors (entered in the main section under the names of the editors; here rearranged under the names of the authors)

Translations from other languages (divided by German, French, English, Italian, Hungarian, Russian, Greek, Latin, Arabic, and Persian; not included in part two)

Additions and corrections (not included in part two)

An index of authors for the entire volume concluded this work.

The overall organization and editing of *Die hebräische Publizistik* was the responsibility of Bernhard Wachstein, and his unique bibliographical method turned this work—originally intended as an index to Hebrew periodicals published in Vienna—into a basic work for the study of the history of the Enlightenment movement, especially in Austria and Galicia. It also became a model of how indexes of this kind should be organized.

## Jacob Rader Marcus: *An Index to Scientific Articles on American Jewish History*

At its annual meeting in 1904, the American Jewish Historical Society (founded 1892) appointed a committee on the indexing of American Jewish periodicals "in order to render their contents more accessible to historical enquirers." The committee met a number of times and submitted a report to the society's annual meeting of 1905.[64] We do not know what the practical results of that report were, but it is a fact that until recent years no collective index of American Jewish periodicals existed.[65] A first step in the direction of compiling such an index was taken in 1971 by the American Jewish Archives, with the publication of *An Index to Scientific Articles on American Jewish History* in Cincinnati.

The new index was edited by Jacob Rader Marcus (born 1896), an eminent American Jewish historian, professor at Hebrew Union College, and founder of the American Jewish Archives.[66] The index was described as "a joint product of the staff of the American Jewish Archives and a number of students on the campus of the Hebrew Union College—Jewish Institute of Religion." Thirteen American Jewish periodicals were indexed,[67] and about 7,000 entries were prepared and arranged in dictionary style (including authors, titles, subjects) in a 420—page volume.

## III. Indexes of Individual Jewish Periodicals

### From Tables-of-Contents to Indexes

Hayyim Nahman Bialik (1873—1934), the great Hebrew poet who was also a successful publisher, addressed an urgent request in 1913 to the librarian of the Strashun Library in Vilna,[68] Mr. Chaikl Lunsky (1881—1942 or 3):

> . . . I am turning to you, sir, with a very important request, to copy [for me] from *Hamelits* a feuilleton . . . by the late Levinsky . . . entitled "Yefifuto shel Yefet." Under this general title, there appeared in *Hamelits* during the years 1893/4, 1894/5, 1895/6, or thereabouts, an entire series of feuilletons [by Levinsky]. We are now issuing the third volume of Levinsky's writings, and we are lacking a great part of one of these [feuilletons], where he talks about clubs, gambling, billiards, etc. This feuilleton begins with the words: "The long nights of Tevet" . . . and it started in *Hamelits* number 19, according to a note on the margin, but it does not say which year. The best guess would be to search for it in the above listed years. . . . [69]

Lunsky's reply to Bialik's letter is not preserved, but we may assume that he was able to find Levinsky's feuilleton in *Hamelits* and copy it for Bialik.[70] Similarly, we may assume that with the clues he received from Bialik Lunsky's task was not too difficult. He had only to examine about three volumes to discover the feuilleton. His task was made even easier by the fact that *Hamelits* published an annual table of contents (divided into several sections, with all feuilletons grouped together into a separate section).[71] Without Bialik's clues and without the tables of contents Lunsky's task would have been formidable. He would have had to examine, page by page, more than thirty volumes, each consisting of several hundred pages.

It was the idea of assisting the scholar, researcher, and librarian in similar tasks that was partially responsible for the printing of annual tables of contents to periodicals. This practice, which became universally accepted during the nineteenth century, soon proved to be inadequate for the needs of modern scholarship. The advent of the modern scientific periodical necessitated a more detailed description of their contents. Thus came into being the idea of publishing semiannual, annual, or multiannual indexes to individual periodicals.

## Monatsschrift für Geschichte und Wissenschaft des Judentums

The first scientific Jewish periodicals of permanent value made their appearance during the second half of the nineteenth century. First came the German *Monatsschrift für die Geschichte und Wissenschaft des Judentums.* [72] Founded and edited by Zacharias Frankel (1801–1875)[73] and published by the Jüdisch-Theologisches Seminar in Breslau,[74] it made its appearance in Breslau in 1851. Heinrich Hirsch Grätz (1817–1891)[75] took over its editorship seventeen years later (1868), and two decades afterwards (1888) decided to suspend its publication. After five years of suspension, publication was resumed in 1893 under the editorship of Marcus Brann (1849–1920),[76] with the assistance of David Kaufmann (1852–1899).[77] After Brann's death editing was assumed by Isaac Heinemann (1876–1957).[78] The final volume (vol. 83) appeared in 1939, with Dr. Leo Baeck (1873–1956)[79] as official editor.

A *Generalregister* of the first seventy-five volumes of the *Monatsschrift* was published in Breslau in 1938. It consisted of two parts:

> List of essays ("Aufsätze") and book reviews ("Rezensionen")
> Index of names and topics ("Namen und Sachregister")

The register was compiled mainly by Arthur Posner and completed by Suse Hallenstein. A supplementary register for Volumes 76–83, consisting only of lists of essays and book reviews, was compiled by Leo Baerwald and published in 1963 as part of a work on the history of the Jüdisch-Theologisches Seminar.[80] A *Gesamtregister* to the *Monatsschrift* was published in Tübingen in 1966. It consisted of a reprint of the *Generalregister* for Volumes 1–75 with the addition of a new *Generalregister* for Volumes 76–83. A chronological list of the published volumes of the *Monatsschrift* concluded the volume.


## Revue des Études Juives

Almost thirty years after the launching of the *Monatsschrift*, the next important scientific Jewish periodical appeared. Entitled *Revue des Études Juives*,[81]
edited by Isidore Loeb (1839—1892),[82] and published by the Société des
Études Juives, it made its first appearance in Paris in the fall of 1880. Editing
passed to Israel Lévi (1856—1939)[83] after Loeb's death. During the following
years, the Revue was edited by several scholars (among others, Julien Weill,
Maurice Liber, and Edmond Fleg), and it continued with few interruptions
until the outbreak of World War II. As soon as the war was over, the *Revue*
reappeared under the editorship of Georges Vajda. It was at first irregular in
appearance and meager in contents, but it gradually recovered some of its
former glory. After eighty years of independent publishing during which 120
volumes were issued, the *Revue* merged in 1962 with the English-language
periodical *Historia Judaica,* which had been published and edited in New
York from 1938 to 1961 by Guido Kisch (born 1889).[84]

When Israel Lévi became editor of the *Revue*, one of his first projects was
to prepare an index for the first twenty-five volumes. The index appeared as
a supplement to Volume 25 (1892), and it was divided into three sections:

    List of essays (arranged by author)
    List of subjects
    List of Hebrew titles

An index for the first fifty volumes (1880—1905) was published as a separate
volume in 1910. It contained the following:

    Index (arranged in dictionary style)
    List of Hebrew words and titles
    List of Greek words and titles
    List of Latin words and titles

An index for Volumes 51 to 100 (1906—1936) was published in 1937. It contained:

    List of subjects

List of Hebrew titles
List of authors

An index for Volumes 101 to 125 (1937—1966) was published in 1974. It consisted of the following seven sections:

List of tables of contents
List of authors
List of reviews (arranged by the names of the authors of the reviewed works)
List of subjects
List of places
List of facsimiles and illustrations
List of Hebrew words

## The Jewish Quarterly Review

In 1888 the first Anglo-Jewish scientific periodical, entitled *The Jewish Quarterly Review,* appeared in London.[85] The new periodical was edited by Israel Abrahams (1858—1925)[86] and Claude Joseph Goldsmid-Montefiore (1858—1938),[87] and it continued publication for a period of twenty years during which twenty volumes appeared. The October 1907 issue (Vol. 20, no. 1) informed the readers of the intention of the editors to cease publication the following July. The board of directors of Dropsie College in Philadelphia, Pennsylvania, therefore decided to acquire publication rights from the editors and to continue publication under its own auspices. The first issue of *The Jewish Quarterly Review* under its new management (designated as New Series) appeared in Philadelphia in July 1910; it was edited by Cyrus Adler (1863—1940)[88] and Solomon Schechter (1847—1915).[89] After Schechter's death Adler continued as sole editor, assisted by a number of scholars, among them Solomon Zeitlin (1892—1977).[90] The latter, together with Abraham Aaron Neuman (1890—1970),[91] became editors in 1940.

In 1966, fifty-eight years after the demise of the original series of *The Jewish Quarterly Review,* a reprint edition of the twenty-volume set was issued in New York by Ktav Publishing House, accompanied by a one-volume *Analytical Index.* The index was prepared by Isaiah Berger, and it consisted of the following:

Author-title index
Subject guide
Book review index (divided into list of authors and list of reviewers)

A *Classified Index* to the first twenty volumes of *The Jewish Quarterly Review,* New Series (1909–1930), was published in Philadelphia in 1932. It was compiled by Paul Romanoff (1898–1943), and consisted of the following:

Index of authors, titles, and catchwords (arranged in a single alphabetical order)
List of Hebrew titles
List of Arabic titles[92]

## *Hashilo'ach*

Nine years after the launching of the original series of *The Jewish Quarterly Review* the first modern scientific-literary Hebrew monthly began to appear in Berlin. The periodical was edited by Achad Ha'am (Asher Ginzberg; 1856–1927),[93] financed by Kalonymos Ze'ev Wissotzky (1824–1904),[94] published by Achiasaf,[95] and entitled *Hashilo'ach* (cf. Isaiah 8:6).[96] It made its first appearance in October 1896. Volumes 1–10 (1896–1902) were edited by Achad Ha'am. Volumes 11–46 (1903–1927) were edited by Joseph Klausner (1874–1958).[97] During the three decades of its existence, *Hashilo'ach* changed its location several times and weathered a number of crises.[98] Volumes 1–6 (1896–1899) and 9–10 (1902) were published in Berlin; Volumes 7–8 (1901) and 11–15 (1903–1905) were published in Cracow; Volumes 16–35 (1907–1918) were published in Odessa, and Volumes 36–46 (1919–1927) were published in Jerusalem. *Hashilo'ach* finally succumbed only a few months after the death of its first editor and founder, Achad Ha'am.[99]

An eight-page index to the first ten volumes of *Hashilo'ach,* arranged alphabetically by the name of the author (and probably compiled by Achad Ha'am himself to signify the end of a period in the life of the periodical), was appended to Volume 10 (1902). Achad Ha'am's secretary during his later years, Johanan Pograbinsky (1895–1959), prepared a complete index to the entire set of *Hashilo'ach,* arranged by author and subject. It remained unpublished.[100] In 1964, however, a volume entitled *Hashilo'ach, 1896–1927: Bibliyografyah,* prepared by Jehoshua Barzilai (Folman), was published in Tel Aviv. It contained the following:

List of authors (including biographical data and list of titles; this section included
    280 authors and 2,141 titles)
Bibliographical notes on works that were later reissued in other periodicals or in
    monographs (arranged by author)
List of titles
List of subjects

## Hatekufah

The Russian Revolution of 1917 lifted the restrictions on establishing new Jewish periodicals in Russia, and it facilitated the launching of one of the most impressive Hebrew quarterlies ever to be published. Edited by David Frishman (1859–1922)[101] and financed by Abraham Joseph Stybel (1884–1946),[102] *Hatekufah* began to appear in Moscow in January 1918.[103] Volumes 1–15 (1918–1922) were edited by Frishman; later volumes were edited successively by Fischel Lachower (1883–1947), Jacob Cohen (1881–1960), Saul Tchernichovski (1875–1943), Ben-Zion Katz (1875–1958), Simon Rawidowicz (1897–1957), Aaron Zeitlin (1898–1974), and Isaac Silberschlag (born 1903).

*Hatekufah,* like *Hashilo'ach,* carried scholarly literary and scientific sections, but most significant and unique was its section of translations from world literature. It was forced to change locations several times due to political and financial crises. Volumes 1–3 (1918) were published in Moscow; Volumes 4–23 (1919–1925) were published in Warsaw; Volumes 24–27 (1928–1930) were published in Berlin; Volumes 28–29 (1936) appeared in Tel Aviv, and Volumes 30/31–34/35 (1946–1950), in New York.

A thirty-one-page author-title index for the first twenty-five volumes of *Hatekufah* was published in 1929 as a supplement to Volume 25. A complete index to all volumes was published in Tel Aviv about three decades later (1961). Entitled *Hatekufah 1918–1950: Bibliyografyah,* compiled and edited by Jehoshua Barzilai (Folman), it was divided into the following three sections:

> List of authors (including biographical data and list of titles; this section included 301 authors)
> List of titles
> List of subjects[104]

## Gilyonot

Jehoshua Barzilai (Folman), who compiled and edited the indexes to *Hashilo'ach* and *Hatekufah,* also compiled an index to a Hebrew monthly that was published in Tel Aviv for a period of twenty-two years. Entitled *Gilyonot,* a publication devoted to "literature, thought, and criticism" and edited and published by Isaac Lamdan (1899–1954),[105] it initially appeared in Tel Aviv in 1933. Thirty-one volumes were published before it ceased appearing in 1955, due to Lamdan's death.[106] *Gilyonot* included among its participants writers of fiction, poets, thinkers, literary critics, and publicists from Palestine, Poland, the United States, and Russia, constituting the cream of modern Hebrew literature.

Barzilai's index, entitled *Gilyonot 1933–1955: Bibliyografyah,* was published in Tel Aviv in 1973 by the Benzion Katz Institute for Research in Hebrew Literature of Tel Aviv University. A welcome improvement over the previously mentioned indexes by Barzilai, it listed in a single alphabet 7,205 entries of authors, titles, and subjects.

## *Ha'achdut, Kuntres* and *Hapoel Hatsair*

In a review of a Hebrew work on the preparation of indexes, Getzel Kressel complained that "up to and including our own days, there is a confusion (in the Hebrew field) between tables of contents and indexes. This is evident from a number of 'indexes' to periodicals that have appeared lately, which are actually just tables of contents."[107] Kressel, who during the 1960s compiled a number of indexes to Hebrew periodicals based on the Wilson system of indexing,[108] did not exaggerate. Compared to the indexes he compiled, most of those mentioned earlier did indeed look like tables of contents.

Kressel's first index, entitled *Mafte'ach Leha'achdut,* was published in 1961 in the Tel Aviv Hebrew periodical *Asufot*[109] (and was also issued as a separate). *Ha'achdut,* the official organ of the Zionist-Socialist group, Poale Zion, was published in Jerusalem from 1910 to 1914, during which period six volumes appeared.[110] Among the participants in *Ha'achdut* were David Ben-Gurion, the first prime minister of the State of Israel, and Itzhak Ben-Zvi, its second president. The *Mafte'ach,* consisting of seventy-three pages, was the first in a planned series, Indexes to the Labor Movement Press in Palestine.

Kressel's second index, entitled *Mafte'ach Lakuntres,* was published in Tel Aviv in 1966 in the same periodical[111] (and it was also issued as a separate). *Kuntres,* the organ of the Zionist-Socialist group Achdut Ha'avodah, began to appear in Tel Aviv in 1919 as a weekly. Three hundred eighty issues appeared between 1919 and 1929, when publication was suspended. Fourteen additional issues appeared between 1943 and 1945, when publication of *Kuntres* was resumed under the auspices of Mifleget

Poale Erets Yisrael—Mapai. The *Mafte'ach,* consisting of 180 pages, was the second in the planned series, Indexes to the Labor Movement Press in Palestine.

Kressel's crowning achievement in indexing came in 1968 with the publication in Tel Aviv of his *Mafte'ach Lehapoel Hatsair. Hapoel Hatsair,* the organ of the Hitagdut Hapoalim Ha'ivrim Hatse'irim Be'erets Yisrael (later changed to: Histadrut Hapoalim Ha'ivrim Be'erets Yisrael; now known as Mifleget Poale Erets Yisrael—Mapai), was founded in Tel Aviv in 1907.[112] The *Mafte'ach,* consisting of 367 pages, covered the first fifty years of the existence of this periodical. It was issued in folio format to match the size of the periodical, and it contained about 100,000 entries.[113] The joint compilation of the volume—by Isa and Getzel Kressel—and its printing took about fourteen years; it constitutes the most massive and scientifically arranged Hebrew index to be published until now.[114]

## Mibifnim

While Kressel was compiling indexes to periodicals of the labor movement in Palestine-Israel, plans were being made by a specially formed group to compile indexes to the periodicals of the Kibbutz movement in Palestine-Israel. This group, named Mif'al Habibliyografyah Hakibutsit (formed jointly by the Institute for Zionist Research in memory of Chaim Weizmann of the Tel Aviv University and the Bibliographic Institute of the Kibbutz Meuchad Center for Study and Research) set as its first goal the compiling of separate indexes to the major periodicals published by four different Kibbutz groups;[115] later, the separate indexes were to be cumulated into a single one.[116]

An "orientation" volume for the preparation of the planned indexes was issued by the Mif'al in 1968,[117] and in 1970 the first volume in the series of "Indexes to Kibbutz Periodicals" appeared in Tel Aviv. It was an index to the first twenty-nine volumes of *Mibifnim,* the organ of Kibbutz Meuchad (formerly Kibbutz Ein Charod), and it was accordingly entitled *Mibifnim; Mafte'ach Lashanim 1923—1967.*[118] The 571-page volume was compiled and edited by Meir Buchsweiler and Daniel Kapri, and it included about 17,000 entries (besides cross-references) arranged in accordance with the Wilson method of indexing.[119]

## Niv Hakevutsah

The second volume in the series of "Indexes to Kibbutz Periodicals," also compiled under the editorship of Meir Buchsweiler and Daniel Kapri, was published in Tel Aviv in 1975. It was an index to the first twenty-eight years of *Niv Hakevutsah,* the organ of Ichud Hakevutsot Vehakibutsim, and it was accordingly entitled *Niv Hakevutsah; Mafte'ach Lashanim 1929—1967.*[120] The 785-page volume, included more than 20,000 entries and was arranged in the same manner as the preceding one.

ʿ

## Miscellaneous Indexes to Hebraica and Judaica Periodicals

The publication of Barzilai's index to *Hatekufah,* in 1961, was such a happy occasion for one Hebrew enthusiast in New York that he was going to call up some friends on the telephone to wish them *mazal tov.*[121] The publication of indexes to Jewish periodicals has made great progress since then, and it is no longer a rarity. A quarter of a century ago, a well-known Hebrew bibliographer, in a survey of indexes to Hebrew periodicals, was able to list no more than seven indexes to large runs of such periodicals, published during the first forty-five years of this century.[122] The number of published indexes for the last two decades alone is much larger than this. The following will briefly describe (in alphabetical order) additional individual indexes to the most important Hebraica and Judaica periodicals:[123]

*American Jewish Year Book.* Publication in progress since 1899/1900. First issued in Philadelphia by the Jewish Publication Society of America, later in New York, jointly with the American Jewish Committee. Indexes "to special articles and features" were added to Volumes 36 (1934/35), 40 (1938/39), 45 (1943/44), 46 (1944/45), 47 (1945/46), and 50 (1948/49). A complete index to Volumes 1—50 (1899/1900—1948/49) was compiled by Elfrida C. Solis-Cohen, and published in New York in 1967 by Ktav Publishing House. See also above, note 67.

*Ariel: A Review of Arts and Sciences in Israel.* Publication in progress since 1962. Issued in Jerusalem by the Cultural Relations Department of the Ministry for Foreign Affairs. An index to numbers 1—30 (1962—1972), compiled by Curtis Arnson, was published in Jerusalem in 1972.

*Hadoar*. Publication in progress since 1921, first as a daily (November 1, 1921 – June 1922), later as a weekly. Issued in New York by Histadruth Ivrith of America. An effort to compile an index to the daily *Hadoar* was made in the 1920s by Zecharia Fishman.[124] Demands for the compilation of a complete index to *Hadoar*, made in 1948 and in 1961 by prominent *Hadoar* writers,[125] were partially fulfilled in 1964 with the publication of Leo Shpall's *Yahadut Amerika Beshule Hadoar* (New York, 1964). The volume, an index to articles dealing with American Jewry published in *Hadoar* from 1921 through 1963, registered more than 1,200 entries, divided into 14 sections.

*Evreiskaia Starina*. Published in thirteen volumes from 1909 to 1930. Issued in Petrograd-Leningrad by Evreiskoe Istoriko-Etnograficheskoe Obshchestvo. An index, compiled by Abraham Gordon Duker (born 1907), was published in *HUCA* 8–9 (1931–32): 525–603 (and also issued as a separate.)

*Gesher*. Publication in progress since 1954. Issued in Tel Aviv by the World Jewish Congress, Israel Executive. A three-part index (authors, titles, subjects), covering issues 1–25 (1954–1960), was published in 1962. An extended index, covering issues 1–41 (1954–1964), was published in 1966.

*Di Goldene Keyt*. Publication in progress since 1949. Issued in Tel Aviv by Hahistadrut Hakelalit shel Haovdim Ha'ivrim Be'erets Yisrael. An author-title index to issues 1–50 (1949–1964) was published in 1964 together with issue number 50.

*Hagoren*. Published in ten volumes from 1898 to 1928. Issued in Berdichev-Berlin by Samuel Abba Horodetzki (1871–1957). A table of contents to all published volumes, together with an alphabetical list of authors and titles, was printed at the end of Volume 10.

*Hebrew Union College Annual*. Publication in progress since 1924.[126] Issued in Cincinnati, Ohio, by the Hebrew Union College–Jewish Institute of Religion. "Tables of Contents of Previous Volumes" was appended to Volumes 4–15 (1927–1940). Beginning with Volume 16 (1941), an author-title index to the preceding issues was added to each volume. An *Analytical Subject Index* to Volumes 1–37 (1924–1966), compiled by Isaiah Berger, was published in New York in 1969 by Ktav Publishing House.

*Historia Judaica*. Published in twenty-three volumes from 1938 to 1961. Merged with *Revue des Études Juives* since 1962. Issued in New York by Guido Kisch. A topically arranged index to Volumes 1–20 (1938–1958), compiled by Kurt Schwerin, was printed in the final volume, pp. 23–166. See also above, note 67.

*Jahrbuch der Gesellschaft für Geschichte der Juden in der Cechoslovakischen*

*Republik.* Published in nine volumes from 1929 to 1938. Issued in Prague and edited by Samuel Steinherz (born 1857). A periodical of a similar nature was the *Zeitschrift für die Geschichte der Juden in der Tschechoslowakei.* Published in five volumes from 1930 to 1938. Issued in Brünn by Jüdischer Buch- und Kunstverlag. A joint index to both periodicals was compiled by Robert Dán and published in the Tel Aviv *Zeitschrift für die Geschichte der Juden* 5 (1968): 180–201.

*Jahrbuch für jüdische Geschichte und Literatur.* Published in thirty-one volumes from 1898 to 1937. Issued in Berlin by Verband der Vereine für jüdische Geschichte und Literatur in Deutschland. An index, compiled by Robert Dán, was published in the above mentioned *Zeitschrift für die Geschichte der Juden* 7 (1970): 136–153.

*Jewish Book Annual.* Publication in progress since 1942. Issued in New York by the Jewish Book Council of America. A "Cumulative Index" to Volumes 1–10 (1942–1951/52) was printed in Volume 11, and to Volume 11–20 (1952/53–1962/63) in Volume 20. A "Cumulative Title and Author Index" to Volumes 1–25 (1942–1967/68) was printed in Volume 25 (and was also issued in 1972 as a separate, together with reproductions of the contents pages of Volumes 26–30).

*Jewish Daily Bulletin.* Published in twelve volumes from 1924 to 1935 (became weekly with Volume 12, no. 3,200; was absorbed on February 18, 1938, by *American Hebrew*). Issued in New York by the Jewish Daily Bulletin Corp. A volume entitled *The Jewish Daily Bulletin Index: A Key to Contemporary Jewish History* was published in New York in 1925. It covered the *Bulletin* from January 1 to December 31, 1924, and it registered more than 10,000 entries.

*Jewish Life.* Publication in progress since 1946 (from January 1946 to February 1959 entitled *Orthodox Jewish Life*). Issued in New York by Union of Orthodox Jewish Congregations of America. An author and subject index for the years 1946–1965, compiled by Micha Falk Oppenheim, was published in New York in 1968.

*Jewish Social Studies.* Publication in progress since 1939. Issued in New York by the Conference on Jewish Relations (later changed to Conference on Jewish Social Studies). Two brief lists, entitled *List and Subject Index* for Volumes 1–14 (1939–1952) and 1–15 (1939–1953), compiled by Lloyd Philip Gartner (born 1927), were issued in 1952 and 1953. A *Jewish Social Studies Cumulative Index* to Volumes 1–25 (1939–1964), compiled by Max M. Rothschild, was published in New York in 1967. See also above, note 67.

*Judaica: Zeitschrift für Geschichte, Literatur, Kunst und Bibliographie.* Published in twenty-six numbers (in 13 issues) from 1934 to 1937. Issued in Pressburg (Bratislava) by Samuel Bettlheim (1873–1942). An index, compiled by Robert

Dán, was published in the *Zeitschrift für die Geschichte der Juden* 4 (1967): 42−54.

*Jüdisches Archiv; Zeitschrift für jüdisches Museal- und Buchwesen, Geschichte, Volkskunde und Familien-Forschung.* Published in two volumes from October 1927 to May-June 1929. Issued in Vienna and edited by Ludwig Moses. An index, compiled by Robert Dán, was published in the *Zeitschrift für die Geschichte der Juden* 6 (1969): 99−106.

*Kiryat Sefer.* Publication in progress since 1924. Issued in Jerusalem by the Jewish National and University Library. Cumulative indexes listing studies and reviews were issued for Volumes 1−15 (1924−1938/39), Volumes 16−25 (1939/40−1948/49), and Volumes 26−35 (1949/50−1959/60). An enlarged index to Volumes 1−40 (1924−1964/65) was issued in 1967 under the title *Maftechot Lema'amarim, Lehe'arot Uledivre Bikoret.*[127]

*Leshonenu.* Publication in progress since 1928. Issued in Jerusalem by Va'ad Halashon Ha'ivrit Be'erets Yisrael (and from Volume 19 by Ha'akademyah Lalashon Ha'ivrit). A six-part index (author-title, subjects, words, book reviews, obituaries, activities of Va'ad Halashon and the Akademyah) for Volumes 1−25 (1928−1961) was issued in 1967.

*Halevanon.* Published in twenty volumes from 1863 to 1886. Issued in Jerusalem-Paris-Mainz-London by Jehiel Brill (1836−1886). An index to material in *Halevanon* dealing with the Jewish community in Palestine, compiled by Rahel Fried and Amikam Kohen, was published in Jerusalem in 1974 by Yad Itzhak Ben-Zvi.[128]

*Luach Erets Yisrael.* Published in twenty-one volumes from 1895 to 1916. Issued in Jerusalem by Abraham Moses Luncz (1854−1918). A list of titles published in volumes 1−10 (1895−1904) was printed in Volume 10.

*Ma'arachot.* Publication in progress since 1940. Issued in Tel Aviv by the publishing house of the Tseva Haganah Leyisrael. A subject index to Volumes 1−20 (1940−1953) was issued as Volume 24 (corresponding to no. 91/92, 1955). In this volume three one-time publications that preceded *Ma'arachot* are also indexed, namely, *Biyeme Ma'arachot* (September 1939), *Ashmurot* (November 1939), and *Machanot* (January 1940). A subject index to Volumes 21−37 (1953−1960) was issued as Volume 38 (corresponding to no. 134, 1961). Also indexed in this volume was *Tsiklon,* a companion periodical to *Ma'arachot,* published in Tel Aviv by Tseva Haganah Leyisrael in 120 numbers from 1953 to 1963.

*Magyar Zsidó Szemle.* Published in sixty-two volumes from 1884 to 1948. Issued in Budapest as a Hungarian-Jewish counterpart to *JQR* and *REJ;* edited by

Wilhelm Bacher (1850—1913), Ludwig Blau (1861—1936), and other Hungarian-Jewish scholars. An index to a select number of topics, compiled by Shemuel Hacohen Weingarten (born 1899), was published in *Areshet,* 2 (1960): 285—308 (also issued as a separate). See also below, p. 304, n. 10.

*Moznayim.* Publication in progress since 1933. Issued as a monthly in Tel Aviv by Agudat Hasofrim Beyisrael.[129] An author index to Volumes 1—18 (nos. 1—100; 1933—1944), compiled by Ithamar Lipshitz, was published in Volume 18.

*Perozdor.* Published in twelve numbers (in 8 issues) from 1962 to 1968. Issued in Tel Aviv by Itzhaq Zimerman (1894—1969). An author index (and separate list of reviews), compiled by Elazar Benyoez, was printed as a supplement to Zimerman's posthumously published work, *Be'enav shel Ma'amin* (Tel Aviv, 1970).

*Publications of the American Jewish Historical Society.* Published in fifty volumes from 1892 to 1961.[130] Issued variously in Philadelphia, Baltimore, and New York by the Society. A detailed index to Volumes 1—20 (1892—1914), compiled by Henrietta Szold (1860—1945) and Elfrida Cowen, was published in 1914.[131] See also above, note 67.

*Sinai.* Publication in progress since 1937. Issued in Jerusalem by the Rabbi Kook Institute and edited for twenty-five years by its founder, Rabbi Yehudah Leib Maimon (1875—1962).[132] An index of authors, titles, and topics for Volumes 1—40 (1937—1957), compiled by Nathaniel Katzburg (born 1922), was printed in *Sinai: Sefer Yovel* (Jerusalem, 1958).

*Tarbits.* Publication in progress since 1929. Issued in Jerusalem by the Hebrew University Press and edited by Jacob Nahum Epstein (1878—1952), Jefim Schirmann (born 1904), and others. An index of authors and topics for Volumes 1—10 (1929—1939) was issued in 1939. An extended index of authors and topics for Volumes 1—20 (1929—1949) was issued in 1950. An index of authors, topics, and book reviews for Volumes 1—30 (1929—1961) was issued in 1963.

*Tel-Talpiyot.* Published in forty-five volumes from 1892 to 1938. Issued and edited in Vácz-Budapest by David Zvi Katzburg (born 1856). A two-volume index, consisting of lists and authors and subjects, was compiled by Menahem Katzburg (a son of the editor and publisher).[133] Volume 1 (lists of authors and places) was published in Jerusalem in 1968 by Machon Ma'ayan Hachochmah. Volume 2 (list of subjects) to be published soon.

*Torah Mitsiyon.* Published in eleven volumes from 1887 to 1906. Issued and edited in Jerusalem by Samuel Zuckerman. An index to Volumes 1—10 (1887—1905), compiled by Asher Leib Brisk (1872—1916) and entitled *Beri'ach Hatichon,* was published in Jerusalem in 1911. (A pamphlet consisting of tables of contents for Volumes 1−10 was published in 1906).

*Tradition.* Publication in progress since 1958. Issued in New York by the Rabbinical Council of America. A subject, author, and book-review index to Volumes 1−10 (1958−1969), compiled by Micha Falk Oppenheim, was published in New York in 1970.

*Tsiklon.* See above, under *Ma'arachot.*

*Year Book of the Central Conference of American Rabbis.* Publication in progress since 1890. Issued in Philadelphia [etc.] Indexes to Volumes 1−25 (1890−1915), 26−30 (1916−1920), and 31−35 (1921−1925) were published in, respectively, 1916, 1921, and 1926. A cumulative index to Volumes 1−50 (1890−1940) was published in 1941.

*Yedi'ot Genazim.* Publication in progress since 1962. Issued in Tel Aviv by Genazim, Machon Biyo-Bibliyografi Al Shem Asher Barash. A detailed index to numbers 1−75 (1962−1971) was issued in 1972.

*Yerushalayim.* Published in thirteen volumes from 1882 to 1919. Issued and edited in Vienna-Jerusalem by Abraham Moses Luncz (1854−1918). An index of titles, topics, and authors for Volumes 1−10 (1882−1913) was printed at the end of Volume 10.

*Zamlbikher.* Published in eight volumes from 1936 to 1952. Issued in New York and edited by Joseph Opatoshu (1886−1954) and Halper Leivick (1888−1962). An author-subject index, compiled by Noe Grüss, was printed in *Pinkes far der Forshung fun der Yidisher Literatur un Press* (New York, 1972), 2:369−384.

*Zeitschrift für die Geschichte der Juden in der Tschechoslowakei.* See above, under *Jahrbuch der Gesellschaft für Geschichte der Juden in der Čechoslovakischen Republik.*[134]

*Zeitschrift für die Geschichte der Juden in Deutschland.* Published in eight volumes from 1929 to 1938. Issued in Berlin by Philo Verlag and edited by Ismar Elbogen (1874−1943), Aron Freimann (1871−1948), and Max Freudenthal (1868−1937). An index, compiled by Robert Dán, was published in the Tel Aviv *Zeitschrift für die Geschichte der Juden* 5 (1968): 29−49.

# IV. Indexes of Jewish Monographic Works

## Marcus-Bilgray: *An Index to Jewish Festschriften*

After the scientific periodical, the most important media for the dissemination of scholarly studies and articles is the Festschrift. Periodicals are published at intervals, and each issue is, in a sense, a continuation of the preceding one; Festschriften are published on special occasions—in honor of or in memory of a person, institution, or organization—and there is no relation between one Festschrift and another. Each is a one-time publication, monographic in nature. But there is a single factor that is common to periodicals and Festschriften: both consist of contributions of articles and essays by various scholars and are, therefore, the end-result of a collective effort.[135] The need for indexes to materials contained therein is, understandably, as important in the case of Festschriften as in the case of periodicals.

A first effort at indexing Jewish Festschriften was made in 1937 by Jacob Rader Marcus[136] and Albert Bilgray (born 1910) with the publication by the Hebrew Union College, Cincinnati, of a mimeographed volume entitled *An Index to Jewish Festschriften.* The volume registered "some 4,000 entries . . . contained in 53 (actually 54) Festschriften." The compilers indexed "all the Festschriften that were available" to them "up to 1936," and they excluded volumes "that limit themselves solely to Biblical and Semitic philological and linguistic materials." The entries were arranged "alphabetically according to the author's surname, the title, and . . . subject. . . . " Each entry in the three categories consisted of:

| *Author Entry* | *Title Entry* | *Subject Entry* |
|---|---|---|
| Author (surname and forename) | Title of article | Subject heading |
| Title of article | Author (surname with initial of forename) | Author (surname with initial of forename) |
| Festschrift (key word) | Festschrift (key word) | Title of article |
| Page numbers | Page numbers | Festschrift (key word) |
| | | Page numbers |

The *Index* was divided into the following three sections:

List of Festschriften indexed (each Festschrift assigned a key word to be used in the entries)

Index
List of Hebrew titles

## Charles Berlin:
### *Index to Festschriften in Jewish Studies*

A quarter of a century after the publication of the Marcus-Bilgray *Index*
another index, of a different nature, appeared, but one which nevertheless
appreciably complemented the former. It was Dorothy Rounds' *Articles on
Antiquity in Festschriften* (Cambridge, Mass., 1962), which registered articles dealing with the ancient Near East, Old Testament, Greece, Rome,
Roman law, and Byzantium. The compiler indexed 1,174 Festschriften for
this purpose, including 180 devoted to Bible studies, an area not covered by
Marcus-Bilgray.

Rounds' index did not meet the need to bring under bibliographic control the thousands of articles in nearly 250 Jewish-content Festschriften that
had become available since 1936. The Rounds index included very little
Hebrew material (and the little that was included suffered from an un-
believable number of misprints and typographical errors); it also overlooked
most of the articles in Festschriften devoted to Jewish studies. The gap was
finally filled in 1971 with the appearance of an almost complete index to
Jewish Festschriften published from 1936 to June 1970.[137] Compiled by
Charles Berlin (born 1936), Judaica bibliographer at Harvard College
Library, and entitled, *Index to Festschriften in Jewish Studies,* the new
volume indexed 243 titles (259 volumes), and it was arranged as follows:

> List of Festschriften indexed (arranged according to the names of the honorees)
> Index of authors (registering about 6,700 articles; each entry consisting of author,
> title, Festschrift, and page numbers)
> Index of subjects (including 13,200 entries arranged in 1,600 subjects; each entry
> consisting of subject, author, title, Festschrift, and page numbers)[138]

The Berlin *Index* "automatically" excluded "any Festschrift indexed by
Marcus-Bilgray" and "Festschriften dealing with Bible . . . indexed by
Rounds." It also omitted about 300 articles, mainly in the area of rabbinic
commentaries, novellae, responsa, and biography. These exclusions and
omissions are regrettable. A unified index to all Festschriften published up
to 1970 would have been of much greater assistance to the prospective user,
especially since the Marcus-Bilgray *Index,* which covered many of the most

important Festschriften published in the field of Jewish studies, is no longer readily available.[139]

## Indexes to the Talmud and Midrash

Indexes to books antedate indexes to periodicals, perhaps by millennia. The book index is actually not much younger than the book itself. In Hebrew literature, the index might have had its beginnings with mnemonic and identification devices. Letters, words, or phrases, placed at the beginning or the end of a chapter or section, helped the student and scholar in memorizing or recalling information,[140] and headings were assigned to works, or to parts of works, to identify and to reveal their contents. From these devices evolved the table of contents, the forerunner of the modern index. Some works came into being with ready-made, built-in indexes: these were massive encyclopedic works, structured and arranged along broad topical lines. In Hebrew literature, the Mishnah, the Talmud, or the later codes of Moses ben Maimon, Jacob ben Asher, and Joseph Caro, to mention just a few examples, belong to this category. Since they were divided into tractates or sections, each devoted to a different subject, familiarization with the arrangement also served as a key to their content.[141]

During the last few centuries, as the number of Hebrew works has grown into the thousands and as the interests of Hebrew scholars and students have diversified, built-in indexes and tables of contents have proved to be insufficient, and the need for precise and detailed indexes to classic Hebrew works has become acute. A number of efforts have been made to prepare auxiliary works for the study of old Hebrew classics. These include, among others, the preparation of encyclopedias, concordances, books of quotations, and collections of phrases and proverbs.[142] A start toward the compilation of a "complete" index to the Babylonian Talmud was made in Jerusalem in 1930 with the publication of *Mafte'ach Hashalem Letalmud Bavli* by Eliyahu Nahum Porush-Glickman (born 1892).

The *Mafte'ach* covered *Berachot,* the first tractate of the Talmud, and it consisted of the following twenty-four sections:

Scriptural references
Rules of interpretation
Ritualistic laws (comprising sections 3—9)
Rules of the Talmud

Controversies among the rabbis of the Talmud
Ethical and folkloristic material (sections 12—13)
The Jewish people, the nations, and their histories (sections 14—15)
The universe, nature, and the supernatural (sections 16—17)
Health and medicine
Human creations
Names of people, places, books (sections 20—23)
Honorary and derogatory titles

Porush-Glickman's hope to compile a "complete" index to the Talmud never materialized beyond the first volume, but about three decades later there appeared an index that embraced the entire Babylonian Talmud. Entitled, *Oznayim Latorah; Subject Concordance to the Babylonian Talmud,* compiled by Lazarus Goldschmidt (1871—1950),[143] and edited by Raphael Edelman (1902—1972), the new volume was published in Copenhagen in 1959.

Goldschmidt planned the index as a supplement to his monumental nine-volume German translation of the Babylonian Talmud.[144] At the same time he intended it to serve as an index to the standard editions of the Talmud. Accordingly, each entry in *Oznayim Latorah* referred the user to both the Goldschmidt edition and the standard editions of the Babylonian Talmud. The index was arranged in a single alphabetical order, with subject key words placed at the beginning of each entry.

Another by-product of a translation of the Babylonian Talmud was an index published in London in 1952. During the years 1935—1948 the Soncino Publishing Society of London issued a complete English translation of the Babylonian Talmud in thirty-four volumes,[145] and in 1952 concluded the achievement with the publication of an *Index Volume to the Soncino Talmud,* compiled by Judah J. Slotki (born 1903). The *Index Volume* consisted of the following sections:

General index
Index of Scriptural references
Rabbinical index (i.e., references to names of rabbis)
Glossary

The Soncino Publishing Society was also responsible for the translation of *Midrash Rabbah* into English, and Judah J. Slotki was again the compiler of an *Index Volume* to the nine-volume set published in 1939.[146] The *Index Volume* contained the following:

Glossary
List of abbreviations
General index
Scriptural references
Talmudic references

## Indexes to *Mishneh Torah* and *Shulchan Aruch*

The two most important and popular codes of Jewish law, the *Mishneh Torah* by Moses ben Maimon—Maimonides (1135–1204)—and the *Shulchan Aruch* by Joseph Caro (1488–1575), attracted the attention of indexers during the last decades. Half a century ago, Moses Avigdor Chaikin (1852–1928), a *dayan* in the London Beth Din, published an index of rabbinic laws and decisions, and added at the end of each letter of the alphabet a section of references to the *Shulchan Aruch*.[147] Thirty-seven years later, Zvi Moskovitz, a Jerusalem publisher and bookdealer, compiled Chaikin's references to the *Shulchan Aruch* into a separate volume and published it under the title *Mafte'ach Ha'inyanim Me'arba Chelke Shulchan Aruch* (Jerusalem, 1960).[148]

A volume entitled *Mafte'ach Lashulchan,* an index to the *Shulchan Aruch,* the *Mishnah Berurah,*[149] and *Mishneh Torah,* was compiled by Isaac Nisenbaum and published in New York in 1965.

Another volume entitled *Mafte'ach Orach Chayim Umishnah Berurah,* compiled by Yehuda Eisenberg (born 1937), was published in Jerusalem in 1967. It was divided into a general and topical index. An index to the laws of *Shulchan Aruch Yoreh De'ah* was compiled by Abraham Drushkowitz (Druskaviciaus) and published in Kaunas in 1933 under the title *Sha'are Hora'ah.*

The most elaborate index of this nature was issued in Jerusalem in 1971. Entitled *Entsiklopedyah Hilchatit Chasde David* (cf. Isaiah, 55:3) and compiled by Eliahu David Slotky and Moshe Klapholtz, it consisted of summaries of the laws in *Mishneh Torah* and *Shulchan Aruch,* arranged in topical order. The volume included the following extra features:

Laws concerning the writing of Torah scrolls, etc.

Comparative table of contents of *Shulchan Aruch* and *Mishneh Torah*
Charts detailing the laws of weights and measures, prohibited work on the
Sabbath, and prayer

## Indexes to Responsa Literature

The last few decades have witnessed appreciable progress in indexing a
related area of rabbinic literature, responsa. Designated as *She'elot
Uteshuvot*, this branch of rabbinic works consists mostly of decisions in
Jewish law rendered by rabbinic authorities in various countries during a
span of about thirteen centuries. Many of these decisions deal with actual
cases and therefore include detailed descriptions of Jewish life and customs
in different communities during specific periods. This makes the responsa
an important source for the study of Jewish history and culture in various
countries and places. A recent estimate places the number of individual
responsa at about 300,000.[150]

The first collections of responsa date back to the Geonic period of the
seventh to the eleventh centuries. They consist of questions directed to the
heads of the rabbinic academies—the Geonim—by Jews of Babylonia and
other countries. Since these questions, and the answers (or decisions) they
solicited, covered almost every area of Jewish life, Jewish communities
began to collect them in volumes. They even prepared tables of contents, for
such volumes for easier reference.[151] The first printed collection of geonic
responsa appeared in Constantinople in 1516,[152] and it was followed fifty-
nine years later (1575) by a second collection.[153] About ten more collections
appeared up to the end of the nineteenth century.[154] Joel Müller (1827–
1895),[155] who himself published several collections of geonic responsa, compiled and issued a volume in Berlin in 1891 entitled *Mafte'ach Liteshuvot
Hageonim.* The volume, consisting of twenty-nine chapters, included the following:

Bibliographical surveys of eleven printed collections of geonic responsa (chapters
1–12)
Bibliographical survey of geonic responsa available in other printed volumes
(chapter 13)
Description of the intellectual activities of thirty-four Geonim (listed in
chronological order) with indexes of their responsa (chapters 14–28)
Topical index of responsa by anonymous Geonim (chapter 29)

Reprint editions of Müller's *Mafte'ach* were published in New York (Menorah Institute) in 1959 and in Jerusalem in 1967.

The discovery of the Cairo Genizah[156] in the 1890s brought to light many thousands of unknown geonic responsa, some of which were published during the first half of this century.[157] This prompted Benjamin Manasseh Lewin (1879–1944), who devoted himself to the study of the geonic period,[158] to compile all the known geonic responsa and other writings and to arrange them according to the order of the tractates of the Babylonian Talmud under the title *Otsar Hageonim.* This arrangement served as a built-in index to an unusually large corpus of geonic writing, and it enabled Hebrew scholars to gain easier access to this much-scattered material. Thirteen volumes of Lewin's *Otsar Hageonim* (*Berachot* to *Baba Metsia*) were published in Haifa-Jerusalem between 1928 and 1944, constituting about two-thirds of the available materials. Plans to continue Lewin's work have only partly materialized.[159]

Efforts to compile indexes to post-geonic responsa began several centuries ago. Some of these compilations were in effect abstracts of responsa, others were in the form of annotated references to various laws, but most of them were arranged either as glosses or as companion volumes to the *Shulchan Aruch.*[160] Plans to compile modern indexes to the responsa literature began to take shape in the early 1920s with the publication in New York of a specimen prepared by Judah David Eisenstein (1854–1956).[161] It consisted of five leaves, each printed on one side, indexing the historical and cultural material to be found in the responsa of Asher ben Jehiel (ca. 1250–1328). At the bottom of the last leaf the compiler noted, "this is an example of a plan to index all subjects relating to Jewish history, culture, and peculiar decisions, found in rabbinical responsa works up to the nineteenth century."

Eisenstein's plan called for the indexing of about one thousand works. This was to have been achieved with the help of a group of scholarly indexers, each one responsible for a certain number of responsa. Afterwards, the material was to have been arranged into a single index. The plan never went further than the specimen,[162] but forty years later (1963) the Institute for Research in Jewish Law of the Hebrew University in Jerusalem established a project to index responsa which was in a sense similar to the one proposed by Eisenstein, with the exception that its stress was rather more on the legal than on the historical and cultural material contained in the responsa literature. As the work progressed, the Institute modified its earlier policy and decided to include equally the legal as well as the historical and cultural materials.

The long-range goal of the Institute is to index all postgeonic responsa. A first step toward that goal is to index the responsa by the Spanish and North African scholars dating from the eleventh to the fifteenth centuries. Such an index would cover about 10,000 responsa, and it would be published in seven volumes divided into the following separate sections:

Index of legal matter
Index of sources (lists references to Bible, Talmud, and posttalmudic literature)
Index of historical material[163]

A sample volume of the Institute's work was published in Jerusalem in 1965. It was a 656-page index of the responsa of Asher ben Jehiel (also used by Eisenstein as a specimen). Entitled, *Mafte'ach Hashe'elot Vehateshuvot: She'elot Uteshuvot Harosh,* and edited by Menachem Elon (born 1923) the director of the Institute, the volume reflected the original indexing policy of the Institute, being devoted almost entirely to legal matter. Another sample volume reflecting the new policy of including all available historical information, was published in Jerusalem in 1973. Entitled, *Mafte'ach Hashe'elot Vehateshuvot: Hamafte'ach Hahistori,* and again edited by Menachem Elon (with the assistance of Avraham Grossman and Shimon Shtober), the new volume indexed historical material available in the responsa of Yom-Tob ben Abraham Ishbili (ca. 1270–1342) and Judah ben Asher (1270–1349).

Based on the two sample volumes, the indexing work done at the Institute, when completed, should prove to be of immeasurable value to Jewish studies in general and to Jewish law and history in particular.[164]

While the Institute for Research in Jewish Law was already deeply involved in responsa indexing, another Jerusalem-based institution, the Machon Maharshal Talmudic Seminary, independently began indexing and abstracting the entire literature of responsa, beginning with the geonic period up to the present. The plan of the Machon was to compile a four-part index:

Index of legal matter (including ritualistic laws, an area not covered by the Institute; arrangement to be according to the order of the *Shulchan Aruch* and *Mishneh Torah*)
Index of commentaries (arranged according to the books of the Bible, Talmud, Codes, etc.)
Index of rules in talmudic law, and topics dealing with the areas of cabala, ethics, etc. (arranged in alphabetical order)
Index of topics not included in the above, such as history, bibliography, biography, linguistics, etc.

The first part of the index of legal matter appeared in Jerusalem in 1971 under the title, *Otsar Hashe'elot Uteshuvot*.[165] Compiled by the students and scholars of the Machon and edited by Menachem Nachum Shapiro (born 1915), the volume included material from about 900 responsa volumes, dealing with matters covered by *Shulchan Aruch Orach Chayim*, sections 1–88.[166] This latest index of responsa should prove to be of great practical importance to rabbinic students and scholars.

## Indexes to Cabalistic and Chassidic Works

Another branch of early Jewish literature that invited indexing was the cabalistic-mystical literature. The *Zohar*, the main work of Hebrew Cabala,[167] was first published in 1558 (simultaneously in two different editions in Mantua and in Cremona), and its first index appeared about eight years later. Entitled *Mafte'ach Hazohar* (Venice, 1566) and compiled by Moses ben Mordecai Galante (died 1608),[168] the thirty-four-page index listed biblical passages and a variety of topics dealt with in the *Zohar*.

A twenty-four-leaf topical index to the *Zohar*, compiled by Abraham ben Michael Raphael Rovigo (ca. 1650–1713),[169] and again entitled *Mafte'ach Hazohar*, was published in Amsterdam in 1710. A much larger and more detailed work entitled *Maftechot Hazohar* was compiled by a cabalist named Samuel, edited by Israel Berechiah ben Joseph Jekuthiel Fontanella (died 1762),[170] and published in Venice in 1744. It was divided into two parts:

    Index of subject
    Index of biblical passages

Reprint editions of *Maftechot Hazohar* were issued in Jerusalem in 1969 and 1970.

A much broader and more modern index to the *Zohar* was compiled by Haim David Halevi (born 1924), Sephardic chief rabbi of Tel Aviv, with the title *Maftechot Hazohar Vera'ayonotav*. The volume, consisting of a 258-page subject index, was published in Tel Aviv in 1971.

The latest and most elaborate index of the *Zohar* was compiled by Eliahu David Slotky. The new volume, entitled *Aderet Eliyahu, Entsiklopedyah: Mafte'ach al Sifre Hazohar* and consisting of close to 10,000 entries, alphabetically arranged by subject and supplemented by cabalistic diagrams, was published in Jerusalem in 1974.

Next in importance to the *Zohar,* in cabalistic literature, are the works of Isaac Luria (Ari; 1534–1572), as transmitted by his closest disciple, Hayyim Vital (1543–1620). A topical index to three works by Vital—*Ets Chayim, Mavo She'arim,* and *Sha'ar Hahakdamot*—was compiled by Jacob Shealtiel Nino[171] and was published in Livorno (Leghorn) in 1843 under the title *Emet Leya'akov.* A reprint edition was issued in Jerusalem in 1968 or 1969.

A more elaborate index which covered the most important works of the Lurianic school of Cabala was compiled by Eliahu David Slotky and published in Jerusalem in 1963 under the title, *Yad Eliyahu: Mafte'ach (Entsiklopedyah) Lekabalat Ha'ari.* The 380-page volume consisted of close to 10,000 topically arranged entries, supplemented by a list of cabalistic terminology and diagrams.

Closely related to the Lurianic school of Cabala is the Chassidic movement, which came into being in Eastern Europe during the eighteenth century; closest to the Lurianic school is the Lubavich-Chabad branch of the Chassidic movement. An index to the major works and publications of the leaders of the Lubavich dynasty was published in Brooklyn, N.Y., in 1966, under the title *Sefer Hamaftechot Lesifre Uma'amare Chasidut Chabad.* The 352-leaf volume consisted of eighteen separate indexes to the works of five early leaders of the Lubavich movement,[172] some of which were compiled by the present leader of the movement, Rabbi Menachem Mendel Schneerson (born 1902); the rest were by Eliyahu Carlebach, a follower of the movement.[173] Since the indexes were compiled during a long period of time and were originally planned as supplements to individual works, they were not uniform. Some were divided into three sections: subjects, biblical references, and names of people and books; others had only two divisions (omitting either the biblical references or the names), and a few indexes listed only subjects.

Another Chassidic group that came into being about the same time as the Lubavich group was the one founded by Rabbi Nahman ben Simhah, of Bratzlav (1770?–1810?), a grandson of Israel ben Eliezer Ba'al Shem Tov (ca. 1700–1760), the founder of the entire Chassidic movement.[174] An index to the works of Rabbi Nahman and his most trusted pupil, Rabbi Nathan, was compiled by Natan Tsevi Kenig, edited by Shemuel Tukatsinski, and published in Bene Berak in 1968 under the title *Pituche Chotam* (cf. Exodus, 28: 11, etc.).

During recent decades the indexing of monographs has become a common practice among traditional rabbinical scholars, resulting in the publication of several individual indexes to well-known rabbinical works.[175] A few efforts were also made at preparing collective indexes to such works.[176] The most ambitious attempt of this kind was made by Mosheh Tsuri'el, of Bene Berak, who indexed the contents of about seventy-seven works (more than one hundred volumes) and published the index under the title, *Migdal Oz* (the numerical value of the Hebrew letters constituting the word *Oz* is 77). The volume, published in Bene Berak in 1973, covered works in the fields of cabala, Midrash, ethics and thought, Chassidism, Holy Land settlement, biography and halachah.

## Lists of Approbations and Subscriptions

Beginning with the 1490s and to the middle of the nineteenth century almost every printed Hebrew book carried one or more approbations by rabbis, scholars, or leaders of Jewish communities. The approbation served as a kind of copyright to protect the author or printer-publisher, and as a kind of censorship of his writings.[177] The censorship function of the approbation was originally forced upon the Hebrew book from the outside—from the ruling Catlolic church—but even afterwards, when this outside pressure was relaxed, the custom of attaching an approbation to a Hebrew book was continued voluntarily, and it is still done in current traditional publications.

During the nineteenth century, scholars already had begun to realize the importance of the information contained in the approbations,[178] and bibliographers began to include the names of approvers in Hebrew book entries for catalogs they compiled.[179] But it was only in 1923 that an index of approbations in Hebrew books was first published. Entitled *Mafte'ach Hahaskamot—Index Approbationum,* compiled and edited by Leopold Löwenstein (1843–1924),[180] and published in Frankfort (and in Berlin), it covered Hebrew works printed between 1490 and 1850. The volume was divided into the following sections:

List of approbations (arranged by the names of the approvers; 3,662 entries)
List of titles (circa 2,700)
List of places

The index was lithographically reproduced from an autograph written in the difficult Gothic script. This made it hard for many scholars to utilize the work to its fullest extent.[181]

Other sources of important information on Jewish life and history are the lists of subscribers printed in many Hebrew (mainly rabbinic) works published during the last two hundred years. The custom of printing such lists arose from the sad situation that most rabbinic authors could not find publishers for their works, and they themselves did not have the means to publish without the financial support of subscribers. These authors would travel from city to city to collect support, and when they succeeded in publishing their works, they usually listed in them the names of their benefactors as an expression of gratitude. The list of subscribers— *prenumerantn* in Yiddish[182]—was usually arranged according to cities or countries and carried the names of scholars, prominent people, and important institutions of various Jewish communities.

Berl Kagan, a librarian at the Jewish Theological Seminary in New York, devoted fifteen years of his life to compiling an index of subscription lists in Hebrew books printed during the last two centuries. The fruit of his labor was a volume of nearly 400 pages, small folio in format, bearing the title *Sefer Haprenumerantn* (New York, 1975).[183] In the introduction to his work—written in Yiddish and in English—Kagan states that he had examined "tens of thousands" of Hebrew books in his search for Hebrew subscription lists, and that he indexed about 70–75 percent of all Hebrew books that carry such lists. *Sefer Haprenumerantn* is divided into the following sections:

List of communities (8,749 Jewish communities in Europe and North Africa; each entry gives titles of works where community is listed)

List of indexed works (about 900)

List of personalities mentioned as subscribers (about 2,000 names of rabbis, well-known scholars, and laymen, selected from a total number of 350,000 names in compiler's file)

List of synagogues (about 300)

List of societies (about 80)

Geographical index (names of communities in Roman characters)

# Retrospective Indexes to Jewish Periodicals

| Title | Compilers or Editors | Places and Dates of Publication | Volumes, Numbers, or Pages | Topics and Period Covered | Frequency | Category* |
|---|---|---|---|---|---|---|
| Bibliografia Historii Żydów w Polsce i w Krajach Ościennych | Majer Balaban | Warsaw, 1939 | 112 pages | History; 1900–1930 | OTP** | II |
| Bibliography of Jewish Social Studies | Salo W. Baron | New York, 1941 | 291 pages | General; 1938–1939 | OTP | I |
| Bibyografishe Yorbikher fun Yivo | Yivo Bibl. Center | Warsaw, 1928 | 446 pages | General; Yiddish lit.; 1926 | OTP | I |
| Hasid's Index to Periodicals and Booklist | Harry S. Linfield | New York, 1932–1937 | Vols. 1–6, nos. 1–2 | General; 1932–1937 | Monthly; irregular | I |
| Die hebräische Publizistik in Wien | Bernhard Wachstein | Vienna, 1930 | 3 parts | Hebrew lit.; 1820–1889 | OTP | II |
| An Index to Scientific Articles on American Jewish History | Jacob R. Marcus | Cincinnati, 1971 | 420 pages | History; 1884–1968 | OTP | II |
| Me'ir Enayim | Meir Wunder | Bene-Berak-Jerusalem, 1968–1972 | Vols. 1–3 | Religion; 1966/7–1968/9 | Biannual | I |
| Die Palästina-Literatur | Peter Thomsen | Leipzig-Berlin, 1908–1960 | Vols. 1–7; A | Holy Land; 1878–1945 | Irregular | II |
| Palestine and Zionism | S.A. Udin, S. Landress | New York, 1946–1956 | Vols. 1–11 | General; 1946–1956 | Bimonthly; annual | II |
| Quellenkunde zur Geschichte der deutschen Juden | Moritz Stern | Kiel, 1892 | 105 pages | History; 19th century | OTP | II |
| Répertoire des Articles Relatifs à l'Histoire et à la Littérature Juives | Moïse Schwab | Paris, 1899–1903; 1914–23: repr. New York, 1971 | 539 pages | General; 1665–1900 | OTP | I |
| Sistematicheskii Ukazatel' Literatury o Evreiakh | Mefitse Haskalah | St. Petersburg, 1892: repr. Cambridge, 1973 | 568 pages | History; 1708–1889 | OTP | II |

\* See list of categories at beginning of Chapter Seven
\*\* One-time publication

## Current Indexes to Jewish Periodicals

| Title | Compilers or Editors | Places and Dates of Publication | Volumes, Numbers, or Pages | Topics and Periods Covered | Frequency | Category* |
|---|---|---|---|---|---|---|
| Index to Jewish Periodicals | Miriam Leikind | Cleveland, 1964— | Vol. 1— | General; 1963— | Annual; semiannual | I |
| Me'ir Letsiyon | Meir Wunder | Jerusalem, 1973— | Vol. 1— | Jewish law; 1969/70— | Biannual | I |
| Reshimat Ma'amarim Bemada'e Hayahadut | Issachar Joel | Jerusalem, 1969— | Vol. 1— | General; 1966— | Annual; semiannual | I |

* See list of categories at beginning of Chapter Seven

## Indexes to Individual Jewish Periodicals; Retrospective and Current

| Name of Periodical* | Compilers of Indexes | Places and Dates of Publication | Volumes, Numbers, or Dates Indexed | Topics Covered | Arrangement |
|---|---|---|---|---|---|
| Ha'achdut | G. Kressel | Tel Aviv, 1961 | Complete | All topics | Dictionary style |
| American Jewish Year Book | Elfrida C. Solis-Cohen | New York, 1967 | Vols. 1–50 | All topics | Dictionary style |
| Ariel | C. Arnson | Jerusalem, 1972 | Nos. 1–30 | All topics | Dictionary style |
| Hadoar | L. Shpall | New York, 1964 | 1921–1963 | American Jewry | Topical arrangement (14 sections) |
| Evreiskaia Starina | A. G. Duker | Cincinnati, 1931/32 (in *HUCA* 8–9) | Complete | All topics | Topical arrangement (20 sections) |
| Gesher | J. Barzilai | Tel Aviv, 1966 (in *ZGJ* 7) | Nos. 1–41 | All topics | Author-title-subject |
| Gilyonot | | Tel Aviv, 1973 | Complete | All topics | Dictionary style |
| Di Goldene Keyt | | Tel Aviv, 1964 | Nos. 1–50 | All topics | Author-title |
| Hagoren | S. A. Horodetzki | Berlin, 1928 (in vol. 10) | Complete | All topics | Table of contents and author-title |
| Hebrew Union College Annual | I. Berger | New York, 1969 | Vols. 1–37 | All topics | Topical arrangement |
| Historia Judaica | K. Schwerin | New York, 1961 (in vol. 23) | Vols. 1–20 | All topics | Topical arrangement |
| Jahrbuch der Gesellschaft für Geschichte der Juden in der Čechoslovakischen Republik | Robert Dán | Tel Aviv, 1968 (in *ZGJ* 5) | Complete | All topics | Author-subject |
| Jahrbuch für jüdische Geschichte und Literatur | Robert Dán | Tel Aviv, 1970 (in *ZGJ* 7) | Complete | All topics | Author-subject |
| Jewish Book Annual | | New York, 1972 (also in vol. 25) | Vols. 1–25 | All topics | Author-title |
| Jewish Daily Bulletin | M. F. Oppenheim | New York, 1925 | Vol. 1 | All topics | Dictionary style |
| Jewish Life | | New York, 1968 | 1946–1965 | All topics | Author-subject |
| Jewish Quarterly Review | I. Berger | New York, 1966 | Complete | All topics | Author-title; subject; book-review |
| Jewish Quarterly Review, New Series | P. Romanoff | Philadelphia, 1932 | Vols. 1–20 | All topics | Dictionary style; Hebrew titles; Arabic titles |

*The bibliographical data on the listed periodicals are given in Chapter Seven, Section III.

Indexes to Individual Jewish Periodicals; Retrospective and Current (cont.)

| Periodical | Compiler | Place, Year | Volumes | Topics | Style |
|---|---|---|---|---|---|
| Jewish Social Studies | M. M. Rothschild | New York, 1967 | Vols. 1–25 | All topics | Dictionary style |
| Judaica | Robert Dán | Tel Aviv, 1967 (in *ZfGJ* 4) | Complete | All topics | Author-subject |
| Jüdisches Archiv | Robert Dán | Tel Aviv, 1969 (in *ZfGJ* 6) | Complete | All topics | Author-subject |
| Kiryat Sefer | | Jerusalem, 1967 | Vols. 1–40 | Studies; reviews | Author-title-subject |
| Kuntres Leshonenu | G. Kressel | Tel Aviv, 1966 Jerusalem, 1967 | Complete Vols. 1–25 | All topics All topics | Dictionary style Author-title-subject |
| Halevanon | R. Fried, A. Kohen | Jerusalem, 1974 | Complete | Jewish community in Erets Yisrael | Dictionary style |
| Luach Erets Yisrael | | Jerusalem, 1904 (in vol. 10) | Vols. 1–10 | All topics | Titles |
| Ma'arachot | | Tel Aviv, 1955; Tel Aviv, 1961 | Vols. 1–20; Vols. 21–37 | All topics | Topical |
| Magyar Zsido Szemle | S. Weingarten | Jerusalem, 1960 (in *Areshet* 2) | Complete | Selection | Topical |
| Mibifnim | M. Buchsweiler, D. Kapri | Tel Aviv, 1970 | Vols. 1–29 | All topics | Dictionary style |
| Monatsschrift für Geschichte und Wissenschaft des Judentums | A. Posner, S. Hellenstein | Breslau, 1938; reprinted and completed, Tübingen, 1966 | Complete | All topics | Title-subject (two sections) |
| Moznayim | I. Lipshitz | Tel Aviv, 1944 (in vol. 18) | Vols. 1–18 (nos. 1–100) 1929–1967 | All topics | Author |
| Niv Hakevutsah | M. Buchsweiler, D. Kapri | Tel Aviv, 1975 | Complete | All topics | Dictionary Style |
| Perozdor | E. Benyoez | Tel Aviv, 1970 (in *Be'enav Shel Ma'amin*) | Complete | All topics | Author-reviews |
| Hapoel Hatsa'ir | I. and G. Kressel | Tel Aviv, 1968 | Vols. 1–50 | All topics | Dictionary style |
| Publications of the American Jewish Historical Society | H. Szold, E. Cowen | Philadelphia, 1914 | Vols. 1–20 | All topics | Dictionary style |

## Indexes to Individual Jewish Periodicals; Retrospective and Current (cont.)

| | | | | | |
|---|---|---|---|---|---|
| Revue des Études Juives | | Paris, 1910; Paris, 1937; Paris, 1974 | Vols. 1–50; Vols. 51–100; Vols. 101–125 | All topics | Dictionary style; Hebrew, Greek, Latin words |
| Hashilo'ach | J. Barzilai | Tel Aviv, 1964 | Complete | All topics | Author-title-subject |
| Sinai | N. Katzburg | Jerusalem, 1958 (in Sinai: Sefer Yovel) | Vols. 1–40 | All topics | Author-title-subject |
| Tarbits | | Jerusalem, 1963 | Vols. 1–30 | All topics | Author-subject-book reviews |
| Hatekufah | J. Barzilai | Tel Aviv, 1961 | Complete | All topics | Author-title-subject |
| Tel-Talpiyot | M. Katzburg | Jerusalem, 1968 | Complete | Names | Authors-places |
| Torah Mitsiyon | L. Brisk | Jerusalem, 1911 | Vols. 1–10 | All topics | Author-title |
| Tradition | M. F. Oppenheim | New York, 1970 | Vols. 1–10 | All topics | Subject-author; book reviews |
| Tsiklon | | Tel Aviv, 1961 (in Ma'arachot 38) | Nos. 1–93 | All topics | Subject |
| Year Book of the Central Conference of American Rabbis | | Philadelphia, 1941 | Vols. 1–50 | All topics | Dictionary style |
| Yedi'ot Genazim | | Tel Aviv, 1972 | Nos. 1–75 | Names | Four sections |
| Yerushalayim | | Jerusalem, 1913 (in vol. 10) | Vols. 1–10 | All topics | Title-subject-author |
| Zamlbikher | Noe Grüss | New York, 1972 (in Pinkes Far der Forshung fun der Yidisher Literatur 2) | Complete | All topics | Author-subject |
| Zeitschrift für die Geschichte der Juden in der Tschechoslowakei | Robert Dán | Tel Aviv, 1968 (in ZfGJ 5) | Complete | All topics | Author-title-subject |
| Zeitschrift für die Geschichte der Juden in Deutschland | Robert Dán | Tel Aviv, 1968 (in ZfGJ 5) | Complete | All topics | Author-title-subject |

## Indexes to Jewish Festschriften and Classic Hebrew Works

| Works Indexed | Titles | Compilers | Places and Dates of Publication | Arrangement | Features |
|---|---|---|---|---|---|
| Festschriften | An Index to Jewish Festschriften | J. R. Marcus, A. Bilgray | Cincinnati, 1937 | Dictionary style | 4,000 entries; 54 titles; cut-off date: 1936 |
| | Index to Festschriften in Jewish Studies | C. Berlin | Cambridge, 1971 | Author-subject (2 sections) | 6,700 articles; 1,600 subjects; 243 titles; cut-off date: 1970 |
| Talmud | Mafte'ach Hashalem Letalmud Bavli | E. N. Porush-Glickman | Jerusalem, 1930 | Topical (24 sections) | Tractate Berachot only |
| | Oznayim Latorah | L. Goldschmidt | Copenhagen, 1959 | Dictionary style | References are given to standard editions of Talmud and also to Goldschmidt's Hebrew-German edition |
| | Index Volume to the Soncino Talmud | J. J. Slotki | London, 1952 | (Four sections): General, scriptural, rabbinical indexes; glossary | Rabbinical index gives references to names of rabbis mentioned in Talmud |
| Midrash | Index Volume to the Soncino Midrash | J. J. Slotki | London, 1939 | (Five sections): Glossary; abbreviations; general, scriptural, and talmudic indexes | |
| Mishneh Torah and Shulchan Aruch | Mafte'ach Ha'inyanim Me'arba Chelke Shulchan Aruch | M. A. Chaikin, Z. Moskovitz I. Nisenbaum | Jerusalem, 1960 | Topical | |
| | Mafte'ach Lashulchan | | New York, 1965 | Topical | Covers Shulchan Aruch, Mishnah Berurah, and Mishneh Torah |
| | Mafte'ach Orach Chayim Umishnah Berurah | Y. Eisenberg | Jerusalem, 1967 | Topical (two sections) | |
| | Sha'are Hora'ah | A. Drushkowitz | Kaunas, 1933 | According to order of the Shulchan Aruch | Indexes Yoreh Deah only |

# Indexes to Jewish Festschriften and Classic Hebrew Works (cont.)

| Category | Title | Author | Place, Date | Style | Notes |
|---|---|---|---|---|---|
| Responsa Literature | *Entsiklopedyah Hilchatit Chasde David* | E. D. Slotky, M. Klapholtz | Jerusalem, 1971 | Dictionary style | Covers Mishneh Torah and Shulchan Aruch; special section on laws concerning writing of Torah scrolls, etc.; comparative table of contents of Shulchan Aruch and Mishneh Torah; summaries of laws |
| | *Mafte'ach Liteshuvot Hageonim* | J. Müller | Berlin, 1891 (reprinted, New York, 1959; Jerusalem, 1967) | Author-subject (29 sections) | Bibliographical survey of printed Geonic responsa; description of life of Geonim |
| | *Mafte'ach Hashe'elot Vehateshuvot: She'elot Uteshuvot Harosh* | M. Elon | Jerusalem, 1965 | Topical (3 sections) | Indexes legal matter mainly |
| | *Mafte'ach Hashe'elot Vehateshuvot: Hamafte'ach Ha-histori* | M. Elon | Jerusalem, 1973 | Topical (2 parts) | Covers historical material in the responsa of Ritba and Judah ben Asher |
| | *Otsar Hashe'elot Uteshuvot, Volume one* | M. N. Shapiro | Jerusalem, 1971 | According to the order of the Shulchan Aruch | Indexes circa 900 volumes of responsa; covers Orach Chayim, sections 1–88 |
| Zohar | *Mafte'ach Hazohar* | M. Galante | Venice, 1566 | Biblical passages; topics (12 sections) | |
| | *Mafte'ach Hazohar* *Mafte'ach Hazohar* | A. Rovigo Samuel, cabalist; I. B. Fontanella | Amsterdam, 1710 Venice, 1744 (reprinted, Jerusalem, 1969 and 1970) | Topical Topics; biblical passages | |
| | *Maftechot Hazohar Vera ayonotav* | H. D. Halevi | Tel Aviv, 1971 | Topical | |

## Indexes to Jewish Festschriften and Classic Hebrew Works (cont.)

| Category | Title | Compiler | Place, Date | Arrangement | Notes |
|---|---|---|---|---|---|
| Lurianic Cabala | Aderet Eliyahu; Mafte'ach al Sifre Hazohar | E. D. Slotky | Jerusalem, 1974 | Topical | 10,000 entries; includes cabalistic diagrams |
| | Emet Leya'akov | J. S. Niño | Livorno, 1843 (reprinted, Jerusalem, 1968/9) | Topical | Indexes Vital's Ets Chayim, Mavo She'arim, Sha'ar Hahakdamot |
| | Yad Eliyahu; Mafte'ach Lekabalat Ha'Ari | E. D. Slotky | Jerusalem, 1963 | Topical | 10,000 entries; included list of cabalistic terminology and diagrams |
| Chassidism | Sefer Hamaftechot Lesifre Uma'amare Chasidut Chabad | M. M. Schneerson, E. Carlebach N. Ts. Kenig, S. Tukatsinski | Brooklyn, 1966 | Topical (18 separate indexes) | Indexes works of five leaders of the Lubavich movement |
| | Pituche Chotam | | Bene Berak, 1968 | Topical | Indexes works of Rabbi Nachman, of Bratzlav, and his disciple, Rabbi Nathan |
| | Migdal Oz | M. Tsuri'el | Bene Berak, 1973 | Topical | Indexes circa seventy-seven works; covers also a selection of classic rabbinic works |
| Approbations and Subscriptions | Index Approbationum | L. Löwenstein | Frankfort (also Berlin), 1923 | Author-title-places | 3,662 entries; circa 2,700 titles |
| | Sefer Haprenumerantn | B. Kagan | New York, 1975 | Topical (six sections) | Lists 8,749 communities; circa 900 works; circa 2,000 personalities; 300 synagogues; 80 societies |

# Chapter Eight

# Miscellaneous
# Jewish Bibliographical Works

Shlomo Shunami: *Bibliography of Jewish Bibliographies*. Gazetteers of Hebrew Printing. Aron Freimann and Moses Marx: *Thesaurus Typographiae Hebraicae*. Abraham Yaari: *Digle Hamadpisim Ha'ivriyim* and Abraham Meir Habermann: *Sha'are Sefarim Ivrim*. Aron Freimann: *Union Catalog of Hebrew Manuscripts*. Hamachon Letatslume Kitve Hayad Ha'ivriyim. Abstracts and book reviews. Research, theses, dissertations.

I

### Shlomo Shunami:
### *Bibliography of Jewish Bibliographies*

INACTIVITY HAS SELDOM existed in the domain of Jewish literature, but the activity that began early in the nineteenth century and has continued unabated up to our own day has been the most spectacular. Jewish literature has branched out in every direction, entering area after area and covering every conceivable topic of Jewish interest. This has necessitated the creation of bibliographical tools, designed to bring some order to this unprecedented literary activity and to help the student and the scholar each find his way in the midst of this activity.

During the second half of the nineteenth century, as we have seen, an increasing number of Jewish bibliographies of various kinds began to appear, among them bibliographical periodicals, dealers' lists, catalogs of private and public institutions, and subject and personal bibliographies. The output of bibliographical tools steadily increased until it became evident that a special tool was needed to sort out, register, and bring order to the many hundreds of Jewish bibliographies and bibliographical works scattered throughout the continents and written in the many languages of civilization. Finally, in the late 1920s Shlomo Shunami, a librarian at the Jewish

National and University Library in Jerusalem, undertook the task of compiling such a work.

Shunami, who was born in Munkács, Hungary, in 1897, emigrated to Palestine in 1921.[1] He joined the staff of the Jewish National and University Library and later attended the American Library School in Paris (1925). During the years 1929–1930, while on leave with the Hebrew Union College Library in Cincinnati, Shunami began to compile "a list of Jewish bibliographies."[2] The collection of Jewish bibliographies at the Cincinnati library became the nucleus of his planned work. To this he added material he had found in other libraries in the United States and in Europe which he visited during his return trip to Jerusalem. He also obtained information by correspondence with various libraries and bibliographers, and the completion of his work was based, on the whole, on the collection of the Jewish National and University Library.

Shunami's work was turned over to the printer in November 1933, and it was published in Jerusalem in 1936 under the title *Bibliography of Jewish Bibliographies*. It was a 399-page volume, divided into twenty-six main sections consisting of 2,078 entries. The entries were "done according to the American Library Association Rules with slight changes," and, whenever possible, the compiler attempted "to conform to the Library of Congress practices" in cataloging similar material. The entries were often annotated, and references were given to reviews of the more important works listed. Hebrew works were annotated in Hebrew, and works in other languages were annotated in English. The title pages, introductions, and table of contents of the *Bibliography* were in both English and Hebrew (the Hebrew title being *Mafte'ach Hamaftechot*). The subject arrangement was "based chiefly on the system of Freidus[3] combined with certain elements of the Decimal Classification of Melvil Dewey." Thus the twenty-six sections were arranged as follows:

Encyclopedias
Bibliography of bibliography
General bibliographies
Catalogs of public collections
Catalogs of private collections
Booksellers' catalogs (a selection)
Bibliographical periodicals
Lists of periodicals
Religion, Philosophy, Cabala
Hebrew language
Bible
Talmudic and Midrashic literature, Halacha, Minhagim, Jurisprudence
Liturgies, Music, Homiletics

Jewish literature, Modern Hebrew literature
Judaeo-German; Yiddish
Judaeo-Spanish (Ladino), Judaeo-Portuguese, Other dialects
Jews and Gentiles
Sociology
Sects
Secular sciences
Palestine, Zionism and nationalism
History
Biography, Bio-bibliography
Personal bibliographies
Hebrew typography, The Hebrew book
Manuscripts

The volume concluded with an index of names and subjects, an index of Hebrew titles, and additions and corrections.

Shunami's *Bibliography of Jewish Bibliographies* was enthusiastically received by librarians, bibliographers, and scholars in the field of Jewish studies,[4] and it was soon out of print. This encouraged the compiler to continue his effort to collect new and omitted material for the purpose of supplementing the original volume. First he planned to bring the volume up to date by issuing occasional supplementary lists or surveys of new bibliographical works. During 1938 and 1939 he published two annual surveys of Jewish bibliographies[5] in a Jerusalem Hebrew weekly and in 1947, in a memorial volume issued in Budapest, he published a list of personal bibliographies that appeared during the years 1939–1947.[6] He soon abandoned this approach and began preparing an entirely new and enlarged edition.

After close to three decades of constant effort, the new edition of Shunami's *Bibliography of Jewish Bibliographies* appeared in Jerusalem in 1965. It was a bulky volume of 992 pages consisting of 4,750 entries, more than twice the number of entries in the first edition.[7] The changes were not only in the number of pages and entries; some improvements were made in the arrangement of the material and in additional annotations, and some were made in extending the original scheme to include new areas. The following subsections, among others, were added:

Dead Sea scrolls (subsection to Bible)
State of Israel (the former section "Palestine, Zionism, nationalism" was divided
    into two: "Zionism, nationalism" and "Palestine, State of Israel," and
    the number of sections was thus increased to twenty-seven)
The Holocaust (added to History)

A number of improvements were also introduced in the indexes, making it easier for the user to utilize this work to its fullest extent.

A photo-offset edition of *Bibliography of Jewish Bibliographies* (with a five-page pamphlet of additional "Corrections") was issued in Jerusalem in 1969. A 464-page *Supplement to Second Edition, Enlarged 1965* was issued in Jerusalem by the Magnes Press in 1975. The volume consisted of more than 2,000 entries, "the great majority . . . published during the last ten years." The compiler considered this supplement as his final effort in compiling a *Bibliography of Jewish Bibliographies.*[8]

# II

## Gazetteers of Hebrew Printing

The history of Hebrew printing is an essential part of Jewish bibliography. Many bibliographical difficultes (such as establishing places and dates of publication for some Hebrew works) would never have been solved without a thorough knowledge of the history of the establishment of Hebrew printing presses in various localities. Johann Christoph Wolf, as was indicated earlier, was the first bibliographer of Jewish literature to note its importance, and in his *Bibliotheca hebraea* he devoted space to the locations of Hebrew printing and to the people who established Hebrew printing presses.[9] Moritz Steinschneider and David Cassel elaborated on Wolf's material, and jointly published a lengthy essay listing locations of Hebrew printing and of the printers and publishers of Hebrew books.[10] Other Jewish bibliographers extended the list immensely,[11] and Steinschneider himself later added numerous additions and corrections to his earlier essay.[12] But it was only in 1917 that a volume devoted entirely to listing Hebrew printing places was first published.

Entitled *A Gazetteer of Hebrew Printing* (London, 1917) and compiled by Elkan Nathan Adler (1861–1946), the 23-page volume listed 547 localities where Hebrew type was used in books at one time or another.[13] Adler, one of the great collectors of Jewish books,[14] based the data in the *Gazetteer* mostly upon his own collection, and there were only "three or four" books in the entire list which he had not seen or handled himself. The arrangement was alphabetical by the place names, and each entry contained the following information:

Place of printing (including places where Hebrew type was used in non-Hebrew books)
Date of publication of first work with Hebrew type ("the earliest instance" known to the compiler)
Author and title of first work in which Hebrew type was used (Hebrew titles registered with translation or description)
Format
References

About three decades after the appearance of Adler's *Gazetteer,* Aron Freimann compiled and published in a New York periodical a new and expanded "Gazetteer of Hebrew Printing",[15] and a year later it was issued as a separate volume with the addition of two appendices. Freimann's *Gazetteer* (New York, 1946) listed 939 localities of Hebrew printing presses in alphabetical order. The entries included the following information:

Place of printing (including places where Hebrew type was used in non-Hebrew books)
Name of printer
Date of publication of first work with Hebrew type (for exceptions to this, cf. compiler's introduction)
Author and title of first work in which Hebrew type was used
References

The appendices were as follows:

Alphabetical table of Hebrew place names (arranged according to the order of the Hebrew alphabet, with equivalents in Roman characters)
Chronological table of Hebrew printing (ranging from 1475 to 1945)

## Aron Freimann and Moses Marx:
### *Thesaurus Typographiae Hebraicae*

For the history of printing in general, and Hebrew printing in particular, works printed during the fifteenth century—incunabula—are of the utmost importance. Since European movable-type printing came into being during the fifteenth century, the volumes produced during that period are the most reliable sources of information about the people and places connected with the early development of the art of printing. Hebrew incunabula are of special importance to the history of printing since very few copies have sur-vived in their complete and original form, externally and internally.[16] The scarcity and incompleteness of Hebrew incunabula volumes have prevented many scholars from undertaking detailed studies of their typographical components, and have caused many bibliographical problems with respect to identification of printers, places of printing, and dates of publication.

This deficiency in early Hebrew literature identification was partially corrected during the years 1924—1931 with the publication in Berlin of a series of portfolios containing facsimiles of leaves of Hebrew incunabula. Published in eight portfolios under the Hebrew-Latin titles *Ha'otsar Limelechet Hadefus Ha'ivri Harishonah Ad Shenat Resh Samech—Thesaurus Typographiae Hebraicae Saeculi XV,* and edited by Aron Freimann and Moses Marx (1885—1973),[17] the work included 332 plates of facsimiles of selected pages in more than one hundred Hebrew incunabula. The selection included works printed in about twenty locations by some thirty printers during a period of twenty-two years (1475—1497), and the plates were .reproductions of complete leaves as well as of colophons, diagrams, illustra-tions, initials, etc. Each plate carried at the bottom a printed legend of iden-tification, in Hebrew and Latin, with references to bibliographies that describe the particular incunabulum. The material in each portfolio (except portfolio seven) consisted of two groups, identified on each leaf with either an initial A (indicating Italian origin) or initial B (indicating Spanish-Portuguese origin). Portfolio seven also featured four plates, identified with the initial C, of the only Hebrew incunabulum printed in Turkey.[18]

A reprint edition of the *Thesaurus,* in which the plates were rearranged into three groups, A, B, and C, and to which was added a table of authors and topics (anonymous works, Bible, Talmud, prayer books, and liturgies), was published in Jerusalem by the Universitas Booksellers, in 1968.

Freimann and Marx originally planned to issue ten portfolios of fac-similes, the final one to include an introduction, a list of abbreviations, and indexes. Due to economic difficulties and the changed political situation in Germany, their plan was not realized. In 1969, however, the publishers of the reprint edition issued a special supplement to the *Thesaurus* which in-cluded, besides introductions by Israel Mehlman and Herrmann Meyer, the following (compiled by Meyer):

Selected literature on Hebrew incunabula (to be used as bibliographical
   references in the short-title list that follows)
Short-title catalog of the Hebrew incunabula and other books illustrated in the

*Thesaurus* (191 entries, of which 187 are *incunabula;* each entry accompanied by
a list of bibliographical references)
Concordances (comparative tables between short-title list and *Thesaurus,* and
between other bibliographies of Hebrew incunabula and the *Thesaurus*)


Abraham Yaari: *Digle Hamadpisim Ha'ivriyim*
and
Abraham Meir Habermann: *Sha'are Sefarim Ivrim*

Other sources of information for the history of printing are the printers'
marks that came into being soon after the invention of printing. The first
printer's mark appeared in the Latin Bible of Füst and Schöffer, printed in
Mayence in 1462. The *Tur Orach Chayim,* by Jacob ben Asher, printed in
Hijar, Spain, in 1485, seems to have been the first Hebrew work to appear
with a printer's mark. The marks usually served a double purpose: a device
of identification for the printer and an ornament for the colophon or title
page.[19] The former made the marks an invaluable source of bibliographic information, except for one obstacle: the difficulty of searching through
hundreds of volumes to identify the right mark. This obstacle was removed
in 1943 with the publication, in Jerusalem, of Abraham Yaari's *Digle
Hamadpisim Ha'ivriyim,* which reproduced in facsimile the printers' marks
used in Hebrew books "from the beginning of Hebrew printing to the end of
the 19th century."[20] Yaari envisaged for his work a triple purpose:

To serve as a "repository of Jewish graphic art through many ages"
To assist in the study of Jewish symbology
To serve as an aid "in identifying defective books," in determining names of
    printers who concealed their identity, and in "tracking the various fortunes
    of printers and the migrations of their presses"

In order to meet his set objectives, Yaari arranged his *Digle Hamadpisim* as
follows:

Facsimiles of Hebrew printers' marks (208 facsimiles in chronological order, with
    location of printing press, name of printer, and dates of printing activity
    printed at the bottom of each page in Hebrew and English)
Explanation and interpretation of marks (including bio-bibliographical data on
    the printers)
List of the owners of Hebrew printers' marks

List of motifs represented on Hebrew printers' marks
List of printing places to be identified through Hebrew printers' marks
List of verses that accompanied some Hebrew printers' marks

A reprint edition of *Digle Hamadpisim,* including the addition of eight marks and their meanings which had been published by Yaari in 1956 in *Kiryat Sefer,*[21] was issued in Farnborough, England, by Gregg International Publishers in 1971.

Complementing Yaari's *Digle Hamadpisim* is a recent book by Abraham Meir Habermann (born 1901) on Hebrew title pages, entitled *Sha'are Sefarim Ivrim* (Safed, 1969).[22] Title pages began to appear in Hebrew books in the early sixteenth century, and in the span of one hundred years they developed from simple identification devices to works of art.[23] Since most title pages were designed for specific printers or printing houses, they became an additional source of information on the history of printing during the seventeenth to twentieth centuries.

Habermann arranged his *Sha'are Sefarim* in the following order (similar to Yaari's arrangement of his *Digle Hamadpisim*):

Facsimiles of title pages (104 facsimiles of ornamented title pages in
   chronological order, beginning with a thirteenth-century manuscript, with
   identification of book, place, and date of publication at bottom of each page)
Explanations of title pages
List of printing places
Chronological list of title pages
List of titles

# III. Hebrew Manuscripts

## Aron Freimann:
### *Union Catalog of Hebrew Manuscripts*

The early bibliographers of Hebraica literature—Johannes Buxtorf, Giulio Bartolocci, and Shabbethai Bass[24]—registered Hebraica manuscripts in their works, in addition to printed Hebraica; and Bartolocci and Bass frequently indicated the locations of manuscripts. Azulai and Benjacob also listed manuscripts in their bibliographic works, and Benjacob added references as well to the sources of his information.[25] Hebraica bibliographers and catalogers, around the middle of the nineteenth century, gradually began to list handwritten and printed Hebraica separately. The last general Hebraica bibliography—Friedberg's *Bet Eked Sefarim*—entirely excluded manuscripts.[26]

Hand in hand with the growth of scientific Jewish scholarship during the first half of this century, interest in Hebraica codices also increased. Although large numbers of printed catalogs of private and public collections of Hebraica manuscripts had appeared since the turn of the century,[27] the absence of a general list of Hebraica manuscripts with information as to their location made it difficult for many scholars to pursue their studies successfully. Aron Freimann, the man who contributed so greatly to Jewish bibliography,[28] devoted many years of his life to preparing such a list. During the years he served at the Frankfurt am Main Stadtbibliothek, Freimann made it his habit to utilize his vacations to visit libraries with Jewish collections. Besides the known collections of the Bodleian Library, British Museum, Vatican Library, etc., he visited unknown institutions with small collections of Hebraica manuscripts or rare printed Hebraica, especially in Germany and Switzerland.[29] When Freimann died he left thousands of handwritten slips describing Hebraica manuscripts, each slip filled with information he had gathered during his visits to the various libraries and augmented by information he culled from printed Hebraica catalogs. The American Academy for Jewish Research, which received Freimann's slips, felt that "although incomplete, the catalog is still worthy of publication," and decided to publish it by reproducing the slips without any changes.

Freimann's slips were photographically reproduced in a 462-page folio volume, published in New York in 1964 under the title *Union Catalog of Hebrew Manuscripts and Their Location*. The volume (designated as Volume Two) consisted of 11,861 entries arranged alphabetically by title. Each entry usually included the following details:

Title (in Hebrew characters)
Author (in Roman characters)
Description (in German; sometimes in English)
Location
Bibliographical sources

The difficulty in deciphering Freimann's writing, abbreviations, and symbols prevented many scholars from utilizing the catalog to its fullest extent.

This difficulty was partially eased in 1973 with the publication of Volume One of the *Union Catalog* which includes, in addition to introductions by Salo Wittmayer Baron and Solomon Dob Goitein,[30] the following aids by Menahem Hayyim Schmelzer:

List of frequently used abbreviations
List of locations, owners of manuscripts, catalogs, and their symbols
Author-title index (in Roman characters; also listing names of scribes or others mentioned in the catalog)

## Hamachon Letatslume Kitve Hayad Ha'ivriyim

In 1947, one year before Freimann's death and while the renowned scholar and bibliographer was still concentrating on compiling in *one* catalog all available information on Hebraica manuscripts,[31] another well-known Jewish scholar, Ben Zion Dinur, advanced the idea of assembling (on microfilm) in *one* place, in Jerusalem, all extant Hebraica manuscripts.[32] David Ben-Gurion (1886–1973), the first prime minister of the State of Israel, adopted Dinur's idea, and three years later (1950) he became instrumental in establishing a special section at the Ministry of Education and Culture called Hamachon Lechitve Hayad Ha'ivriyim. The purpose of the Machon was to microfilm Hebraica manuscripts available in the many private and public libraries around the world and to make them accessible to scholars working in various areas of Jewish studies. Twelve years later the Machon became part of the Jewish National and University Library in Jerusalem, and to its name was added the word Tatslume, to underscore its microfilm function.

During the first twenty-five years of its existence, the Machon accumulated microfilms of more than 30,000 codexes and tens of thousands of fragments of Hebrew manuscripts. Between 1957 and 1968, the Machon also issued three volumes, entitled *Reshimat Tatslume Kitve Hayad Bamachon*. Volume 1 listed manuscripts microfilmed at Austrian and German libraries; Volume 2 listed manuscripts microfilmed in Belgium, Denmark, Holland, Spain, and Switzerland; and Volume 3 recorded manuscripts microfilmed at the Vatican Library. Each of the three volumes included author, title, and subject indexes.

## IV. Abstracts and Book Reviews

Dealers' lists and bibliographies of current or retrospective publications, even the most scientific ones, do not transmit complete information on books. Bibliographical information is simply not meant to cover every facet of a book. In a bibliography every work is an "item" or "entry" deserving equal treatment. Bibliography is neutral in its descriptions; it expresses no opinions. The task of describing a work in its entirety, by examining every aspect of the work, is left to the abstracter and reviewer. In many specialized fields of literature the importance of the abstract or review surpasses that of the bibliography.

In the field of Jewish literature, the first effort at issuing a publication devoted to reviews of current works was made by the Jewish Book Council of America in New York in 1945. Issued monthly under the title *In Jewish Bookland,* the publication mostly concentrated on reviewing Jewish belles lettres written in the English language.[33]

Another effort at regularly presenting reviews and abstracts of current Jewish literature began in 1954 with the publication of *Hebrew Abstracts.* The first issue, published by the National Association of Professors of Hebrew in American Institutions of Higher Learning, was edited by Abraham I. Katsh; and it contained "brief descriptions of articles, books, and periodicals published in Hebrew or in other languages about the Hebrew language, literature, philology, exegesis, bibliography, and methodology."

Volumes 1−4 (1954−1957) were issued successively in conjunction with *The Shane Quarterly* and *Encounter* of the School of Religion, Butler University, Indianapolis. Beginning with Volume 5 (1958), *Hebrew Abstracts* became an independent publication, and it is currently published annually at the University of Louisville, Kentucky, under the editorship of Israel T. Naamani.

The idea of regularly publishing abstracts and reviews of current Hebrew books was adopted in Israel in 1965 by the Institute for the Translation of Hebrew Literature in Tel Aviv, with the publication of a periodical entitled *Hebrew Book Review.* The purpose of the new publication was "to help the reader not versed in Hebrew to keep track of the literary scene in Israel." *Hebrew Book Review* was first published annually; later it was published semiannually, and it is currently being published quarterly. Each issue contains essays, translations, and reviews of current Hebrew literature.

In 1968 a publication in Hebrew began to appear in Jerusalem with the title *Al Sefarim Chadashim; Leket Divre Bikoret,* which was later reversed to read *Leket Divre Bikoret Al Sefarim Chadashim*. Published by the Center for Public Libraries in Jerusalem, the new periodical originally consisted of photographically reproduced reviews that had appeared in Hebrew dailies in Israel. Beginning with number 23/24 (December 31, 1974), the material has been reproduced from typewritten copy. *Leket Divre Bikoret* is issued in a large folio format. First it appeared at irregular intervals, later it became a monthly, and it is currently a biweekly publication. Each issue contains reviews of current books in the areas of Hebrew belles lettres, literary biography, poetry, and juvenile literature.

A 175-page volume entitled *Mivchar Sefarim* also appeared in Jerusalem in 1970/71. The volume consisted of abstracts of current Hebrew literature that had appeared originally as supplements to circulars issued by the Committee for Recommending Books for Teachers at the Ministry of Education and Culture during the years 1967/68−1970/71. The abstracts, written by Meshullam Halevi, were compiled into a single volume and arranged into the following fifteen categories:

    Education and teaching
    Psychology
    Judaism
    Bible
    Language
    Literature
    General history and archeology
    Jewish history and history of Jews in Palestine
    Jewish demography
    The Holocaust
    Zionism and citizenship
    Sociology
    Geography and knowledge of the Land (of Israel)
    Exact sciences and biology
    Art

Author and title indexes concluded the volume.

Another volume of abstracts of Hebrew literature was published in Jerusalem in 1973, entitled *Mivchar Hasefer Ha'ivri*. Edited by Simhah Raz and published jointly by the World Hebrew Union and the Center for Public Libraries, the 319-page volume concentrated on Hebrew works in the field of Jewish studies published during 1970/71−1972/73. The material was arranged in the following ten major groups:

    Bible and language
    Literature

Rabbinica
Jewish thought
History and folklore
Erets Yisrael
Education
Theater
Reference works

Title and author indexes completed the volume.


# V. Research, Theses, Dissertations

The registration and periodic publication of lists and abstracts of theses and dissertations accepted at institutions of higher learning in Europe and in the United States began in the nineteenth century. The first lists were prepared by libraries based on their holdings of such material.[34] Later, most institutions of higher learning began to publish their own lists and abstracts of accepted theses and dissertations.

In the field of Jewish studies, Dropsie College of Philadelphia seems to have been the first to publish lists of doctoral theses in order "to aid the prevention of duplication of effort in scholarly investigation."[35] But the first effort to compile one volume containing a list of research, theses, and dissertations in the Jewish field conducted at American schools of higher learning, was made in 1958 by Raphael Patai (born 1910), director of research of the Theodor Herzl Institute in New York.

The volume, entitled, *Current Jewish Social Research* (New York, 1958), edited by Patai and published by the Theodor Herzl Institute, registered 1,128 investigations, completed and in progress, in the area of Jewish studies. The editor interpreted as "current" every unpublished thesis or dissertation. Thus he was able to list research done even in the nineteenth century. The term "social" was also interpreted by the editor in the most liberal manner, since the material listed in the volume covered the entire field of Jewish studies. This is evident from the division of the material into forty sections, listed in alphabetical order on the contents page.

Patai planned to issue additional volumes biannually, but this plan did not materialize. Several years later, however, Isacque Graeber compiled and published a list of 452 dissertations on "Jewish themes" granted by fifty-two American universities and seminaries during a thirty-year period (1933–

1962).[36] The list was arranged in chronological order, divided into the following groups:

Religion and philosophy
Sociology, psychology, anthropology, and economics
Literature and languages
History
Education[37]

Graeber's list was the forerunner of an annual publication entitled *Doctoral Dissertations and Master's Theses Accepted by American Institutions of Higher Learning* which made its appearance in New York in 1966. Designed as part of a series of "Guides to Jewish Subjects in Social and Humanistic Research" and "compiled for the Yivo Clearinghouse for Social and Humanistic Research in the Jewish Field,"[38] the first issue covered the academic year 1963/64. The volume, compiled by Wita Ravid, registered seventy-seven entries divided into nine subject areas, followed by an index of authors. Beginning with issue two, covering the academic year 1964/65, the material was compiled by Phyllis Disenhouse. A double issue, covering the years 1968/69–1969/70, was published in 1974; it included 215 entries divided into twenty subject areas, followed by a cumulative author index to the first six issues.

Useful lists of doctoral theses in Jewish studies, accepted or in progress at a number of Jewish schools of higher learning in Israel and in the United States, began to appear in the *Newsletter* of the World Union of Jewish Studies in Jerusalem in the spring of 1971 (issue number 3).[39] The information covered the following institutions: in Israel—Hebrew University, Jerusalem, Tel Aviv University, and Bar-Ilan University; in the United States—Hebrew Union College and Yeshiva University. The *Newsletter* also includes in each issue useful information about ongoing research projects in the field of Jewish studies at various Israel and American institutions.

An effort to compile a worldwide list of Jewish research in progress was made in 1974 by the American Section of the World Jewish Congress, with the publication of a twenty-page pamphlet entitled *A Survey of Current Jewish Research* (New York, 1974). The list consisted of more than 360 entries arranged by topics. The compilers are planning to issue updated lists and supplements periodically.

Lists of current research, dissertations, and theses devoted to specific areas of Jewish studies have also made their appearance during the last several decades. In 1940 Mordecai Soltes published a list of dissertations and theses in the field of Jewish education.[40] Isacque Graeber augmented Soltes's list fourteen years later[41] with a bibliography of surveys and theses in the field of American Jewish education prepared during the years 1890–1953.[42] Walter Crosby Eells, three years later, supplemented both lists[43] with a bibliography of dissertations dealing with Jewish education outside the United States.

In the same issue of *Jewish Education* in which Eells' bibliography appeared, Joshua A. Fishman began publishing an annual review of current research relating to Jewish education.[44] But Frank Rosenthal, with the assistance of Judah Pilch, outdid them all with the publication of a 137-page volume entitled *Abstracts of Doctoral and Masters' Dissertations in Jewish Education and Related Areas* (Los Angeles, 1965?). The volume, published jointly by the University of Judaism and the Jewish Theological Seminary of America, listed 223 entries arranged alphabetically by author, followed by indexes of titles and subjects. For the benefit of the user the compiler also provided a list of American doctoral dissertations in Jewish studies written since the 1920s.

The Washington-based Middle East Institute published three volumes during the years 1956–1958 entitled *Current Research on the Middle East.* These volumes registered and abstracted completed and published research projects, as well as those in process during the years 1955–1957. They included, among others, research in such areas as Palestine, Judaism, Old Testament, Dead Sea scrolls, and Samaritan religion.

University Microfilms of Ann Arbor published a 57-page volume in 1961, prepared by Martin J. Buss, entitled *Old Testament Dissertations, 1928–1958,* which listed "dissertations having a bearing on the Old Testament or on the inter-testamental period, including a good number of Near Eastern studies judged to be of interest to the Old Testament specialist." The material was divided into dissertations written in North America, the British Isles, and other countries. Each entry carried location references.

In Europe, a one-man effort over a period of forty years produced two volumes listing dissertations on Jewish topics in the German language. Guido Kisch, the editor and compiler of these volumes, first published a list of forty-six dissertations in 1931[45] dealing with German Jewish history that were written in Germany during the years 1922–1928. More than a quarter of a century later, Kisch, jointly with Kurt Roepke, compiled a 49-page volume entitled *Schriften zur Geschichte der Juden; eine Bibliographie der in Deutschland und der Schweiz 1922–1955 erschienenen Dissertationen* (Tübingen, 1959). The volume was the fourth in a series of scientific publications issued by the Leo Baeck Institute of Jews from Germany,[46] and it listed 381 dissertations arranged in twelve main sections, preceded by an essay reviewing the history of Jewish bibliography in Germany, and followed by an index of authors.[47]

The second volume, compiled and edited entirely by Kisch, was entitled *Judaistische Bibliographie; ein Verzeichnis der in Deutschland und der Schweiz von 1956 bis 1970 erschienenen Dissertationen und Habilitationsschriften* (Basel—Stuttgart, 1972). The volume listed 508 dissertations arranged in ten main sections, preceded by an enlarged essay on the history of Jewish bibliography in Germany since the nineteenth century, and followed by indexes of topics and authors.

A companion work to Kisch's volumes is Wolfdieter Bihl's *Bibliographie der Dissertationen über Judentum und jüdische Persönlichkeiten, die 1872— 1962 an österreichischen Hochschulen (Wien, Graz, Innsbruck) approbiert wurden* (Vienna, 1965). The fifty-one page volume lists 448 dissertations arranged by subject, followed by indexes of personalities and authors. An additional fifty-nine dissertations are listed at the end of the volume.

A few decades ago in Israel, the Hebrew University of Jerusalem began to publish short lists of Ph.D. recipients and research students, periodically, together with the titles of their dissertations or research projects.[48] Then, in 1964, the university published a volume for the first time entitled *Abstracts of Theses Approved for the Degrees of Doctor Philosophiae (Ph.D.) and Doctor Juris (Jur. D.).*[49] The volume covered the academic year 1961/62, and it was divided into two parts. Part one listed theses in the areas of humanities, social science, and law; part two listed theses in the areas of science and agriculture. About ten theses in the field of Jewish studies were included in part one. The *Abstracts* were later issued in two separate bilingual (English-Hebrew) volumes, one devoted to natural sciences, medicine, and agriculture, and the other to humanities, social sciences, and law. The volume devoted to the humanities was published in Jerusalem in 1968, and it covered the academic years 1962/63—1965/66. This volume also included more than thirty dissertations in the field of Jewish studies arranged in six sections (Bible, Talmud, Hebrew literature, Jewish philosophy and mysticism, Hebrew language, Jewish history).[50]

A bilingual (English-Hebrew) volume entitled *Ph. D. Degrees and Abstracts* was issued in 1972 by the Tel Aviv University. The volume covered the academic years 1970 to 1972, and it included four dissertations in the field of Jewish studies.[51]

Several years ago the Institute of Contemporary Jewry at the Hebrew University of Jerusalem began to compile an *Inventory of Current Studies in*

*Contemporary Jewry*. The *Inventory* is to register ongoing research in the area of Jewish studies dealing with the post-World War I period, and "it will include both masters theses and doctoral dissertations in process as well as theses and dissertations which have been completed since 1967 but not yet published." A *Preliminary Register of Studies in Israel* was issued by the Institute in 1970 as a sample of how the *Inventory* would look when completed. The thirty-page *Preliminary Register* listed and described more than fifty research projects being conducted at schools of higher learning in Israel.

Frank Joseph Shulman, a professional bibliographer in the field of Asian Studies at the Center for Japanese Studies at the University of Michigan, compiled and edited for Xerox University Microfilms a twenty-five page volume entitled *American and British Doctoral Dissertations on Israel and Palestine in Modern Times* (Ann Arbor, Michigan, 1973).[52] The volume listed about 530 postwar dissertations "dealing in whole or in part with the land of Israel since the early 1880's." The material was divided into five main sections, followed by indexes of authors and institutions.

A list of theses and dissertations dealing with the history of Palestine from the time of the Arab conquest (636 C.E.) to the establishment of the State of Israel (1948), completed or in progress at Israel universities, was compiled by Ya'akov Barnay for Yad Izhak Ben Zvi and published in a sixty-five page volume under the title *Mechkar Erets-Yisrael Vehayishuv Hayehudi Bah Ba'universita'ot Yisrael* (Jerusalem, 1974). The volume was divided into two parts. Part one, divided into four sections, listed and described seventy-eight doctoral and masters theses completed up to the end of 1973. Part two listed, in alphabetical author order, fifty-four theses still in preparation. An author index completed the volume.

# Notes

Notes to Chapter One:
*General Hebraica Bibliographies*

1. *Baba Batra* 14b–15a. N. Sarna, "The Order of the Books," in *Studies in Jewish Bibliography, History and Literature in Honor of I. Edward Kiev,* ed. C. Berlin (New York, 1971), pp. 407–411, suggests that the purpose of the discussion in the Talmud was to establish cataloging and shelving rules for ancient Jewish libraries. A. M. Habermann, *EI* vol. 8, p. 264 and *EJ* (1971), vol. 4, p. 970, thinks that the purpose of the discussion was to establish rules of order for copyists of the Holy Scriptures.

2. *Shabbat* 13b; *Ketubot* 110b; *Sanhedrin* 100b, among others. Cf. also *Mishnah Yadayim* 3:5.

3. Cf. *Igeret Rav Sherira Gaon,* ed. B. M. Lewin (Haifa, 1921; reprinted, Jerusalem, 1971/72); Abraham ben David, ha-Levi, *A Critical Edition with a Translation and Notes of the Book of Tradition (Sefer Ha-qabbalah),* ed. Gerson D. Cohen (Philadelphia, 1967); Abraham ben Samuel Zacuto, *Yuchasin Hashalem,* ed. H. Filipowski (London and Edinburgh, 1857; second edition with introduction by A. C. Freimann, Frankfort, 1924; reprinted with additions, Jerusalem, 1962/63); Gedaliah Ibn Yahya, *Shalshelet Hakabalah* (Venice, 1587; improved edition, Jerusalem, 1961/62); David Gans, *Tsemach David* (Prague, 1592; improved edition, Jerusalem, 1966).
During the last hundred years numerous handlists of books dating back to the eleventh century and owned by private collectors or bookdealers have been uncovered. About 80 percent of these lists were discovered in the Cairo Genizah. Cf. N. Allony, "Arba Reshimot Sefarim Mehame'ah Ha'yud-bet," *KS* 43 (1967): 121. For references to published booklists, cf. S. A. Poznanski, *ZfHB* 12 (1908): 111; Jacob Mann, *Texts and Studies in Jewish History and Literature* (Cincinnati, 1931; reprinted, Ne York, 1972), 1:643; Alexander Marx, *Studies in Jewish History and Booklore* (New York, 1944), p. 200, n. 6; E. E. Urbach, *KS* 15 (1938/39): 237, n. l; S. Assaf, *KS* 18 (1941): 273, nn. 1 and 2; N. Allony, *KS* 43 (1967): 123 ("Luach Kitsurim"). Additional lists and corrections to previously published lists appear in *KS* 24 (1947/48): 248–249; 25 (1948/49): 203–205; 26 (1949/50): 72–95; 27 (1950/51): 283; 30 (1954/55): 445–446; 39 (1963/64): 427–428; 40 (1964/65): 133–135; 44 (1968/69): 124, 125, 546–548; 48 (1972/73): 152–172; *Sefer Asaf* (Jerusalem, 1953), pp. 33–39. See also Solomon Dob Fritz Goitein, *Sidre Chinuch Bime Hageonim* (Jerusalem, 1962), pp. 149–150. A fifteenth-century list of Hebrew authors and titles was published by Isaac Benjacob in *Devarim Atikim* (Leipzig, 1846), 2: (7)–10. The practice of preparing short handlists by owners of Hebrew books is mentioned by Judah Ibn Tibbon (ca. 1120–1190) in his last will to his son. Cf. *Tsava'ot Geone Yisrael,* ed. Israel Abrahams (Philadelphia, 1926), 1:81.

4. The most complete bio-bibliographical essay on Gesner was written by J. C.

Bay, "Conrad Gesner (1516—1565), the Father of Bibliography: An Appreciation," *The Papers of the Bibliographical Society of America,* vol. 10, no. 2 (Chicago, 1916): 53—86.

5. The title page of the first volume of Gesner's *Bibliotheca* reads as follows: "Bibliotheca universalis; sive, catalogus omnium scriptorum locupletissimus, in tribus linguis, latina, graeca, et hebraica, extantium et non extantium, ueterum et recentiorum in hunc usq, diem, doctorum et indoctorum, publicatorum et in bibliothecis latentium. . . ."

6. An examination of Gesner's *Bibliotheca* (especially vols. 2 and 3, entitled *Pandectarum sive partitionum universalium* and *Partitiones theologicae, pandectarum universalium*) reveals relatively few entries for Jewish authors and topics, fewer than the entries for non-Jewish authors of anti-Jewish works. There is also a curious duplication of some entries. Maimonides, for example, is entered under different forms: Moses Cordubensis, R. Mose filij Maimon Aegyptij, and simply R. Moysi. Places and dates of publication of most Hebrew works are omitted. Moritz Steinschneider, *Bibliographisches Handbuch über die theoretische und praktische Literatur für hebräische Sprachkunde* (Leipzig, 1859; reprinted with additions, Jerusalem, 1937), p. xvi, lauds Gesner for being the first to introduce Hebrew bibliography into general bibliography, and Leopold Zunz, *Gesammelte Schriften* (Berlin, 1875) 1:49, names him as the first bibliographer to publish a dealer's list of Hebrew works (in his *Pandectae*). See also Julius Fürst, "Zur Geschichte der jüdischen Bibliographie" (in his *Bibliotheca Judaica*, vol. 3), p. lxxii, and A. Freimann, "Daniel Bombergs Bücher-Verzeichnis," *ZfHB* 10 (1906): 38—39.

7. For additional bio-bibliographical data on the Buxtorfs, cf. *JE* vol. 3, pp. 444—447; *EJ* vol. 4, pp. 1232—1234; *EJ (1971),* vol. 4, pp. 1543—1544; Zalman Reisen, *Leksikon far der Yudisher Literatur un Prese* (Warsaw, 1914), pp. 94—95.

8. Steinschneider, *Bibliographisches Handbuch* p. xv, describes the reasons for Christian interest in Hebrew studies during the sixteenth century:

"Das Interesse an der hebr. Sprachkunde beruhte vorherrschend auf dem Bedürfnisse selbstständiger Erforschung der jüdischen Bibel als Basis der christlichen. Wäre es möglich gewesen das hebräische aus andern als jüdischen Quellen zu holen, so hätte man es gewiss vorgezogen, denn das Verhältniss zur jüdischen Literatur war, abgesehen von den allgemeinen, philosophischen Wissenschaften, im Mittelalter im Ganzen mehr ein, von Renegaten genährtes, polemisches. . . . So erzeugte zunächst die hebräische Philologie sprachliches und sachliches Interesse an dem jüdischen Schriftenthum des Mittelalters überhaupt, und es entsteht die *hebräische Bibliographie* die sich später zur *jüdischen* entwickelt, aber stets nur als Anhang zur christlichen Theologie figurirt. . . ."

See also Steinschneider's remarks in *HB* 17 (1877): 90, and in his *Jewish Literature from the Eighth to the Eighteenth Century* (London, 1857; reprinted, New York,

1965), p. 210. See also M. Kayserling's evaluation of Buxtorf, the father, in *JE* vol. 3, p. 445.

9. Cf. Kayserling, *JE* vol. 3, p. 445. Nonetheless, it later appeared in several editions under the title *Synagoga Judaica*. It was also translated into other languages. Buxtorf's bias against Judaism did not affect his private relations with Jews. Cf. Leopold Zunz, *Die Synagogale Poesie des Mittelalters* (Berlin, 1855), p. 341; Bernhard Friedberg, *Toldot Hadefus Ha'ivri* (Antwerp, 1937), pp. 7–8; Kayserling, *JE* vol. 3, p. 445.

10. Buxtorf's contribution to Hebrew (and Yiddish) lexicography will be discussed in Volume Three of this work.

11. Buxtorf published a new edition of the Hebrew Bible (Basel, 1618–1619) with rabbinical commentaries and Masoretic punctuation, and supplemented it with a volume entitled *Tiberias, sive commentarius masoreticus triplex* (Basel, 1620).

12. Buxtorf's edition of the Hebrew concordance will be discussed in Volume Three of this work.

13. *Institutio epistolaris Hebraica* (Basel, 1610). The appendix was printed in the second edition (Basel, 1629).

14. Cf. Steinschneider, *Jewish Literature*, p.210.

15. On Eliyahu Bachur and his achievements, see Volume Three of this work.

16. The volume *De abbreviaturis hebraicis* will be discussed in Volume Three of this work.

17. For centuries the term "rabbinica" was applied by Christian theologians to the entire postbiblical Hebrew literature. Cf. Zunz, *Gesammelte Schriften* (Berlin, 1875), 1:58, where he explains the origin of this term:

> "Der Namen 'rabbinisch' hat die jüdische Literatur gleichfalls von den Theologen erhalten. Diese haben jüdische Bücher stets nur aus einen einseitigen Standpunkte, und die Juden nur als Kirchenmaterial betrachtet: als Zeugen oder als Widersacher eines siegenden Christenthums. Jüdische Autoren erschienen ihnen daher immer als Vertreter des bekämpften Prinzips, d. h. als Rabbiner. . . ."

Steinschneider, "Jüdische Literatur," *Allgeneine Encyclopädie der Wissenschaften und Künste*, ed. Ersch and Gruber, 2d section H–N (Leipzig, 1850), p. 357, advances a different explanation:

> ". . . Auch ist die jüdische Literatur nicht etwa vorzugsweise durch eigentliche, d. h. in Amt stehende, Rabbiner Vertreten; sondern die im Mittelalter, vielleicht durch Opposition der Karäer, herrschend gewordene Sitte, dem Namen jedes Schriftkundigen, also auch jedes Verfassers, den Ehrentitel Rabbi vorzusetzen, hat christliche Gelehrte veranlasst, solche als Rabbiner zu bezeichnen und den Namen Rabbinische Literatur zu schaffen, welcher keinen wissenschaftlichen Begriff einschliesst."

Both Steinschneider and Zunz preferred to use the terms "neuhebräische" or "jüdische Literatur." Cf. Zunz, *Schriften*, p. 3, n. l, and Steinschneider, "Jüdische Literatur," idem, *Bibliographisches Handbuch*, p. xviii.

18. Buxtorf's Hebraica library was later augmented by his son and also by his nephew, and it was sold in 1705 to the public library of Basel for one thousand Reichsthaler. Cf. E. Kautzsch, *Johannes Buxtorf der ältere* (Basel, 1879), p. 26; *JE* vol. 3, p. 446. Concerning the sources used by Buxtorf in compiling the *Bibliotheca*, see Menahem Mendel Slatkine, *Reshit Bikure Habibliyografyah* (Tel Aviv, 1958), pp. 23, 25, 40, 44.

19. Even yeshiva students of modern days would find it difficult to identify the authors of such popular rabbinic works as *Pene Yehoshua* and *Sha'agat Aryeh*, or the acronyms of Rashba and Ritba, to mention just a few.

20. Roman lived in Turkey during the late sixteenth and early seventeenth centuries. He was a linguist and bibliographer, and he assisted the younger Buxtorf in acquiring Hebrew books. He planned to translate and publish Hebrew classical works, and began to translate *Tiberias* by Buxtorf, the elder. Kayserling, *JE* vol. 10, pp. 442–443, identifies Roman as the Ya'akov Romano, of Jerusalem, listed in David Conforte's *Kore Hadorot* (cf. David Cassel's edition [Berlin, 1846; reprinted, New York, 1944, and Jerusalem, 1968/69], p. 41a). He also identifies him as one of a group of Jewish elders who were imprisoned for ransom by Mohammed ibn Faruk in 1625. Cf. *Charvot Yerushalem* ed. Eliezer Rivlin (Jerusalem, 1927/28), pp. 20–21; Steinschneider, "Statthalter-Wirtschaft in Jerusalem," *Sippurim* ed. W. Pascheles, 4th series (Prague, 1856), p. 53. *OY,* vol. 10, pp. 281–282, accepts Kayserling's identification as fact, but Rivlin, in Aryeh Loeb Frumkin's *Toldot Chachme Yerushalayim* (Jerusalem, 1927/28; reprinted, Tel Aviv, 1968/69), 2:16–17, questions this identification.

21. The Herborn Nassau 1708 edition was compiled and published by Johann Adam Faber, Johann Heinrich Schramm, and Georg Christian Burcklin, according to Fürst, "Zur Geschichte der jüdischen Bibliographie," p. lxxii. Among the new Hebrew works listed in this edition was Shabbethai Bass's *Sifte Yeshenim.*

22. Plantavit compiled a *Florilegium rabbinicum* (Lodova, 1645) and appended to it a *Bibliotheca rabbinica.* As to whether Plantavit was a student of Leone da Modena, cf. Steinschneider, "Miszellen und Notizen," *ZfHB* 9 (1905): 188; L. Blau, "Plantavits Lehrer im Rabbinischen," *ZfHB* 10 (1906): 113–117.

23. Hottinger included a list of Hebrew books, divided into eleven major categories, in his *Promtuarium; sive, bibliotheca orientalis* (Heidelberg, 1658). A narrower subject division for Hebrew literature was developed earlier by Manasseh ben Israel (1604–1657) in his *Conciliator* (Amsterdam, 1632–1651). The Hottinger family, like the Buxtorfs, supplied three generations of Hebraists. Cf. *Encyclopedia Britannica,* 11th ed., vol. 13, p. 807; Steinschneider, "Christliche Hebraisten," *ZfHB* 3 (1898):49; J. W. Parkes, "Early Christian Hebraists," *SBB* 6 (1962/63): 20, n. 114; 22, n. 164.

24. Cf. Slatkine, *Reshit Bikure Habibliyografyah,* pp. 25–31; idem, *Shemot Hasefarim Ha'ivrim* (Tel Aviv, 1954), 2:6–21.

25. The biographical details on Bartolocci and Battista are based on Fürst, "Zur Geschichte der Jüdischen Bibliographie," pp. lxxiii–lxxv; Steinschneider, *ZfHB* 2 (1897): 51; Zunz, *Gesammelte Schriften* (Berlin, 1875), 1:52; *JE* vol. 2, pp. 547–548; *EJ* vol. 3, pp. 1102–1103; *EJ (1971)*, vol. 4, pp. 264–265.

26. A history and description of the Vatican Library Hebrew manuscript collections is given by Umberto Cassuto (1883–1951) in his *I manoscritti Palatini ebraici della Biblioteca apostolica vaticana e la loro storia* (Vatican City, 1935). In 1956 Cassuto's list and description of 115 codices in the Vatican Library was published. A description of 30 Hebrew manuscripts was published by Naftali Ben-Menahem under the title *Miginze Yisrael Bavatikan* (Jerusalem, 1944), and a list of 801 Hebrew manuscripts from the Vatican Library, available on microfilm at the Institute of Microfilmed Hebrew Manuscripts in Jerusalem, was published in 1968.

27. Fürst, "Zur Geschichte der jüdischen Bibliographie," pp. lxxv–lxxvi.

28. Cf. his introduction to vol. 1. He also credited these bibliographers as sources for some of the works that he did not see.

29. For example, studies on the wars of the Hasmoneans; origins of Chanuka, Pesach, the Hebrew calendar, customs of reading weekly portions from the Pentateuch, and musical notes with explanations of synagogal Bible cantilations; long discourses with texts and translations of *Megilat Antiyochus* (cf. *JE* vol. 1, p. 637; *EI* vol. 22, p. 148), *Eldad Hadani* (cf. Abraham Epstein's edition [Pressburg, 1891], reprinted in his *Kitve* vol. 1, ed. A. M. Habermann [Jerusalem, 1949/50]), *Sipur Rav Amnon* (cf. *JE* vol. 1, pp. 525–526; *EJ (1971)*, vol. 2, p. 861), Ben Sira (cf. *JE* vol. 2, pp. 679–680; *EI* vol. 9, pp. 165–167; *EJ (1971)*, vol. 4, pp. 548–553).

30. Fürst, "Zur Geschichte der jüdischen Bibliographie," p. lxxv (from Richard Simon's *Bibliotheca critica*). Sabbatai Ambrun, an Italian-Jewish scholar, prepared a new *Bibliotheca rabbinica* in 1712, "to point out Bartolocci's hostility to the Jews, and to correct his errors" (according to Steinschneider, *Jewish Literature*, p. 252), but he was prevented by Christian as well as Jewish authorities from publishing it (according to Fürst, "Zur Geschichte der jüdischen Bibliographie," p. lxxxiii). For bio-bibliographical information on Ambrun, see Fürst, *Bibliotheca Judaica* (Leipzig, 1863), 3:183; Isaac Benjacob, *Otsar Hasefarim*, p. 159, no. 181.

31. Bartolocci quotes frequently from *Sefer Hakabalah* and *Yuchasin* (see above, n. 3).

32. The inclusion of the format of *printed* Hebrew books in bibliographical descriptions was introduced earlier by Buxtorf, the son, in the 1640 edition of his father's *Bibliotheca rabbinica*.

33. Bass's original surname might have been Strimers, which was the name of his brother who is mentioned on the title page of his *Sifte Yeshenim* (see below, p.10; also n. 41). The biographical information on Bass here is based mainly on Bernhard Friedberg, *Toldot Hadefus Ha'ivri* (Antwerp, 1937), pp. 55–64; A. M. Habermann, "Rabi Shabtai Meshorer Bas," *YL* 3 (1953): 157–163; Itzhak Raphael, *Rishonim Ve'acharonim* (Tel Aviv, 1957), pp. (171)–200; Slatkine, *Reshit Bikure Habibliyografyah*, pp. 12–20. For the period of his activities as printer and publisher, cf. L. Oelsner, *R. Sabbathai Bassista und sein Prozess* (Leipzig, 1858); M. Brann,

"Geschichte und Annalen der Dyhernfurter Druckerei," *MGWJ* 40 (1896): 477–480, 515–526, 560–574.

34. Bass, *Sifte Yeshenim*, p. 106b.

35. Särtels flourished in Prague in the first half of the seventeenth century. The first edition of his *Be'er Mosheh* was published in Prague in 1605.

36. Rashi, Rabbi Solomon ben Isaac (1040–1105), the most popular commentator on the Pentateuch and the Talmud, was a master of brevity, and his interpretations, especially on the Pentateuch, invited explanations. A few hundred supercommentaries on Rashi are known to have been written. Cf. J. M. Toledano, *Apiryon* (Jerusalem, 1905), supplemented in *ZfHB* 9 (1905): 137–138; Israel Schapiro, "Parshane Rashi al Hatorah," *Bitsaron* 2 (1940): 426–437 (reprinted separately, New York, 1940); Aron Freimann, "Manuscript Super-Commentaries on Rashi's Commentary on the Pentateuch," *Rashi Anniversary Volume* (New York, 1941), pp. 73–114 (reprinted separately, New York, 1941).

37. *Masechet Derech Erets* (Amsterdam, 1680). Text in Yiddish; title page in Hebrew. It will be described in the supplement to Volume Three of this work.

38. Entitled *Sifte Chachamim*, it was published together with the text of the Pentateuch. The second edition appeared in Amsterdam in 1685–1686. It is now a standard commentary, printed in every rabbinic edition of the Pentateuch.

39. On titles of Hebrew books, cf. Solomon Schechter, *Studies in Judaism*, 1st series (Philadelphia, 1896; reprinted several times), pp. 270–281; Abraham Berliner, "Hebräische Büchertitel," *JJLG* 2 (1904): (331)–350 (translated into Hebrew by A. M. Habermann and published under title *Shemot Sefarim Ivriyim* [Berlin, 1933/34]); Slatkine, *Shemot Hasefarim Ha'ivrim* (Neuchatel, Tel Aviv, 1950–1954); P. Pick, "Shemot Sefarim Ivriyim Atikim," *YL* 6 (1959/62): 196–201; M. Catane, "Shemotehem Shel Hasefarim Ha'ivriyim," *Machanayim*, no. 106 (1966), pp. 38–43; *EJ (1971)*, vol. 8, pp. 71–77.

40. See Bass, *Sifte Yeshenim*, p. 6b (first numbering), where he lists a few more reasons for the title of the work.

41. Some of the writers of approbations also mentioned that Bass was a brother of the famous cabalist. Habermann, *YL* 3 (1953): 157, thinks that Bass studied under his brother. This would explain Bass's cabalistic inclinations (see below, n. 42), the reason for inscribing his brother's name on the title page of this work, and the reference to him in the introduction to *Sifte Chachamim*. Cf. also H. C. Zafren, "The Value of 'Face Value', " *HUCA* 40–41 (1969–1970): 559.

42. Bass also composed two special prayers to be recited after pronouncing the names of the books (cf. *Sifte Yeshenim*, leaves 8–9, first numbering). Fürst, in "Zur Geschichte der jüdischen Bibliographie," pp. lxxvii–lxxviii, sees in Bass's first "benefit" a sign of the spiritual degeneration of German Jewry during the seventeenth century. Israel Zinberg, in *Di Geshichte fun der Literatur bay Yidn* (Vilna, 1935), 5:180–181 (Hebrew edition, [Tel Aviv, 1958], 3:246–247), sees in the first "benefit" a reflection of the "suspicion and hatred" of Polish and German Jews against anything new. Habermann, in "Rabi Shabtai Meshorer Bass," p. 160, expresses a similar opinion. But Slatkine, in *Reshit Bikure Habibliyografyah*, pp. 68–

69, disagrees. Secular books in Hebrew were published during the same period, and earlier, without objections. Bass, according to Slatkine, was a good businessman. He knew that a bibliographic work would find few customers, and he hit on a "gimmick" to save his investment (*Reshit Bikure Habibliyografyah*, pp. 71−72). Slatkine maintains that the prayerbook (without title page), bound together with some copies of *Sifte Yeshenim*, was printed by Bass as part of his plan to pass off the *Sifte Yeshenim* as a holy book, thereby attracting more cutomers. Cf. *ZfHB* 10 (1906): 62, 123, 127; M. Beit-Arié, "Sefatayim Dovevot," *KS* 40 (1964−1965): 126, n. 6; (could one of these two copies be that mentioned in *ZfHB* p. 62?). H. Liberman, *KS* 38 (1963): 276, differs with Slatkine and points out that a date (1678), printed on one of the leaves of the prayerbook, precedes the publication of *Sifte Yeshenim* by two years. Liberman speculates that Bass published the prayerbook separately; and by the time he published his *Sifte Yeshenim* only "a small number of copies (of the prayerbook) without title pages" remained, and "he did not know what to do with them, so he attached them to the *Sifte Yeshenim*." Cf. *KS* 39 (1964): 280.

43. Slatkine, *Reshit Bikure Habibliyografyah*, pp. 9−10, 21.

44. Cf. his preface to the author index, *Sifte Yeshenim*, p. 93b, and his "apology" on p. l06b.

45. Bass, *Sifte Yeshenim*, p. 107a.

46. Cf. Slatkine, *Reshit Bikure Habibliyografyah*, pp. 24−35 and Raphael, *Rishonim Ve'acharonim*, pp. 188−190, nn. 14−17, 22−25. See also Slatkine, *Reshit*, pp. 45−64 for a detailed listing of numerous errors in *Sifte Yeshenim* (some of these already pointed out by Azulai in his *Shem Hagedolim* and by I. Benjacob in his *Otsar*).

47. Cf. Beit-Arié, *KS* 40 (1964−1965): 126, 132; Habermann, 'Rabi Shabtai Meshorer Bas," p. 161.

48. Fürst, "Zur Geschichte der jüdischen Bibliographie," p. lxxxi, lists various attempts to translate the *Sifte Yeshenim* into Latin or German. Cf. M. Brann, *Das bibliographische Handbuch des Schabtai Bass in der lateinischen Übersetzung Clanners* (Breslau, 1882); Raphael, *Rishonim Ve'acharonim*, pp. 189−190; *JE* vol. 2, p. 584.

49. On Rubinstein as a printer, cf. Friedberg, *Toldot Hadefus Ha'ivri Bepolonyah* 2d ed. (Tel Aviv, 1950), p. 84.

50. *Da'at Sifre Shorashim, sive: Historia lexicorum hebraicorum . . .* (Würtemberg, 1705).

51. *Notitia karaeorum* (Hamburg, 1721).

52. Cf. *Bibliotheca* vol. 1 (introduction), p. 118; vol. 2, p. 312; also introduction to vols. 3 and 4. On the Oppenheimer Collection, see below, pp. 38−40.

53. Fürst, "Zur Geschichte der jüdischen Bibliographie," p. xc.

54. Steinschneider, *Bibliographisches Handbuch*, p. xviii; cf. Fürst, "Zur Geschichte der jüdischen Bibliographie," p. lxxxiii. Marx, *Studies in Jewish History and Booklore*, p. 216, calls Wolf "the greatest bibliographer of Hebrew letters that ever lived (except Steinschneider)." Steinschneider himself complained elsewhere about Wolf's biased attitude to Judaism. Cf. *HB* 17 (1877): 90. Zunz may have had in mind Wolf's attitude to Judaism, when he stated ". . . das Werk [ist] fast eben so leer

an Geist wie das Eisenmengerische. . . ." (*Gesammelte Schriften,* 1:53). On the other hand, Moses Hagiz (1671?–1750), a contemporary of Wolf, in one of his works describes in flowery language a visit to Wolf's house and a theological discussion he had with him. Cf. Hagiz's introduction to his *Mishnat Chachamim* (Wandsbeck, 1733), p. 4a (I am grateful to Professor Meir Benayahu for calling my attention to this source).

55. On Steinschneider's *Catalogus,* see below, Chapter 2.

56. *Specimen observationum philologicarum in I Sam. ii* (Jena, 1772); *Stricturarum antimasorethicarum in Kirjam et Chtib ad librum judicum specimen* (Jena, 1780); *Versuch einer Erklärung der Geschichte Saul's mit der Betrügerin zu Endor* (Gera, 1780).

57. Steinschneider, *Bibliographisches Handbuch,* p. xviii, and n. 2; Fürst, "Zur Geschichte der jüdischen Bibliographie," pp. xci–xcii.

58. The *Seder Hadorot* was printed posthumously in Karlsruhe, 1769. The bibliographic section in that edition was called *Shemot Ba'ale Mechabrim Vechol Hasefarim.* It was changed to *Seder Mechabrim Veseder Sefarim* by N. Maskileison in his edition of the *Seder Hadorot* (Warsaw, 1878–1882). The Maskileison edition is considered the most reliable. A detailed discussion on Heilprin and his work will be found in Volume Two of this work.

59. See above, pp. 11–12 and note 44.

60. Cf. Maskileison's foreword to this section; Raphael, *Rishonim Ve'acharonim,* p. 190, n. 22.

61. For further bibliographical data on Fürst, cf. Samuel Joseph Fünn, *Kneset Yisrael* (Warsaw, 1886), pp. 438–440; A. M. Habermann, "Yulyus First," *YL* 2 (1950/51): 102–105; *JE* vol. 5, pp. 533–534; *EJ* vol. 6, pp. 1209–1210; *EJ (1971),* vol. 7, pp. 213–214.

62. Fürst's edition of the Hebrew concordance will be discussed in Volume Three of this work.

63. For a list of Fürst's major works, cf. *JE* vol. 5, pp. 533–534; and Shlomo Shunami, *Bibliography of Jewish Bibliographies* (Jerusalem, 1965) no. 3542.

64. Cf. *JE* vol. 3, p. 200; A. Fraenkel, introduction to 1968 edition of Freimann's *Katalog* p. III*.

65. Cf. introduction to part 3 of the *Bibliotheca Judaica* (p.vi).

66. Ibid., p. vii.

67. Azulai and his bibliographic achievements will be discussed below, in Chapter 3.

68. Leopold Zunz (1794–1886), who ushered in the era of modern Jewish studies with his essay *Etwas über die rabbinische Literatur* (Berlin, 1818), contributed greatly to the development of Jewish bibliography with his essays on Hebrew books and printers. Cf. his *Zur Geschichte und Literatur* (Berlin, 1845), pp. 214–303. Zunz's contributions to modern Jewish scholarship will be discussed in the supplement to Volume Three of this work.

69. About Steinschneider, see below, pp. 40–44 and 140–143.

70. For details, see below, Chapter 2.

71. For details, see below, Chapter 6.

72. See above, pp. 17–18.

73. The biographical data on I. Benjacob are based on the chapter "Toldot Yitschak" in *Otsar Hasefarim,* pp. (xxi)–xxviii and Jacob Benjacob's introduction to that work, p. xiii. For additional information, cf. Slatkine's introduction to his *Otsar Hasefarim Chelek Sheni,* pp. 7–12; A. M. Habermann, "Yitschak Aisik Ben-Ya'akov Ba'al Otsar Hasefarim," *YL* 3 (1951): 1–6; G. Kressel, "Yitschak Aisik Ben-Ya'akov," *JBA* 20 (1962/63): 95-99; idem, *Leksikon Hasifrut Ha'ivrit Bedorot Ha'acharonim* (Merchavya, 1965–1967), 1:281–282; *Hamagid* 7 (1863): 234–235; *KS* 2 (1925/26): 69–70, 74–75; *Ale Hadas,* ed. M. E. Beilinson (Odessa, 1865), pp. 24–27.

74. Among the Hebrew books which Benjacob published in Leipzig were two pamphlets of medieval texts and other minor works, entitled *Devarim Atikim* (Leipzig, 1844–46); a eulogy by Solomon Ibn Gabirol, entitled *Za'akat Shever* (Leipzig, 1846); and Bahya Ibn Pakuda's *Chovot Halevavot* (Leipzig, 1846). Together with Z. G. Stern, he also published in Leipzig in 1844 a sixteen-page booklet of corrections to Azulai's *Shem Hagedolim* under the title *Kuntres Shinuye Shem Vetikune Va'ad.* This booklet served as the forerunner to his later, scientific edition of the *Shem Hagedolim* (see below, pp. 78–79).

75. Cf. his letters to Isaac Baer Levinsohn, *Fun Noentn Ovar* 1 (1937): 27–39 (published earlier in Hebrew translation in *Hakerem* [1887], pp. 41–62), and Levinsohn's reply in Bernard Natanson's *Sefer Hazichronot* (Warsaw, 1876), p. 114. Cf. also Baruch Halevi Epstein, *Mekor Baruch* (Vilna, 1928; reprinted, New York, 1954), pp. 1090–1091.

76. Published in Vilna, 1848–1853. Besides the standard Rashi commentary, Benjacob and Lebensohn added the translation and commentaries by Moses Mendelssohn and his disciples, together with additional materials of their own.

77. On Benjacob's plan and the controversy it created, cf. S. Y. Stanislavski, "Chomer Lenisyono Shel Ben-Ya'akov Leyased Hotsa'at Sefarim Ivrit Berusyah," *Reshumot,* 2d ed. (Tel Aviv, 1925), 1:317–332 (this article also includes biographical material on Benjacob); A. Yaari, "Letoldot Hamolut Ha'ivrit," *Moznayim* 3, no. 27 (1931): 10–12; T. Preshel, "Kiryat Sefer Lechochmat Yisrael," *Hadoar* 43 (1964): 301–303; G. Kressel, "Hacheruz Harishon Shel Chevrat Mekitse Nirdamim," *Areshet* 4 (1966), 465–468.

78. Jacob Benjacob states in the introduction to the *Otsar* p. xv, that his father was in the book trade for about twenty years and that he worked on the *Otsar* for "decades" (p. xiii). That could indicate that Benjacob began both activities around the same time.

79. Jacob Benjacob, "Vorbemerkung" to *Otsar.* Cf. Zunz, *Zur Geschichte und Literatur,* p. 248.

80. Cf. I. Benjacob's introduction to Azulai's *Shem Hagedolim,* p. 4 (first numbering). The various stages of development of the *Otsar* described here are based on J. Benjacob's "Magid Mereshit," in *Otsar* pp. xiii–xv.

81. Slatkine, in the introduction to his supplement to the *Otsar,* p. 9, marvels over Steinschneider's friendly relations to Benjacob, since "generally he was not

pleasant to people and was highly pedantic. . . ." Cf. below, p. 278, n. 40 and pp. 296–297, n. 9–12, 14.

82. With the exception of the letter *tav*, which was revised only up to number 880. Cf. *Otsar*, bottom of p. 676.

83. Benjacob earlier might also have revised the letter *nun*. Cf.*Otsar*, bottom of p. 406.

84. Cf. *Hatsefirah* 3, (1876), no. 24.

85. For biographical details on Jacob Benjacob, cf. *Literarishe Bleter* 2 (1926), no. 98, p. 192 (where an *Otsar Hasofrim* by Jacob Benjacob is mentioned, consisting of 18,000 bio-bibliographies of writers, translators, editors, and publishers of Jewish works); *Haolam* 14 (1926): 290; ibid. 22 (1934):707; M. Schorr, "Ben-Ya'akovs Oytser Hasforim," *YB* 8 (1935): 139, n. 2.

86. Cf. M. Schorr, "Aus einem Briefwechsel betreffend Benjacob's Thesaurus," *Jewish Studies in Memory of George A. Kohut* (New York, 1935), pp. 528–548. Steinschneider's special interest and assistance in the printing of the *Otsar* is reflected in his letters to J. Benjacob, ibid., pp. 543–548. J. Benjacob acknowledged Steinschneider's assistance by listing his name on the title page of the *Otsar*, and by inserting the initials רמש"ש into numerous entries annotated by Steinschneider. Another important contributor to the *Otsar* was Raphael Nathan Rabinowitz (1835–1888), author of *Dikduke Soferim*. Isaac Benjacob himself utilized a bibliographical pamphlet prepared by Rabinowitz around 1854, and he credited this source with the initials שי"ג meaning שפתי ישנים ג', since Rabinowitz chose to remain anonymous. Cf. list of abbreviations to the *Otsar* and Rabinowitz's letter to J. Benjacob in *Jewish Studies in Memory of George A. Kohut* p. 539.

87. Cf. Slatkine's introduction to his *Otsar Hasefarim Chelek Sheni*, pp. 8–9; S. Wiener, *Kohelet Mosheh*, p. 46; *EJ (1971)*, vol. 4, p. 521 (where the figure of 8,480 manuscripts is erroneous). Steinschneider suggested to Benjacob that he not include manuscripts in the *Otsar*, but Benjacob wanted the *Otsar* to contain all the features of *Sifte Yeshenim*; cf. *HB* 6 (1863): 108–109.

Lists of duplicate entries in the *Otsar* were published by Friedberg, *Jüdisches Archiv* 2 (1929): 49–51 (also issued as a "Separatabdruck"), and in his *Bet Eked Sefarim* (Antwerp, 1931), pp. 839–844 (see below, p. 25).

88. Although Benjacob abandoned his intention of preparing an extended edition of *Sifte Yeshenim*, he made the latter the basis for the *Otsar*. Cf. Steinschneider, *HB* 6 (1863):108: "Er hatte nach Form und Inhalt des Sifte yeschenim des Sabbatai zu grunde gelegt. . ." See also Slatkine, *Shemot Hasefarim Ha'ivrim*, 2:7. Benjacob made good use of an annotated copy of *Sifte Yeshenim* that included additions written by Bass and Solomon Dubno (1738–1813). Cf. M. Beit-Arié, *KS* 40 (1964/65): 126–127.

89. Cf. Schorr, "Aus einem Briefwechsel," especially the letters by David Kaufmann (p. 531), R. N. Rabinowitz (p. 540), and Steinschneider (p. 548). For reviews, cf. (among others) *MGWJ* 30 (1881): 375–384, 570–572 (by M. Brann), *JJGL* 5–6 (1883): 217–221 (by N. Brüll).

90. Besides the additions and corrections included in the above-mentioned

reviews (note 89), there also appeared additional material by A. E. Harkavy (1835–1919) in *Hayekev* 2 (1894): 42–48, *Hagat* (1897), pp. 83–95 (reprinted in his *Chadashim Gam Yeshanim,*[Jerusalem, 1970], pp. 92–98, 269–281), and by Aron Freimann, *ZfHB,* beginning with vol. 8 (1904). Characteristic of Harkavy's relations with Steinschneider is his brief introduction to his additions and corrections to the *Otsar;* cf. *Hayekev* p. 42; *Chadashim Gam Yeshanim* p. 92.

91. Cf. title page of *Otsar;* also introduction, pp. xiv, xvii.

92. Cf. Steinschneider's letters to J. Benjacob, *Jewish Studies in Memory of George A. Kohut,* pp. 543–544, 548.

93. The information on J. Benjacob's version of the *Otsar* is based on the descriptions by M. Schorr, *SB* 2 (1927), 38–40; *YB* 8 (1935), 138–147. For additional information, cf. Slatkine's introduction to his *Otsar Hasefarim Chelek Sheni,* pp. 10–11.

94. For bio-bibliographical information on Schorr, cf. J. Guzik, "Mosheh Shor," in *Ishim Udemuyot Bechochmat Yisrael Be'eropah Hamizrachit lifne Shekiatah,* ed. S. K. Mirsky (New York, 1959), pp. 207–222; *Hapoel Hatsa'ir* 55 (1961/62), no. 15, pp. 17-18; *EJ (1971),* vol. 14, pp. 997–998.

95. The CCAR is not identical with Agudat Harabanim, as Habermann thought; cf. *YL* 3 (1951): 5.

96. According to Habermann, *ibid.*

97. See above, note 93. Schorr's report in *YB* was accompanied by a facsimile of a sample page of the new edition; cf. *YB* 8 (1935): 147.

98. Shunami, *Bibliography,* no. 80, dates this edition as "1948/49?" Library of Congress's "1943/44" seems to be too early. A new reprint edition was recently announced by Gerstenberg Reprints (cf. their Catalog 71/72).

99. *Shemot Hasefarim Ha'ivrim,* 2 vols. (Neuchatel, Tel Aviv, 1950–1954).

100. *Reshit Bikure Habibliyografyah* (Tel Aviv, 1958). On Slatkine and his literary activities, cf. E. Ben-Ezra, *Hadoar* 29 (1949/50): 952; D. Persky, ibid. 38 (1958/59): 597; Kressel, *Leksikon* 1:746; idem, *Moznayim* 20 (1964/65): 420. Cf. also *Igrot Cha'im Nachman Bialik,* (Tel Aviv, 1938), 1:62 and n. 3.

101. Cf. Slatkine's introduction to his *Otsar Hasefarim Chelek Sheni,* pp. 11–13.

102. Cf. ibid., pp. 20–21, where he lists manuscript collections that changed hands during the last hundred years.

103. Cf. S. R. Brunswick's review, *JSS* 29 (1967): 113–114.

104. Cf. Brunswick, ibid., p. 114, about the shortcomings of Slatkine's index to the *Otsar.*

105. In introduction to *Bet Eked Sefarim.*

106. *Rabenu Yosef Karo* (Drohobycz, 1895).

107. For biographical details on Friedberg, see Habermann, *Anshe Sefer Ve'anshe Ma'aseh* (Jerusalem, 1974), pp. 62–63; Kressel, *Leksikon,* 2:659.

108. *Toldot Hadefus Ha'ivri Bepolonyah* (Antwerp, 1932), with additions to *Bet Eked Sefarim,* pp. 109–111; 2d ed. (Tel Aviv, 1950); *Toldot Hadefus Ha'ivri Bimedinot Italyah, Aspamyah-Portugalyah, Togarma Ve'artsot Hakedem* (Antwerp,

1934); 2d ed. (Tel Aviv, 1956); *Toldot Hadefus Ha'ivri Be'arim Ha'eleh Shebe'eropah Hatichonah* (Antwerp, 1935); *Toldot Hadefus Ha'ivri Be'arim Ha'eleh Shebe'eropah* (Antwerp, 1937).

109. In introduction to *Bet Eked Sefarim* first edition; with minor changes also in the second edition.

110. Cf. Aryeh Tauber, *KS* 5 (1928/29): 206–208; 6 (1929/30): 452–456 (reprinted in his *Mechkarim Bibliyografiyim* [Jerusalem, 1932], pp. [78]–85) and H. Liberman's letter to Daniel Persky in *Hadoar* 41 (1961/62): 54.

111. See above, note 87.

112. Cf. Tauber's reviews in *KS* (n. 110 above), where Friedberg is criticized, among others, for his unscientific way of registering pagination of works (giving total numbers without distinguishing between the introduction, foreword, and similar sorts of materials, and the body of the book). See also Abraham Yaari, *KS* 11 (1934/35): 111–116, about the gap in Ladino works. Joseph Klausner, on the other hand, published a favorable review in *Haolam* 19 (1931): 1006–1008. Klausner's only major objection was to Friedberg's inclusion of works in Jewish dialects among the Hebrew works.

113. The actual number of individual titles, according to N. Ben-Menahem, *YL* 6 (1959/62): 205, was 28,234.

114. Cf. Ben-Menahem, "Bet Eked Sefarim," *Sinai* 30 (1952): 144-155 (also issued as a separate); G. Elkoshi, *Gilyonot* 27 (1952): 108–111, where the *Bet Eked* is called " the work of a dilettante." According to Elkoshi, "over fifty percent of the publications of modern Hebrew literature are missing" in *Bet Eked,* and "the Hebrew periodical is almost not visible in the present bibliography." Also, the number of errors and blunders is "terrifying." Elkoshi also objected to the financial support given to Friedberg by the Ministry of Education and Culture of the State of Israel to publish the *Bet Eked.*

115. Cf. S. Shunami, *Al Sifriyot Vesafranut* (Jerusalem, 1969), pp. 30–31 (published originally in the Tel Aviv daily *Davar,* February 18, 1938).

116. Cf. Ben-Menahem, "Mif'al Habibliyografyah Ha'ivrit," *YL* 6 (1959/62): 202–203.

117. Cf. Gershom Scholem's introduction to *Choveret Ledugmah* (1964), p. 7.

118. Shunami, *YL* 7 (1964): 149 (reprinted in his *Al Sifriyot,* pp. 130–133), pointed out that *Mif'al* should be translated as *project;* the Hebrew equivalent for *institute* is *mosad.*

119. For a list of the "Executive Organs of the Institute," cf. *Choveret Ledugmah* (1964) and *Mif'al Habibliyografyah Ha'ivrit* (Jerusalem, n. d.).

120. Scholem, *Choveret Ledugmah,* p. 7.

121. Ben-Menahem, "Mif'al Habibliografyah Ha'ivrit," p. 205; Scholem, *Choveret Ledugmah,* p. 7.

122. Ben-Menahem, "Mif'al Habibliyografyah Ha'ivrit," p. 205.

123. Ibid., pp. 203–204; Scholem, *Choveret Ledugmah,* pp. 9–10.

124. For the significance of approbations, see below, p. 235.

125. Some of the "rules" were already violated in the specimen entries; cf. Shunami, *YL* 7 (1964): 149 and *Al Sifriyot,* pp. 131—132.

126. In September 1972, Mr. Ben-Menahem (1911—1974) informed this writer that the *Mif'al* had already completed the author registration up to the letter *samech* and that the first volume of the bibliography would be in the printer's hands sometime in 1975, with publication to commence about a year later. The first volume would cover part of the letter *alef.* The untimely death of Ben-Menahem has considerably altered this schedule of publication.

Notes to Chapter Two:
*Catalogs of Hebraica Book Collections*

1. On Jewish book collectors and their collections, see Leopold Zunz, *Zur Geschichte und Literatur* (Berlin, 1845), pp. 230—248; Alexander Marx, *Studies in Jewish History and Booklore* (New York, 1944), pp. 198—237; Shlomo Shunami, *Bibliography,* sections IV—V, XXVI; *JE* vol. 3, pp. 310—312; *EJ (1971),* vol. 4, pp. 973—976.

2. For a complete history of the Bodleian Library, see W. D. Macray, *Annals of the Bodleian Library* (Oxford, 1890); E. Craster, *History of the Bodleian Library, 1845—1945* (Oxford, 1952).

3. The biographical sketch of David Oppenheimer and the history of his book collection are based on L. Löwenstein's "David Oppenheim," in *Gedenkbuch zur Erinnerung an David Kaufmann* (Breslau, 1900), pp. 538—559; C. Duschinsky, *Toldot Hagaon R' David Openhaimer* (Budapest, 1922; reprinted from *Hatsofeh Lechochmat Yisrael* 5 [1921]: 39—45, 145—155; 6 [1922]: 26—37; (C. Duschinsky, "Rabbi David Oppenheimer," *JQR* n. s. 20 (1929—1930): 217—247; H. Meyer, "Materialien zur Geschichte der Bibliothek David Oppenheims," *SB* 2 (1927): 59—80; Marx, *Studies,* pp. 213—219, 238—255.

4. Duschinsky, *Toldot,* p. 73, lists twenty-one works by Oppenheimer. Zunz, *Zur Geschichte und Literatur,* p. 244, mentions twenty-four manuscripts by Oppenheimer in the possession of a private collector in Viasen, near Vilna. Heimann Joseph Michael, *Or Hachayim* (Frankfort, 1891), pp. 315—318, lists eighteen works, mostly manuscripts, in his possession. The first volume of Oppenheimer's responsa, entitled *Nish'al David* recently was published from a manuscript in the Bodleian Library (Jerusalem, 1971/72).

5. Cf. Duschinsky, "Rabbi David," p. 242.

6. Marx, *Studies,* p. 214; see also p. 239, where the figure of 460 is given. Cf. also Michael, *Or Hachayim,* p. 317, no. 18.

7. Cf. Löwenstein, "David Oppenheim." p. 545; *JE* vol. 9, p. 419.

8. Cf. Marx, *Studies*, pp. 214, 243–244; Duschinsky, *Toldot*. pp. 78–79.

9. Löwenstein, "David Oppenheim," p. 546.

10. Duschinsky, *Toldot*, pp. 78–79. Oppenheimer became quite wealthy through inheritance and marriage.

11. Cf. Löwenstein, "David Oppenheim," pp. 546–547.

12. Duschinsky, "Rabbi David," p. 240, relates a different version.

13. Cf. *HB* 6 (1863): 35–39.

14. Marx, *Studies*, p. 216; also n. 56.

15. Ibid., p. 215. This is also the number of volumes acquired later by the Bodleian Library. Wolf, *Bibliotheca hebraea*, (Hamburg, 1715), 1:290, estimated 7,000 printed and 1,000 handwritten works. The books occupied 106 shelves, forty of which were taken up by manuscripts. See also Marx, *Studies*, p. 244.

16. *Verzeichnis verschiedener hebräischen und rabinischen Bücher, welche insgesamt aus der Hand auf die Nacher angeführte Bedingungen verkauft verden sollen* (Hannover, 1764). Cf. Shunami, *Bibliography*, no. 349.

17. For the text of Moses Mendelssohn's evaluation, cf. Meyer, "Geschichte der Bibliothek," p. 67.

18. *Reshimah Tamah*, comp. Israel Breslau (Hamburg, 1782); cf. Shunami, *Bibliography*, no. 350.

19. *Kohelet David*, comp. Isaac Metz (Hebrew part) and Eleazar Solomon von Embden (Latin part) (Hamburg, 1826), with an index by Jacob Goldenthal, published in Leipzig, 1845. Cf. Shunami, *Bibliography*, nos. 351–352.

20. The interest in the Oppenheimer Collection among Christian scholars is described by Meyer, "Geschichte der Bibliothek," pp. 59–80.

21. Cf. Cecil Roth, "An Episode in the History of the Oppenheimer Collection," *The Bodleian Library Record* 5 (1954): 104–108, reprinted in his *Studies in Books and Booklore* (Westmead, 1972), pp. 243–247. Cf. also M. Benayahu, "Igrot Rabi Mosheh Chayim Morpurgo," *Areshet* 1 (1958): 228, 250. On the Paris Sanhedrin, cf. Diogène Tama, *Transactions of the Parisian Sanhedrin*, translated from French by F. D. Kirwan (London, 1807; Cincinnati, 1956); *JE* vol. 11, pp. 46–48; *EJ (1971)*, vol. 14, pp. 840–842.

22. Craster, *The Bodleian Library* p. 21, and Roth, *Books and Booklore* p. 247, convert this sum to £2,080; Duschinsky, "Rabbi David," p. 218, *Toldot*, p. 4, converts it to £1,350. Interestingly enough, the cost of honorarium and printing of Moritz Steinschneider's *Catalogus* was £2,050. Cf. Craster, *The Bodleian*, p. 106.

23. The biographical sketch of Steinschneider here is based on S. Bernfeld, "Zichron Lachachamim," *Hashilo'ach* 17 (1907): 306–310; Reuben Brainin, "Mosheh Shtainshnaider," *Hatoren* 4, no. 32 (1917/18): 7–10, reprinted in his *Kol Kitve* (New York, 1940), 3:81–87; *Hatoren* 7, no. 31 (1920/21): 8; Marx, *Studies*, pp. 364–368; Marx, *Essays in Jewish Biography* (Philadelphia, 1947), pp. 112–184; A. M. Habermann, "Mosheh Shtainshnaider," *YL* 1 (1947): 239–242; J. Bloch, "Moritz Steinschneider," *JBA* 15 (1957/58): 88–93; A. R. Malachi, "Mosheh Shtainshnaider," *Perakim* 2 (1960): 129–141; S. W. Baron, "Moritz Steinschneider's Contributions to Jewish Historiography," *Alexander Marx Jubilee Volume* (New

York, 1950), English section, pp. 83−148, reprinted in his *History and Jewish Historians* (Philadelphia, 1964), pp. 276−321; D. S. Löwinger, "Mosheh Shtainshnaider," *Chochmat Yisrael Bema'arav Eropah* (Jerusalem, 1965), 3:331−344; G. Kressel, "Mosheh Shtainshnaider," *Katif* 4/5 (1967): 306−310.

24. Details about the plan will be found in Volume Two of this work.

25. Entitled "Jüdische Literatur," it occupied pp. 357−471 (seven times more than the original amount of space allotted for such a topic) of section two, part 27, of the *Allgemeine Encyklopädie der Wissenschaften und Künste* (Leipzig, 1850). An English translation of the article by William Spottiswoode (in which the first two pages of the original article were left out) was published in London in 1857, under the title *Jewish Literature from the Eighth to the Eighteenth Century* (reprinted, New York, 1965). A Hebrew translation, omitting many footnotes, was prepared by Henry Malter and published in Warsaw in 1897−1900, under the title *Sifrut Yisrael* (reprinted, Warsaw, 1923; Jerusalem, 1970/71).

26. Published in part 28 (Leipzig, 1851; reprinted as a separate, Jerusalem, 1938).

27. About Michael and his bio-bibliographical work, see below, pp. 88−90.

28. See below, p. 47.

29. The *Specimen* included the entries on Moses Maimonides, Saadia Gaon, Salomo Ibn Gabirol, Salomo Isaki (Rashi), and Samuel Nagid.

30. The list of printers, etc., included many corrections to "Jüdische Typographie und jüdischer Buchhandel," written jointly by Steinschneider and Cassel. See above, p. 41.

31. *Conspectus codd. mss. hebraeorum in bibliotheca Bodleiana* (Berlin, 1857).

32. Marx, *Essays*, p. 150.

33. Ibid., pp. 150−152. Solomon Schechter, *Seminary Addresses* (Cincinnati, 1915; New York, 1959), p. 122, called Steinschneider's *Catalogus* "the Urim and Thummim (oracle) of every Jewish student." Julius Fürst, on the other hand, devoted two pages of his "Zur Geschichte der jüdischen Bibliographie" (in his *Bibliotheca Judaica* vol. 3), pp. xlix−li, to denigrate the importance of Steinschneider's achievement.

34. Marx, *Essays*, p. 151.

35. Ibid.

36. Brainin, *Kol Kitve*, p. 85.

37. Marx, *Studies*, p. 229.

38. Brainin, *Kol Kitve*, p. 81.

39. Steinschneider's major works included: *Allgemeine Einleitung in die jüdische Literatur des Mittelalters* (published originally in *JQR* 15−17 [1903−1905]; reprinted as a separate [Jerusalem, 1938]); *Die arabische Literatur der Juden* (Frankfort, 1902; reprinted, Hildesheim, 1964); *Bibliographisches Handbuch über die theoretische und praktische Literatur für hebräische Sprachkunde* (Leipzig, 1895; 2d ed. with additions and corrections [Jerusalem, 1937]); *Die hebräischen Übersetzungen des Mittelalters und die Juden als Dolmetscher* (Berlin, 1893; reprinted, Graz, 1956); *Polemische und apologetische Literatur in arabischer Sprache, zwischen Muslimen, Christen und Juden* (Leipzig, 1877; Nendeln: Kraus Reprint, 1966); *Vorlesungen über*

*die Kunde hebräischer Handschriften, deren Sammlungen und Verzeichnisse* (Leipzig, 1897; reprinted, Jerusalem, 1937); translated into Hebrew by Y. Eldad and published under the title *Hartsaot al Kitve Yad Ivriyim* (Jerusalem, 1965). A volume of Steinschneider's *Gesammelte Schriften* was edited by H. Malter and A. Marx, and published in Berlin in 1925. See also below, notes 52−55, for some of the more important catalogs prepared by Steinschneider.

40. Cf. Brainin, *Hatoren* 7, no. 31 (1920/21): 8, and Marx, *Essays*, p. 183, for statements that Steinschneider was always helpful to students and scholars; Bernfeld, "Zichron Lachachamim," p. 269, claims just the opposite: —"he was jealous of every young scholar. . . ." According to Marx, *Essays*, p. 181, he was possessed by "deep inner modesty"; according to Bernfeld, "he believed that Jewish scholarship will die when he will die, and that nobody like him will survive in Israel." Brainin and Marx testify to his wit. Bernfeld agrees, although he characterizes it as "biting and painful jests." All his biographers agree that his writing was mostly dry. On Steinschneider's feuds with Carmoly, Fürst, and other scholars, cf. Marx, *Essays*, pp. 170−175; Baron, *Alexander Marx Jubilee Volume*, pp. 115−120 (in his *History and Jewish Historians*, pp. 299−303), also footnotes. See also below, Chapter 6. Steinschneider's attitude toward living Judaism is summed up by Brainin in the following words: "He liked the research about the dead Judaism much more than he liked the present living Jews and living Judaism." According to Bernfeld, "when he used to sit and work on his bibliographical notes and compilations, he imagined that he is researching the tombstones of a people that was buried thousands of years ago." See also Gershom Scholem's essay "Mitoch Hirhurim al Chochmat Yisrael," *Luach Ha'arets*, 1944/45, p. 102. Steinschneider, in his younger days, was just the opposite; cf. Marx, *Essays*, pp. 120−123; S. W. Baron, "Abraham Benisch's Project for Jewish Colonization in Palestine (1842)," *Jewish Studies in Memory of George A. Kohut* (New York, 1935), pp. 72−85. See also below, Chapter 6.

41. Arthur Ernest Cowley, in his preface to *A Concise Catalogue of the Hebrew Printed Books in the Bodleian Library*. Adolf Neubauer, in his preface to volume one of his *Catalogue*, suggests that the *Catalogus* "should rather be called Bibliotheca Judaica."

42. Cf. Marx, *Essays*, pp. 136−137, for the reaction of the curators of Bodleian Library to the *Catalogus*.

43. See below, p. 48.

44. Ibid.

45. *Aramaic Papyri of the Fifth Century B. C.* (Oxford, 1906, 1923, 1967); *The Samaritan Liturgy* (Oxford, 1909); *Jewish Documents of the Time of Ezra* (London, 1919); and, together with Neubauer, *The Original Hebrew of a Portion of Ecclesiasticus* (Oxford, 1897).

46. A. Kahana, *Moznayim* 1, no. 25 (1929): 15. The reviewer praised the "condensation and clarity" of Cowley's entries in the *Catalogue* and his "abbreviating and condensing of the title pages for the sake of a clear definition and emphasis on the nature of the books." His only criticism was that the compiler did not prepare a detailed introduction providing the history of the collection, the

number of books listed in the catalog, statistics about the various languages and subjects, etc.

47. Quoted by Marx, *Essays,* p. 137.

48. See above, p. 42; also n. 31.

49. E. N. Adler in *Studies in Jewish Bibliography and Related Subjects in Memory of Abraham Solomon Freidus* (New York, 1929), pp. 31–54, published a bibliography of Neubauer listing 300 entries. Another 109 entries were added later by Boaz Cohen in *KS* 10 (1933): 365–371. The biographical data on Neubauer here is based on I. Ben-Reshef, "Adolf Noibauer," *Chochmat Yisrael Bema'arav Eropah,* (Jerusalem, 1965), 3:242–245; Kressel, *Leksikon,* 2:449–450; *JE* vol. 9, pp. 234–235; *EJ (1971),* vol. 12, pp. 1,003–1,005.

50. For data on Firkovich and his collection, cf. *JE* vol. 5, pp. 393–394; *EE* vol. 15, pp. 289–293; *EJ (1971),* vol. 6, pp. 1,305–1,306. An interesting episode about Firkovich's "corrections" of old Hebrew manuscripts is related by Jacob Saphir, *Even Sapir* vol. 2 (Mainz, 1874), footnote to pp. 178–179.

51. During his years in England, Neubauer prepared and published a number of important texts, among them *The Book of Hebrew Roots* by Abu'l-Walîd Marwân ibn Janâh (Oxford, 1875; reprinted, Amsterdam, 1968); *Mediaeval Jewish Chronicles and Chronological Notes* (Oxford, 1887–1895; reprinted, Jerusalem, 1967). He also collaborated with Ernest Renan (1823–1892) on *Les Rabbins français du commencement du XIVe siècle* (Paris, 1877; reprinted, Farnborough, 1969), and compiled a *Catalogue of the Hebrew Manuscripts in the Jews' College, London* (Oxford, 1886).

52. *Catalogus codicum hebraeorum bibliothecae academiae Lugduno-Batavae* (Leyden, 1858).

53. *Die hebräischen Handschriften der K. Hof- und Staatsbibliothek in München* (Munich, 1875); 2d ed., (Munich, 1895).

54. *Catalog der hebräischen Handschriften in der Stadtbibliothek zu Hamburg und der Sich Anschliessenden in anderen Sprachen* (Hamburg, 1878).

55. *Verzeichniss der hebräischen Handschriften* (Berlin, 1878–1897).

56. *Catalogues des manuscrits hébreux et samaritains de la bibliothèque imperiale* (Paris, 1866).

57. *Catalogue of the Hebrew Manuscripts Preserved in the University Library* (Cambridge, 1876).

58. *Catalog der hebräischen Bibelhandschriften der Kaiserlichen Öffentlichen Bibliothek in St. Petersburg* (St. Petersburg, Leipzig, 1875).

59. Cf. G. Margoliouth's review of Neubauer's *Catalogue* vol. 2, in *JQR* 19 (1907): 589: "Steinschneider cultivates extraordinary fullness of detail, and he is never tired of tracing a name, a date, or any other interesting point, through all its possible bibliographical windings."

60. The literature dealing with the accusations against Firkovich of forging some colophons in his collections of manuscripts are listed in the sources noted above, n. 50.

61. Cf. also Margoliouth's review of Neubauer's *Catalogue, JQR:* "Neubauer limits himself to what he regards as the details necessary for cataloging purposes. He

indeed very often puts in a hint or two to guide the student on his path of further research, but his descriptions are all the same uniformly concise and circumscribed in range."

62. See above, p. 40; also notes 15, 22.

63. See above, pp. 41–42, and below, p. 48. On Michael, see below, pp. 88–90.

64. Cf. *MGWJ* 35 (1886): 460–461, where the reviewer of this volume praises Neubauer's "plaine Englisch" (!) as contrasted to Steinschneider's "holprige Latein" in his *Catalogus.*, "das noch dazu mit Citatengestrüpp und mit fragwürdigen Fragezeichen und 'sic' gespickt, den Leser wirre macht."

65. Cf. Craster, *Bodleian Library*, pp. 210–212. On the Cairo Genizah discovery, cf. P. E. Kahle, *The Cairo Genizah* (London, 1947; 2d ed., Oxford, 1959); A. M. Habermann, *Hagenizah Vehagenizot* (Jerusalem, 1971); *EJ (1971)*, vol. 7, pp. 404–407.

66. Printed in Venice by Daniel Bomberg, 1520–1522/23. On Bomberg's editions of the Talmud, cf. R. N. Rabinowitz, *Ma'amar al Hadfasat Hatalmud* 2d ed. with additions by Habermann (Jerusalem, 1951/52). On Bomberg and his printing shop, cf. *JE* vol. 3, pp. 299–300; *EJ (1971)*, vol. 4, pp. 1195–1196.

67. Quoted from Solomon Schechter, *Studies in Judaism,* first series (Philadelphia, 1896), p. 255. Cf. also Habermann, "Shlomoh Dekosta Meyased Hamachlakah Ha'ivrit Bamuzeon Habriti," *Ve'im Bigevurot Minchah Lire'uven Mas* (Jerusalem, 1974), pp. (173)–177. The original is in the British Museum. Cf. *Catalogue of the Hebrew and Samaritan Mss.,* vol. 3, no. 1053.

68. Schechter, *Studies.*

69. J. Leveen, "Joseph Zedner," *SBB* 1 (1953): 159.

70. The manuscripts from the Michael collection were sold to the Bodleian Library: see above, p. 47.

71. On Joseph Almanzi, cf. *JE* vol. 1, pp. 429; *EJ (1971)*, vol. 2, pp. 660–661, also n. 82 below.

72. The data on Zedner is based on M. Steinschneider, *Gesammelte Schriften* (Berlin, 1925), pp. 628–634; J. Leveen, "Joseph Zedner," *SBB* 1 (1953): 159–160; A. M. Habermann, *Anshe Sefer* (Jerusalem, 1974), pp. 36–43; *JE* vol. 12, pp. 650–651.

73. See above, Chapter 1.

74. For a description of Zedner's nonbibliographical works, cf. Habermann, *Anshe Sefer,* pp. 37, 39, 42–43.

75. Giovanni Bernardo de Rossi, *Annales Hebraeo-typographici sec. xv* (Parma, 1795); *Annales Hebraeo-typographici ab an. MDI ad MDXL* (Parma, 1799; reprinted in a single volume, Amsterdam, 1969). On De Rossi, see below, pp. 85–86.

76. Leveen, "Zedner," p. 160. See also review in *Jüdische Zeitschrift für Wissenschaft und Leben* 5 (1867): 182–183; R. N. Rabinowitz's letter to Jacob Benjacob, *Jewish Studies in Memory of George A. Kohut,* p. 540; Wiener's introduction to *Kohelet Mosheh* fascicle one, p. iii, fascicle two, p. (vii).

77. *HB* 10 (1870): 87–88.

78. Wiener, introductions to *Kohelet Mosheh.*

79. Cf. *JE* vol. 12, p. 401; Shunami, *Bibliography,* no. 157.

80. *JQR* 19 (1907): 589–590.

81. Business deeds from the Anglo-Norman period.

82. The nucleus of Joseph Almanzi's collection came from his father, who owned the Azulai collection (about Azulai, see below, pp. 75–78). The British Museum also acquired some of the printed Hebraica in the Almanzi collection (see above, p. 49); the remainder was sold to Temple Emanuel in New York, and was presented later to the library of Columbia University.

83. Shapira was a well-known but ill-fated antiquarian bookseller during the second half of the nineteenth century. Born in Poland in 1830, he committed suicide in Rotterdam in 1884, after attempting to sell to the British Museum Hebrew antiquities considered to be forged. With the discoveries of the Dead Sea scrolls in the 1940s, some scholars recalled the case and questioned whether the antiquities offered by Shapira were not genuine after all. Cf. M. Mansoor, "The Case of Shapira's Dead Sea (Deuteronomy) Scrolls of 1883," *Transactions of the Wisconsin Academy of Sciences, Arts and Letters* 47 (1958): 183–225 (reprinted as a separate, Madison, Wisconsin, 1959); J. Allegro, *The Shapira Affair* (Garden City, N. Y.,: 1965); O. K. Rabinowitz, "The Shapira Scroll," *JQR*, n. s. 56 (1965/66): 1–21 (reprinted as a separate, Philadelphia, 1965).

84. Moses Gaster (1856–1939), *Chacham* of the Sephardic community of England, linguist, folklorist, and bibliophile, amassed sizable collections of Hebrew and Samaritan manuscripts. The Hebrew manuscripts were sold to the British Museum in 1925, and were therefore not included in the *Catalogue;* the Samaritan manuscripts were sold to the John Rylands Library in Manchester and were listed in vol. 2 of the library's *Catalogue of the Samaritan Manuscripts* (Manchester, 1962). The bulk of Gaster's printed book collection, together with additional manuscripts, was sold to a Jerusalem bookseller, and from there they made their way to the library of the University of California, Los Angeles.

85. Leveen also compiled the second part of the catalog of Hebrew manuscripts in the Cambridge University Library (see above, also n. 57); it remained unpublished. Cf. *JQR*, n. s. 53 (1962/63): 76.

86. Cf. A. Marx, *JQR*, n. s. 7 (1916/17): 124.

87. I. Elbogen, *JQR* 19 (1907): 402.

88. Fürst, "Zur Geschichte der Jüdischen Bibliographie," p. xxviii, estimated that it was perhaps the largest collection of this nature in Germany during that period.

89. The data on the history of the Bibliotheca Rosenthaliana is based largely on the prefaces to its *Systematische Catalogus*, vols. 1 and 6. See also below, Chapter 5, for a description of the Judaica catalog of the Rosenthaliana.

90. For additional biographical details on Roest, cf. L. Fuks, "Meijer Roest Mz., de eerste conservator van de Bibliotheca Rosenthaliana," *Studia Rosenthaliana* 1 (1967): 4–12; Habermann, *Anshe Sefer*, pp. 44–45.

91. Almost all of the auction catalogs compiled by Roest were published without the name of the compiler. Cf. Shunami, *Bibliography* index, p. 953.

92. *De Israelitische Letterbode* (1875/76–1888). Among the participants in this

periodical were Steinschneider, Neubauer, and other well-known Jewish scholars.

93. L. Fuks, *Studia Rosenthaliana* 1 (1967): 13—21.

94. The change of printers explains why page 501 in the *Anhang* is set in a different type.

95. The number of manuscripts in the Rosenthaliana later grew to several hundred, and a *Catalogue of the Manuscripts of the Bibliotheca Rosenthaliana* compiled by L. Fuks and R. G. Fuks-Mansfeld, was published in Leiden in 1973, as part one of the *Hebrew and Judaic Manuscripts in Amsterdam Public Libraries.* Concerning the development of the Judaica section of the Rosenthaliana, see below, pp. 119—120.

96. When Jacob Benjacob was preparing his father's *Otsar* for publication (see above, pp. 20–21), he was advised by R. N. Rabinowitz and Steinschneider to rely on the catalogs of Zedner and Roest "because they are very exact" (cf. *Jewish Studies in Memory of George A. Kohut*, pp. 540, 545).

97. Cf. introductions to Zedner's and Roest's catalogs. Some paragraphs in Roest's introduction read like translations from Zedner's. See also above, pp. 50–51, the description of Zedner's rules of entry.

98. Wiener, *Kohelet Mosheh,* fascicle one, p. iii; fascicle two, p. (vii).

99. On the Pale of Settlement, cf. *JE* vol. 9, pp. 468—470; *EJ (1971)*, vol. 13, pp. 24—28.

100. Cf. *JE* vol. 4, pp. 514; Wiener, *Kohelet Mosheh,* fascicle one, p. (i).

101. Wiener, *Kohelet Mosheh,* fascicle two, pp. ix—xi, lists the major collections acquired by Friedland.

102. For the reaction among Russian Jews to Friedland's announcement, cf. Baruch ha-Levi Epstein, *Mekor Baruch* (Vilna, 1928; reprinted, New York, 1954), 1:726—730; A. I. Katsh, "Mosheh Aryeh Leib Fridland Vesifriyato Hamefursemet," *Perakim* 3 (1963): 178—179, reprinted in *Sefer Avraham Yitschak Kats* (Tel Aviv, 1969), p. 145. Cf. also E. L. Levinsky, *Kitve,* 2d ed. (Tel Aviv, 1935), pp. 477—480 (reprinted from *Hamelits*).

103. Katsh, "Mosheh Aryeh Leib Fridland," pp. 185—190, *Sefer Katz,* pp. 152—156, published the letter (by Rabbi David Friedman of Karlin) and Friedland's reply. Katsh interprets Friedland's action as an expression of disillusionment with the "people of the book" who did not care to protect the physical survival of their books, and as a protest against the lack of order and organization in Jewish life. S. Dubnow, *Dos Bukh fun Mayn Lebn* (Buenos Aires, 1962/63), 1:214, accuses Wiener, Friedland's librarian, of talking Friedland into giving his library to the Asiatic Museum. Wiener, according to Dubnow, needed residency rights in St. Petersburg, and his position as a cataloger of the *Friedlandiana* at the Asiatic Museum helped him to acquire such rights. Dubnow says Wiener intentionally worked at a slow pace while cataloging the collection, in order to hold on to his residency rights indefinitely. See also A. Marx, *Hadoar* 8 (1928/29): 387. Friedland's letter, published by Katsh, partially absolves Wiener from Dubnow's accusations.

104. For additional information on Samuel Wiener, cf. E. Deinard, *Zichronot Bat-Ami* (New Orleans, 1920), 2:52—53; Habermann, *Anshe Sefer,* pp. 56—61; Kres-

sel, *Leksikon,* 1:664—665; also the eulogies by S. Ernst, *Mizrach Uma'arav* 3 (1929): 460—462; A. Marx, *Hadoar* 8 (1928/29): 387; A. Tauber, *KS* 6 (1929/30): 108; and n. 103 above. Wiener published two works: *Da'at Kedoshim* (St. Petersburg, 1897—98; reprinted, Jerusalem? 1969/70), written by I. T. Eisenstadt (died 1893), and edited, annotated, and appended by Wiener; and *Bibliographie der Oster-Haggadah, 1500— 1900* (St. Petersburg, 1902; reprinted, New York, 1949). Cf. also Shunami, *Bibliography,* index, p. 983. Wiener devoted many years of his life to compiling a complete Hebraica bibliography, and to writing a history of Hebrew printing in Russia. It is not known what became of his efforts.

105. Cf. Marx, *Hadoar* 8 (1928/29): 387.

106. Cf. n. 103, above, Dubnow's explanations for the slow pace of Wiener's cataloging activity. Marx, *Hadoar,* related Wiener's own explanation that "Orientalists" at the Asiatic Museum interfered with his work out of envy. Ernst, *Mizrach Uma'arav* 3 (1929): 460—462, feels that Wiener was a slow worker by nature. It is worth noting that Wiener's descriptions of works in letters *yod* and *kaf* (fascicles six—seven) were less elaborate than the preceding ones.

107. Around the turn of the century the collection consisted of 30,000 volumes, plus 5,000 in Yiddish, according to Wiener, in the introduction to his *Bibliographie der Oster-Haggadah.*

108. Tauber, *KS* 6 (1929/30): 108.

109. During the last two decades, only a few Western scholars have succeeded in gaining access to Russian libraries in order to examine their Jewish collections. Cf. A. I. Katsh's introduction to his *Catalogue of Hebrew Manuscripts Preserved in the USSR Acquired (on microfilm) by Abraham I. Katsh* (New York, 1957).

110. For biographical details on Wachstein, cf. M. Balaban, "Bernhard (Dov Ber) Vakhshtayn," *YB* 13 (1938): 193—227; reprinted in *Vakhshtayn Bukh* (Vilna, 1939), pp. 193—227; Habermann, "Duber (Bernhard) Vachshtain—Bibliograf Vechoker," *YL* 5 (1958/59): 163—165; reprinted in his *Anshe Sefer,* pp. 52—55; N. M. Gelber, "Dr. Dov Bernhard Vachshtain," *Chochmat Yisrael Bema'arav Eropah* 1 (Jerusalem, 1958): 232—240; M. Ungerfeld, "Ha'iluy Mitlustah," *Hapoel Hatsair,* 61, no. 21 (1967/68): 24.

111. *Mafteach Hahespedim* (Vienna, 1922—32); *Literatur über die jüdische Frau* (Vienna, 1931); "Mafteach Hatsavaot" *KS* 11 (1934/35): 235—244, 372—383; 12 (1935/36): 98—108); *Hebräische Autographen* (Vienna, 1927). Wachstein also periodically issued lists of additions to the collections of the *Bibliothek.* Cf. Shunami, *Bibliography,* nos. 191—198. His *Hebräische Publizistik* will be discussed below, Chapter 7.

112. *Die Inschriften des Alten Judenfriedhofes in Wien* (Vienna and Leipzig, 1912—1917).

113. *Die Grabschriften des alten Judenfriedhofes in Eisenstadt* (Vienna, 1922); *Urkunden und Akten zur Geschichte der Juden in Eisenstadt und den Siebengemeinden* (Vienna, 1926).

114. Cf. S. Chajes, *Bibliographie der Schriften Bernhard Wachsteins* (Vienna, 1933), which lists 146 entries.

115. Halberstam was known to Hebrew scholars as שזח״ה. According to a notice in *Hamagid Leyisrael* 5 (1896): 368, Salo Cohn paid 6,000 Reichskrone for the Halberstam volumes. The rest of the Halberstam collection was sold to the Judith Montefiore College in Ramsgate, England (412 manuscripts) and to Judge Mayer Sulzberger for the Jewish Theological Seminary in New York (5,000—6,000 volumes including 140 manuscripts). Cf. Marx, *Studies,* pp. 230—234. For additional biographical details on Halberstam, cf. Moses Reines, *Dor Vechachamav* (Cracow, 1890), pp. 86—92; Gershom Bader, *Medinah Vechachameha* (Vienna, 1934), pp. 75—76; *JE* vol. 6, pp. 166—167; *EJ* vol. 7, pp. 865.

116. Friedmann was a member of the Ruzhin-Sadagora dynasty. His father as well as his father-in-law were both sons of Rabbi Israel, the founder of the dynasty. He acquired his collection through purchases and gifts. Many Chassidim who came to visit his uncle and father-in-law, the Rebbe, presented rare books to the young bibliophile. Some of these books carried inscriptions with requests to pray for their donors. He also received a substantial number of volumes through inheritance. As a true bibliophile, Friedmann indicated on each book, with a special stamp, the source of its acquisition (purchase, inheritance, or gift; on some books he stamped the words *matnat ger,* "a gift of a proselyte"). Cf. Habermann (Heman Hayerushalmi), *Gevilim* (Tel Aviv, 1941/42), pp. 100—101. The entire collection consisted of about 4,000 volumes, most of which were later sold at an auction in London. Cf. Shunami, *Bibliography,* no. 264.

117. M. Weinreich, *YB* 8 (1935): 157.

118. A. Yaari, *KS* 12 (1935/36): 97.

119. According to Balaban, *YB* 13 (1938): 206, Wachstein compiled a geographical index to the entire collection of the *Bibliothek.* He began to print it, and reached the work "Bayern" (for a total of 1955 entries). It was not published.

120. Cf. the histories of major Jewish book collections in the U. S., published in *JBA,* beginning with volume 20 (1962/63).

121. *A Catalog of Books Represented by Library of Congress Printed Cards* (Washington, 1942—46), 167 volumes; supplemented in 1948 by 42 volumes; title changed to *Author Catalog* beginning with 1953; became *National Union Catalog* in 1958. *Subject Catalogs* began appearing in 1955.

122. Cf. A. Berger, "The Jewish Division of the New York Public Library," *JBA* 23 (1965/66): 42—47.

123. Cf. J. Bloch, "The Classification of Jewish Literature in the New York Public Library," *Studies in Jewish Bibliography and Related Subjects, in Memory of Abraham Solomon Freidus* (New York, 1929), pp. 1—lxxvii (reprinted as separate, New York, 1929). On Freidus, cf. the articles by P. Wiernik and R. Kohut, ibid., pp. xxiii—xxx, xl—xliii. A Freidus bibliography (by Joshua Bloch) was printed in the same volume, pp. xii—xxii (also issued as a separate).

124. On Joshua Bloch, cf. A. L. Lebeson, "Joshua Bloch: An Appreciation," *The Joshua Bloch Memorial Volume* (New York, 1960), ix—xix, and the bibliography by D. Steinglass, pp. 180—216.

125. For a detailed description of the development of the HUC library, cf. A. S.

Oko, *A History of the Hebrew Union College Library and Museum* (Cincinnati, 1944; reprinted from his larger article entitled "Jewish Book Collections in the United States," *AJYB* 45: [1943]: 67–96); H. C. Zafren, "The Hebrew Union College Library," *JBA* 20 (1962/63): 45–52.

126. For biographical details, see *JE* vol. 8, p. 296.

127. For biographical details, see *EJ (1971)*, vol. 11, pp. 716–717.

128. For biographical details, see *EJ (1971)*, vol. 14, pp. 976–977.

129. For biographical details, see *EJ (1971)*, vol. 12, p. 1,355.

130. G. K. Hall also published the *Manuscript Catalog of the American Jewish Archives* (Boston, 1971), which is part of HUC-JIR at Cincinnati.

131. Harvard's Judaica catalog will be described below, Chapter 5. On the Yiddish collection at Harvard, cf. A. A. Roback, "The Yiddish Collection in the Harvard Library," *Harvard Alumni Bulletin* 31, no. 29 (1929): 843–853 (translated with modifications into Yiddish and published in *Bibliotek-Bukh, 1914–1934* (Montreal, 1934), pp. 54–56.

132. For details on the history of Harvard's Judaica collection, cf. H. A. Wolfson, "Hebrew Books in Harvard," *Harvard Alumni Bulletin* 34 (1932); reprinted as a separate (Cambridge, 1968); C. Berlin, "The Judaica Collection at Harvard," *JBA* 26 (1968/69): 58–63; reprinted as a separate (Cambridge, 1971); cf. also Berlin's introduction to the *Catalogue*.

133. "Of which 40,000 are in Hebrew, 10,000 in Yiddish, and the remainder in other languages" (Berlin, introduction to the *Catalogue*).

134. Wiener was also responsible for launching the Yiddish collection. For biographical details on Wiener, see J. Shatzky, "Leo Viner," *YB* 15 (1940): 247–256; *Leksikon,* 3:447–449; *UJE* vol. 10, p. 514; *EJ (1971)*, vol. 16, pp. 499–500. See also below, p. 130, and p. 295, n. 48.

135. For biographical details, see *EJ (1971)*, vol. 7, pp. 186–187.

136. For biographical details, see *EJ (1971)*, vol. 14, pp. 203–204. See also below, p. 130, and p. 295, n. 49.

137. Also published as a separate (Cambridge, 1972); it is described below, pp. 127–128.

## Notes to Chapter Three:
*Bio-Bibliographical Works*

1. The biographical data on Azulai are largely based on Meir Benayahu, *Rabi Chayim Yosef David Azulai* (Jerusalem, 1959).

2. *Sha'ar Yosef* (Livorno, 1757).

3. For a complete bibliography of Azulai's works, see Benayahu, *Rabi Chayim,* part one, pp. 177–252.

4. Azulai's diary is known as *Ma'agal Tov,* first published in Livorno in 1879, reprinted in Przemisl in 1885, and in Piotrków in 1910 ?. A scientific edition, based on the author's manuscript, edited and annotated by Aron Freimann under the title *Ma'agal Tov Hashalem,* was published in Berlin-Jerusalem in 1921−1934, reprinted in Jerusalem? in 1967?.

5. This is especially true of scholars known by their acronyms, such as רשב"א, ראב"ד, etc.

6. For example, תולדות אדם, ספר הפרדס, מלחמות ה'. Cf. Isaac Benjacob's *Otsar Hasefarim* under these entries.

7. *Helem Davar,* published in *Sinai* 43 (1958): 301−314, reprinted as a supplement to *Shem Hagedolim* (Tel Aviv, 1959/60) and (Jerusalem?, 1967?).

8. Only a few of Azulai's contemporaries were mentioned in his work. Cf. introduction to Hazan's *Hama'alot Lishelomoh.*

9. *Chasde Avot.* It was reprinted as a separate (Bartfeld, 1927) and (Lemberg? n. d.); appeared also in several editions together with Moses Alshech's commentary on *Pirke Avot.*

10. *Rosh David* (Mantua, 1776), *Ledavid Emet* (Livorno, 1786), and *Simchat Haregel* (Livorno, 1782).

11. *Midrash Temurah;* reprinted in *Midrash Agadat Bereshit,* lst ed. (Vilna, 1802), and in Jellinek's *Bet Hamidrash,* vol. 1, lst ed. (Leipzig, 1853).

12. Cf. *Va'ad Lachachamim,* p. 2a, where it is designated as *Shem Hagedolim,* part three.

13. *Tuv Ayin;* reprinted as a separate (Husiatyn, 1904).

14. *Kikar La'aden* (Livorno, 1801), leaves 202−208.

15. Cf. Benayahu, *Rabi Chayim,* part one, p. 86. Fürst, "Zur Geschichte der jüdischen Bibliographie," p. xcvi, gives the figure of 2,200.

16. Cf. Isaac Benjacob's introduction to Azulai's *Shem Hagedolim,* note to p. vi. See also Menaham Mendel Slatkine's introduction to his own *Otsar Hasefarim Chelek Sheni,* pp. 6−7.

17. Among others, he corrected some errors in Shabbethai Bass's *Sifte Yeshenim* and in Heilprin's *Seder Hadorot.* Cf. *Shem Hagedolim,* part two, letters *tet,* no. 12, and *nun,* no. 29.

18. Cf. *Shem Hagedolim,* part one, letters *yod,* no. 89, 128, and *mem,* no. 35, to mention just a few.

19. Cf. Isaac Benjacob's introduction to *Shem Hagedolim,* note to p. iv.

20. The biography was by Eliakim Carmoly (1802−1875); the notes were by Carmoly, Aaron Fuld (1790−1847), and Raphael Kirchheim (1804−1889).

21. The rearrangement consisted of inserting the additions *Bet Va'ad* in part two, and placing *Va'ad Lachachamim* in *Shem Hagedolim,* part two, together with Azulai's additions, after each letter of the alphabet.

22. Cf. Isaac Benjacob and Zalman Stern, *Kuntres Shinuye Shem Vetikune Va'ad* (Leipzig, 1844). This work was the forerunner of Benjacob's edition of *Shem Hagedolim.* See also Benjacob's *Otsar Hasefarim,* p. 591, no. 803.

23. On Isaac Benjacob, see above, Chapter 1.

24. Cf. Steinschneider's eulogy on Isaac Benjacob, *HB* 6 (1863): 108, where he relates that he had suggested to Benjacob the division into authors and works in one volume and anonyms in the other.

25. Cf. above, n. 20. Isaac Benjacob revised and expanded this essay.

26. For other notes and additions, printed and in manuscripts, cf. Benayahu, *Rabi Chaim,* part one, pp. 217—218, 233, no. 18.

27. For a complete list of the later editions of *Shem Hagedolim,* cf. ibid., pp. 215—217.

28. For additional biographical data on Walden, cf. Benzion Eisenstadt, *Dor Rabanav Vesofrav,* (Vilna, 1901), 3:13—14; J. Rubinstein, "He'arot al Hasefer Shem Hagedolim Hechadash," *Hadarom* 16 (1962): 140—142. On Rabbi Menaham Mendel of Kotsk, see Abraham Joshua Heschel, *Kotsk: In Gerangl Far Emesdikayt* (Tel Aviv, 1973) and *Passion for Truth* (New York, 1973).

29. Steinschneider, *HB* 8 (1865): 109, punning, suggested that the work be renamed *Shem Hakedoshim.* Cf. also William Zeitlin's *Bibliotheca Hebraica,* p. 403.

30. According to Steinschneider, *HB* 8 (1865): 108, *EJ (1971),* vol. 16, p. 248, he mentions more than 1,600 works. This figure is also mentioned by Rubinstein, *Hadarom* 16 (1962): 141.

31. Walden later published a volume of Chassidic tales entitled, *Kahal Chasidim* (Warsaw, n. d., reprinted several times).

32. Cf. introduction to Hazan's *Hama'alot Lishelomoh.* See also *Hakarmel* 6 (1866): 181—182, 190—191; Rubinstein, *Hadarom* 16 (1962): 140—150; 18 (1963): 167—180.

33. Cf. Hazan, *Hama'alot Lishelomoh,* 113b.

34. The title reads: המעלות לשלמה, הוא שם הגדולים מהדורא תנינא.

35. Azulai did not list his contemporaries. Cf. above, p. 77, also n. 8.

36. Such as rabbis Hayyim Ozer Grodsenski, Eliezer Gordon, Raphael Shapira, Isaac Jacob Reines, and others.

37. When Markovich's achievement became known, a number of Hebrew writers published articles about him in the Hebrew press. In the introduction to the second edition of his work, Markovich himself lists articles in *Hatsefira,* no. 84 (1899); *Hamelits,* no. 152 (1899); *Hed Hazeman* (1910); and in the Russian-Jewish *Voskhod* (1900).

38. *Lekorot Ir Rasein Verabaneha; Lekorot Ir Kaidan Verabaneha;* and *Lekorot Ir Navardok Verabaneha* (all three were published in Warsaw in 1913; the last volume was reprinted in Tel Aviv in 1968/69).

39. It seems that in his later years he finally learned to master writing. Cf. B. Z. Shurin, *Keshet Giborim* (Jerusalem, 1964), p. 184; N. Ben-Menahem, *Chachme Lita* (Jerusalem, 1969), p. 66.

40. An effort at compiling a bio-bibliography of Hungarian rabbis was made earlier by Leopold Greenwald (1889—1955). He succeeded in publishing only the first volume of a planned five-volume work under the title *Hayehudim Be'ungarya* (Vacz, 1912; reprinted, Jerusalem? 1968/69). Greenwald's *Pe'ere Chachme Medinatenu* (Marmarossziget, 1910) will be discussed in Volume Two of this work.

41. Cf. N. Ben-Menahem, "R' Avraham Yehudah Hakohen Shvarts," *Areshet* 4 (1966): 427–435.

42. Medieval Hebrew sources refer to Hungary as Erets Hagar. Cf. Elias Levita, *Tishbi,* 1st ed. (Isny, 1541), s. v. הונגר.

43. Part one originally carried a supplement, *Milu'im Leshem Hagedolim Me'erets Hagar,* that included a number of Reform rabbis. It was removed due to protests by Orthodox rabbis. Cf. *Areshet* 2 (1960): 354, no. 1620.

44. The supplements will be described in Volume Two of this work.

45. The biographical data on Ben Naim is based on A. Elmaleh, "Habibliyograf Harav Yosef Ben Naim," *OYS* 5 (1962): 118–124.

46. According to some sources, his library consisted of about 30,000 volumes; in actuality he possessed only about 7,000 volumes. Cf. Elmaleh, "Yosef Ben Naim," p. 122.

47. Elmaleh, ibid., 124–125, compiled a complete bibliography of Ben Naim's works.

48. Other bio-bibliographical works dealing with North African Jewish communities were begun by a number of scholars but were never completed. Cf. Shunami, *Bibliography,* nos. 2379, 2382–2383. Isaac Michael Badhab (1859–1947), a Jerusalem bibliophile and bibliographer, compiled a work on Jerusalem authors and works, which he called *Shem Hagedolim Hakelali.* Cf. M. Benayahu, "Rabi Yitschak Badhab," *Yerushalayim* 1 (1948): (58)–60; Kressel, *Leksikon,* 1:169–170.

49. Cf. his introduction to the *Dizionario,* p. iv.

50. *JE* vol. 10, p. 486.

51. The results were published in his *Variae lectiones veteris testamenti* (Parma, 1784–1788).

52. *De hebraicae typographiae origine ac primitiis seu antiquis ac rarissimis hebraicorum librorum editionibus seculi xv . . .* (Parma, 1776); 2d ed. (Erlangen, 1782; reprinted, Amsterdam, 1969).

53. *De typographia hebraeo-ferrariensi commentarius historicus quo ferrarienses Judaeorum editiones hebraicae* (Parma, 1780); *Annali Ebreo-Tipografici di Sabbioneta* (in Affo, Ireno, *Vita di Vespasiano Cozaga* [Parma, 1780], pp. 137–167; 2d enlarged ed., Erlangen, 1783).

54. *Annales hebraeo-typographici sec. xv* (Parma, 1795) and *Annales hebraeo-typographici ab an. 1501 ad 1540* (Parma, 1799). The term "post-incunabula" is sometimes applied to Hebrew books printed between the years 1501 and 1540.

55. *Bibliotheca Judaica antichristiana* (Parma, 1800; reprinted, Amsterdam, 1964). This bibliography was a by-product of his *Della Vana Aspettazione degli Ebrei del Loro Re Messia* (Parma, 1773).

56. *Mss. codices hebraici biblioth. I. B. De-Rossi* (Parma, 1803). De Rossi made a number of curious mistakes in this catalog. Cf. B. Dinaburg (Dinur), "Me'archiyono shel Shir," *KS* 2 (1925): 72–73, also n. 1; M. Weinreich, *Bilder fun der Yidisher Literaturgeshikhte* (Vilna, 1928), pp. 114–116. According to Weinreich, Zunz and Harkavy were misled by De Rossi's identification of Yiddish manuscripts as "Codices Polonici." A Polish-Jewish authoress with assimilationist tendencies con-

cluded on the basis of the same description that Polish Jews in the sixteenth century prayed in Polish.

57. *Libri Stampati di Letteratura Sacra Ebraica ed Orientale* . . . (Parma, 1812).

58. *Annali Ebreo-Tipografici di Cremona* (Parma, 1808).

59. In a bibliography of his own works, published in Parma in 1809, De Rossi listed 41 printed works and 81 manuscripts.

60. See above, Chapter 1.

61. Cf. Leopold Zunz, *Gesammelte Schriften* (Berlin, 1876), 3:122–128; *Wissenschaftliche Zeitschrift für jüdische Theologie* 4 (1839): 419–448.

62. "De Rossi's Dictionary of Hebrew Authors," translated and annotated by Mayer Sulzberger, *Occident* 24–26 (1867–1869).

63. The biographical data on Nepi are based on Samuel Joseph Fünn, *Kneset Yisrael* (Warsaw, 1886), pp. 370–371; *Zichron Le'avraham Eliyahu* (St. Petersburg, 1908; reprinted, Jerusalem, 1968/69), pp. 471–472; Fürst, "Zur Geschichte der jüdischen Bibliographie," pp. xcvii–xcviii; *JE* vol. 9, p. 224; *EJ (1971)*, vol. 12, pp. 963–964.

64. See above, pp. 6–8, 13–15.

65. Fürst, "Zur Geschichte," p. xcvii, n. 3, gives date as 1835.

66. *Tocho Ratsuf Ahavah* (Pisa, 1818). He began writing it at the age of sixteen. The biographical data on Ghirondi are based on his son's sketch at the end of *Toldot Gedole Yisrael*, pp. 374–375; Fürst, "Zur Geschichte" pp. xcvii–xcviii; *JE* vol. 5, p. 656; *EJ (1971)*, vol. 7, p. 548.

67. Ghirondi's unpublished works are in the Judith Montefiore College in Ramsgate, England. Cf. Hartwig Hirschfeld, *Descriptive Catalogue of the Hebrew Mss. of the Montefiore Library* (London, 1904), in which 34 works are listed. Ghirondi's annotations to Azulai's *Shem Hagedolim* appeared in the Brooklyn, 1958 edition of that work. See above, p. 79.

68. According to Fürst, "Zur Geschichte," p. xcviii, the original title was *Toldot Gedole Italyah*.

69. Fürst, "Zur Geschichte," p. xcviii. Nepi prepared a second version of *Zecher Tsadikim* containing material not available in the printed version. Cf. *Zichron Le'avraham Eliyahu*, pp. 477–483; reprinted as a separate (Ferrara, 1909); *Scritti in Memoria di Sally Mayer* (Jerusalem, 1956), Hebrew section, pp. 99–109 (reprinted in the Jerusalem? 1967/68 edition of *Toldot Gedole Yisrael*).

70. On Löwenstein, see below, Chapter 7.

71. *ZfHB* 17 (1914): 171–183; reprinted as a separate (Frankfort, 1915).

72. *JJLG* 4 (1906), Hebrew section, p. 29. About Michael's book collection, see above, pp. 47 and 48.

73. Cf. *Hashachar* 2 (1871): 26–46, 137–151.

74. *JJLG* 4 (1906), Hebrew section, p. 72.

75. The designation "rabbinic" should not be taken literally; Michael included many nonrabbinic authors and works. About the origin of this term, see above, Chapter 1, n. 17.

76. See above, pp. 41–42. A list of Michael's non-Hebrew books was published

earlier under the title *Verzeichnis einer Sammlung von Büchern aus der Bibliothek des H. J. Michael* (Hamburg, 1847). Zunz, in his introduction to the Hebrew catalog, praised the non-Hebrew collection, especially the works listed on pp. 63 to 101 of the list of non-Hebrew books, and concluded: "Diese interessante Sammlung hätte verdient, dass mit ihr ein Grund gelegt worden zu einer nichthebräischen Bibliothek für die Wissenschaft des Judenthums." The prompt publication of both lists was due to the financial difficulties of the Michael family, which necessitated a quick sale of the collection. Cf. also *MGWJ* 60 (1916): 331–333, about efforts by Zunz and others to retain the collection in Germany.

77. See Berliner's introduction to *Or Hachayim*, note to p. vii, on the reasons for naming this bio-bibliography *Or Hachayim*.

78. Alexander Marx, *Studies in Jewish History and Booklore* (New York, 1944), p. 221. Corrections of dates in *Or Hachayim* were published in *Jüdisches Litteratur-Blatt* 20 (1891): 73, 77. Steinschneider, in *Central-Anzeiger für jüdische Literatur* 1 (1891): 100, noted the lack of an index in this work. S. Raz, *Hapoel Hatsair* 59, no. 8 (1965/66), p. 22, suggested a number of indexes to be attached to *Or Hachayim*, among others, for titles and subjects.

79. This edition included, besides an introduction by N. Ben-Menahem, a translation of Berliner's introduction from the German and notes by Solomon Joachim Halberstam.

80. Kohn also wrote two other works: *Yom Lashanah* (Botosani, 1902), a record of memorial dates of famous Jewish personalities (to be discussed in Volume Two of this work); and *Yevakesh Nirdaf* (Botosani, 1929), on Hebrew synonyms.

81. Abraham ben Elijah (ca. 1750–1808) was the son of the Gaon of Vilna. His midrashic index was entitled *Rav Pe'alim* (Warsaw, 1894; reprinted, New York, 1958/59; Tel Aviv, 1967?).

82. Cf. title page of 1922 edition.

83. Cf. *Bet Eked Sefarim*, 2d ed., 4:1065, note to no. 421. Cf. also *Hamaor* 10, no. 4 (1960), pp. 28–29, where Chones is castigated for including "heretical ideas" in his work.


Notes to Chapter Four:
*Subject Bibliographies of Hebraica Literature*

1. The biographical information on Zeitlin is based on A. M. Habermann, "Vilyam (Ze'ev) Tsaitlin Habibliyograf Shel Sifrut Hahaskalah," *YL* 2 (1950/51): 146–150; reprinted in his *Anshe Sefer* (Jerusalem, 1974), pp. 46–51; *JE* vol. 12, pp. 653–654; *EJ (1971),* vol. 16, pp. 976; Kressel, *Leksikon* 2:716.

2. See Fischel Lachower, *Rishonim Ve'acharonim* (Tel Aviv, 1943), 2:72–73; 2d ed. (Tel Aviv, 1965), pp. 267–268.

3. Published in *Magid Mishneh* (Lemberg, 1872), p. 59.

4. Published in *Hamagid* 17 (1873): 5—6. This was the first list of Hebrew periodicals ever compiled. Cf. editor's note.

5. *Tav-Zikaron Letsiyon. Bibliotheca Sionistica; hebräische Schriften über Zionismus, 1852—1905* (Frankfort, 1909); published originally in *ZfHB* 12—13 (1908—1909). For other bibliographies compiled by Zeitlin, cf. Shunami, *Bibliography*, index, p. 989. Zeitlin also participated in compiling material for Peter Thomsen's *Palästina-Literatur*. See below, pp. 205—207.

6. *Ta'alumot Sofrim. Anagramme, Initialen und Pseudonyma neuhebräischer Schriftsteller und Publizisten* (Frankfort, 1905); published originally in *ZfHB* 9 (1905). Additions were published, ibid. 14 (1910), 15 (1911), 18 (1915); to be described in Volume Three of this work.

7. Giulio Bartolocci was the first bibliographer to use *Kiryat Sefer* as a title for a Hebraica bibliography. Cf. above, Chapter 1. Zeitlin's title *Bibliotheca Hebraica* is reminiscent of Johann Christoph Wolf's *Bibliotheca hebraea*, discussed above, Chapter 1.

8. Cf. note preceding his "Sterbedaten," *ZfHB* 19 (1916): 37.

9. Habermann, *YL* 2 (1950/51): 149; idem, *Anshe Sefer*, p. 50.

10. Cf. *Hadoar*, 28 (1948/49): 1004.

11. Cf. his introduction to *Bibliographisches Lexicon*, Neue Serie, p. viii.

12. The biographical information on Lippe is based on Gershom Bader, *Medinah Vechachameha* (New York, 1934), pp. 131—132; *EJ*, vol. 10, pp. 992—993; Kressel, *Leksikon*, 2:276—277.

13. *Shishah Michtavim Hamefitsim Or al Sichsuche Ha'emunah Begalil Erets Hagar Ha'elyon* (Košice, 1866).

14. This publication will be described below, Chapter 6.

15. The idea for an added Hebrew title as well as the Hebrew title itself could have come to Lippe from Steinschneider's *Hamazkir-Hebräische Bibliographie*. Cf. below, Chapter 6.

16. Cf. entries: Alliance Israélite Universelle; Anglo-Jewish Association; Hollander, Leo; Lippe, C.; and others.

17. This new policy was indicated on the title page and explained fully in his lengthy introduction, pp. ix—x.

18. For other subject catalogs issued by the Jewish National and University Library during the 1920s and 1930s, cf. Shunami, *Bibliography* index, p. 901.

19. *Chanukat Ha'aron* (Venice, 1729). The year 1729 is also the birthdate of Moses Mendelssohn, with whom William Zeitlin begins the era of modern Hebrew literature in his *Bibliotheca Hebraica*. Joseph Klausner and Fischel Lachower, in their histories of modern Hebrew literature, also differed on the beginning date. Klausner's *Historyah Shel Hasifrut Ha'ivrit Hachadashah* begins with Mendelssohn, and Lachower's *Toldot Hasifrut Ha'ivrit Hachadashah* begins with Luzzatto.

20. *KS* 6 (1929/30): 119—138, 277—290; 7 (1930/31): 282—289. Both supplements also appeared as off-prints.

21. The actual publication date was 1931. Cf. A. Yaari, "Targumim Ivrim,"

*Moznayim* 3, no. 36 (1932), p.12, n. 1. The list originally appeared in *Studies in Jewish Bibliography and Related Subjects, in Memory of Abraham Solomon Freidus* (New York, 1929), pp. 182—218, and was later issued with the addition of indexes. On translations into Hebrew during medieval days, cf. Moritz Steinschneider, *Die hebräischen Übersetzungen des Mittelalters* (Berlin, 1893; reprinted, Graz, 1956). Brief lists of translations into Hebrew from ancient days to modern times were published in the *JE* vol. 12, pp. 219—226. On Schapiro, cf. *Genazim* 2 (1965): 63—64.

22. *JBA* 8 (1949/50), Hebrew section, 36—47.

23. *Yad Lakore* no. 5/6 (1944), pp. 11—22.

24. Current translations into Hebrew, published in Israel, are listed in *Index Translationum.*

25. *JBA* 7 (1948/49), Hebrew section, 18—27.

26. Ibid., pp. 63—72.

27. Ibid., 11 (1952/53): 136—153. The first English book to be translated into Yiddish was Daniel Defoe's *Robinson Crusoe,* published in Metz in 1764.

28. The biographical information on Kasher is based on Kressel, *Leksikon,* 2:155—156; *EJ (1971),* vol. 10, pp. 807—808.

29. The *Torah Shelemah* was planned to consist of thirty-five volumes. Twenty-seven volumes have appeared up to the end of 1975, covering Genesis, Exodus, and a part of Leviticus.

30. An effort to compile a bibliography of rabbinical literature from the closing of the Talmud to the appearance of the *Shulchan Aruch* was made by Solomon Zucrow (1870—1932) in his *Sifrut Hahalachah,* published posthumously in New York in 1932.

31. The first edition of the *Shulchan Aruch* appeared in Venice in 1564—1565.

32. About this supplement, cf. *Sinai* 61 (1967): 316—320.

33. *Sefer Adam-Noach . . . Zikaron Ler' Adam-Noach Dr. Braun* (Jerusalem, 1969). Gad Ben-Ami Tzarfati published in the same volume (pp. 196—299) notes on *Sare Ha'elef.*

Notes to Chapter Five:
*Judaica Bibliographies*

1. Cf. above, pp. 3—8; 13—16.

2. Ibid, p. 8.

3. Ibid, pp. 17—19.

4. Cf. above, pp. 103—105.

5. *Biblioteca Espãnola-Portugueza-Judaica* (Strasbourg, 1890); reprinted, with additions by Steinschneider, J. S. da Silva Rosa, M. Weisz, and the author, and with a prolegomenon by Y. H. Yerushalmi (New York, 1971). Mention should also be

made of the printed card catalogs of New York Public Library's Jewish Collection and the Hebrew Union College Library in Cincinnati that include sizable amounts of Judaica literature. Cf. above, pp. 63–65, and below, pp. 126–128

6. The biographical data on Freimann are based mainly on the "Necrology" by Alexander Marx and Boaz Cohen in *PAAJR* 17 (1947–48): xxiii–xxviii; eulogy by S. D. Goitein in *KS* 25 (1948–49), 109–110; biographical sketch by M. Eliash in *Chochmat Yisrael Bema'arav Eropah,* (Jerusalem, 1958), 1:407–425; also Abraham Yaari, *Moznayim* 3, no. 24 (1931/32), pp. 12–13; *JE* vol. 5, p. 507; *EJ* vol. 6, pp. 1,159–1,160; Kressel, *Leksikon,* 2:666.

7. Rabbiner Seminar für das Orthodoxe Judenthum; founded in 1873 by Israel Hildesheimer (1820–1899).

8. Marx-Cohen, "Necrology," p. xxiii.

9. The Mekize Nirdamim society was founded in Germany in 1864 with the aim of publishing old Hebrew works from manuscripts.

10. *Zeitschrift für die Geschichte der Juden in Deutschland* (Berlin, 1929–1938).

11. *Germania Judaica* (Frankfort, 1917–1934). It will be discussed in Volume Two of this work.

12. *Inyane Shabtai Tsevi* (Berlin, 1912; reprinted, Jerusalem? 1967/68).

13. *Ma'agal Tov Hashalem* (Jerusalem, 1934; reprinted, Jerusalem? 1967?).

14. *Festschrift zum 70. Geburtstage A. Berliners* (Frankfort, 1903); *Festskrift i Anledning af Professor David Simonsens 70-arige Fodselsdag* (Copenhagen, 1923); *Livre d'Hommage à la Mémoire du Samuel Poznanski* (Warsaw, 1927); and others.

15. Among others, *Geschichte der Israelitischen Gemeinde Ostrowo* (Ostrów, 1896), and *Frankfort* (Philadelphia, 1929).

16. *Zeitschrift für hebräische Bibliographie;* to be described in Chapter 6, below.

17. A bibliography of Freimann's writings up to 1931 lists several hundred entries. Cf. *Festschrift für Aron Freimann zum 60. Geburtstage* (Berlin, 1935), pp. 5–16.

18. Freimann's *Thesaurus* will be described in Chapter 8, below.

19. Freimann's *Gazetteer* will be described in Chapter 8, below.

20. *Union Catalog of Hebrew Manuscripts;* to be described in Chapter 8, below.

21. Marx-Cohen, "Necrology," p. xxviii.

22. Ibid.

23. Cf. preface to Freimann's *Stadtbibliothek zu Frankfurt a. M. Ausstellung hebräischer Druckwerke* (Frankfort, 1902), p. 8.

24. On Brüll, see below, pp. 143–144.

25. Cf. A. Fraenkel's preface to the new edition of the *Katalog:* "Der Katalog... erscheint hier im Neudruck, nicht mehr also Bibliothekskatalog, sondern als bibliographisches Handbuch."

26. See above, pp. 54–57.

27. Ibid.

28. Cf. preface to part one of the *Systematische Catalogus,* p. ix.

29. On Frank and his activities, cf. H. Heiber, *Walter Frank* (Stuttgart, 1966).

30. *Forshungen zur Judenfrage* (Hamburg, 1937–1944). For a description of these volumes, cf. Heiber, *Walter Frank,* pp. 458–461.

31. Cf. Heiber, ibid., pp. 429–432.

32. Only a few non-German works were included.

33. Cf. Shunami, *Bibliography,* no. 2276. See also Heiber, *Walter Frank,* p. 455; *Forshungen zur Judenfrage* (1941), 6:263. About Jewish and Nazi evaluations of Eichstädt's bibliography, see Heiber, *Walter Frank,* pp. 455–456.

34. *Books on Persecution, Terror, and Resistance in Nazi Germany* (London, 1949; 2d enlarged ed., London, 1953).

35. *From Weimar to Hitler; Germany 1918–1933* (London, 1951).

36. The Wiener Library continues to compile "Post-War Publications on German Jewry," and publishes it annually in the *Year Book* of the Leo Baeck Institute, published in London since 1956. The lists are also issued separately.

37. M. Kreutzberger, "The Library and Archives of the Leo Baeck Institute in New York," *JBA* 29 (1971/72): 47. Also issued separately.

38. Ibid.

39. Cf. editor's preface to *Judaica,* where a detailed description of the classification of the catalog is also given.

40. See above, pp. 65–66.

41. To the deficiencies of the shelflist belong such omissions as added entries for joint authors, and the lack of cross-references. Under human errors may be listed this entry for 1854 in the chronological listing: "Ashkenazi, Tovia. A Bibliographical History of Writings, 1922–1954. Washington, 1854."

42. See above, p. 66.

43. *JBA* 8 (1949/50): 68–76. For a partial list of earlier translations from Hebrew into other languages, cf. *JE* vol. 12, pp. 226–229.

44. *The Jewish Caravan; Great Stories of Twenty-Five Centuries* (New York, 1935; rev. and enl. ed., New York, 1965); *A Golden Treasury of Jewish Literature* (New York, 1937); *Memoirs of My People through a Thousand Years* (Philadelphia, 1943).

45. *JBA* 16 (1958/59): 55–67. Cf. also D. Patterson, "Hebrew Literature: The Art of the Translator," ibid., pp. 68–80.

46. The inclusion of this section was questioned by G. Kressel, *YL* 10 (1969/70): 46, on the ground that it opens the door to countless translations of current events and history.

47. Cf. M. Bakal, "Di Noytvendikayt fun a Bibliyografye oyf Yidish," *Yidishe Kultur* 8, no. 8 (1946), pp. 56–57. Cf. also ibid., no. 12, pp. 47–49 and vol. 9 no. 11 (1947), pp. 57–58. An effort to establish a center for Yiddish bibliography at the Yivo Institute in Vilna was made in the 1920s. Cf. *Literarishe Bleter* 2 (1925–1926): 116–117, 256–257. A sizable number of Yiddish subject and personal bibliographies appeared during the last half century. Cf. M. Starkman, "Yidish Bibliyografye in di Fareynikte Shtatn," *Tsukunft* 56 (1951):79–86. But until now not even one major bibliography of Yiddish has been produced. Jacob Shatzky (1894–1956) worked on compiling an "exhaustive bibliography" of Yiddish literature prior to 1800. Cf. *JTS Register* (New York, 1926), p. 144. According to a notice in *Haolam* 16 (1928): 738, Shatzky's bibliography, entitled "A Bibliography of Yiddish Imprints

(from the Fifteenth Century to 1850)," was to appear in the fall of 1928. Max Weinreich, *Bilder fun der Yidisher Literaturgeshikhte* (Vilna, 1928), p. 44, mentions that Shatzky was preparing a two-part bibliography: part one to be "a complete bibliography of all Yiddish imprints from the beginning up to Isaac Meir Dick" (1807?–1893); part two to "deal with Yiddish manuscripts." Cf. also *Bibliologisher Zamlbukh* (Kharkov, 1930), p. 215. A bibliography of Old Yiddish works, based on a catalog of the Oppenheimer collection, was prepared by Steinschneider and published in *Serapeum* 9–10 (1848–1849); additions published ibid., 25 (1864), registering, altogether, 450 entries; reprinted as a separate volume under the title *Jüdisch-deutsche Literatur* (Jerusalem, 1961). A bibliography of works dealing with modern Yiddish literature was published by Ephim H. Jeshurin in his *Hundert Yor Moderne Yidishe Literatur* (New York, 1965).

48. *Songs of the Ghetto,* by Morris Rosenfeld (1862–1923). Wiener printed the original Yiddish text in German Gothic characters, together with his (literal) translation, on opposite pages. Wiener also published *A History of Yiddish Literature in the Nineteenth Century* (New York, 1899), and included in it a number of translations from Yiddish literature. Leo Wiener (1862–1939), Professor of Slavic languages at Harvard University, was responsible for establishing a Yiddish book collection at Harvard University Library. Cf. above, p. 65, and p. 285, n. 134.

49. Abraham Roback (1890–1965), psychologist and authority on Yiddish, helped to develop the Yiddish book collection at Harvard. Cf. above, p. 65, and p. 285, n. 136.

50. *JBA* 7 (1948/49): 67–74. About the nature of English translations from Yiddish, cf. J. Leftwich's survey, ibid., 31 (1973/74): 49–57. See also his article in *Yidishe Dyalogn* (Paris, 1968), pp. 184–190.

51. *Hapoel Hatsair* 59, no. 1/2 (1965/66), p. 23; reprinted in Sadan's *Pulmus Ushaveh Pulmus* (Jerusalem, 1972), p. 254.

52. Cf. above, p.28, and p. 275, n. 126.


Notes to Chapter Six:
*Bibliographical Periodicals*

1. Cf. *Börsenblatt für den deutschen Buchhandel und für die mit ihm verwandten Geschäftszweige* (Leipzig, 1834+); *Organ des deutschen Buchhandels oder Allgemeines Buchhändler Börsenblatt* (Berlin, 1834+); *Serapeum; Zeitschrift für Bibliothekwissenschaft* (Leipzig, 1840+); *Allgemeine Bibliographie für Deutschland* (Leipzig, 1843+).

2. Among others, Abraham Geiger's *Wissenschaftliche Zeitschrift für jüdische Theologie* (Frankfort, 1835+); Ludwig Philippson's *Allgemeine Zeitung des Judenthums* (Leipzig, 1837+); Julius Fürst's *Literaturblatt des Orients* (Leipzig,

1840+); and Zecharias Frankel's *Zeitschrift für die religiösen Interessen des Judenthums* (Berlin, 1844+).

3. See above, pp. 41 and 49.

4. *Hamazkir* is mentioned five times in the Hebrew Bible as an official title of the state chronicler or recording officer. Cf. 2 Samuel 20:24; I Kings 4:3, etc.

5. The first few issues also included a third section: "Bulletin des Antiquariats von A. Asher & Co." This was later dropped, and the publisher was satisfied with the legend on the front page, below the dateline: "Die in dieser Bibliographie angezeigten Bücher sind von A. Asher & Co. zu beziehen," and with occasional supplements of lists of books wanted or offered by Asher & Co.

6. Beginning with volume 9 (1869), Hebraica were also arranged by author.

7. Interestingly enough, one of the early German bibliographical periodicals was entitled *Repertorium der gesammten deutschen Literatur* (Leipzig, 1834+).

8. First to be "hit" was *Hamagid,* the first Hebrew weekly. For a reply to this attack and to those that followed, cf. *Hamagid* 2 (1858): 158.

9. Cf. *HB* 2 (1859): 99, n. 2, and his *Bibliographisches Handbuch,* pp. xxxii– xxxvi. Characteristic is his obituary on Jost, *HB* 3 (1860): 117: "Jost (M. J.) ist am 20. November hingeschieden und gehört nunmehr selbst der Geschichte an, die er vor ungefähr 40 Jahren nicht ohne Verdienst zu bearbeiten begonnen. Seine literarische Thätigkeit in den letzten Jahren war leider eine solche, dass wir mit der Todesanzeige keine Kritik derselben verbinden wollen."

10. Cf. Abraham Geiger's attack on Grätz displayed prominently in *HB* 3 (1860): 1–4, and Steinschneider's comments, ibid., 103–104; 12 (1872): 131; 14 (1874): 77; 21 (1881/82): 13. According to S. Bernfeld, *Hashilo'ach* 17 (1907): 270, Grätz came under attack because of the nationalistic ideas expressed in his works, to which Steinschneider was bitterly opposed. Evidence for a more personal reason for these attacks can be found in Steinschneider's obituary on Fürst (cf. n. 12 below), where a veiled accusation of plagiarism is noted. Cf. also, Salo Wittmayer Baron, *History and Jewish Historians* (Philadelphia, 1964), p. 302.

11. His attacks on Carmoly reached their climax in the following obituary in *HB* 15 (1875): 134: "15. Februar kehrte auch zu Frankfurt a. Main in 'die Wahrheit' ein der ehemaliger Rabbiner zur Brüssel, Elijakim Carmoly (ursprünglich Getsch Sulz aus Colmar), nachdem er dieselbe durch Fälschungen aller Art und freche Plagiate in zahlreichen Schriften und Artikeln verläugnet und misshandelt hatt. . . . Als er den Geist aufgab, hatte letzterer ihn selbst längst aufgegeben. . . . Wenn es aber die Aufgabe der Kritik ist, 'der Wahrheit die Ehre zu geben,' so bleibt dem Andenken Carmoly's kein Segen der Gerechten übrig." A detailed discussion of Carmoly and his feud with Steinschneider will be found in Volume Two of this work.

12. In his obituary on Fürst, Steinschneider was able to hit three targets with one stone in *HB* 13 (1873): 140: "Fürst hat sich um die Einfürung der literarischen In-dustrie in jüdischen Kreise verdient gemacht. In der Kunst, Fremdes Gut zu eigenen Ruhm und Vortheil zu verwenden hinterlässt er nun einen Meister C(armoly) und einen hoffnungsvollen Schüler G(rätz). Er gab durch 12 Jahre Seinesgleichen Auf-munterung und Gelegenheit in den Brunnen zu speien, aus dem sie geschöpft hat-ten."

13. *Hashilo'ach* 17 (1907): 269.

14. Steinschneider included attacks on his contemporaries even in his lectures, and this sometimes created resentment among his students. George Alexander Kohut, Steinschneider's most beloved pupil, reveals such an occurrence *(Studies in Jewish Bibliography and Related Subjections,* p. 115, n. 89): "My friend, Dr. Immanuel Löw, told me verbally, in September 1928, that he considered Steinschneider's attitude as destructive as antisemitism and that in his own student days, he and the entire class had boycotted his *Vorlesungen* because of his bitter invective and the merciless manner in which he lampooned some of the most revered personalities of the day."

Judah Loeb Gordon (1831–1892), on the other hand, felt flattered after being attacked in *HB*. In a letter to a friend he boasts *(Igrot Yalag* [Warsaw, 1894], 1:46): "I forgot to tell you the good news that Dr. Steinschneider scolded me in the last number of Hamazkir . . ." Cf. also ibid. pp. 51, 92, and 115, where Gordon accuses Steinschneider of plagiarism.

15. Beginning with Volume 5 (1862), *HB* listed the assistance of a number of scholars and bibliographers such as Isaac Benjacob, Abraham Geiger, Meyer Kayserling, Samuel David Luzzatto, Meijer Roest, Joseph Zedner, Leopold Zunz, and others. Their assistance was visible in the first eight volumes only in section two; in the renewed *HB* they became visible also in section one.

16. It was actually published in March 1883.

17. *Hapoel Hatsair* 36, no. 51 (1942/43), p. 8.

18. The bio-bibliographical data on Brüll are based on *JE* vol. 3, pp. 402–403; *Otsar Hasifrut* (Cracow, 1888), 2:277–278; B. Cohen, "Nehemiah Brüll," *Studies in Jewish Bibliography and Related Subjects,* pp. 219–246 (also issued as a separate). Cf. also Hamagid 35 (1891):60.

19. A subsection entitled "Recensionen" was originally added to section two, but it was later dropped.

20. *Hapoel Hatsair* 36, no. 51, p. 8.

21. The biographical data on Brody are based on *JE* vol. 3, pp. 393–394; G. Kressel, *Leksikon,* 1:326–327; *Chochmat Yisrael Bema'arav Eropah,* 1:92–97; *EJ (1971),* vol. 4, pp. 1,399–1,400.

22. A bibliography of Brody's writings up to 1930, consisting of 564 entries, was compiled and published by M. and H. Wollstein in *Festschrift für Heinrich Brody* (appeared as *SB* 3, no. 2–4 [July 1930], pp. 9–36 (85–112). H. Wollstein later extended the bibliography to include Brody's writings up to 1938, listing an additional 131 entries, and published it in *Yediot Hamachon Lecheker Hashirah Ha'ivrit* 5 (1939): xi–xvi.

23. On Freimann, see above, pp. 117–119. On the J. Kauffman firm, cf. *EJ* vol. 9, pp. 1,094–1,095; *EJ* (1971), vol. 10, pp. 840–841.

24. Cf. Shunami, *Bibliography,* no. 484.

25. The data on Kreppel are based on Reisen, *Leksikon (1927),* 3:790–796; *EJ* vol. 10, pp. 807–808; E. R. Malachi, *Hadoar* 22 (1941/42): 148, 158; 30 (1949/50): 885–886; Meir Henish, *Mibayit Umichuts* (Tel Aviv, 1961), pp. 276–277; *Eleh*

*Ezkerah* (New York, 1965), 6:259–264; G. Kressel, *Hapoel Hatsair* 61, no. 15 (1967/68), pp. 17–18.

26. On Zupnik, cf. Kressel, *Leksikon* 1:727–728. The data in *JE* vol. 12, p. 705, are questionable.

27. Among others, Zupnik published *Drohobyczer Zeitung,* a weekly German publication in Hebrew characters (1883–1912), and *Tsiyon,* a literary Hebrew monthly (1885–1888; 1896–1897).

28. Cf. Henish, *Mibayit Umichuts,* p. 276, where he relates the history of Kreppel's first literary "work," the composing of "the continuation and the end" of the missing part of a *Techinah.*

29. He edited *Tsiyon* for 1896–1897.

30. During 1903–1904, Kreppel published two dailies; one in Hebrew (*Hayom*) and one in Yiddish (*Tageblat*), a Yiddish weekly (*Der Emeser Yud*) and a Yiddish monthly (*Der Shtrahl*). In 1905 he traveled to New York in an unsuccessful attempt to establish a Hebrew newspaper there. From 1909 to the outbreak of World War I, he published a Yiddish daily (*Der Tog*), a Yiddish weekly (*Di Yudishe Ilustrirte Tsaytung*) with a monthly satirical supplement (*Di Havdole*), and a Hebrew literary monthly (*Bet Yisrael*).

31. *Der Weltkrieg und die Judenfrage* (Vienna, 1915).

32. *Juden und Judentum von Heute . . .* (Vienna, 1925); *Handwörterbuch für Politik und Wirtschaft der Gegenwart . . .* (Vienna, 1927–1930).

33. Printed in Przemysl between 1924 and 1930.

34. Cf. Henish, *Mibayit Umichuts,* p. 277.

35. Prior to the publication of *Yerushalayim,* Kreppel launched a newspaper in German entitled *Jüdische Volksstimme,* with a monthly literary supplement entitled *Jerusalem.* The Hebrew *Yerushalayim* was thus an outgrowth of the German *Jerusalem.*

36. The subtitle in the first four issues of *Yerushalayim* reads: השקפה על ספרת ישראל בכל הלשונות. In issue number five it was corrected to read: השקפה על ספרות ישראל בכל הלשונות. The outdated "ספרת" thus gave way to the more modern "ספרות."

37. Cf. *Das Buch* 1 (4), nos. 1 (13)–2 (14) (Vienna, 1927–1928).

38. Malachi, *Hadoar* 30 (1949/50): 885–886.

39. *Hapoel Hatsair,* 1, no. 10/11 (1908) p. 27. Agnon signed this review with the pseudonym Adandon. Cf. Kressel, ibid., 61, no. 15 (1947/48), p. 17; Arnold Band, *Nostalgia and Nightmare* (Berkeley, 1968), p. 29.

40. *Ha'omer* was published in Jerusalem during 1907–1908. In Volume 2 (1908), pp. 53–65, a short story, "Agunot," appeared, signed by a penname "Shai Agnon," which later became Samuel Josef Czaczkes's official name. Cf. Kressel, *Leksikon.* 2:544.

41. *Bisedeh Sefer* (Leipzig, 1921), 3:107–108.

42. Kressel, in *Hapoel Hatsair* 61, no. 15 (1947/48), p. 18, wonders that both reviewers of *Yerushalayim,* Agnon and Berdichevsky, indicated that they were not aware of the publication of a first volume of that periodical. "Was it concealed from Berdichevsky and Agnon that there really existed a first volume?" he asks. It is quite

possible that Agnon did not know about the first volume, since he was only about twelve years old when it appeared, although it seems that he knew who Kreppel was, and he may have participated in one of Kreppel's publications. About Berdichevsky, it is hard to believe that he would not know about a publication in which a critical review of four of his books appeared.

43. *Midrash Bereshit Raba* (Theodor-Albeck edition), 85: 3; cf. also Rashi commentary on Genesis, 44: 87.

44. *Kiryat Sefer* was published in Warsaw but printed in Cracow due to restrictions by the Russian government on permits for issuing Hebrew periodicals. On Scheinfinkel, cf. E. Halpern's "Zikhroynes," *YB* 35 (1951): 241−242.

45. Based on the article in *JE* vol. 3, pp. 199−202.

46. For additional biographical details on Kotik, cf. Reisen, *Leksikon (1927)*, 3:418−424.

47. A publication with the same title and aims was published in New York fifteen years later by the American Branch of the Yivo Institute. It appeared as a quarterly during the years 1927−1929.

48. According to information published in the *Yohrbukh*, there were about one thousand Jewish libraries in Russia in 1911, of which only about three hundred were legal. The effort to establish and legalize Jewish libraries in Russia was spearheaded by the various branches of the Mefitse Haskalah society.

49. Books objected to by the authorities were declared "confiscated," and libraries were ordered to remove them from their shelves. Libraries were severely punished for disregarding the order. Cf. *Yohrbukh*, pp. 128−129.

50. On the history of the Bund, cf. *EJ* (1971), vol. 4, pp. 1,497−1,507; Gregor Aronson (ed.), *Di Geshikhte fun Bund* (New York, 1960- ).

51. For a list of the founders of the Kultur-Lige in Kiev and Warsaw, cf. Reisen, *Leksikon* (1927) 2:382.

52. For a list of the editors of the renewed *Bikher Velt*, cf. Reisen, *Leksikon* (1927), 2:382.

53. A number of important bibliographies were published in *Bikher Velt*, such as J. Yashunski's bibliography of the Yiddish press since 1917 (in issues 1−3, 1922) and Z. Reisen's list of Yiddish periodicals that appeared in various countries during 1921 (in issues 4−5, 1922).

54. Also published as a separate under the title *Dos Yidishe Bukh in F.S.S.R. far di Yorn 1917−1921* (Kiev, 1930).

55. Lists of Yiddish publications in the Soviet Union covering the years 1923−1927 were published in *Af di Vegn tsu der Nayer Shul* (Moscow, 1924−1928); lists covering the years 1928−1930 were published in *Ratnbildung* (Kharkov, 1929−1931). Cf. M. Shapiro, "Mer Ernst tsum Inyen Biblyografye," *Yidishe Kultur* 9, no. 11 (1947), pp. 57−58.

56. Yiddish book production in the Soviet Union during 1940 was covered by *Dos Yidishe Bukh in F.S.S.R.* (Kharkov, 1941), acording to M. Shapiro (in his article cited above, n. 55). Y. Y. Kohen, in *Pirsumim Yehudiyim Biverit Hamoetsot* (Jerusalem, 1961), doubted if such a book was actually published. Shapiro also

claimed that a bibliography of Yiddish books published in the Soviet Union during the World War II years was being prepared for publication by the Emes-Farlag in Moscow.

57. Zechariah Fishman's bio-bibliographical activities will be discussed in Volume Two of this work.

58. For two opposing views of *En Hakore,* cf. *Hatekufah* 19 (1923): 497–498, and *Hatoren* 10, no. 2 (1923), p. 92.

59. The history of the Soncino Gesellschaft is told in *SB* 1 (1925–1926): 112. A more detailed history is given by Abraham Horodisch, "Ein Abenteuer im Geiste: Die Soncino-Gesellschaft der Freunde des jüdischen Buches," *Bibliotheca Docet; Festgabe für Carl Wehmer* (Amsterdam, 1963), pp. 181–208. Cf. also F. Homeyer, *Deutsche Juden als Bibliophilen und Antiquare,* 2d ed. (Tübingen, 1966), pp. 67–69; 128–133.

60. On the Soncino family of printers, cf. G. Manzoni, *Annale Typographiche dei Soncino* (Bologna, 1886); A. M. Habermann, *Hamadpisim Bene Sontsino* (Vienna, 1933). Cf. also D. W. Amram, *The Makers of Hebrew Books in Italy* (Philadelphia, 1909; reprinted, London, 1963).

61. *Soncino Nachrichten,* appended to *SB* 1 (1925–1926): i.

62. For a complete list of works published by the Soncino Gesellschaft, cf. Horodish, "Ein Abenteuer im Geiste," pp. 198–208.

63. Volume 3, number 2–4 (July, 1930) was also called *Festschrift für Heinrich Brody.*

64. Freimann's Judaica *Katalog* of the Frankfort Stadtbibliothek, although published in 1932, was actually prepared much earlier.

65. The history and development of the Jewish National and University Library up to 1920 are fully described in Abraham Yaari's *Toldot Bet Hasefarim Hale'umi Vehauniversita'i Ad Shenat Tav-Resh-Peh* (Jerusalem, 1930). For later developments, cf. *Bet David Volfson* (Jerusalem, 1930).

66. *Kiryat Sefer* was earlier used by Bartolocci and Zeitlin as the title for their Hebraica bibliographies (cf. above, Chapters 1 and 4). Scheinfinkel was the first to use this title for a Hebrew bibliographical periodical (cf. above, p. 150).

67. Among the editors were listed Hugo Bergmann, Hermann Pick, Simcha Assaf, Benzion Dinaburg (Dinur), L. A. Mayer, Gershom Scholem, and Aryeh Tauber. The actual editor of the first three volumes and part of Volume 4 was Scholem; afterwards it was edited by Issachar Joel. Cf. Shunami, *Bibliography,* no. 4507.

68. The statement of purpose was written by Benzion Dinur. Cf. Kressel, *Leksikon,* 1:552.

69. Supplements were issued to several volumes of *Kiryat Sefer.* They included the following independent bibliographical works:

> *Kirve-Yad Bekabalah . . .* ed. Gershom Scholem in cooperation with Issachar Joel (Jerusalem: 1930). Supplement to Volume 7.
>
> *Reshimat Sifre Ladino . . .* comp. Abraham Yaari (Jerusalem, 1934). Supplement to Volume 10.

*Reshimat Kitve-Hayad Ha'ivriyim* . . . comp. Issachar Joel (Jerusalem, 1934). Supplement to Volume 11.

*Hadefus Ha'ivri Be'artsot Hamizrach,* comp. Abraham Yaari (Jerusalem, 1936—1940). Supplement to Volumes 13 and 17.

*Digle Hamadpisim Ha'ivriyim* . . . by Abraham Yaari (Jerusalem, 1943). Supplement to Volume 21.

*Hadefus Ha'ivri Bekushta* . . . by Abraham Yaari (Jerusalem, 1967). Supplement to Volume 42.

Aryeh Tauber's *Mechkarim Bibliyografiyim,* published as a supplement to Volume 9, consisted of a collection of essays published earlier.

70. *Hapoel Hatsair* 36, no. 51 (1942/43), p. 9.
71. *Haolam* 17 (1929): 238.
72. *Hapoel Hatsair* 26, no. 19 (1932/33), p. 14.
73. *Moznayim* 2 (1934): 220.
74. For additional biographical details on Lippe, see above, pp. 103—105.
75. It is safe to assume that Lippe borrowed from Steinschneider, not only the idea of a Hebrew-German title, but also the title itself, since there is a relation in the Bible between the words *hamazkir* and *me'asef.* Cf. II Kings, 18: 18, 37; Isaiah, 36: 3, 22, where the name Asaf Hamazkir appears. Asaf is a name, but it is also the root letters of *measef.* Lippe later used the words Asaf Hamazkir as the Hebrew title for his *Bibliographisches Lexicon.* Cf. above, pp. 104—105; also p. 291, n. 15.
76. Cf. Lippe's preface to his *Bibliographisches Lexicon,* pp. iii—iv. See also above, p. 103.
77. Cf. Lippe's preface to his *Bibliographisches Lexicon.*
78. See above, pp. 104—105.
79. The only bibliographical work worth mentioning is Ephraim Deinard's *Kohelet Amerika* (St. Louis, 1926). Of interest also are the dealers' lists: one by Alter Hebrew Book Company, New York, *Reshimat Hasefarim Me'otsar Hasefarim* (New York, 1925), and the other by Bloch Publishing Company, *General Judaica: A Catalogue of Practically All Available Books in English of Special Jewish Interest Including Fiction, Poetry, Drama* (New York, 1927).
80. For bio-bibliographical details on Margulies, cf. Kressel, *Leksikon,* 2:421—423; *Sefer Margaliyot* (Jerusalem, 1973).
81. Bernstein also began to publish, in fascicles, a supplement to *Alim* (beginning with Volume 3, number 1), consisting of the *Divan* of the Spanish-Jewish poet of the fourteenth century, Solomon ben Meshullam Dapiera. Only a 24-page introduction and 128 pages of the text were printed before *Alim* ceased publication; the complete text was published by Bernstein in New York in 1946.
82. While in Berlin, Mass published a 124-page list in 1929 of modern Hebrew works available at his store. Entitled *Yalkut Sefarim,* it registered 2,067 entries, arranged by subject, supplemented by an index, and preceded by an introduction by Simon Bernfeld.
83. The Bialik Institute was founded in Jerusalem in 1935 by the World Zionist

Organization as a publishing house in memory of Hayyim Nahman Bialik.

84. A bulletin described as "private," issued by the group during 1945—1946, offered Hebrew book-publishing news and announcements of new publications.

85. See below, p. 167.

86. Volumes 1—2 (1959/60—1960/61) featured scenes reproduced from illuminated Hebrew manuscripts; Volumes 3—5 (1961/62—1963/64) featured Hebrew printers' marks reproduced from Abraham Yaari's *Digle Hamadpisim Ha'ivriyim* (about this work, see below, pp. 252–253); and, from Volume 6 on, there began to appear reproductions of Jewish ex libris.

87. Poznanski was the son of Abraham Samuel Poznanski, well-known Hebrew scholar and founder of the society. Cf. Kressel, *Leksikon,* 2:577.

88. A small number of works with 1933 and 1935 imprints were also listed. Cf. introduction.

89. The idea was also transplanted to Israel, where an annual Hebrew Book Week is sponsored jointly by the Book Publishers Association and the Ministry of Education and Culture. Book buying during Hebrew Book Week is encouraged by offering large discounts. For this purpose the association publishes a collective catalog of books offered at a 40 percent discount.

90. The subtitle was changed as follows: Volumes 3—6, "Riv'on Lesafranut Ulebibliyografyah"; Volumes 7—8, "Ketav Et Lesafranut Ulebibliyografyah"; from Volume 9 on, "Ketav Et Lesafranut, Lebibliyografyah Ulearchiyoniut."

91. Volume 1 was published jointly by the Histadrut and Hakibuts Hame'uchad; Volumes 2—3, by the Department of Libraries of the Histadrut; Volumes 4—8, no. 1—2, jointly by the Union of Civil Servants and the Israel Library Association; beginning with Volume 8, number 3, by the Center for Public Libraries. Volumes 1—6 were edited by Shlomo Shunami; Volumes 7—10, by Mordecai Nadav; from Volume 11, by V. Arad.

92. The last issue of Volume 1 was dated August—October 1947, and the first issue of Volume 2, April 1950; the first issue of Volume 3, October 1951; the last, April 1953; followed by the first issue of Volume 4 in July 1956. Volume 6 began in 1959 and was completed in 1962, etc.

93. The supplement was entitled *Reshimat Sefarim Ivriyim* (Tel Aviv, 1950/51). It was compiled by Reuben Levi and edited by Shlomo Shunami.

94. Cf. Volumes 1 to 4, especially Habermann's biographical essays on Steinschneider, Fürst, Benjacob, and others.

95. After sharing publication of the first three volumes, the Hebrew Book Publishers separated to found their own periodical (see above, p. 165).

96. A retrospective issue, covering publications from September 1950 through March 1951, was published later.

97. With the exception of Volumes 1960/61, 1964/65, and 1965/66.

98. *Mivchar Hasefarim Ha'ivrim . . . Shenitkablu Besifriyat Hakneset . . .* (Jerusalem, 1956+).

99. Dingell Amendment to Public Law 83—480. For a study on the background and evolution of PL-480, cf. David S. McLellan and Donald Clare, *Public Law 480:*

*The Metamorphosis of a Law* (New York, 1965; Eagelton Institute Cases in Practical Politics, Case 36).

100. The effect of the Israel PL-480 program on American libraries is discussed by Charles Berlin in "The Israel PL-480 Program, 1964—1969: A Review," *JBA* 27 (1969/70): 48—55; also produced as a separate. For a review of the program in general, cf. Mortimer Graves, *The Library of Congress PL-480 Foreign Acquisitions Program: User's Eye View* (New York, 1969; *ACLS Newsletter,* Special Supplement, September 1969).

101. For a number of years, the Book and Printing Center of the Israel Export Institute reproduced the *Accession List: Israel* under the title *List of Books and Serials Published in Israel* and mailed it to interested parties abroad. In 1973, after the *Accession List* ceased publishing, the center began reproducing the bibliography section of *Kiryat Sefer* as *A List of Books and Serials Published in Israel (New Series)*.

102. A number of American institutions have periodically published lists of acquisitions. Among them are the Cincinnati, Los Angeles, and Jerusalem libraries of the Hebrew Union College-Jewish Institute of Religion and the Jewish Studies Collection of the University of California at Los Angeles. The libraries of Yeshiva University and the Yivo Institute for Jewish Research in New York began issuing such lists in 1973 and 1974 respectively.

103. See above, p. 171.

104. *Studies in Jewish History and Booklore* (New York, 1944).

105. The Rabbi Kook Institute was founded in 1937 by Rabbi Yehudah Leib Maimon (1875—1962) in memory of the late Chief Rabbi Abraham Isaac Kook (1865—1935). The purpose of the institute was to conduct rabbinic research and to publish rabbinic works.

106. A publication with the same title was edited by Raphael in 1944. It was the first of a planned annual publication to be issued by the union of religious Hebrew writers in Jerusalem. No more were published.

107. Also published as a separate volume. Cf. above, Chapter 2, n. 39.

108. See above, n. 105.

109. "Defus Rom Bevilna," by Samuel Sheraga Feigensohn (1838—1932), one of the managers of that printing and publishing house. Published completely in *Yahadut Lita* (Tel Aviv, 1960), 1:196—268.

110. Margulies' bibliography appeared in every issue, and it covered several tractates of the Talmud. It was also published in four separate pamphlets.

111. Frenkel compiled the list for nos. 1—7. Y. Y. Kohen compiled the list for no. 8, adding to it an index of titles, authors, and editors, and an index of publishers. Elazar Hurvitz compiled the list for no. 9, adding an index of printing places. Kohen's and Hurvitz's lists were also issued separately.

Notes to Chapter Seven:
*Indexes to Jewish Periodicals and Monographs*

1. On Poole and Wilson and their indexing systems, cf. John Lawker, *The H. W. Wilson Company; Half a Century of Bibliographic Publishing* (Minneapolis, 1950).

2. The French bibliographic index for books and periodicals, *Polybiblion,* began to appear in Paris in 1868.

3. For biographical data on Schwab, cf. *Otsar Hasifrut* 3 (1889/90): 83−86, the section, "Toldot Anshe Shem"; *Hashilo'ach* 35 (1918): 376−377; *Hatsefirah* no. 10 (March 7, 1918), pp. 9−10; *JE* vol. 11, p. 117; *EJ (1971),* vol. 14, p. 1,015.

4. Paul Hildenfinger's *Bibliographie des Travaux de Moïse Schwab* (Paris, 1905) lists 410 entries. Additions, bringing the list to 428 entries, were published in *REJ* 56 (1908): 292−293.

5. *Le Talmud de Jérusalem* (Paris, 1871−1889; reprinted in 1932−1933 and 1960).

6. The publication date of the first *Hame'asef* was 1783, when it was issued in Königsberg by the disciples of Moses Mendelssohn. The index also included some earlier material.

7. The decision to lithograph the author's handwritten copy instead of printing it in type was made because of financial problems and also because Schwab considered it only a preliminary work. Cf. S. Poznanski, *ZfHB* 4 (1900): 143−145; *Hashilo'ach* 35 (1918): 377.

8. Cf. M. Brann, *MGWJ* 44 (1900): 92−95; Poznanski, *ZfHB.*

9. Cf. Poznanski, ibid.

10. In compiling the first volume, Schwab was assisted, on a limited scale, by Immanuel Löw (1854−1944) and Flavio Servi (1841−1904). The former indexed *Ben Chananja* and *Magyar Zsido Szemle,* published in Hungary, and the latter indexed *Vessilo Israelitico,* published in Italy. In this connection, Poznanski also felt that Hungarian titles should have been translated, and that Hebrew titles should have been explained.

11. Additional improvements included translations and explanations of Hungarian and Hebrew titles, as suggested by Poznanski. See above, n. 10.

12. Cf. B. Wachstein, "Randbemerkungen," *JJLG* 19 (1928): 225−235 (also issued as an offprint), in which he offers 232 corrections to the *Répertoire;* J. Pograbinski, *KS* 8 (1931/32): 248.

13. See above, n. 12.

14. Cf. Schwab's introduction to the first edition of the *Répertoire;* S. Feigin, "Hatsaot Bibliyografiyot," *Hadoar* 7 (1927/28): 180−184; idem, *Moznayim* 3, no. 30 (1931), pp. 10−12, where he stresses the benefits to scholars from the realization of his proposals. Cf. also Bruno Kirschner, *MGWJ* 76 (1932): 257, about the importance of a periodical index for Jewish scientific work.

15. This attitude was expressed as late as 1924 in the introduction to the first issue of *Kiryat Sefer.* See above, p. 158.

16. Issue nos. 9—10 of Volume 2 consisted of a biennial subject and author index.

17. Cf. announcement on verso of title page to Volume 3 (1934).

18. Cf. Arnold J. Band, "Jewish Studies in American Liberal-Arts Colleges and Universities," *AJYB* 67 (1966): 3—27. For references to earlier studies on this topic, see his n. 3.

19. *A Social and Religious History of the Jews* (still in progress).

20. *JSS* 2, no. 3—4 (1940).

21. M. Kosover, in *YB* 19 (1947): 268—270, offered a number of additions and corrections to Baron's *Bibliography*. See also on pp. 265—266 his criticism of the practice of translating titles.

22. Cf. Shmuel Hugo Bergmann, "Tarbut Bibliyografit," *YL* 1, no. 1—2 (1946), pp. 1—4, where he suggests, among others, a joint effort by a number of institutions at establishing a bibliographical institute. Cf. also Benzion Dinur, "Avodah Meshutefet Umif'alim Meshutafim Bemada'e Hayahadut Uderachim Le'irgunam," *Hakinus Haolami Lemada'e Hayahadut* (Jerusalem, 1952), p. 35.

23. See above, p. 28.

24. *Betoch Kitve-et*. See above, p. 158.

25. Ibid. Of more practical value was the approach of *Kuntres Bibliyografi,* which interfiled periodicals with books in its subject scheme. See above, p. 175

26. Excluding Hebrew poetry, an area reviewed annually in *Kiryat Sefer* by Jefim Schirmann (also available in offprint).

27. For example, Bible commentaries were arranged in the order of the books of the Bible, subdivided in each book by chapter and verse; the language subsection "idioms, specific words," was arranged alphabetically according to the words; the subsection "biography, letters, memoirs," was arranged alphabetically by the names of the personalities, the subjects of the biography, or by the author of the letters or memoirs. Other sections and subsections were arranged chronologically or alphabetically by author.

28. Cf. foreword to this issue.

29. See above, p. 5, and p. 286, n. 39.

30. "Palestine" and the "State of Israel" were merged into one; the "Six Day War" was eliminated; and the section beginning with "Ethics" was changed to read "Ethics, homiletics, thought, chassidism."

31. A bulletin by the Center of Torah Libraries and a bibliography of the writings of the late Reuben Margulies.

32. The editor is also planning to issue periodic indexes covering biographical materials on Jewish religious personalities, under the title *Enecha Ro'ot.*

33. See above, p. 197.

34. *Jewish Literary Annual,* 1904, pp. 109—146. Also issued as offprint.

35. See above, p. 102.

36. Cf. K. J. Silman, "Orot Meofel," *Ha'arets,* August 11, 1921. Cf. also D. Persky, *Ivri Anochi* (New York, 1948), p. 150; idem, *Hadoar* 40 (1960/61): 207. Dinur's file, covering 167 Hebrew periodicals published from 1784 to 1920 and con-

sisting of 70,000 cards arranged by subjects, was turned over to Yad Vashem in 1955. Cf. *Yedi'ot Yad Vashem* nos. 4–5 (June 1955), p. 7, and no. 6–7 (January 1956), pp. 20, 29.

37. Cf. S. Feigin, "Hatsaot Bibliyografiyot," *Hadoar* 7 (1927/28): 180–184. Feigin also proposed that Hebrew periodicals should publish annual summaries of important essays of Jewish interest published in scholarly magazines. Feigin returned to the idea of the index several years later in *Moznayim* 3, no. 30 (1931), pp. 10–12.

38. The original plan also called for indexing Jewish periodicals in Hebrew and in European languages. It had to be abandoned due to lack of funds.

39. Cf. introduction ("A Vort Frier").

40. Cf. *Bikher Velt* no. 3 (March 1929), pp. 38–45; *Bibliologisher Zamlbukh,* pp. 215–228. The reviewer in this publication attacked Yivo mainly for its "yidishist, middle-class, nationalistic-reactionary ideology."

41. Cf. M. Kosover, *YB* 19 (1947): 265.

42. *Zeitschrift für die Geschichte der Juden in Deutschland* 2 (1888): 1–46, 109–149.

43. The publishers of the reprint edition, in a credit statement on the verso of the title page erroneously ascribed the compiling of the *Ukazatel'* to V. I. Mezhov. Cf. J. Weizman, "Biblyografye fun der Yidisher Prese," *YB* 9 (1936): 136; Shunami, *Bibliography,* no. 2445. See also introduction to *Ukazatel'.*

44. Cf. last page of *Ukazatel'.* A plan to prepare supplements to the *Ukazatel'* was discussed in 1928 by the Moscow Society of the Study of the Yiddish Language, Literature, and History. Cf. *Visenshaftlekhe Yorbikher* 1 (1929): 251.

45. Balaban's contribution to Jewish history, in general, and to Polish Jewish history, in particular, will be discussed in the supplement to Volume Three of this work.

46. *Kwartalnik Historyczny* 22 (1908). Also issued separately (Lwów, 1908).

47. *Przeglad Historyczny* 15 (1911): (230)–248, (369)–385. During the same period Balaban also published similar lists in the Petrograd-based *Evreiskaia Starina*

48. For detailed information on Thomsen, cf. "In Memoriam Peter Thomsen," *Palästina-Literatur* 6 (1956), preceding "Vorwort."

49. *Zeitschrift des Deutschen Palästina-Vereins* (Leipzig, 1878–    ).

50. Cf. *MGWJ* 53 (1909): 499. Thomsen implemented this suggestion beginning with Volume 2.

51. On Zeitlin, see above, pp. 101–102.

52. A reviewer of this volume observed that the section on Jewish history included editions of the Mishnah and works and articles dealing with the Talmud and medieval Hebrew literature not related to Jewish history. Cf. *KS* 4 (1927/28): 143. Similar criticism was also voiced concerning Volume 3, in *MGWJ* 61 (1917): 235.

53. See above, p. 194.

54. An annotated *Bibliographical Bulletin* (issued separately in English, German, and Hebrew) was published bimonthly in Jerusalem during 1936–1941 by the

Central Zionist Archives. It listed only books and pamphlets. The bulletin in Hebrew was published first in *Haolam,* beginning with Volume 25, no. 5 (October 22, 1936). Guides to books and articles dealing with Zionism appeared earlier. Cf. *Ukazatel' Literatury o Sionizme* (St. Petersburg, 1903), consisting of 3,886 entries (about the compilers, cf. *YB* 9 [1936]: 136; 14 [1939]: 178); Benzion Dinaburg (Dinur), *Madrich Lebibliyografyah Tsiyonit* (Jerusalem, 1931), consisting of 598 annotated entries.

55. On the Wilson Company, see above n. 1.

56. The term "Publizistik" in the title was used in its broadest form, encompassing everything published in periodicals.

57. On Wachstein, see above, p. 61.

58. The followers of Moses Mendelssohn launched a periodical in 1783 entitled *Hame'asef,* ushering in with it the Enlightenment movement. The nine periodicals indexed by Wachstein were: *Bikure Ha'itim* (1821–1831), *Kerem Chemed* (1833–1856), *Bikure Ha'itim* (1844), *Bikure Ha'itim Hachadashim* (1845), *Kochve Yitschak* (1845–1873), *Meged Geresh Yerachim* (1848), *Avne Nezer* (1853), *Otsar Nechmad* (1856–1863), *Bikurim* (1864–1865).

59. For biographical data on Taglicht, cf. N. M. Gelber, "Doktor Yisrael Taglicht," *Chochmat Yisrael Bema'arav Eropah* (Jerusalem, 1963) 2:111–114; C. Bloch, "Dokter Yisroel Taglikht," *YB* 23 (1944): 249–54; 24 (1944): 138–139.

60. The two periodicals were *Bet Hamidrash* (1865) and *Bet Talmud* (1881–1889), both edited by Isaac Hirsch Weiss (1815–1905).

61. For biographical data on Kristianpoller, cf. *EJ (1971)* vol. 10, p. 1,266.

62. The four periodicals were *Hashachar* (1868–1883/84), *Hamabit* (1878), *Hamabit Leyisrael* (1878), *Ha'emet* (1877).

63. Smolenskin edited the first two periodicals listed above, n. 62.

64. Cf. *PAJHS* 13 (1905): xix–xxiii.

65. It is possible that the publication of an index for the first twenty numbers of the society's *Publications* in 1914 was the result of the effort begun in 1904. About individual indexes to other American Jewish periodicals, see below, pp. 219–224.

66. For biographical and bibliographical data on Marcus, cf. *Essays in American Jewish History* (Cincinnati, 1958), pp. 1–22, 493–512. The Marcus-Bilgray *Index to Jewish Festschriften* will be disscused below, p. 225.

67. The indexed periodicals were: *American Jewish Archives* 1–20 (1948–1968), *American Jewish Historical Quarterly* and *Publications of the American Jewish Historical Society* 1–58 (1892–1968), *American Jewish Yearbook* 1–69 (1899–1968), *The American Jews Annual* 1–10 (1884–1896); *Contemporary Jewish record* 1–8 (1938–1945); *Historia Judaica* 1–23 (1938–1961); *Jewish Journal of Sociology* 1–10 (1959–1968); *Jewish Quarterly Review,* n. s. 1–58 (1910–1968); *Jewish Social Studies* 1–30 (1939–1968); *Michigan Jewish History* 1–8 (1960–1968); *The Record* (Jewish Historical Society of Greater Washington) 1–3 (1966–1968); *Rhode Island Jewish Historical Notes* 1–4 (1954–1966); *Yivo Annual* 1–13 (1946–1965).

68. On Strashun and his library, cf. Z. Harkavi's introduction to Strashun's *Mekore Harambam* (Jerusalem, 1956), pp. 8–10, especially notes, 13, 19; idem,

"Rabi Matityahu Strashun," *Chochmat Yisrael Bema'arav Eropah* (Jerusalem, 1965), 3:345–355, also notes 2, 41. See also M. Shalit, "Vilner Bibliyotekn," *Vilner Zamlbukh* 1 (1916): 31–37; S. Federbush, *Chikre Yahadut* (Jerusalem, 1965), p. 324; I. Klausner, "Bate-Eked Sefarim Birushalayim Delita," *Sefer Rafa'el Mahler* (Merchavia, 1974), pp. 6–12.

69. *Igrot Byalik* (Tel Aviv, 1938), 2:142–143. On Lunsky, cf. Klausner, *Sefer Refa'el Mahler,* pp. 74–77; *Leksikon* 5:14–15; Kressel, *Leksikon* 2:218–219.

70. Cf. *Kitve E. Levinski* (Odessa, 1913), 3:294–305.

71. *Hamelits* was founded in Russia in 1860 as a Hebrew weekly, and it became a daily in 1886. In 1878, it began to print an annual table of contents. Cf. A. R. Malachi, "Maftechot Kelaliyim Ba'itonut Ha'ivrit," *Hadoar* 28 (1948): 38–44.

72. On the history of the *Monatsschrift,* cf. the articles by P. F. Frankel, "Erinnerungen und Hoffnungen dieser Monatsschrift," *MGWJ* 34 (1885): 1–16; M. Brann, "Zur Geschichte der Monatsschrift," ibid., 51 (1907): 1–16; G. Kressel, "Lezecher Chacham Ve'achsanyah," *Me'asef Davar* (Tel Aviv, 1955) pp. (357)–372; D. S. Löwinger, "Yarchon Lehistoryah Ulemada'e Hayahadut," *Chochmat Yisrael Bema'arav Eropah* (1958), 1:529–542; K. Wilhelm, "Die Monatsschrift für Geschichte und Wissenchaft des Judentums; ein geistesgeschichtlicher Versuch," *Das Breslauer Seminar* (Tübingen, 1963), pp. 327–349.

73. For biographical and bibliographical data on Frankel, cf. S. P. Rabinowitz *R' Zecharyah Frankel* (Warsaw, 1898); L. Ginzberg, *Students, Scholars and Saints* (Philadelphia, 1928), pp. 195–216; *MGWJ* 25 (1876): 12–26; ibid., 45 (1901): 193–278, 336–352, 558–562; *EJ* vol. 6, pp. 1,090–1,094; *EJ (1971),* vol. 7, pp. 80–82; Kressel, *Leksikon,* 2:684–686.

74. On the history of the Seminar, cf. M. Brann, *Geschichte des Jüdisch-theologischen Seminars (Fraenkel'sche Stiftung) in Breslau* (Breslau, 1904?); G. Kisch, ed. *Das Breslauer Seminar* (Tübingen, 1963).

75. For biographical and bibliographical data on Grätz, cf. E. Schmerler, *Chaye Grets* (New York, 1921); *Das Breslauer Seminar,* pp. (187)–237; S. W. Baron, *History and Jewish Historians* (Philadelphia, 1964), pp. 269–275; *MGWJ* 61 (1917): 321–391, 412–421, 444–491; ibid., 62 (1918): 5–15, 125–151, 231–269; *EJ* vol. 7, pp. 645–652; *EJ (1971),* vol. 7, pp. 845–850.

76. For biographical and bibliographical data on Brann, cf. *MGWJ* 63 (1919): 81–97; ibid., 64 (1920): 241–249; *EJ* vol. 4, pp. 277–278; *EJ (1971),* vol. 4, pp. 1,307–1,308.

77. For biographical and bibliographical data on Kaufmann, cf. *Gedenkbuch zur Erinnerung an David Kaufmann* (Breslau, 1900), pp. i–lxxxvii; *EJ* vol. 9, pp. 1,095–1,099; *EJ (1971),* vol. 10, pp. 842–843; Kressel, *Leksikon,* 2:739–740.

78. For biographical details on Heinemann, cf. E. Urbach, "Prof. Yitschak Haineman," *Chochmat Yisrael Bema'arav Eropah* (1958), 1:219–222; *EJ (1971),* vol. 8, pp. 277–278. For a bibliography of his writings, cf. *MGWJ* 80 (1936): 294–297.

79. For biographical details on Baeck, cf. *EJ (1971),* vol. 4, pp. 76–77.

80. "Register für die Jahrgänge 76 bis 83 der Monatsschrift," *Das Breslauer Seminar,* pp. 351–373.

81. For a history of the *Revue* up to World War II, cf. J. K. Mikliszanski, "Hariv'on Hatsarfati Lechochmat Yisrael," *Chochmat Yisrael Bema'arav Eropah* (1958), 1:543—553.

82. For biographical data on Loeb, cf. *JE* vol. 8, pp. 148—149.

83. For a detailed biography of Levi, cf. Mikliszanski, *Cochmat Yisrael Bema'arav Eropah,* 1:297—309.

84. For additional biographical data on Kisch, cf. *EJ (1971),* vol. 10, pp. 1,062—1,063. On the history of *Historia Judaica,* cf. the articles by Kisch, Grayzel, and Grünwald in *HJ* 23 (1960): 3—22. The same issue also carries an index to the first twenty volumes of *HJ.* See below, p. 220.

85. On the history of the old and new series of *JQR,* cf. S. Zeitlin, "Seventy-Five Years of the Jewish Quarterly Review," *The Seventy-Fifth Anniversary Volume of the Jewish Quarterly Review* (Philadelphia, 1967), pp. 60—68; idem, introduction to *Studies and Essays in Honor of Abraham A. Neuman* (Leiden, 1962), pp. xi—xii; T. Preschel, "Hariv'on Ha'angli," *Chochmat Yisrael Bema'arav Eropah* (1963), 2:360—370.

86. For biographical and bibliographical data on Abrahams, cf. *Jewish Studies in Memory of Israel Abrahams* (New York, 1927), pp. v—lxvi.

87. For additional biographical data on Montefiore, cf. *Speculum Religionis* (Oxford, 1929), pp. 1—17; N. D. M. Bentwich, *Claude Montefiore and His Tutor in Rabbinics* (Southamptom, 1966; Montefiore Memorial Lecture, 6); *UJE* vol. 7, pp. 628—629; *EJ (1971),* vol. 12, pp. 268—269.

88. For biographical and bibliographical data on Adler, cf. *UJE* vol. 1, pp. 88—89; *EJ (1971),* vol. 2, pp. 272—274.

89. For complete biographical and bibliographical data on Schechter, cf. N. D. M. Bentwich, *Solomon Schechter* (London, 1931; Arthur Davis Memorial Lecture); idem, *Solomon Schechter; A Biography* (Cambridge, 1938; Philadelphia, 1938, 1940, 1948); idem, *Claude Montefiore and His Tutor in Rabbinics;* A. S. Oko, *Solomon Schechter; A Bibliography* (Cambridge, 1938); *UJE* vol. 9, pp. 393—394; *EJ (1971),* vol. 14, pp. 948—950.

90. On Zeitlin, cf. *Bitsaron* 50, no. 1 (1964), pp. 13—44, 61—62; S. B. Hoenig, *Solomon Zeitlin: Scholar Laureate; An Annotated Bibliography, 1915—1970, with Appreciations of His Writings* (New York, 1971); *EJ (1971),* vol. 16, pp. 975—976.

91. On Neuman, cf. S. Zeitlin's introduction to *Studies and Essays in Honor of Abraham A. Neuman,* pp. vii—xiii; *EJ (1971),* vol. 12, pp. 1,009—1,010.

92. S. Feigin, *Haolam* 22 (1934): 212—213, sharply criticized the arrangement of the author index. For additional indexing of *JQR* n. s., see above, n. 67.

93. The biographical and bibliographical materials relating to Ginzberg are summarized in *EI,* vol. 2, pp. 400—408; *EJ (1971),* vol. 2, pp. 440—448; Kressel, *Leksikon,* 1:60—71. See also Shunami, *Bibliography,* nos. 3,556—3,557; Jerusalem, Institute for Hebrew Bibliography, *Choveret Ledugmah* (Jerusalem, 1964), pp. 11—13. Ginzberg's contribution to Jewish research literature will be discussed in Volume Two of this work.

94. On Wissotzky, see Volume Two of this work.

95. On the history of "Achiasaf," cf. E. Kaplan, *Hashkafah al Ma'aseh Hachevrah 'Achiasaf'* (Warsaw, 1897); *Ben Avigdor Lechag Yovlo* (Warsaw, 1917), p. 4; J. Pograbinsky, "Letoldot Hamolut Ha'ivrit," *JBA* 9 (1950/51), Hebrew section, pp. 39−44. See also Volume Two of this work.

96. For the new periodical, Ginzberg intentionally selected the name of the "slow moving" water spring near Jerusalem because it reflected his editorial policy: slow, quiet, noncontroversial writing. On the history of *Hashilo'ach,* cf. B. Shohetman and B. Elizedek, "Kitve Yosef Klozner," *Sefer Klozner* (Tel Aviv, 1937; also issued as separate), pp. 475−528 (especially pp. 525−526, where detailed bibliographical data on *Hashilo'ach* are given); B. Shohetman, "Hashilo'ach; Çhamishim Shanah Lereshit Hofo'ato," *Gilyonot* 21 (1947−48): 101−107; T. Preschel, "Hashilo'ach," *Chochmat Yisrael Bema'arav Eropah,* 2:317−328; J. Barzilai (Folman), *Hashilo'ach, 1896−1927: Bibliyografyah* (Tel Aviv, 1964), pp. 1−6 (first numbering).

97. For a detailed biography and bibliography on Klausner, cf. J. Becker and H. Toren, *Yosef Klozner; Ha'ish Ufo'olo* (Tel Aviv, 1946); J. Nedava (ed.), *Yosef Klozner Lidemuto; Kovets Lezichro* (Tel Aviv, 1960); S. Kling, *Joseph Klausner* (New York, 1970); *EJ (1971), vol. 10, pp. 1,091*−1,096; Kressel, *Leksikon,* 2:758−764; Shunami, *Bibliography,* nos. 3,798−3,800. See also Volume Two of this work for Klausner's contribution to Jewish research literature. Besides Ginzberg and Klausner, *Hashilo'ach* also had other editors. The last part of Volume 6 (1899) was edited by S. Bernfeld; Volumes 13−15 (1904−1905) were edited jointly by H. N. Bialik and Klausner, and Volume 16 (1907) by Bialik alone; volumes 45−46 (1925−1927) were edited jointly by J. Fichman and Klausner.

98. The crises were sometimes financial and sometimes political. The financial difficulties were most severe during the years of Ginzberg's editorship, and they were the result of his editorial policies. The political difficulties were the result of the political situation in Russia. After the 1905 revolution, *Hashilo'ach* was closed by the government, together with the entire Jewish press in Russia. It was again closed during the years of World War I. In 1919 it was declared counterrevolutionary by the Bolshevik regime, and its publication was prohibited. Cf. *Hashilo'ach* 36 (1919/20): 214, note.

99. The last issue (Volume 46, no. 3−6) was dated June−September 1926, but it was actually printed in March 1927, two months after Ginzberg's death.

100. Cf. Pograbinsky's letter in *Hadoar* 28 (1948/49): 474.

101. For biographical and bibliographical details on Frishman, cf. *Sefer Habikoret* attached to *Kol Kitve David Frishman* (Warsaw, 1914); *Komets-Alim al Kever David Frishman* (New York, 1922); Reisen, *Leksikon,* 3:204−228; *Leksikon,* 7:505−513; Kressel, *Leksikon,* 2:668−675; *EJ (1971),* vol. 7, pp. 198−203; Shunami, *Bibliography,* nos. 3,536−3,537.

102. On Stybel and his publications, cf. Daniel Persky, *Hatoren* 6, no. 5 (1919/20), pp. 11−13; idem, *Hadoar* 26 (1946/47): 32−34 (cf. also ibid., pp. 45−46); G. Kressel, *Yad Lakore* 1 (1946): 111−114 (also ibid., p. 218); J. Twersky and N. Touroff, *Hatekufah* 32/33 (1947): 11−32; S. Rawidowicz, *Metsudah* 5/6 (1948):

627—630; J. Pograbinsky, *JBA* 10 (1951/52), Hebrew section, pp. 37—40; *EJ (1971)*, vol. 15, pp. 465. A series of letters and articles dealing with Stybel publications, written by F. Lachover, Ben-Zion Katz, and Stybel himself, were published in *Hatsefirah* 1927, nos. 6, 12, 24, 36, 42, 48, 54, and 60.

103. On the history of *Hatekufah,* cf. T. Preschel, "Hatekufah," *Chochmat Yisrael Bema'arav Eropah,* 2:329—333; J. Barzilai, *Hatekufah 1917—1950: Bibliyografyah* (Tel Aviv, 1961), pp. 1—3 (first numbering).

104. Cf. *Hadoar* 40 (1960/61): 206—207, D. Persky's reaction to the publication of the index. See also below, p. 219.

105. For biographical and bibliographical details on Lamdan, cf. Leon I. Yudkin, *Isaac Lamdan* (Ithaca, N. Y., 1971); *EI* vol. 21, pp. 903—904; Kressel, *Leksikon,* 2:285—287; *EJ (1971)*, vol. 10, pp. 1,363—1,365.

106. The final volume was published after Lamdan's death by a group of friends.

107. *YL* 9 (1967/68): 124.

108. Kressel spent some time in the United States working for Wilson (cf. his introduction to the index of *Hapoel Hatsair*). Kressel's contributions to Jewish research literature will be discussed in Volume Two of this work.

109. Cf. *Asufot* 7 (1961): 115—185.

110. For a history of *Ha'achdut,* cf. Y. Zerubavel, "Perakim al Ha'achdut," *Asufot* 4 (1954): 68—89; 5 (1957): 121—133; also the various articles in Volume 7 (1961) devoted to *Ha'achdut.*

111. *Asufot* 11 (1966): 3—180.

112. For a history of *Hapoel Hatsair,* cf. the articles by Kressel in *Asufot* 4 (1954): 4—65, and 5 (1957): 108—120.

113. One reviewer of the index felt that the number of entries could have been substantially reduced by grouping together the regular monthly features of the periodical under one heading instead of listing them separately. The same reviewer also noticed a lack of cross-reference in a number of key topics. Cf. *YL* 10 (1969/70): 46—47.

114. One box of index cards was lost during that period, and it was not replaced. Cf. introduction to index and note to page 350. A by-product of the index was the compiler's solving of a large number of pen-names and pseudonyms used by writers of *Hapoel Hatsair.*

115. The Israel kibbutz movement is divided into the following four groups: Hakibuts Hameuchad (which has published *Mibifnim* since 1923); Ichud Hakevutsot Vehakibutsim (which has published *Niv Hakevutsah* since 1929); Hakibuts Ha'artsi (which has published *Hedim* since 1934); and Hakibuts Hadati (which has published *Amudim* since 1938). For a description of the kibbutz movement and the ideological differences among these four groups, cf. *EJ (1971)*, vol. 10, pp. 963—973.

116. About the aims and work of the *Mif'al,* cf. M. Buchsweiler, "Al Mif'al Habibliyografyah Hakibutsit," *YL* 11 (1970/71): 213—214, 217.

117. *Mafte'ach Lechitve-Et Shel Hatenuah Hakibutsit: Choveret Ledugmah* (Tel Aviv, 1968).

118. The history of *Mibifnim* is related in the introduction to the index, pp. 4—6.

A 39-page index to twnety years of *Mibifnim* (1931—1951) was compiled earlier by S. Even-Shoshan, and it was published as a supplement to *Mibifnim* 16 (1952/53).

119. The compilers laid special stress on deciphering the pen-names and initials used by some authors in the periodical and on establishing their present names.

120. The history of *Niv Hakevutsah* is related in the introduction to the index, pp. 4—7.

121. Cf. above, n. 104.

122. Cf. E. R. Malachi, "Maftechot Kelaliyim Ba'itonut Ha'ivrit," *Hadoar* 28 (1948/49): 38, 43—44. See also J. Pograbinsky's letter and Malachi's reply, ibid., p. 474.

123. Due to technical difficulties, the indexes to the following three periodicals could not be described: *Bama'aleh, Ketuvim* (both mentioned by Malachi, in his above-mentioned article), and *Tefutsot Yisrael.* A list of articles dealing with Jewish history, Palestine, and Zionism, printed in the Hungarian-Jewish yearbook *Evkönyv* (1895-1948), was compiled by Juda Spiegel and published in *Sinai* 34 (1953/54): 207—208. Some of the materials published in the Jerusalem *Hame'asef* (1896—1914), edited by Ben-Zion Koenka, was indexed in Koenka's *Tiferet Tsiyon* (Jerusalem, 1970/71). A card-file index of the London Jewish Chronicle for the years 1841—1880 and 1881—1890, is available on microfilm. A more elaborate index to the Tel Aviv daily *Ha'arets* and *Jerusalem Post,* to be available on microfilm, is now in process of preparation by S. Shihor. Cf. *YL* 13 (1973): 168—169, and circulars by Shihor's Encyclopedic Index, dated March and April 1974.

An effort to index the Tel Aviv daily *Davar* was made by G. Kressel in the 1940s. He succeeded in compiling the first four years (1925—1929). The index remained unpublished (from a private communication by Kressel; cf. also the above mentioned article by Malachi, p. 44).

The compiling of a *Gesamtindex* to the most important German-Jewish periodicals is currently being attempted at the Leo Baeck Institute in New York (cf. "Einleitung" to *Katalog* of the Leo Baeck Institute, p. xxxiii).

Indexing of the Philadelphia *Occident* was in process at the American Jewish Archives in Cincinnati during the 1950s; cf. J. Trachtenberg, "Jewish Bibliography in America," *SBB* 2 (1955/56): 101.

124. Cf. D. Persky, "Toldot Hadoar Vedarko," *Sefer Hayovel Shel Hadoar Limelot Lo Sheloshim Shanah* (New York, 1952), p. 25.

125. Cf. E. R. Malachi, *Hadoar* 28 (1948/49): 44, and D. Persky, ibid., 41 (1961): 22.

126. A publication with the same title appeared originally in 1904. It did not continue.

127. For a detailed description of this *Mafte'ach* see above, p. 159. See also G. Kressel's criticism in *JBA* 32 (1974/75): 64.

128. The volume is part of a monumental project in progress at Yad Itzhak Ben-Zvi in Jerusalem to index all periodicals containing material relating to the Jewish community in the Holy Land, from the time of the destruction of the Temple to the establishment of the State of Israel. On the history of the *Halevanon,* cf. Shoshana Halevy's introduction to this volume.

129. *Moznayim* was published as a weekly from 1929 to 1933; the monthly *Moznayim* was suspended from June 1947 to 1954 and was replaced by a biweekly *Moznayim* from September 1947 to April 1948.

130. The *Publications* have been continued since September 1961 by the *American Jewish Historical Quarterly*.

131. On pp. 588–600 was printed "An Index to the Jewish Encyclopedia, containing references to articles that deal with the history of the Jews in the United States," compiled by Samuel P. Abelow.

132. On the history of *Sinai*, cf. *Sinai: Sefer Yovel* (Jerusalem, 1958), pp. 5–7, 602–606.

133. For biographical details on Katzburg, cf. introduction to *Peletah Hanisheret Mimechabere Vesofre Tel-Talpiyot*, vol. 1 (Jerusalem, 1971).

134. Excluded from this list are the indexes to *Ketavim Lecheker Hachakla'ut, Hateva Veha'arets*, and *Teva Va'arets*, since they do not belong to the category of Jewish studies. The indexes to individual volumes of *Devar Hashavua* (published in recent years in the last issue of each volume) and the indexes to the stenographical reports of the Zionist congresses (being published currently by the Institute for Zionist Research of Tel Aviv University) were also omitted, because indexes to individual volumes are outside the scope of this work.

135. For a description of Jewish Festschriften literature, cf. C. Berlin, *Festschriften in Jewish Studies* (offprinted from *Harvard Library Bulletin* 19, no. 4 [October 1971], pp. 366–374), and his introduction to the *Index to Festschriften in Jewish Studies*. Cf. also *EJ* (1971), vol. 6, pp. 1,246–1,247.

136. On Marcus, cf. above, p. 210, also p. 307, n. 66.

137. A few volumes were included that were officially published later but had been supplied to the compiler in advance of publication; a few volumes were omitted that were published about the time of the cut-off date but were not available to the compiler on time.

138. The list of subjects was followed by corrigenda and errata, consisting mainly of articles in the English section of the Wolfson Festschrift not included in the *Index*.

139. Cf. also S. R. Brunswick's review in *College and Research Libraries* 34 (1973) 4:316–318.

140. For a complete list of mnemonic devices in rabbinic literature, cf. Phinehas Jacob Kohn, *Sefer Hasimanim Hashalem* (London, 1952). See also his introduction, where he summarizes the literature dealing with mnemonics in Jewish literature. Cf. also *JE* vol. 8, pp. 631–632; *EJ (1971):* vol. 12, pp. 187–190.

141. About indexes in Hebrew literature, cf. Menahem Zvi Barkay, *Miftuach* (Jerusalem, 1968). On indexes in general literature, cf. Robert Lewis Collison, *Indexes and Indexing* (New York, 1953, etc.).

142. The special encyclopedias, concordances, etc., will be described in Volumes Two and Three of this work.

143. For biographical details on Goldschmidt, cf. Z. Werba, "Doktor Eliezer Goldshmidt, Hachoker Vehamevaker," *Hadoar* 22 (1942/43): 307–308; Samuel Abba Horodezky, *Zichronot* (Tel Aviv, 1957), pp. 158–162 (based on earlier article

in *Moznayim* 3, no. 29 [1931/32], pp. 13–14); *EJ (1971)*, vol. 7, pp. 729–730.

144. *Der babylonische Talmud* . . . nebst Varianten . . . (Berlin-Leipzig-The Hague, 1896–1935). On the history of this translation, cf. Goldschmidt's memoirs in *Areshet* 2 (1960): 309–330.

145. *The Babylonian Talmud* . . . Translated into English with Notes, Glossary, and Indices under the editorship of Isidore Epstein (London, 1935–1948).

146. *Midrash Rabbah,* translated into English with notes, glossary, and indices under the editorship of H. Freedman and Maurice Simon (London, 1939).

147. *Kelale Haposkim Umar'eh Mekom Hadinim Beshulchan Aruch* (London, 1922/23).

148. The *Mafte'ach* was also issued bound with the Jerusalem (1960) edition of Rabinowitz's *She'elot Uteshuvot Hageonim.*

149. *Mishnah Berurah* is a popular commentary on *Shulchan Aruch Orach Chayim,* by Israel Meir Kagan, commonly known as *The Chofets Chayim* (1838–1933).

150. Cf. Menachem Elon's introduction to *Mafte'ach Hashe'elot Vehateshuvot; Hamafte'ach Hahistori* (Jerusalem, 1973), p. 9, n. 1. According to Elon, these responsa are scattered in more than 3,000 volumes by different authors. For detailed discussions of the responsa literature, cf. Boaz Cohen, *Kuntres Hateshuvot* (Budapest, 1930; reprinted, Jerusalem, 1969/70, and Farnborough, 1970), pp. 3–36; Solomon Bennett Freehof, *The Responsa Literature* (Philadelphia, 1955; reprinted, New York, 1973); Menachem Elon, *Hamishpat Ha'ivri* (Jerusalem, 1973), pp. 1,213–1,277 (vol. 3); *JE* vol. 11, pp. 240–250; *EJ (1971)*, vol. 14, pp. 83–95. For a bibliography of printed responsa volumes, cf. Boaz Cohen's above-mentioned *Kuntres Hateshuvot* and S. B. Freehof's supplement in *SBB* 5 (1961), Hebrew section, pp. 30–41.

151. Cf. S. Abramson, "Mahadurot Rishonot Shel Otsar Hageonim," *Sinai* 14 (1944):208; idem, "Maftechot Liteshuvot Geonim," *Harry Austryn Wolfson Jubilee Volume* (Jerusalem, 1965), Hebrew section, pp. 1–23.

152. *Halachot Pesukot min Hageonim* (Constantinople, 1516).

153. *She'elot Uteshuvot Mehageonim* (Constantinople, 1575; reprinted, Prague, ca. 1590, Mantua, 1596).

154. For a list and description of these collections, cf. Joel Müller's *Mafte'ach,* chapters 2–12 (see below).

155. For biographical and bibliographical details on Müller, cf. *JE* vol. 9, pp. 106–107; Kressel, *Leksikon,* 2:352–353; *Hamagid Leyisrael,* 4 (1895): 344.

156. See above, p. 280, n. 65.

157. For a list of geonic responsa published up to the 1950s, cf. M. M. Kasher's *Sare Ha'elef* (see above, Chapter 4), pp. 246–248. Many geonic responsa still await publication. Cf. S. Abramson, "Maftechot Liteshuvot Geonim," p. 18, n. 2.

158. For biographical and bibliographical details on Lewin, and for his contributions to the study of geonic literature, cf. *Sefer Hayovel Ledoktor B. M. Levin* (Jerusalem, 1940), pp. (1)–32; *Sinai* 14 (1944): 185–191, (195)–203, (213)–214; 35 (1954): 66–73; *Chochmat Yisrael Bema'arav Eropah,* 2:(163)–169; *EJ (1971)*, vol.

11:169–170; Kressel, *Leksikon,* 2:197–198. Lewin's edition of *Igeret Rav Sherira Gaon* will be discussed in Volume Two of this work.

159. Rabbi Kook Institute of Jerusalem is planning to continue Lewin's work. A volume entitled *Otsar Hageonim Lemasechet Sanhedrin,* edited by Chayim Tsevi Taubes, was published by the Institute in 1966.

160. Among the glosses may be included Hayyim Mordecai Margulies's *Sha'are Teshuvah* on *Shulchan Aruch Orach Chayim* and Abraham Zevi Eisenstadt's *Pitche Teshuvah* on the other parts of the *Shulchan Aruch* (printed in the standard editions). Among the companion volumes: Isaac Jeshurun's *Panim Chadashot* (Venice, 1651; Frankfort, 1670?), supplemented by Moses Hagiz's *Leket Hakemach* (Amsterdam-Hamburg, 1697–1715), and the monumental work by Hayyim Benveniste, *Keneset Hagedolah* and *Shiyore Keneset Hagedolah* (Livorno-Constantinople, etc., 1657–1731). Cf. also J. M. Gold's *Me'asef Lechol Hamachanot* (Munkács, 1937) and J. Z. Katz's *Leket Hakemach Hechadash* (London, 1960–1964).

161. On Eisenstein and his contributions to Jewish research literature, cf. Volume Two of this work.

162. Eisenstein reprinted the specimen several years later in his *Otsar Zichronotai* (New York, 1929), pp. 358–363, with the following note (on p. 363): "Rabbi Dr. Revel . . . took this index . . . removed my name . . . signed his own name . . . and mailed it to some rabbis suggesting that he is the compiler of the index . . . ." Cf. also *Choveret Ledugmah* (Jerusalem, 1964), issued by Mif'al Habibliyografyah Ha'ivrit, p. 28, no. 30. Efforts to refute Eisenstein's accusations were recently made in two works on Revel. Cf. Sidney B. Hoenig, *The Scholarship of Dr. Bernard Revel* (New York, 1968), p. 118, n. 2; reprinted in *Studies in Judaica in Honor of Dr. Samuel Belkin* (New York, 1974), p. 463, n. 2; Aaron Rothkoff, *Bernard Revel; Builder of American Orthodoxy* (Philadelphia, 1972), pp. 36–37.

163. Cf. *Divre Hakongres Haolami Lemada'e Hayahadut* (Jerusalem, 1973), 5:69–70, 76–77; M. Elon's introduction to *Mafte'ach Hashe'elot Vehateshuvot: Hamafte'ach Hahistori,* pp. 10–11.

164. For criticism of the two indexes published by the Institute, cf. I. Ta-Shema's reviews in *Deot,* no. 30 (Fall 1965), pp. 274–278; *KS* 49 (1973/74): 194–198.

165. Rabbi Mordecai Shochetman, of New York (died 1948?), devoted a large part of his life to indexing and abstracting legal matter in responsa literature, which he planned to publish under a similar name, *Otsar Hateshuvot.* Cf. *Talpiyot* 7, no. 2/3 (1960), pp. 261–262, 267–268. It is not known what became of the materials he compiled.

166. A volume containing abstracts of responsa was published in Berlin-Antwerp, 1936, under the title *Frucht vom Baum des Lebens-Otsar Perot Ets Chayim.* The editor, Menko Max Hirsch, abstracted and translated into German 953 responsa by the rabbis of the Amsterdam Yeshiva Ets Chayim, which were issued in pamphlets entitled *Peri Ets Chayim* during a period of one hundred and sixteen years. A project to computerize large segments of responsa, for the purposes of instant retrieval of information on any given subject, came into being several years ago in Israel as a joint effort of scientists connected with the Weizmann Institute of

Science and Bar-Ilan University. By mid-1973, the Responsa Literature Information Storage and Retrieval Project succeeded in keypunching on I.B.M. cards and transferring to magnetic tape nineteen volumes of responsa totaling 3,479,000 words. Another 3.5 million words were in process of being transferred to magnetic tape (from information supplied by Dr. Aviezri Frenkel, of the Weizmann Institute).

167. For the latest and most elaborate reviews of the *Zohar* and Cabala, cf. Gershom Scholem's articles in *EI* vol. 16, pp. 631–648; *EJ (1971)*, vol. 10, pp. 489–653; vol. 16, pp. 1,193–1,215.

168. For additional biographical information on Galante, cf. *JE* vol. 5, p. 547; *EJ (1971)*, vol. 7, pp. 260–261.

169. For additional biographical information on Rovigo, cf. *EJ (1971)*, vol. 14, pp. 355–356.

170. For additional biographical information on Fontanella, cf. *JE* vol. 5, p. 430.

171. For additional biographical information on Nino, cf. Ghirondi, *Toldot Gedole Yisrael,* 359, no. 91.

172. The five leaders of the Lubavich movement indexed in this volume were Shneor Zalman ben Baruch (1747–1812), Dob Baer ben Shneor Zalman (1773–1827), Menahem Mendel Schneersohn (1789–1866), Shalom Dov Ber Schneersohn (1860–1920), and Joseph Isaac Schneersohn (1880–1950).

173. On Carlebach, cf. *Hamaor* 18, no. 6 (1966), p. 48; ibid., 15, no. 3 (1964), p. 33.

174. For recent works on Rabbi Nahman, cf. Natan Tsevi Kenig, *Neveh Tsadikim* (Bene-Berak, 1968/69; contains also bibliography of Rabbi Nahman's works and the works of his disciples); Gedaliah Fleer, *Rabbi Nachman's Fire* (New York, 1972). Cf. also *EI* vol. 25, pp. 39–40; *EJ (1971)* vol. 12, pp. 782–787.

175. Some of these indexes were published in reprint editions of rabbinic works, and some were issued separately. Cf. the reprint editions of Hayyim Hezekiah Medini's *Sede Chemed* (Brooklyn, 1949–1953; New York, 1962–1963; Bene Berak, 1962/63–1967) and Shalom Mordecai Schwadron's *She'elot Uteshuvot Maharsham* (Jerusalem, 1973/74). Cf. also the separate *Maftechot* to Joseph Babad's *Minchat Chinuch* (Jerusalem, 1971/72) and to Joseph Ber Soloveichik's *Bet Halevi* (Bene Berak, 1966/67), among others.

176. A number of such indexes, arranged according to the order of the tractates of the Talmud, were issued in mimeographed form and were distributed among students of yeshivot in Israel and the United States.

177. On the origin and history of Hebrew approbations (*Haskamot*), cf. William Popper, The *Censorship of Hebrew Books* (New York, 1899; reprinted, New York, 1969), especially chaps. 10 and 11; Moshe Carmilly-Weinberger, *Sefer Vasayif* (New York, 1966), index, p. 284 (Haskamot); N. Rakover, *Hahaskamot Lisefarim Kiyesod Lizechut Hayotsrim* (Jerusalem, 1970); Meir Benayahu, *Haskamah Ureshut Bidefuse Venetsyah* (Jerusalem, 1971); *JE* vol. 2, pp. 27–29; *EI* vol. 14, pp. 882–884; *EJ (1971)*, vol. 7, pp. 1,453–1,454. See also Ludwig Blau's notes concerning approbations in *JQR* 10 (1898): 175–176, 383–384.

178. Cf. Blau, *JQR* 10 (1898): 176.

179 See above, pp. 56, 60, and 62.

180. For additional data on Löwenstein, cf. *EJ* 10:1,150–1,151; *EJ (1971)*, vol. 11:451–452.

181. Additions and corrections to the *Index* were published by Bernhard Wachstein in his review of this work in *MGWJ* 71 (1927): 123–133. A list of approbations by the Council of Four Lands in Poland was published by I. Halpern in *KS* 11 (1934/35): 105–110, 252–264; 12 (1935/36): 250–253 (partially published earlier by L. Lewin in *JJLG* 3 [1905]: 124–130). Asher Leib Brisk published texts of rare Hebrew title pages, colophons, introductions and approbations under the title *Divre Kohelet* (Jerusalem, 1905–1914). The pamphlets were issued covering eighty-eight works published from 1486 to 1594.

182. From the German *Pränumeranten*.

183. The introduction also includes bibliographical material dealing with *prenumerantn* phenomena. The compiler's reference to *KS* 8:144, as a source about "a tentative attempt" by Isaac Benjacob to compile such an index is entirely erroneous. The quoted passage in *KS* refers to Benjacob's private list of subscribers (*prenumerantn*) to his planned series of books under the title *Kiryat Sefer Lechochmat Yisrael* (see above, p. 20, also p. 271, n. 77).

# Notes to Chapter Eight:
## Miscellaneous Jewish Bibliographical Works

1. For additional biographical information on Shunami, cf. his introduction to the first edition of *Bibliography of Jewish Bibliographies* and Kressel's *Leksikon*, 2:892.

2. All quotations that follow are taken from Shunami's introduction to the first edition of *Bibliography of Jewish Bibliographies*.

3. Abraham Solomon Freidus, first head of the Jewish Division of the New York Public Library, prepared a most elaborate scheme for the classification of Jewish material which was adopted by a number of American Jewish libraries. See above, p. 63, also p. 284, n. 123.

4. Cf. reviews by S. H. Bergman, *KS* 13 (1936): 35; N. Fried (Ben-Menahem), *Haolam* 24 (1936): 362; I. Halpern, *Gilyonot* 4 (1936/37): 218; M. Kossover, *YB* 9 (1936): 273–274; B. Weinryb, *MGWJ* 80 (1936): 497–499.

5. Cf. *Haolam* 26 (1937/38): 377–379 (see also additions by N. Wahrmann, ibid., p. 780); 27 (1938/39); 491, 512, 532; reprinted as separates with additions (Jerusalem, 1938 and 1939). Shunami's first survey of current Jewish bibliographies seems to have been published in *Moznayim* 3 (1931/32), no. 22, pp. 13–14; no. 23, pp. 12–13.

6. Cf. *Semitic Studies in Memory of Immanuel Löw* (Budapest, 1947), Hebrew section, pp. 169–195. Also issued as separate (Budapest, 1947).

7. The most dramatic growth was noticeable in the section of personal bibliographies which tripled since the publication of the first edition. Isaac Rivkind, in reviewing the new edition in *Hadoar* 45 (1965/66): 205, marveled at the fact that a Jewish bibliographical work was made available again in an enlarged form, prepared by the author himself thirty years after the appearance of the original edition: "Second editions of bibliographical works are very rare, except for some volumes reissued by photo-offset. Enlarged editions are almost nonexistent. . . . This is truly an occurrence that merits the blessing of Shehechiyanu!"

8. Cf. compiler's preface to *Supplement*, p. xiv: "I feel it my duty to inform the readers that I have no intention of continuing this work. . . . However, I am prepared to help anyone willing to take up the challenge."

9. Cf. Wolf, *Bibliotheca hebraea*, 2:941–962; 4:447–453. See also above, Chapter 1.

10. See above p. 41, also p. 277, n. 26.

11. Cf. A. Freimann (compiler), *Ausstellung hebräischer Druckwerke* (Frankfort, 1902); Joseph Jacobs, *JE* vol. 12, pp. 238–330; Zedner, *Catalogue of the Hebrew Books in the Library of the British Museum*, pp. 890–891; Wachstein, *Katalog der Salo Cohn'schen Schenkungen*, 1: ix–xvii.

12. Cf. Steinschneider, *Catalogus*, columns 3,095–3,104. See also above, p. 42, also p. 277, n. 30.

13. Steinschneider-Cassel listed 155 printing locations; Freimann listed 179; Joseph Jacobs, 300. Alexander Marx, in a review of Adler's *Gazetteer, JQR, n. s.* 11 (1920–1921): 265–276, extended the list of printing places to 626. For other additions and corrections to the *Gazetteer*, cf. *ZfHB* 21 (1918): 5. An important contribution to the history of Hebrew printing is Herrmann Meyer's "Index Topo-Bibliographicus," *SB* 3 (1929–1931): 243–258, which listed all of the important studies on Hebrew printers and printing locations in 119 entries arranged by place names.

14. For biographical details on Adler, cf. *EJ (1971)*, vol. 2, pp. 275–276. Adler's unique collection of manuscripts and printed books was acquired by the Jewish Theological Seminary Library in New York and by the Hebrew Union College Library in Cincinnati.

15. Cf. *Bulletin of the New York Public Library* 49 (1945): 355–390; 456–468; 530–540; 913–939. On Freimann, see above, Chapter 5.

16. About Hebrew incunabula, cf. *JE* vol. 6, pp. 575–580; *JL* vol. 3, pp. 15–22; *EJ (1971)*, vol. 8, pp. 1,319–1,344. About textual changes between incunabula and later editions of Hebrew books, cf. Marx, *Studies in Jewish History and Booklore*, p. 286, n. 39; *JE* vol. 3, pp. 642–652.

17. Moses Marx was also the publisher of the *Thesaurus*, but he "insisted on not having his name mentioned" on the work (according to Alexander Marx, *Studies*, p. 287). Moses Marx was among the founders of the Soncino Gesellschaft in Berlin (see above, p. 156), and he published, among other things, a number of bibliophile editions of short stories by his brother-in-law, Samuel Josef Agnon. In 1926 Marx

joined the staff of the library at Hebrew Union College of Cincinnati; and after retirement he settled in Israel, where he died in 1973.

18. *Turim,* by Jacob ben Asher, which was believed by many bibliographers to have been printed in Constantinople in 1503. Freimann's investigation proved it to be an incunabulum printed in 1493. For other information gained by using the *Thesaurus,* cf. Marx, *Studies,* pp. 287–295.

19. For detailed discussions on Hebrew printers' marks, cf. Yaari's introduction to *Digle Hamadpisim;* H. C. Zafren, "The Value of 'Face Value'," *HUCA* 40–41 (1969–1970): 555–580; *JE* vol. 10, pp. 200–201; *EJ (1971),* vol. 13, pp. 1,095–1,096.

20. For biographical and bibliographical data on Yaari, cf. Uri Ben-Horin, *Chibure Avraham Ya'ari* (Jerusalem, 1949); *Beohole Sefer; Lezichro Shel Avraham Ya'ari* (Jerusalem, 1966/67; reprinted from *KS* 42 [1966/67]: 246–251, 252–257); Kressel, *Leksikon,* 2:92–93; *EJ (1971),* vol. 16, pp. 690–691. See also above, p. 106.

21. *KS* 31 (1955/56): 501–506 (also issued as separate).

22. For biographical and bibliographical data on Habermann, cf. Kressel, *Leksikon,* 1:(568)–569; *EJ (1971),* vol. 7, p, 1,024.

23. About Hebrew title pages, cf. Habermann's introduction to *Sha'are Sefarim;* M. Ben-Yehuda, *Sha'are Sefarim Vekotrot* (Tel Aviv, 1967; reprinted from *Ta'aruchat Sha'are Sefarim Ivriyim Mehame'ah Hachamesh Esreh Ve'ad Sof Hame'ah Hatesha Esreh* [Tel Aviv, 1965]); *JE* vol. 12, pp. 152–156.

24. See above, pp. 4, 7, and 11.

25. See above, pp. 21 and 77.

26. See above, pp. 25–26.

27. Cf. Shunami, *Bibliography,* pp. 537–561, where about 125 catalogs of public and private Hebrew manuscript collections are listed.

28. See above, pp. 117–118.

29. Cf. "Necrology," by Marx and Cohen, *PAAJR* 17 (1947–1948): xxvii–xxviii.

30. Goitein's eulogy was originally published in Hebrew in *KS* 25 (1948/49): 109–112.

31. Cf. Marx and Cohen, "Necrology," p. xxviii.

32. Cf. *Hakinus Haolami Lemada'e Hayahadut* (Jerusalem, 1952), p. 34.

33. *In Jewish Bookland* has been published as section two of *JWB Circle* since 1950. A guide to reviews of Yiddish works published in the Soviet Union was prepared earlier by Khatskl Nodel and I. Eliovich, entitled *Onvayzer fun Retsenzyes un Kritishe Artiklen, 1922–*1928 (Kharkov, 1929).

34. In 1834 the Bodleian Library issued a list of dissertations from various universities available at the library. The Bibliothèque Nationale began publishing such lists in 1884, and the Library of Congress issued its first list in 1913.

35. Cf. *JQR,* n. s. 24 (1933–1934): 101–102.

36. I. Graeber, "Jewish Themes in American Doctoral Dissertations," *Yivo Annual* 13 (1965): 279–304.

37. The list of dissertations in Jewish education covered only the period of

1953–1962, since Graeber had earlier published such a list for the years 1890–1953 (see below).

38. On Yivo, see above, Chapter 7. On the Yivo Clearinghouse, cf. compiler's introduction to the first issue.

39. The *Newsletter* is an English-Hebrew publication that began to appear in 1970/71. Its Hebrew title is *Yedi'on*.

40. M. Soltes, "Doctoral Dissertations and Master's Theses on Jewish Education and Kindred Themes," *Jewish Education* 11, no. 3 (January 1940), pp. 188–196.

41. I. Graeber, "Research in American Jewish Education," *Jewish Education* 24, no. 3 (1954), pp. 49–55, 57.

42. Cf. above, n. 37.

43. W. C. Eells, "American Graduate Dissertations on Jewish Education Outside the United States of America," *Jewish Education* 28, no. 2 (Winter 1957/58), pp. 61–63.

44. J. A. Fishman, "Social Science Research Relevant to American Jewish Education," ibid., pp. 49–60. Fishman's reviews were interrupted a few years later.

45. G. Kisch, "Dissertationsliteratur zur Geschichte der Juden aus den Jahren 1922 bis 1928," *ZGJD* 3 (1931): 117–123.

46. *Schriftenreihe Wissenschaftlicher Abhandlungen des Leo Baeck Institute of Jews from Germany.*

47. For a critical review with additions to this volume, cf. S. Ash, *KS* 36 (1960/61): 462–466.

48. *Reshimat Mekable Te'udot Doktor Lefilosofyah*, issued by the Office for Research Students for the years 1935/36–1957/58, and *Talmide Mechkar*, issued by the above office during later years.

49. Identical volumes were issued in English and in Hebrew; the Hebrew volume had a separate title, *Tamtsiyot Shel Avodot Sheushru Lekabalat Hato'ar Doktor Lefilosofyah Vedoktor Lemishpatim.*

50. Dissertations in Jewish studies approved at the Hebrew University are currently listed in the *Newsletter* of the World Union of Jewish Studies. See above, p. 259.

51. Lists of dissertations in Jewish studies approved at the Tel Aviv University are currently being published in the *Newsletter* of the World Union of Jewish Studies. See above, p. 259.

52. This volume is a preliminary edition of a much larger work being prepared by Shulman under a tentative title, *Doctoral Dissertations in Judaica and Related Subjects, 1945–1972.* The planned volume would consist of "an international, multilingual listing of over 3000 entries."

# INDEX

*Note:* Hebrew words, phrases, or titles beginning with the article *ha* are alphabetized in this index under the letter following the article (e.g., *Hadoar* under D, and *Hashilo'ach* under S).